Econometric Society Monographs in Quantitative Economics

Advances in Economic Theory

Econometric Society Publication No. 1

Books in both the Econometric Society Monographs in Pure Theory and the Econometric Society Monographs in Quantitative Economics are numbered in a single sequence for the purposes of the Econometric Society. A complete listing of books in the Econometric Society Monographs in Quantitative Economics are given on the following page.

Econometric Society Monographs in Quantitative Economics

Edited by
Angus Deaton, *University of Bristol*
Daniel McFadden, *Massachusetts Institute of Technology*
Hugo Sonnenschein, *Princeton University*

The Econometric Society is an international society for the advancement of economic theory in relation to statistics and mathematics. The Econometric Society Monograph Series in Quantitative Economics is designed to promote the publication of original research contributions of high quality in mathematical economics and in theoretical and applied econometrics.

Other titles in
Econometric Society Monographs in Quantitative Economics:
W. Hildenbrand: *Advances in Econometrics*

Advances in Economic Theory

INVITED PAPERS FOR THE FOURTH WORLD CONGRESS
OF THE ECONOMETRIC SOCIETY
AT AIX-EN-PROVENCE, SEPTEMBER 1980

Edited by
WERNER HILDENBRAND
Rheinische Friedrich-Wilhelms-Universität Bonn

with the assistance of Heike Schmidt

CAMBRIDGE UNIVERSITY PRESS

Cambridge
London   New York   New Rochelle
Melbourne   Sydney

Published by the Press Syndicate of the University of Cambridge
The Pitt Building, Trumpington Street, Cambridge CB2 1RP
32 East 57th Street, New York, NY 10022, USA
296 Beaconsfield Parade, Middle Park, Melbourne 3206, Australia

First published 1982

Printed in the United States of America

Library of Congress Cataloging in Publication Data
Main entry under title:

Advances in economic theory.

(Econometric Society monographs in
quantitative economics; no. 1)
1. Economics—Congresses. 2. Economics,
Mathematical—Congresses. I. Hildenbrand,
Werner, 1936-   . II. Econometric Society.
III. Series.
HB21.A33   330'.028   81-38500

ISBN 0 521 24443 9   AACR2

Contents

Contents

Contributors

Jean-Pascal Benassy
Centre d'Études Prospectives d'Économie
Mathématique Appliquées à la Planification
Paris, France

Theodore Groves
Department of Economics
University of California, San Diego
La Jolla, California, U.S.A.

Jean-Jacques Laffont
Université des Sciences Sociales de Toulouse
Centre de Recherches Economiques et Statistiques
Toulouse, France

Andreu Mas–Colell
Department of Economics
Harvard University
Cambridge, Massachusetts, U.S.A.

Eric Maskin
Department of Economics
Massachusetts Institute of Technology
Cambridge, Massachusetts, U.S.A.

Jean-François Mertens
Center for Operations Research and Econometrics
Louvain-la-Neuve, Belgium

Roy Radner
Bell Laboratories
Murray Hill, New Jersey, U.S.A.

Richard Schmalensee
Alfred P. Sloan School of Management
Massachusetts Institute of Technology
Cambridge, Massachusetts, U.S.A.

Hugo Sonnenschein
Department of Economics
Princeton University
Princeton, New Jersey, U.S.A.

John B. Taylor
Woodrow Wilson School of Public and International Affairs
Princeton University
Princeton, New Jersey, U.S.A.

Yves Younès
Centre d'Études Prospectives d'Économie
Mathématique Appliquées à la Planification
Paris, France

Editorial preface

All the contributions published in this book and in its companion volume, *Advances in Econometrics,* have been presented as "invited symposia" at the Fourth World Congress of the Econometric Society at Aix-en-Provence, in September 1980. The topics and speakers for the sixteen invited symposia were chosen by the Program Committee. The purpose of these symposia was to survey as completely as possible those areas in economic theory and econometrics where important research has come to light during the last five years since the Third World Congress. All but one of the invited symposia are included in these volumes and, according to subject, they are published either in this volume on economic theory, or in the volume on econometrics.

The Editor would like to acknowledge the cooperation of the contributors and the assistance of Heike Schmidt in the preparation of the manuscript.

Werner Hildenbrand
Chairman of the Program Committee
of the Fourth World Congress
of the Econometric Society

PART I

ECONOMICS OF INCENTIVES

CHAPTER 1

On theories of incentive compatible choice
with compensation

Theodore Groves

1   Introduction

The issue of incentives is one of the grand themes of economics; it is a
main thread on which the rich tapestry of economic theory is woven.
Notions of self-interested behavior are at the foundation of all microeconomics or theories of individual agents' behavior. Until quite recently,
however, most investigations have been concerned with analyzing self-
interested behavior under market institutions, as for example, in consumer theory or the theory of the firm.

An early exception to the focus on incentives in a market context was
the famous debate in the early years of this century over the feasibility of
market socialism – known as the socialist controversy. Here, the issue of
incentives arose in a new form – namely, given a specified procedure or
rules for allocating resources and making economic decisions in a socialist
state, will the agents, in fact, have any incentive to behave as specified
by the procedure or in accordance with the rules?

More recently, this question has been posed and analyzed in a variety
of models arising from different literature – some models have been very
general while others have been very specific. Two main branches in this
new, growing field are the theory of economic mechanisms – an out-
growth and development of the theory of socialist and other planning –
and social choice theory. However, in both these branches, interestingly
enough, the problem of incentives was not one of the first issues
explored – although it was raised early by some. In the social choice
literature, although the question of honest voting was raised by Vickrey

1

(1960), nearly twenty years passed after Arrow's original work, c.f. Arrow (1963, 2nd ed.), before the contributions of Farquharson (1969), Gibbard (1973), and Satterthwaite (1975) on strategic voting and straightforward or nonmanipulability of social choice rules.

In the other line of literature – that of general resource allocation mechanisms – it was over ten years from Hurwicz's landmark paper on resource allocation mechanisms, Hurwicz (1959), to Hurwicz's work on incentive compatibility, Hurwicz (1972). Groves's paper on incentives in teams, Groves (1973), given at the Second World Congress in 1970, was a formal treatment of the same question of the incentives decentralized managers might have that was addressed informally in the socialist controversy. There were also other early independent contributions, notably a 1961 paper by Vickrey and others in the early 1970s by Clarke (1971) and Smets (1973).

A related third line of literature, game theory, has recently joined the other two, although game theoretic methods and models have been used in a fundamental way in many of the social choice and resource allocation mechanism papers on incentives. This work originating from game theoretic roots analyzed games that represent some nongame description of market allocations – for example, games giving Walrasian allocations or other market-type allocations in models with money at Nash equilibria, c.f. papers by Shubik, Shapley, Schmeidler, Hurwicz, Postlewaite. One branch of this literature has led to the work on Nash-Cournot theory while another branch has merged with mechanism theory.

Since the first papers appeared approximately a decade ago, a large number of papers dealing with incentives have appeared – numbering in the several hundreds. In addition, over twenty papers at the Fourth World Congress are on this subject. Two major collections of papers surveying much of this growing field are Laffont (ed.) (1979) and the Review of Economic Studies (1979) Symposium. I shall not survey this entire literature. Instead I follow one line – that of general resource allocation mechanisms. And even in this line I examine the development of incentive theory in the context, primarily, of a particular model. Some of the results discussed here were surveyed earlier in Groves (1979).

In this model, there exists at least one private good that can be transferred among many decision makers or agents to induce agreement or to stimulate accurate revelation of preferences. Thus, a medium of *compensation* exists. The alternative *theories* of the title refer to different equilibrium concepts or theories of what the relevant behavior would be in the games defined by the mechanisms.

In Section 2, the general model with compensation is defined. A choice mechanism or procedure for choosing alternatives is then seen as defining an n-person game of incomplete information. Different equilibrium concepts or behavioral theories of how such a game would be played are discussed, including the dominant strategy, Nash, and Bayesian equilibria concepts.

A particular general mechanism, the demand-revealing mechanism, is formulated in Section 3 and analyzed in the case in which the preferences of the agents for alternative collective decisions are independent of the amount of the compensatory private good they receive. Under the demand-revealing mechanism in this case, honest revelation of preferences is a dominant strategy equilibrium. Several applications of this model are discussed in Section 3.3.

A basic limitation of this mechanism is that it does not yield fully efficient outcomes at dominant strategy equilibria, however. In Section 4, it is shown that the demand-revealing mechanism can be modified so that efficient outcomes are achievable at Bayesian equilibria in the case of special quasi-linear preferences. In the case of more general preferences, some recent work of Wilson on optimal risk sharing is discussed.

2   The collective choice model with compensation

2.1   *The model*

We consider a collective choice model with a private good to serve as a medium of compensation or for transferring utility. A group of $n \geqslant 3$ agents, indexed $i = 1, \ldots, n$, face the collective choice problem of choosing an *alternative y* from a set Y of possible alternatives. In addition to choosing y, they can also redistribute among themselves a particular commodity called *money*; that is, choose a vector $t = (t_1, \ldots, t_n)$ of *transfers,* where t_i denotes the amount of money transferred to agent i. Feasibility of the vector t of transfers requires that the sum of its coordinates is nonpositive. Thus, let Z denote the set of (complete) *feasible alternatives* $z = (y, t)$ where:

$$Z \equiv Y \times T \quad \text{and} \quad T \equiv \left\{ t \in \mathbf{R}^n \mid \sum_i t_i \leqslant 0 \right\}$$

Now each agent is assumed to possess a preference relation R_i over alternatives z in Z. However, to justify calling money a private good and to support its use as compensation we assume these preferences satisfy the following conditions:

R_i is representable by a utility function $u_i : Z \to \mathbf{R}$ satisfying
  (a) $u_i(y, t)$ is constant in t_j, all $j \neq i$; henceforth we write $u_i(y, t_i)$;

that is, i cares only about the alternative y chosen and his own transfer t_i (money is a purely private good),

(b) $u_i(y, t_i)$ is strictly increasing in t_i, that is, i is never satiated in money, and

(c) for every $y \in Y$, $t_i \in \mathbf{R}$, if $y' \in Y$, then there exists some $\Delta t_i \in \mathbf{R}$ such that $u_i(y, t_i) = u_i(y', t_i + \Delta t_i)$ that is, i can always be compensated by at least Δt_i (or is willing to pay up to $-\Delta t_i$) to have alternative y' chosen rather than y, given the initial level of transfer t_i (every alternative has its price for an agent).

Let $\mathfrak{R}^\circ$ denote the space of all such preference relations; $R = (R_1, \ldots, R_n)$ denote a *preference profile*; and $\mathfrak{R}^\circ \equiv (\mathfrak{R}^\circ)^n$ denote the space of all profiles.

A *social decision function* (*SDF*) F is a mapping from preference profiles R to alternatives z. We may interpret an *SDF* F in either of two ways: First, an *SDF* may express normative judgments about desirable alternatives z for any given profile R. Alternatively, it may simply represent the outcome of whatever procedure the group of agents uses to determine their choice, given their preferences.

Now, whatever procedure the group uses, we suppose that the individual agents alone know their own preferences. Thus, in order for the alternative z chosen to be related at all to the preferences, some communication or signaling of preference information is required. Formally, a decision procedure, or *mechanism D*, is a pair $(M, \rho(\cdot))$, where M is a *message space* consisting of alternative messages or signals m_i an agent may select, and $\rho(\cdot)$ is an *outcome function* specifying an alternative z for every joint message $m \equiv (m_1, \ldots, m_n) \in M^n$; viz. $z = \rho(m)$.

Given a mechanism D, the agents face a game situation. Individually they choose their own messages (strategies) m_i and then realize the payoff associated with the outcome $\rho(m) = z$ selected by the mechanism. In normal form, the game, $G(R, D)$, is specified as

$$\{I, \langle S_i \rangle_{i=1}^n, \langle w_i \rangle_{i=1}^n\}$$

where: (a) $I = \{1, \ldots, n\}$ is the player set, (b) $S_i = M$ is each player's strategy set, and (c) w_i is player i's payoff function defined over joint strategies $m \in S \equiv X_i S_i = M^n$ as the composition of the player's utility function u_i and the mechanism's outcome function $\rho(\cdot): w_i(m) = u_i[\rho(m)]$ for every $m \in M^n = S$. (Recall, $u_i(\cdot)$ represents the player's preferences R_i over alternatives $z \in Z$.)

In the language of game theory, the game $G(R, D)$ is an n-person game of incomplete information because each player's preferences are known only to himself. Given any solution or equilibrium concept or theory of behavior for such games, a mapping from the space of profiles $\mathfrak{R}^\circ$ to the joint-strategy space $S = M^n$ is defined implicitly. We call this

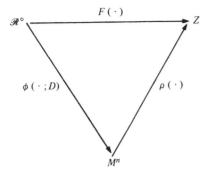

Figure 1.1

mapping a *joint-behavior rule* and denote it by $\phi(R;D)$ where its dependence on the mechanism D is explicitly recognized. Note that any given joint-behavior rule may be empty or multiple-valued at any given profile R.

Once a mechanism D and a joint-behavioral rule are specified, an *SDF* is defined by composition of the outcome and behavioral rules: $F(\cdot) \equiv \rho[\phi(\cdot;D)]$, as illustrated schematically in Figure 1.1. A broad category of questions may be asked within this framework. One is the *implementation problem*, which poses the question whether or not it is possible to implement a given *SDF* $F(\cdot)$ with some mechanism $D = (M, \rho(\cdot))$ and "appropriate" joint-behavioral rule; that is, does Figure 1.1 commute, that is, $F(\cdot) = \rho \cdot \phi(\cdot;D)$? A variation on this question asks if there exists a mechanism D such that for an "appropriate" behavior rule ϕ, the outcome $\rho \cdot \phi(R;D)$ is a subset of $F(R)$ for every R (possibly only in some given subset of $\mathcal{R}^\circ$). Such a question is natural if $F(R)$ is multiple-valued; for example, if $F(R)$ is the set of Pareto-optimal alternatives z in Z. Another variation asks if a given *SDF* $F(\cdot)$ can be implemented with a mechanism of a particular type. For example, if M is restricted to be $\mathcal{R}^\circ$, that is, each message m_i may be interpreted as an announced preference of player i, and if $\rho(\cdot)$ is specified to be identical to $F(\cdot)$, the implementation question then is equivalent to the *revelation question*, that is, asking if "truth telling" or "honest revelation of preferences" is an appropriate joint-behavior rule or a "likely" outcome of the game. For an excellent survey of results in general models, see Dasgupta, Hammond, and Maskin (1979).

2.2 *"Appropriate" joint-behavior rules*

As noted the collective choice problem of the agents, given a particular mechanism, is an n-person game of incomplete information. In the literature on the implementation problem many solution or equilibrium concepts have been investigated. Among these are the dominant strategy equilibrium, the (simple) Nash equilibrium, and the (Harsanyi) Bayesian equilibrium. All are noncooperative concepts which is appropriate if a mechanism is viewed as the formal representation of all opportunities the agents have for exchanging information and coordinating their choice. The strongest of these concepts is the dominant strategy equilibrium.

Definition 1: Given the game $G(R, D)$ defined by a mechanism $D = (M, \rho(\cdot))$ and profile R, a *dominant strategy equilibrium* is a joint strategy $\hat{m} \in M^n$ such that, for every i,

$$u_i[\rho(m/\hat{m}_i)] \geq u_i[\rho(m/m_i)]$$

all $m_i \in S_i \equiv M$, all $m \in S \equiv M^n$ where $(m/\hat{m}_i) \equiv (m_i, \ldots, \hat{m}_i, \ldots, m_n)$.

If a game has a dominant strategy equilibrium, then each player has a strategy that is individually best for him regardless of the strategy chosen by any other player. Thus, if noncooperative behavior is assumed, each player would have a strong incentive to play his dominant strategy.

In the broadest collective choice context, the design of general mechanisms with this strong incentive property is sharply limited by the Gibbard/Satterthwaite Theorem. In essence, this theorem states that no nondictatorial nonimposed *SDF* with a range of at least three alternatives z in Z can be implemented (for all profiles R) by any mechanism and the dominant strategy equilibrium joint-behavioral rule. For any given mechanism, either a dominant strategy equilibrium will not exist at some profile or the mechanism will not select $z = F(R)$ at $\hat{m}$, that is, $\rho(\hat{m}) \notin F(R)$ where $\hat{m} = \hat{\phi}(R, D)$ is a dominant strategy equilibrium for the game $G(D, R)$. In particular, for the revelation question, the implication of this theorem is that truth telling or honest revelation of preferences cannot be a dominant strategy equilibrium in all circumstances.

As will be discussed below, however, for a special class of preferences in the model of Section 2.1 – namely, those for which an individual's preference rankings over alternatives y are independent of the amount of their transfer t_i – it is possible to design mechanisms to pick optimal alternatives y such that honest revelation of preferences is a dominant strategy for each player. But these mechanisms are not wholly satisfactory even for these special preferences because it is generally not possible to achieve allocations that are fully efficient or Pareto optimal. Typically some surplus money is left undistributed.

For both reasons – the nonexistence of dominant strategy equilibria for nondictatorial mechanisms in the general case and the nonefficiency of the particular mechanism in the restricted preference case – it is of interest to explore weaker equilibrium concepts. Two others that have been examined with positive results are the (simple) Nash equilibrium and the Bayesian equilibrium concepts.

Definition 2: Given the game $G(R, D)$ defined by a mechanism $D = (M, \rho(\cdot))$ and profile R, a (simple) Nash equilibrium is a joint strategy $m^* \in M^n$ such that, for every i,

$$u_i[\rho(m^*)] \geqslant u_i[\rho(m^*/m_i)], \quad \text{all} \quad m_i \in S_i = M$$

In contrast to a dominant strategy equilibrium, this weaker concept requires only that each player's equilibrium strategy be best against the other players' equilibrium strategies and not necessarily against all their other strategies.

It turns out that with the Nash equilibrium joint-behavioral rule $\phi^*(\cdot, D)$ mechanisms D can be found that will implement a broad class of social decision functions F. See Maskin (1977) for a formulation of a general mechanism. Hurwicz, Maskin and Postlewaite (1979) apply this mechanism to the problem of implementing Walrasian allocations by Nash equilibria. On this subject, see also the important papers of Hurwicz (1979a, b), Hurwicz and Schmeidler (1978), Postlewaite and Schmeidler (1978), and Schmeidler (1980). Groves and Ledyard (1977a) adopt the Nash equilibrium approach in developing a mechanism to overcome the free-rider problem in public goods models. Other mechanisms for public goods models using the Nash equilibrium are by Hurwicz (1979a) and Walker (1979).

However, a severe conceptual problem exists with the (simple) Nash equilibrium as applied to the games defined by the social choice procedures or mechanisms as discussed above. Because these games are characterized by incomplete information, in general, no player can compute, in one step, even his own Nash equilibrium strategy. Thus, the appropriateness of this concept is at least open to question.

Two approaches have been investigated for overcoming this difficulty. The first is to consider an iterative, tâtonnement-type procedure for playing the game. If the message space M of the mechanism is simple – say a low dimensional Euclidean space rather than a general function space – then one can conceive of the game being played in a sequence of iterations where at each stage a player announces a message m_i. A Nash equilibrium joint strategy m^* is then a possible equilibrium of this iterative process. Of course, whether or not the procedure would ever converge or if the behavior of the agents in playing the iterative game would lead to the (simple) Nash equilibrium joint strategy are immediate important questions. Although the theoretical results are sparse, a variety of experimental results of Smith and others, cf. Smith (1979), suggest that a (simple) Nash equilibrium is often the outcome of such iterative procedures.

The other approach is to reject the (simple) Nash equilibrium concept in favor of the Bayesian equilibrium solution concept for games of incomplete information. This approach requires that the structure of the model be enriched somewhat. Each player is assumed to have a probability distribution over the preferences of all the other players. The Bayesian equilibrium is then the joint strategy where each player's strategy is a function from his preferences to the message space of the mechanism that maximizes his conditional expected payoff, where the probability distribution is the player's distribution over the *other* players' preferences.

Formally, to define this concept let every preference $R_i \in \mathcal{R}^\circ$ be parameterized by an element α_i in some measurable space A_i. Thus, each player knows his own α_i, but none of the others' α_j, $j \neq i$. However, each player is assumed to have beliefs about the others' parameters, represented by a conditional probability measure $P_i(\cdot \mid \alpha_i)$ over the others' joint parameter space $A_{-i} \equiv X_{j \neq i} A_j$, conditioned on his parameter α_i, where $\alpha_{-i} \equiv (\alpha_1, \ldots, \alpha_{i-1}, \alpha_{i+1}, \ldots, \alpha_n)$.

Definition 3: Given the game $G(R, D)$ defined by a mechanism $D = (M, \rho(\cdot))$ and profile R, a Bayesian equilibrium for the probability measures $P_1(\cdot \mid \cdot), \ldots, P_n(\cdot \mid \cdot)$ is a joint-strategy $\delta^* = (\delta_1^*, \ldots, \delta_n^*)$, where $\delta_i^* : A_i \to M$, such that, for every i,

$$\int_{A_{-i}} u_i[\rho(\delta^*(\alpha)); \alpha_i] \, dP_i(\alpha_{-i} \mid \alpha_i)$$

$$\geq \int_{A_{-i}} u_i[\rho(\delta^*(\alpha)/m_i); \alpha_i] \, dP_i(\alpha_{-i} \mid \alpha_i)$$

for all $m_i \in M$, where $\delta^*(\alpha) \equiv [\delta_1^*(\alpha_1), \ldots, \delta_n^*(\alpha_n)]$ and $(\delta^*(\alpha)/m_i) \equiv [\delta_1^*(\alpha_1), \ldots, m_i, \ldots, \delta_n^*(\alpha_n)]$. Note that the utility functions $u_i(\cdot; \alpha_i)$ are parameterized by the variable α_i in this formalization.

The results obtained from the approach of the Bayesian equilibrium are more fragmentary than for either of the other two equilibrium concepts. Most attention for the collective choice model of the previous section has focused upon the special case in which the players' preferences over alternative choices y are independent of their money transfer t_i. Additionally, the results tend to depend on some rather strong assumptions on the players' probability distributions over the others' preferences.

2.3   *Willingness to pay, quasi-linear preferences, and Pareto optimality*

Given the collective choice model with money transfers of Section 2.1, each agent's preferences in $R°$ can be completely described in terms of the money compensation required to leave him indifferent between any choice y' and any given alternative (y, t_i).

Proposition 1: Let $Z = Y \times T$. For any $R_i \in \mathcal{R}°$, which is representable by the utility function $u_i(\cdot)$, the function $\mu_i : Y \times Y \times \mathbf{R} \to \mathbf{R}$ defined by: $\mu_i(y'; y, t_i) = v_i$ where $\mu_i(y, t_i) = u_i(y', t_i - v_i)$ is such that: $u_i(y, t_i) \geqslant u_i(y', t_i')$ if and only if $t_i - t_i' \geqslant \mu_i(y'; y, t_i)$.

Proof: Immediate from the restrictions on preferences in $\mathcal{R}°$.

The function $\mu_i(\cdot)$ is called the *willingness to pay* function since $v_i = \mu_i(y'; y, t_i)$ is the maximum amount of money agent i would be willing to pay to move to $(y', t_i - v_i)$ from (y, t_i). (If v_i is negative, $-v_i > 0$ is the minimum compensation i would require and still be willing to accept the move.)

Now, in general, an agent's willingness to pay to have y' chosen instead of y depends on the transfer amount t_i associated with y. That is, his preferences for y are not independent of money, thus his preferences exhibit income effects. But a special case of considerable interest is when the preferences over Y are independent of money t_i.

Definition 4: An agent's preferences R_i in $\mathcal{R}°$ on $Z = Y \times T$, represented by $u_i(y, t_i)$ is said to be *quasi-linear in money*, t_i, if for any (y, t_i), $(y', t_i') \in Y \times \mathbf{R}$, such that $u_i(y, t_i) = u_i(y', t_i')$, then $u_i(y, t_i + v) = u_i(y', t_i' + v)$ for all $v \in \mathbf{R}$. We denote the class of all quasi-linear preferences by $\mathcal{R}^L$.

In the case of quasi-linear preferences, the willingness to pay function, μ_i, is constant in the amount of t_i and preferences are representable by a utility function that is additive and linear in t_i.

Proposition 2: If $R_i \in \mathcal{R}^L$, that is, R_i is quasi-linear in money, then

(a) R_i is representable by a utility function of the form $u_i(y, t_i) = t_i + v_i(y)$ for some function $v_i : Y \to \mathbf{R}$ and

(b) the willingness to pay function $\mu_i(y; y^0, t_i) = v_i(y) - v_i(y^0)$ for every $(y, y^0, t_i) \in Y \times Y \times \mathbf{R}$.

Proof: For (a) see Katzner (1970, Theorem 2.3-3, p. 25); (b) is immediate.

An advantage of representing preferences with the willingness to pay function $\mu_i(\cdot)$ instead of the utility function $u_i(\cdot)$ is that Pareto-optimal alternatives can be easily characterized in terms of aggregate willingness to pay.

Proposition 3: Let $Z = Y \times T$ and $R_i \in \mathfrak{R}^\circ$ all i. Alternative $z^* = (y^*, t^*)$ is efficient (Pareto-optimal) if and only if

(a) $\sum_i t_i^* = 0$ and

(b) y^* maximizes $\sum_i \mu_i(y; y^*, t_i^*)$ over $y \in Y$; that is, y^* maximizes aggregate willingness to pay to move from y^*, where $\mu_i(\cdot)$ represents R_i.

In the special case of quasi-linear preferences, the characterization is particularly simple:

Corollary 1: If preferences are quasi-linear in money, $R_i \in \mathfrak{R}^L$ all i, then $z^* = (y^*, t^*)$ is efficient (Pareto-optimal) if and only if

(a) $\sum_i t_i^* = 0$ and

(b) y^* maximizes $\sum_i v_i(y)$ over $y \in Y$ where $v_i(y) - v_i(y^0) = \mu_i(y; y^0, t_i)$ for all y, y^0, t_i.

In this special case, of course, all efficient alternatives y^* are independent of the transfer vector t.

3   Demand-revealing mechanisms

3.1   *The general form of the mechanism*

In view of Proposition 3 and Corollary 1, efficient or Pareto-optimal allocations are characterized by maximizing aggregate willingness to pay. Thus, to implement efficient outcomes with some mechanism one might take the message space M to be alternative willingness to pay functions. That is, the mechanism asks agents to report their willingness to pay for various alternatives y in Y. Then, the outcome function, in part, will choose that alternative y that maximizes the sum of the reported willingness to pay.

Formally, let the message space M^* be defined by:

(3.1) $M^* \equiv \{m_i : Y \to \mathbf{R}\}$

that is, the space of all real-valued functions of Y. And, let the outcome function $\rho^*(\cdot) \equiv (y^*(\cdot), t_1^*(\cdot), \ldots, t_n^*(\cdot))$ be defined in the first component by:

$$(3.2) \quad y^*(m) = y\text{-argmax} \sum_j m_j(y)$$

over Y, all $m \in M^{*n}$.

Now in the case of quasi-linear preferences, or the no income effects case, an agent may be said to be "telling the truth," or honestly reporting his willingness to pay, if his message $m_i(\cdot)$ satisfies, for every pair (y', y),

$$m_i(y') - m_i(y) = v_i(y') - v_i(y) = \mu_i(y'; y, t_i)$$

(see Corollary 1).

In the case of general preferences, an agent's true willingness to pay depends on his transfer t_i. But because his transfer is specified by the outcome function – the component $t_i(\cdot)$ – we say that agent i is telling the truth if, given the messages $m_j(\cdot)$ of all the *other* agents, $j \neq i$, his own message $m_i(\cdot)$ satisfies, for every pair (y', y),

$$(3.3) \quad m_i(y') - m_i(y) = \mu_i[y'; y, t_i(m)]$$

Thus, because his transfer $t_i(m)$ depends on all messages m_j, for an agent to tell the truth, he must, implicitly at least, take into account how all messages, including his own, will affect his transfer. Also, it is important to note that it is not possible for an agent to tell the truth or honestly report his willingness to pay unless he knows what his transfer will be for each message he sends – something that depends in general on the messages the other players send. Hence, telling the truth could not possibly be a dominant strategy for a player in the general case, although in the quasi-linear case it perhaps could be because willingness to pay is independent of the transfer.

With the message space M^* and choice rule $y^*(\cdot)$, defined by (3.1) and (3.2), if all agents tell the truth at m and the aggregate transfers balance, then the selected outcome z is efficient.

Proposition 4: If $m_i(\cdot)$ satisfy (3.3), all i, and $\sum_i t_i^*(m) = 0$, then $z^*(m) = (y^*(m), t^*(m))$ is efficient.

Proof: At m, $m_i(y') - m_i(y^*(m)) = \mu_i(y'; y^*; t_i^*)$. Thus, $y^*(m)$ maximizing $\sum_j m_j(y)$ implies y^* maximizes $\sum_i \mu_i(y; y^*, t_i^*)$ which, by Proposition 3 implies z^* is efficient.

Although the message space M^* and choice rule $y^*(\cdot)$ are designed to pick efficient outcomes when all agents truthfully report their willingness to pay, it may not be in an agent's self-interest to tell the truth. By falsely reporting his willingness to pay, he may hope to receive a greater transfer than required to compensate him for any change in y caused by his false report. For example, by professing little willingness to pay for a public good, an agent may hope to reduce his cost share sufficiently to compensate for the otherwise lower quantity of the public good provided, thereby being a free rider on the amounts provided by others.

Whether or not such misrepresentations can benefit an agent depends on the specific transfer rules $t_i(\cdot)$ specified by the mechanism. In the classic public goods problem, it was long thought that no transfer rules (i.e., cost shares or tax functions) exist which would remove the advantage of being a free rider. In the past ten years, however, this view has been shown to be wrong or excessively pessimistic at least by the discovery and elaboration of the demand-revealing mechanism.

These mechanisms are specified by the message space M^* and the choice rule $y^*(\cdot)$ defined above and any set of transfer rules $t^*(\cdot) = (t_1^*(\cdot), \ldots, t_n^*(\cdot))$ defined by:

$$(3.4) \quad t_i^*(m) \equiv \sum_{j \neq i} m_j(y^*(m)) - A_i(m_{-i})$$

where A_i is a real-valued function of the $(n-1)$ messages m_j, $j \neq i$, satisfying

$$(3.5) \quad \sum_i A_i(m_{-i}) \geq (n-1) \sum_j m_j(y^*(m)), \quad \text{all} \quad m \in M^{*n}$$

(Inequality (3.5) ensures that no deficit can result; that is, $\sum_i t_i^*(m) \leq 0$.) As a particular example of the function $A_i(\cdot)$, consider

$$(3.6) \quad A_i^o(m_{-i}) \equiv \max_{y \in Y} \sum_{j \neq i} m_j(y) = \sum_{j \neq i} m_j[y^*(m/\bar{m}_i)]$$

where $\bar{m}_i(\cdot)$ is any constant function. In this case, the transfers are given by:

$$(3.7) \quad t_i^*(m) = -\left\{ \sum_{j \neq i} [m_j(y^*(m/\bar{m}_i)) - m_j(y^*(m))] \right\}$$

This particular demand-revealing mechanism has been called by Green and Laffont (1976) the *pivot mechanism* since each agent is charged (note: $t_i^*(m) \leq 0$ for all m) only when his message changes the choice of y from what it would be if he professed complete indifference (that is, sent $\bar{m}_i(y) = \text{constant}$). Thus, by being a complete free rider an agent maximizes his transfer or minimizes his cost. The transfer rule charges each agent for the full reported willingness of the others to pay for their collective best alternative $y^*(m/\bar{m}_i)$ rather than receive the alternative $y^*(m)$ actually chosen. Nevertheless, free riding is not optimal behavior.

3.2 *Properties of the demand-revealing mechanism in the quasi-linear case*

The main property of the demand-revealing mechanisms is that in the case of quasi-linear preferences, telling the truth or honestly revealing one's willingness to pay or one's demand are the only dominant strategies.

Theorem 1 (Vickrey, Clarke, Groves): If preferences R_i are quasi-linear, $R_i \in \Re^L$ all i, then under any demand-revealing mechanism $D^* = [M^*, (y^*, t^*)]$

   (a) $m_i^*(\cdot) \equiv v_i(\cdot) + constant$ is a dominant strategy for agent i, and
   (b) $m^*(\cdot)$ is a dominant strategy equilibrium if and only if $m_i^*(\cdot) = v_i(\cdot) + constant$ for all i.

Proof: Vickrey (1961) and Clarke (1971) independently proved (a) for particular examples of the mechanism. Groves (1970) independently established (a) and (b) (if part) in a more general model, and Groves (1976a) proved (b, only if). (See also Groves and Loeb (1975).)

Since efficient alternatives y in Y are independent of the transfer vectors t and are characterized by maximizing the aggregate willingness to pay (or $\sum_j v_j(\cdot)$), at any dominant strategy equilibrium the mechanism will select an efficient alternative y. Furthermore, an important theorem of Green and Laffont (1977) established that the class of demand-revealing mechanisms is essentially the only class of mechanisms with this property.

Theorem 2 (Green and Laffont): Suppose preferences are quasi-linear, $R \in \Re^L$, all i. Let $D = (M, (y, t))$ be a mechanism with the properties

   (i) A dominant strategy equilibrium $\hat{m}$ exists.
   (ii) $y(\hat{m})$ is an efficient alternative for all dominant strategy equilibria $\hat{m}$.

Then there exists a function $\psi : M \to M^*$ and a demand-revealing mechanism $D^* = (M^*, (y^*, t^*))$ such that:

   (a) $y(\hat{m}) = y^*(\psi(\hat{m}))$
   (b) $t_i(\hat{m}) = t_i^*(\psi(\hat{m})) + B_i(\hat{m}_{-i})$

where $\psi(\hat{m}) = (\psi(\hat{m}_1), \ldots, \psi(\hat{m}_n))$ and B_i is some real-valued function of the messages $\hat{m}_j, j \neq i$.

Proof: See Green and Laffont (1977) or Groves (1976b, Theorem 4, p. 169) or Holmstrom (1979) for a more general result.

Now, although honest revelation of preferences is a dominant strategy under any demand-revealing mechanism and at any dominant strategy equilibrium an efficient alternative y is chosen, generally the aggregate transfers $\sum_i t_i^*(m)$ will not balance. Hence, an overall Pareto-optimal alternative $z^* = (y^*, t^*)$ in general is not selected by these mechanisms. This result is implied by the more general result of Hurwicz and Green, Kohlberg and Laffont, that there is no mechanism such that a dominant strategy equilibrium will always exist and produce an efficient alternative z^*. (Note that because the space $Z = Y \times T$ is open in the transfer components t_i and preferences are strictly increasing in t_i, a dictatorial mechanism will not have a dominant strategy equilibrium.)

Theorem 3 (Hurwicz [1975] and Green, Kohlberg and Laffont [1976]): There exists no mechanism $D = (M, (y, t))$ such that, for all quasi-linear preference profiles $R \in (\Re^L)^n$, a dominant strategy equilibrium m of the game $G(D, R)$ exists such that $z(m)$ is efficient.

Proof: See Walker (1978) and (1980) for the most general result.

How serious the failure of the demand-revealing mechanisms to guarantee fully efficient outcomes is a matter of some controversy, and perhaps, interpretation. One view is that in any realistic situation with large numbers of agents and relatively small elasticities of demand for y, the size of the surplus, $-\sum_i t_i^*(m)$, will be insignificant (see Tideman and Tullock [1976]). Although this indeed may be the usual case, to my knowledge no reasonably general theorem has yet been proved that delineates clearly the circumstances under which the size of the surplus goes to zero as the number of agents increases. Another view is that the surplus may be used, say, for general tax reduction without practically distorting incentives because individuals would not take into account the effect of their messages on the size of their share of the surplus. This view, of course, introduces a less rigorous behavioral assumption than that of strict rationality, as maintained in all the formal models. A final suggestion by Tideman is to auction the surplus off; that is, sell the right to collect whatever surplus is generated to the highest bidder. The proceeds of the auction would be redistributed to all agents in any lump-sum manner. Then the incentives of all agents *except* the winner of the auction would not be disturbed and the winner might be expected to be sufficiently small to not distort the choice of y significantly. Of course, this proposal is not suggested as a counter-example to Theorem 3 but to minimize the inefficiency that might be associated with merely wasting the surplus collected. But here again, to my knowledge, a precise and rigorous result has yet to be given.

3.3   *Some special models*

In this section, a few special cases of the general model of Section 2.1 will be described with the application of the demand-revealing mechanism to these special cases.

Case 1. The auction model: Suppose the choice y to be made in the allocation of a single item to one of a group of n agents. Thus, we may take Y to be the set $\{y_1, \ldots, y_n\}$ where y_i denotes the allocation of the item to agent i.

Further, suppose each agent only values the allocation in which he receives the item. Then, assuming quasi-linear preferences representable by $u_i(y, t_i)$ where $u_i(y, t_i) = t_i + v_i(y)$ where

$$v_i(y_j) = \begin{cases} v_i > 0 & \text{if } j = i \\ 0 & \text{if } j \neq i \end{cases}$$

communicating the value $v_i(y_i) = v_i$ is equivalent to communicating the entire willingness to pay function $v_i(\cdot)$.

Now, consider the pivot mechanism D° in which the message space M° may now be taken to be the real line and each message is interpreted as agent i's bid for the item. The allocation rule $y^\circ(m)$ which maximizes the aggregate reported willingness to pay is easily seen to allocate the item to the highest bidder, that is,

$$y^\circ(m) = y_j \quad \text{where} \quad m_j = \max\{m_1, \ldots, m_n\}$$

Furthermore, the pivot mechanism transfers are computed from (3.7) to be:

$$t_i^*(m) = \begin{cases} 0 \text{ if } y^\circ(m) \neq y_i \\ -\max\{m_1, \ldots, m_{i-1}, m_{i+1}, \ldots, m_n\} \text{ if } y^\circ(m) = y_i \end{cases}$$

Only the agent winning the auction (that is, with the highest bid) pays anything, and his cost is equal to the second highest bid price.

It is, of course, a result of Theorem 1 that under these rules of the auction, each agent has a dominant strategy to bid his true value for the object being auctioned.

This example is due to Vickrey (1961).

Case 2. The public good model: Suppose the choice y to be made is the quantity of some public good and the cost shares of each agent for the public good. That is, let $y = (y_0, y_1, \ldots, y_n)$ where y_0 is the amount of some public good and $y_i \equiv \alpha_i p \cdot y_0$ is agent i's share of the cost of y_0, p is the unit price of y_0, and α_i is a *fixed* cost share parameter. Also, assume the agents have quasi-linear preferences representable by $\mu_i(y, t_i)$ where agent i cares only about the amount of the public good y_0 and his cost (plus transfer t_i): $\mu_i(y, t_i) = t_i + v_i(y) \equiv t_i + \phi_i(y_0) - \alpha_i p \cdot y_0$. Thus, communicating the willingness to pay function $\phi_i(y_0)$ is equivalent to communicating the function $v_i(y)$.

The pivot mechanism $D° = M°, (y^*, t^*))$ for this model is then given by:

$$M° = \{ m_i : \quad Y_0 \to \mathbf{R} \}$$

$$y_0^*(m) = y \quad \text{maximizing} \quad \sum_i m_i(y_0) - p \cdot y_0 \quad \text{and}$$

$$t_i^*(m) = \max_y \sum_{j \neq i} ((m_j(y) - \alpha_j p \cdot y))$$

$$- \sum_{j \neq i} (m_j(y_0^*(m)) - \alpha_j p \cdot y_0^*(m))$$

Agent i's total cost for the public good is

$$\alpha_i p \cdot y_0^*(m) - t_i^*(m) = \alpha_i p \cdot y_0^*(m) + \max_{y_0} \sum_{j \neq i} (m_j(y_0) - \alpha p \cdot y_0)$$

$$- \sum_{j \neq i} (m_j(y_0^*(m)) - \alpha_j p \cdot y_0^*(m))$$

or, consists of an assigned fraction of total cost $\alpha_i p \cdot y_0^*(m)$ plus an amount $t_i^*(m)$ interpretable as the aggregate willingness to pay of all the other agents to have the quantity y_0 chosen that would maximize their (net) willingness to pay rather than receive $y_0^*(m)$ (which maximizes total willingness to pay).

The basic result is, of course, that under the pivot mechanism each agent has a dominant strategy to honestly reveal his true demand for the public good – even though he is free to be a free rider.

The pivot demand-revealing mechanism was developed for the public good model by Clarke (1971) and independently later by Groves and Loeb (1975). Green and Laffont in a series of papers and a monograph, Green and Laffont (1979), have explored this model in rich detail.

Case 3. Decentralized firm model: Another example of the general model is that of a decentralized firm with a number n, say, of separate divisions. The choice y is a vector of decisions that affect more than one division's profit $v_i(y)$. For example, y may specify a capital budget allocation or a quantity of a transferred good between two divisions. Thus, from the overall point of view of the firm, the choice of the decisions y should be coordinated to maximize total profits $\sum_i v_i(y)$.

To achieve this objective, the coordinating agent, called the center, must have information about the effects of the decision y on all the divisions. Yet each division's manager, if he were to be evaluated solely on the basis of his own division's profit $v_i(y)$, would not have the same interest as the overall firm and hence might be expected to be overly optimistic regarding those decisions increasing his profits and overly pessimistic regarding decisions having a negative impact on his profits. By modifying the measure of performance of the division manager, however, the center can align the manager's interest with that of the overall firm. This is accomplished by crediting (or assessing) the division an amount determined by the transfer rule $t_i^*(\cdot)$ of a demand-revealing mechanism so that a division manager's performance is evaluated on the basis of his division's profits $v_i(y)$ plus his transfer $t_i^*(m)$. Thus, to maximize his evaluation, he has an incentive to provide accurate information, thus also permitting the choice of the overall firm optimal decision $y = y^*(v)$.

The class of demand-revealing mechanisms was first developed by Groves (1970) for a generalized version of this model. Subsequent papers by Groves (1976b), Loeb (1975), Cohen (1977), Groves and Loeb (1979), and Pratt and Zeckhauser (1980), have further developed this model.

Other models: An interesting and ingenious application of the demand-revealing mechanism is by Dolan (1978) to the problem of optimally servicing customers randomly arriving in a queue with varying costs to waiting. The optimal queue discipline is to serve the customer with highest waiting cost first. Yet these costs are not observable and individuals might generally be expected to exaggerate their true costs if by doing so they could reduce their waiting time. But Dolan develops a version of the demand-revealing mechanism to elicit truthful revelation of agents' waiting costs. The (negative) transfers are interpreted as the cost of a particular position in the queue that depends on all waiting customers' true waiting time costs.

Another recent application of the demand-revealing mechanism is that of Leonard, Monash, and Zeckhauser (1980), who analyze the problem of allocating priority claims to a commodity in random supply. Firms must commit themselves to some expenditures, for instance, investment, before the total supply of a resource is known and hence before the firm knows exactly how much resource it will receive. The efficient ex post allocation of the resource depends on the ex ante firm decisions. Thus, for overall efficiency both the ex ante firm decisions and the ex post allocation of the resource must be coordinated. This is done through an ex ante allocation of priorities to the resource supply once it is realized. The demand-revealing mechanism is developed for this problem to induce firms to both reveal their true information so that they receive an efficient priority assignment and to make efficient ex ante firm decisions.

3.4   Properties of the demand-revealing mechanism in the case of general preferences

In the case of general preferences, that is, in the presence of income effects, as discussed in Section 3.1, an agent's willingness to pay for any alternative y depends on his transfer t_i. Thus, under a demand-revealing mechanism, to honestly report his preferences with a message $m_i(\cdot)$, that is, satisfy (3.3), he must take into account how all agents' messages affect his transfer $t_i(m)$. Hence, telling the truth cannot be a dominant strategy. It is, however, a best response strategy.

Theorem 4 (Groves and Ledyard): Given preferences $R_i \in \Re^\circ$ all i and a demand-revealing mechanism $D^* = [M^*, (y^*(\cdot), t^*(\cdot))]$ defined by (3.1), (3.2), and (3.4–5)

(a) $m_i^*(\cdot)$ is agent i's best response strategy given any m_j, $j \neq i$, if

$$m_i^*(y) = \mu_i[y; y^*(m/m_i^*), t_i(m/m_i^*)] + constant, \quad \text{for all} \quad y \in Y \quad \text{and}$$

(b) m^* is a Nash equilibrium joint strategy if

$$m_i^*(y) = \mu_i[y; y^*(m^*), t_i(m^*)] + constant, \quad \text{for all} \quad y \in Y, \quad \text{for all } i$$

Proof: See Groves and Ledyard (1977a, Section 3, and 1977b).

Although truthful revelation of preferences is a Nash equilibrium for a demand-revealing mechanism, fully efficient outcomes are not selected. As in the quasi-linear case, the transfer rules $t_i^*(\cdot)$ cannot in general ensure that aggregate transfers equal zero, as required for efficiency. Other mechanisms, however, do exist with the property that at Nash equilibrium joint strategies, fully efficient or Pareto-optimal alternatives are selected. See the discussion in Section 2.2.

$$(4.3) \quad t_i^+(a) \equiv \int_{A_{-i}} \left\{ \sum_{j \neq i} v_j(y^+(\alpha/a_i); \alpha_j) \right\} dP_i(\alpha_{-i} \mid a_i)$$

$$- \frac{1}{n-1} \sum_{j \neq i} \int_{A_{-j}} \left\{ \sum_{k \neq j} v_k(y^+(\alpha/a_j); \alpha_k) \right\} dP_j(\alpha_{-j} \mid a_j)$$

Several observations may be made of these transfer rules. First, it is easy to see that the sum of the transfer is zero for every joint strategy a; summing (5.3) over all i gives:

$$\sum_i t_i^+(a) = \sum_i \int_{A_{-i}} \left\{ \sum_{j \neq i} v_j(y^+(\alpha/a_i); \alpha_j) \right\} dP_i(\alpha_{-i} \mid a_i)$$

$$- \sum_j \int_{A_{-j}} \left\{ \sum_{k \neq j} v_k(y^+(\alpha/a_j); \alpha_k) \right\} dP_j(\alpha_{-j} \mid a_j) = 0$$

Thus, if all agents tell the truth, that is, $a = \alpha$, then the outcome $z^+ = \rho^+(\alpha) \equiv (y^+(\alpha); t^+(\alpha))$ will be fully efficient or Pareto-optimal.

Second, it is important to note that these transfer rules depend on each agent's probability measure $P_i(\cdot \mid \cdot)$. Thus, if an agent's beliefs about the other agents' parameters is subjective, a subtle issue of interpretation is involved. Essentially, the parameter α_i must in this case be taken to characterize not only agent i's preferences R_i but also his subjective beliefs about the other agents' parameters α_j. That is, each element a_i not only completely defines the function $v_j(\cdot, a_i)$ but the probability measure $P(\cdot \mid a_i)$ as well.

But, as will be seen below, in order to prove positive results for this mechanism, some strong assumptions on the agents' probability measures are required. One assumption implies that the true beliefs of any agent are common knowledge. Thus, under this assumption it is perhaps not unreasonable that the transfer rules $t_i^+(\cdot)$ depend on these beliefs. But, of course, the assumption is especially strong and in any particular case may itself not be reasonable.

Third, it is interesting to compare these transfer rules with the demand-revealing mechanism's transfer rules. Recall (3.4); the demand-revealing mechanisms rules $t_i^*(\cdot)$ are given by:

$$t_i^*(m) = \sum_{j \neq i} m_j(y^*(m)) - A_i(m_{-i}).$$

Now, in this particular case where each agent's message m_i is a reported parameter a_i, suppose the functions $A_i(m_{-i}) \equiv A_i(a_{-i})$ are given by:

$$(4.4) \quad A_i(a_{-i}) \equiv \frac{1}{n-1} \sum_{j \neq i} \int_{A_{-i}} \left\{ \sum_{k \neq j} v_k(y^+(\alpha/a_j); \alpha_k) \right\} dP_j(\alpha_{-j} \mid a_j)$$

4   Bayesian efficient mechanisms

4.1   *The non-stochastic quasi-linear case*

As discussed in Section 2.2 the Bayesian equilibrium conce
equilibrium concept to consider for the collective choic
game of incomplete information. It also turns out that it
define mechanisms such that, in the quasi-linear case at le
cient outcomes are selected at Bayesian equilibrium joint s
is to be compared with the results discussed in the previou
The demand-revealing mechanisms, while admitting don
equilibria in the case of quasi-linear preferences, do not
cient outcomes. Also, while Nash-efficient mechanisms a
least some questions remain concerning the validity of the
equilibrium for the games of incomplete information
mechanism in the collective choice model.

Consider, then, the collective choice model in which a
erences are quasi-linear in money, $R_i \in \mathfrak{R}^L$. Further, supp
preference is parameterized by an element α_i of some be
able space A_i; thus

(4.1) $\mu_i(y, t_i) \equiv t_i + v_i(y, \alpha_i)$

That is, the parameter α_i completely characterizes the fu
and, hence, the agent's preferences R_i. Although each
only his own parameter α_i, he is assumed to have a pro
$P(\cdot \mid \alpha_i)$ defined over the other agents' joint parameter spac

Now we define a mechanism similar in some respec
revealing mechanism. This mechanism was developed
and Gerard-Varet (1979) whose results we follow in
equivalent mechanism was also independently devel
(1979). As under the demand-revealing mechanism, each
some preferences, here, by reporting an element a_i
space A_i. Telling the truth means, of course, that his re
is equal to his true parameter α_i. Then, the outcome
$(y^+(\cdot), t_1^+(\cdot), \ldots, t_n^+(\cdot))$ is defined in the first comp

(4.2) $y^+(a) = y\text{-argmax} \sum_j v_j(y; a_j)$

over Y, all $a \in X_j A_j$. That is, the function $y^+(\cdot)$ s
optimal outcome in the event that all agents tell the tru
rule is equivalent to that for any demand-revealing m
The transfer rules $t_i^+(\cdot)$ are defined by the formul

Then, the two transfer rules $t_i^*(a)$ and $t_i^+(a)$ are given by:

$$t_i^*(a) = \sum_{j \neq i} v_j(y^+(a); a_j) - A_i(a_{-i}) : \text{ demand-revealing and}$$

$$t_i^+(a) = \int_{A_{-i}} \sum_{j \neq i} v_j(y^+(a); a_j) - A_i(a_{-i}) : \text{ Bayesian}$$

Or, alternatively, letting

$$h_j(a) \equiv \sum_{k \neq j} v_k(y^+(a); a_k) \quad \text{and}$$

$$\bar{h}_j(a_j) \equiv \int_{A_{-j}} h_j(\alpha/a_j) \, dP_j(\alpha_{-j} | a_j) \quad \text{then}$$

$$t_i^*(a) = h_i(a) - \frac{1}{n-1} \sum_{j \neq i} \bar{h}_j(a_j) : \text{ demand-revealing}$$

$$t_i^+(a) = \bar{h}_i(a_i) - \frac{1}{n-1} \sum_{j \neq i} \bar{h}_j(a_j) : \text{ Bayesian}$$

Thus, the difference between these two transfer rules for agent i is just the random variable: $\Delta(a) = t_i^*(a) - t_i^+(a) = h_i(a) - \bar{h}_i(a_i)$, whose conditional expected value is zero:

$$\int_{A_{-i}} \Delta(\alpha/a_i) \, dP(\alpha_{-i} | a_i) = 0 \quad \text{for all} \quad a_i \in A_i$$

Thus, agent i's *expected* utility under either mechanism is identical. Note, however, that with the functions A_i defined by (5.4), the sum of the transfers $t_i^*(a)$ may be positive at some joint messages a. So, this particular demand-revealing mechanism is not always feasible. It shows the close similarity with the Bayesian mechanism, however.

As just noted, the Bayesian mechanism is closely related to the demand-revealing mechanism in the quasi-linear case. In view of Theorem 2, however, because the Bayesian mechanism is not a demand-revealing mechanism, telling the truth, that is, the Bayesian equilibrium joint strategy, is not a dominant strategy equilibrium. But, under a demand-revealing mechanism, telling the truth is, of course, a Bayesian equilibrium joint strategy (as it is a dominant strategy equilibrium). This was first proved directly by Groves (1970) in a more general model in which agents (a) were not necessarily able to know the parameter α_i exactly, (b) were not necessarily able to communicate their full information, and (c) were possibly required to take some other decisions affecting their pay-off before they knew what the collective decision y was.

The main theorem for the Bayesian mechanism is that under a strong independence condition on the probability measures, telling the truth is a Bayesian equilibrium and results in an efficient or Pareto-optimal outcome.

Theorem 5 (d'Aspremont and Gerard-Varet, and Arrow): Consider the Bayesian mechanism defined by the message space $A = X_i A_i$ and the rules $y^+(\cdot)$ and $t_i^+(\cdot)$ (cf. 3.2 and 5.3). Suppose the beliefs of the agents satisfy the following independence condition:

(4.5) $P_i(\cdot \mid \alpha_i) = P_i(\cdot \mid \alpha_i')$ for all $\alpha_i, \alpha_i' \in A_i$,   all i.

Then, the joint strategy $\delta^* = (\delta_1^*, \ldots, \delta_n^*)$ where $\delta_i^*(\alpha_i) = \alpha_i$, that is $\delta_i^*(\cdot)$ is the identity function, is a Bayesian equilibrium and thus, $z^* = [y^+(\delta^*(\alpha)), t^+(\delta^*(\alpha))]$ is efficient for all $\alpha \in A$.

Proof: See d'Aspremont and Gerard-Varet (1979, Theorem 6).

As mentioned above, the independence condition (5.5) implies that every agent's beliefs about the others' parameters is common knowledge. This assumption rules out certain kinds of informational externalities in which some agent knows something about another agent that is not also known by a third agent. Although this independence condition can be weakened somewhat (see d'Aspremont and Gerard-Varet, [1979], Theorem 7), what the general minimal conditions are is still an open question. Laffont and Maskin (1979) provide an interesting partial result that in the dependent case, if each agent believes himself to be dissimilar to the other agents (e.g., has much higher or much lower valuations for the decision y than the group average), then it is possible to find a Bayesian-efficient mechanism. However, if all agents believe themselves similar to the others, then their results suggest no Bayesian-efficient mechanism exists.

4.2   *The general case: optimal risk sharing*

Unfortunately, in the case of general preferences $R_i \in \mathfrak{R}^\circ$, representable by $u_i(y, t_i)$, no general mechanisms are known under which at Bayesian equilibria fully efficient outcomes are selected. In a special class of interesting problems, however, some results have been obtained by Wilson (1979). This class of problems concerns optimal risk sharing.

4.2.1   *The basic risk-sharing model*

Following Wilson, we define the risk-sharing model as follows: Suppose the return resulting from the choice y (e.g., investment) depends on a stochastic variable, ω, whose value is unknown at the time of the decision y, but whose distribution, say, $F(\omega)$, is known. Let $\pi(y, \omega)$ denote the net return resulting from the choice y and the realization ω of the random variable.

The agents $i = 1, \ldots, n$ who collectively make the choice y are assumed to care only about their individual shares of the net return. That is, the transfers t_i in this case are functions of the net return specifying each agent's share of π and thus are subject to the constraint: $\sum_i t_i(\pi) = \pi$. Their preferences over shares t_i of money are assumed representable by von Neumann–Morgenstern utility functions $v_i(t_i; \alpha_i)$ where α_i parameterizes their utility. Because these are von Neumann–Morgenstern utility functions, the agent's preferences over alternative decision-sharing rule pairs $(y; t_i(\cdot))$ are given by the expected utility of their share $t_i(\pi)$ given $\pi = \pi(y, \omega)$:

$$u_i(y, t_i(\cdot); \alpha_i) = E_\omega[v_i[t_i(\pi(y, \omega)); \alpha_i]]$$

where the expectation over ω is taken with respect to the distribution $F(\cdot)$.

Efficient or Pareto-optimal decision-sharing rule pairs $(y^*, \{t_i^*(\cdot)\})$ are defined in the ex ante sense.

Definition: $(y^*, \{t_i^*(\cdot)\})$ is Pareto-optimal or efficient if there is no other pair $(y, \{t_i(\cdot)\})$ with $\sum_i t_i(\pi) = \pi$, all π such that

$$u_i(y, t_i(\cdot); \alpha_i) \geqslant u_i(y^*, t_i^*(\cdot); \alpha_i) \quad \text{all } i$$

with strict inequality for some i.

Note that for the case of quasi-linear preferences, that is,

$$u_i(y, t_i(\cdot); \alpha_i) = E_\omega[t_i(\pi(y, \omega))],$$

any decision-sharing rule pair $(y, \{t_i(\cdot)\})$ such that $t_i(\cdot)$ is monotonic increasing in π, $\sum_i t_i(\pi) = \pi$, and y maximizes $E_\omega[\pi(y, \omega)]$ is Pareto-optimal. Quasi-linear preferences in this case, of course, are linear preferences in the transfer and hence exhibit risk neutrality. Thus, the problem of designing efficient mechanisms – that is, mechanisms to produce efficient outcomes – is trivial in this case. No communication with the agents is required because knowing their preferences are linear is the same as knowing their exact preferences. Furthermore, an efficient decision y is independent of the sharing rules – it just maximizes expected return.

In the case of varying risk preferences, however, efficient decisions will depend on how the return is to be shared and also on the various risk tolerances of the individual agents. Although I know of no general solution for the problem of designing efficient mechanisms, Wilson has analyzed a particularly suggestive special case.

4.2.2   *Wilson's model I: constant risk aversion*

Three assumptions in the model outlined above define Wilson's special case. First, suppose the stochastic variable ω is taken to be the net rate of return and is assumed to be normally distributed with (known) mean μ and variance σ^2. Second, suppose the return function exhibits constant returns to scale in the decision variable y so that $\pi(y, \omega)$ is given by: $\pi(y, \omega) = y \cdot \omega$. Third, assume preferences display constant risk aversion or that the utility functions $v_i(t_i; \alpha_i)$ are given by:

$$v_i(t_i; \alpha_i) = -\alpha_i e^{-t_i/\alpha_i}$$

The parameter α_i is just the reciprocal of the Arrow–Pratt local measure of absolute risk aversion and is called the agent's *risk tolerance.*

Now, for this model, efficient decision-sharing rule pairs are composed of linear sharing rules which divide net returns π (marginally) in the proportions α_i/α_0, where $\alpha_0 \equiv \Sigma_j \alpha_j$, and decisions y that are given by $y = \alpha_0 \mu/\sigma_2$. Here, the efficient decision y is the same for all Pareto-optimal pairs $(y, \{t_i(\cdot)\})$; the different efficient pairs are specified by the constant terms on the linear sharing rules $t_i(\pi) = \bar{t}_i + (\alpha_i/\alpha_0)\pi$, where $\Sigma_i \bar{t}_i = 0$. This property of efficient decision-sharing rule pairs is analogous to the property of efficient decision-transfer vector pairs (y, t) in the quasi-linear case where the same decision y is compatible with all Pareto-optimal pairs.

In view of this characterization of efficient decision-sharing rules, Wilson considers the mechanism in which each agent reports a risk tolerance parameter a_i, receives the share $(a_i/\Sigma a_j)\pi$, which results from the decision $y(a) = \Sigma a_j \mu/\sigma^2$. Thus, if each agent reports his true risk tolerance, $a_i = \alpha_i$, then an efficient decision-sharing rule pair results. Wilson shows that reporting his true risk tolerance is an agent's dominant strategy.

Theorem 6 (Wilson): For the game defined by the risk-sharing model and the mechanism

$$t_i(\pi; a) = (a_i / \sum_j a_j) \pi \qquad y(a) = \sum_j a_j \mu / \sigma^2$$

a^* is a dominant strategy equilibrium where $a_i^* = \alpha_i$ is agent i's true risk tolerance parameter.

Proof: See Wilson (1979).

Thus, in this model one is able to get truth telling as a stronger equilibrium – a dominant strategy equilibrium – instead of as only a Bayesian equilibrium. But in Wilson's next model, truth-telling is a Bayesian equilibrium but not a dominant strategy equilibrium.

4.2.3 *Risk sharing with independent information*

This model is an extension of the basic risk-sharing model in which each agent receives some private information about the random variable ω. In this case, an efficient decision y would depend on the agents' information, as well as on their risk tolerances. Thus, an efficient mechanism should induce the agents to reveal accurately their information as well as their risk parameters.

To formalize, suppose each agent i has an independent observation σ_i on the random variable ω, and denote by $F_i(\cdot \mid \omega, \beta_i)$ the conditional distribution of the observation σ_i given ω and a privately known parameter β_i. Thus, we may denote i's private information regarding ω by the observation parameter pair $\gamma_i = (\sigma_i, \beta_i)$ and his total private characteristic by the triple $\epsilon_i = (\alpha_i, \sigma_i, \beta_i)$, which includes his utility function parameter α_i. The full-information posterior distribution of ω given $\gamma = (\gamma_1, \ldots, \gamma_n)$, we denote by $F(\cdot \mid \gamma)$.

An efficient or Pareto-optimal decision-sharing rule pair $(y^*, \{t_i^*(\cdot)\})$ is defined relative to full information.

Definition: $(y^*, \{t_i^*(\cdot)\})$ is Pareto optimal or efficient given γ, if there is no other pair $(y, \{t_i(\cdot)\})$ such that

$$E_{\omega \mid \gamma}[v_i(t_i[\pi(y, \omega]; \alpha_j)] \geq E_{\omega \mid \gamma}[v_i(t_i^*[\pi(y^*, \omega]; \alpha_i)]$$

for all i, with strict inequality for some i, where the (conditional) expectation is taken with respect to the (conditional) full-information posterior distribution of ω, $F(\cdot \mid \gamma)$.

Wilson's Model II specializes this model by three assumptions. First, the conditional distribution of the observation σ_i given ω and parameter β_i is assumed, for all i, to be normal with mean ω and precision β_i (or variance $1/\beta_i$), *and* the posterior of ω given γ is normal with mean

$$\mu_0 \equiv \frac{\Sigma_i \, \sigma_i \beta_i}{\Sigma_i \, \beta_i}$$

and precision

$$\beta_0 \equiv \sum_i \beta_i \quad \left(\text{variance } \frac{1}{\Sigma_i \, \beta_i} \right).$$

Second, as with Model I, the return function exhibits constant returns to scale: $\pi(y, \omega) = y \cdot \omega$. Third, utility functions are the same constant absolute risk aversion functions

$$v_i(t_i; \alpha_i) = -\alpha_i e^{-t_i/\alpha_i}$$

where α_i is agent i's risk tolerance.

Analogous to the previous model, efficient (i.e. full-information Pareto-optimal) decision-sharing rule pairs are such that the sharing rules divide net returns π (marginally) in the proportions α_i/α_0 and the decision $y = \alpha_0 \mu_0 \beta_0$. Here, however, in order to implement efficient decision-sharing rule pairs, information from the agents must be received about not only their risk tolerances α_i, but also their private information (observation-parameter pair) $\gamma_i = (\sigma_i, \beta_i)$. Thus, the mechanism must attempt to elicit all this information.

Wilson considers the mechanism in which each agent reports a risk tolerance parameter a_i *and* (in effect) a reported product $c_i = b_i s_i$ of his observation and parameter. As before, each agent receives the proportion $a_i/\Sigma a_j = a_i/a_0$ of total net returns π resulting from the decisions $y(a, c) = \Sigma_i \, a_i \Sigma_i \, c_i = (a_0 \Sigma_i \, s_i b_i)$. Note that if everyone reports the truth, that is, $a_i = \alpha_i$ and $c_i = \beta_i \sigma_i$, then an efficient decision-sharing rule pair results. Wilson shows that truthful reporting is a best strategy for each agent under the assumption that all the other agents are reporting truthfully.

Theorem 7 (Wilson): Given the game defined by the risk-sharing model with independent information and the mechanism

$$t_i(\pi; a) = \left(a_i / \sum_j a_j \right) \pi, \qquad y(a, c) = \sum_i a_i \sum_i c_i$$

consider the truthful joint strategy δ^* that is, where $\delta^*(\alpha_i, \beta_i \sigma_i) = (\alpha_i, \beta_i \sigma_i)$. For each agent i, the first component of his truth-telling strategy δ_i^*, that is, reporting $a_i = \alpha_i$ is best, irrespective of the other strategies δ_j, and the second component, that is, reporting $b_i s_i = \beta_i \sigma_i$ is best, given that the other agents are also reporting truthfully, that is, $b_j s_j = \beta_j \sigma_j$. That is: for every $a_{-i}, \beta \sigma_{-i}$,

(4.6) $(\alpha_i, \beta_i\sigma_i)$ maximizes $E_{\omega|\gamma_i}[v_i(t_i[\pi(y(a, \beta\sigma/c_i), \omega), a]; \alpha_i)]$

where the conditional expectation is taken over ω, given agent i's private information $\gamma_i = (\sigma_i, \beta_i)$ only. Thus, in particular, δ^* is a Bayesian equilibrium.

Proof: See Wilson (1979).

Note that since the truthful messages $(\alpha_i, \beta_i\sigma_i)$ solve the maximization in (5.6) for every a_{-i} and $\beta\sigma_{-i}$, it is not necessary to consider agents' beliefs about the other agents' parameters. Thus, the equilibrium δ^* is actually stronger than just a Bayesian equilibrium and, a fortiori of course, the mechanism also is independent of the agents' beliefs, in contrast to the d'Aspremont–Gerard-Varet Bayesian mechanism discussed in Section 5.1.

REFERENCES

Arrow, K. (1963). *Social choice and individual values,* 2nd ed. New York: Wiley.
Arrow, K. (1979). The property rights doctrine and demand revelation under incomplete information. In M. Boskins (ed.), *Economics and human welfare: essays in honor of Tibor Scitovsky.* New York: Academic Press.
Clarke, E. (1971). Multipart pricing of public goods. *Public choice* 11: 17–33.
Cohen, S. (1977). Incentive compatible control of the multidivisional firm with iterative communication, Ph.D. dissertation, Northwestern University.
Dasgupta, P., Hammond, P., and Maskin, E. (1979). The implementation of social choice rules: some general results on incentive compatibility. *Review of Economic Studies* 46(2): 185–216.
D'Aspremont, C. and Gérard-Varet, L. A. (1979). Incentives and incomplete information. *Journal of Public Economics* 11: 25–45.
Dolan, R. (1978). Incentive mechanisms for priority queuing problems. *The Bell Journal of Economics* 9(2): 421–436.
Farquharson, R. (1969). *Theory of voting.* New Haven: Yale University Press.
Gibbard, A. (1973). Manipulation of voting schemes: A general result. *Econometrica* 41: 587–601.
Green, J. and Laffont, J. J. (1976). Revelation des preferences pour les biens publics. *Cahiers du Seminaire d'Econometrica.* C.R.N.S., Paris.
Green, J. and Laffont, J. J. (1977). Characterization of satisfactory mechanisms for the revelation of preferences for public goods. *Econometrica* 45: 417–438.
Green, J. and Laffont, J. J. (1979). *Incentives in public decision making.* Amsterdam: North-Holland.
Green, J., Kohlberg, E., and Laffont, J. J. (1976). Partial equilibrium approach to the free rider problem. *Journal of Public Economics* 6: 375–394.
Groves, T. (1970). The allocation of resources under uncertainty , Ph.D. dissertation, University of California, Berkeley.
Groves, T. (1973). Incentives in teams. *Econometrica* 41: 617–631.
Groves, T. (1976a). Information, incentives, and the internalization of production externalities. In Lin, S. A. (ed.), *Theory and measurement of economic externalities.* New York: Academic Press.

Groves, T. (1976b). Incentive compatible control of decentralized organization, In Ho, Y. C. and Mitter, S. (eds.), *Directions in large-scale systems.* New York: Plenum Press.

Groves, T. (1979). Efficient collective choice when compensation is possible. *Review of Economic Studies* 46(2): 227–241.

Groves, T. and Ledyard, J. (1977a). Optimal allocation of public goods: a solution to the 'free rider' problem. *Econometrica* 45: 783–809.

Groves, T. and Ledyard, J. (1977b). Some limitations of demand revealing processes. *Public Choice* 29(2): 107–124.

Groves, T. and Loeb, M. (1975). Incentives and public inputs. *Journal of Public Economics* 4: 211–226.

Groves, T. and Loeb, M. (1979). Incentives in a divisionalized firm. *Management Science* 25(3): 221–230.

Holmstrom, B. (1979). Groves's scheme on restricted domains. *Econometrica* 47: 1137–1144.

Hurwicz, L. (1959). Optimality and informational efficiency in resource allocation processes. In Arrow, K., et al. (eds.), *Mathematical methods in the social sciences.* Stanford: Stanford University Press.

Hurwicz, L. (1972). On informationally decentralized systems. In Radner, R., and McGuire, C. (eds.), *Decision and organization.* Amsterdam: North-Holland.

Hurwicz, L. (1975). On the existence of allocation systems whose manipulative Nash equilibria are Pareto-optimal, unpublished paper presented at Third World Congress of the Econometric Society, Toronto.

Hurwicz, L. (1979). Outcome function yielding Walrasian and Lindahl allocation at Nash equilibrium points. *Review of Economic Studies,* pp. 217–225.

Hurwicz, L. (1979b). On allocation attainable through Nash equilibria. *Journal of Economic Theory* 21: 140–165.

Hurwicz, L. and Schmeidler, D. (1978). Construction of outcome functions guaranteeing existence and Pareto optimality of Nash equilibria. *Econometrica* 46: 1447–1174.

Hurwicz, L., Maskin, E., and Postlewaite, A. (1979). Feasible implementation of social choice correspondence by Nash equilibria, unpublished manuscript dated July 12, 1979.

Katzner, D. (1970). *Static demand theory.* London: Macmillan.

Laffont, J. J. (ed.). (1979). *Aggregation and revelation of preferences.* Amsterdam: North-Holland.

Laffont, J. J. and Maskin, E. (1979). A differential approach to expected utility maximizing mechanism. In Laffont, J. J. (ed.), *Aggregation and revelation of preferences.* Amsterdam: North-Holland.

Leonard, H., Monash, C., and Zeckhauser, R. (1980). Efficient and near efficient allocation of commodities in stochastic supply, unpublished manuscript dated May 1980.

Loeb, M. (1975). Coordination and informational incentive problems in the multi-divisional form, Ph.D. dissertation, Northwestern University.

Maskin, E. (1977). Nash equilibria and welfare optimality. *Mathematics of operations research* (forthcoming).

Postlewaite, A. and Schmeidler, D. (1978). Approximate efficiency of non-Walrasian Nash equilibria. *Econometrica* 46: 127–135.

Pratt, J. and Zeckhauser, R. (1980). Incentive-based decentralization: expected externality payments induce efficient behavior in groups. Discussion Paper 83D, J. F. Kennedy School of Government, Harvard University.

Review of economic studies. (1979). Symposium on Incentive Compatibility 46(2).

Satterthwaite, M. (1975). Strategy-proofness and Arrow's condition: existence and correspondence theorems for voting procedures and social welfare functions. *Journal of Economic Theory* 10: 187–217.

Schmeidler, D. (1980). Walrasian analysis via strategic outcome functions. *Econometrica* 48: 1585–1593.

Shapley, L. and Shubik, M. (1976). Trade using one commodity as a means of payment. Discussion Paper R1-1851-NSF, Rand Corporation, Santa Monica, Calif.

Smets, H. (1973). Le principe de la compensation réciproque un instrument économique pour la solution de certains problèmes de pollution transfrontière. O.C.D.E. Direction de l'Environnement.

Smith, V. (1979). Incentive compatible experimental processes for the provision of public goods. In Smith, V. (ed.), *Research in experimental economics,* vol. 1. Greenwich: JAI Press.

Tideman, T. and Tullock, G. (1976). A new and superior principle for collective choice. *Journal of Political Economy* 84: 1145–1159.

Vickrey, W. (1960). Utility, strategy, and social decision rules. *Quarterly Journal of Economics* 74: 507–535.

Vickrey, W. (1961). Counterspeculation, auctions, and competitive sealed tenders. *Journal of Finance* 16: 8–37.

Walker, M. (1978). A note on the characterization of mechanisms for the revelation of preferences. *Econometrica* 46: 147–152.

Walker, M. (1979). A simple incentive compatible scheme for attaining Lindahl allocation: a non-confiscatory solution to the free rider problem, private communication.

Walker, M. (1980). On the nonexistence of a dominant strategy mechanism for making optimal public decision. *Econometrica* 48: 1521–1540.

Wilson, R. (1979). Incentive compatible risk sharing, technical report, IMSSS, Stanford University.

CHAPTER 2

The theory of incentives: an overview

Jean-Jacques Laffont and Eric Maskin

The theory of incentives is concerned with the problem that a planner (alternatively called a designer, principal, or government, depending on context[1]) faces when his own objectives do not coincide with those of the members of society[2] (whom we shall call agents). This lack of coincidence of goals distinguishes incentives theory from the theory of teams (Marschak and Radner, 1972), which postulates identical objectives, but which otherwise shares many features with our subject. In turn, the assumption that the planner, often the surrogate for society itself, has well-defined objectives separates incentives theory from most of social choice theory, which, since Arrow (1951), examines the possibility of *deriving* social objectives from those of individual preferences.

For an incentive problem to arise, noncoincidence of goals is not enough; the planner must care about either what agents know or what they do. That is, his objective function must depend either on agents' *information* or on their *behavior.*

An example of pure informational dependence is provided by the literature on resource allocation mechanisms. There, the planner's objective – social welfare – is a function of consumers' (agents') preferences and endowments. The incentive problem is, typically, that of eliciting this information.

Pure behavioral dependence is exhibited by an employee-employer relationship in which the employer is interested only in the employee's output. In this case, incentives pertain not to revealing what the employee knows but to inducing him to work hard. Of course, incentive problems typically involve both kinds of dependence.

The planner pursues his objectives by the choice of an incentive

31

scheme,[3] a rule that specifies, in advance, the planner's behavior on the basis of his perceptions of agents' information and actions.[4]

This choice is nontrivial if either (1) some of the agents' payoff-relevant information is not known, a priori, to the planner or else (2) the planner cannot observe agents' actions perfectly. (If the planner both knew all relevant information and could precisely monitor actions, he could presumably force agents to take the optimal action based on this information by promising dire consequences otherwise.)

The first difficulty is frequently called the problem of adverse selection. It is not necessary that the planner's own objective function depend on agents' information – as in the allocation literature – for adverse selection to arise; it is enough that agents' payoffs should. Consider, for example, a monopolist wishing to maximize his (expected) revenue using a nonlinear price schedule. Although his revenue function does not depend directly on consumers' taste parameters – only on their demand – such information is obviously relevant to his choice of schedule. The monopolist's problem is, indeed, a prime example of pure adverse selection.

At the other extreme is the employer-employee relationship mentioned before. Imagine that the employee possesses no information not known to the employer. Suppose, furthermore, that the employee's output depends stochastically on his effort, which is unobservable by the employer. Then, the employer faces a problem of the second kind – a *moral hazard* problem. His failure to induce the "optimal" effort level by the agent derives solely from his limited ability to monitor this effort.

The theories of adverse selection and moral hazard are similar, but there are some important differences between them. It is useful, therefore, to keep them separate conceptually, as we do in Section 2.

The planner's choice of an incentive scheme entails a double maximization: He chooses that scheme which maximizes his (typically, expected) payoff subject to the constraint that, given this scheme, agents will maximize their own objective functions. In many contexts agents must be guaranteed a minimal expected payoff to induce them to participate in the scheme at all. In such cases the planner must maximize subject to the additional constraints that agents obtain these minimal levels. The planner is, therefore, the "leader" in a two-move game; his move consists of selecting a scheme.

What it means for an agent to "maximize his objective function" may be complex if there are other agents, for his payoff then depends on their responses to the planner's scheme as well his own. Thus, with more than one agent, an incentive scheme induces a *game* among the agents, and the planner optimizes subject to the agents' being in *equilibrium*. Of course, to say what an equilibrium is, one must specify an equilibrium concept. Even restricting to noncooperative (noncollusive) behavior by agents, at least four solution concepts (not including their refinements) figure prominently in the incentives literature. We shall have more to say about them later.

We have informally indicated the subject matter of incentives theory in general terms. Of course, questions of incentives are rarely analyzed at this level of generality. Nonetheless, it may be helpful to have a framework within which to relate the disparate pieces of the large incentives literature. To this purpose, we present a formal model in Section 1 and discuss certain modeling difficulties. In Section 2 we show how the literature consists of studies of special cases of this model. Finally, in Section 3, we analyze as an illustrative example a particular, but much studied, special case – a model of public project selection.

1   A general framework

1.1   *The model*

We consider a model consisting of a planner and n agents (indexed $i = 1, \ldots, n$). Each agent i has private information represented by $\theta^i \in \Theta^i$. On the basis of this information, he sends a message $m^i \in M^i$ to the planner. The planner replies to these messages with response $r \in R$. The agent then chooses action $a^i \in A^i$. The planner cannot, in general, observe a^i directly but observes the outcome $y^i \in Y^i$ of a^i, θ^i, and his own response r, where y^i is, in general, the value of the realization of a random function $\tilde{y}^i(a^i, \theta^i, r)$. Finally, the planner selects decision $d \in D$.

An *incentive scheme* is a choice by the planner of message spaces $M^1, \ldots, M^n$ (the other spaces, A^i, R, Y^i, and D are exogenous), response function $\rho : M \to R$, and decision function $\delta : M \times Y \to D$, where $M = \Pi M^i$ and $Y = \Pi Y^i$. Thus we can represent an incentive scheme by (M, ρ, δ). For reasons discussed in Section 1.4, efficiency will ordinarily be improved if the planner can take ρ and δ to be random functions. Thus, we shall often write an incentive scheme as $(M, \tilde{\rho}, \tilde{\delta})$ where the tildes indicate possible randomness.

This is not the most general model of incentives that one could imagine, but it is sufficiently broad to accommodate virtually all work on incentives to date.[5] To see how the elements of this model fit together, suppose that agents are production units and that the planner wishes to allocate capital efficiently across these units. Each agent i produces output from capital and labor according to the production process θ^i, known, ex ante, only to him. The planner asks each agent to provide data about his process. Thus m^i consists of possible messages that i could send about his production technology. Based on this data, the planner allocates capital across units. Thus r is an allocation, and ρ an allocation rule. Given his capital, agent i then chooses a quantity of labor a^i. Capital, labor, the production process, and, perhaps, nature combine to produce output $\bar{y}^i(a^i, \theta^i, r)$. Finally, production units are rewarded by the planner according to the rule δ on the basis of their output and the information they provided.

For another, quite different, example that illustrates the model well, suppose that the planner is an insurance company that insures agents against accidents. Based on the message m^i he provides about his accident-proneness θ^i, agent i is offered an insurance policy r. Whether or not he has an accident (the value of y^i) depends (randomly) on his accident-proneness and the level a^i of preventive care he chooses. (Notice that, in this example, y^i does not depend directly on r.) His ultimate compensation, d, depends on y^i and his policy. Because the policy itself depends on the information he provides, we can write δ as a function of m^i directly.

We shall suppose that agent i's payoff depends on his information θ^i, his action a^i, and the planner's decision d. We shall represent his preferences by the von Neumann-Morgenstern utility function

$$u^i : D \times A^i \times \Theta^i \to \mathbf{R}$$

Agent i's behavior presumably depends on θ^i. Thus, given θ^i, we can represent his behavior by the strategy $\sigma^i(\theta^i) = (\mu^i(\theta^i), \alpha^i(\theta^i, \cdot))$, where $\mu^i(\theta^i) \in M^i$ and, for all r, $\alpha^i(\theta^i, r) \in A^i$. (Throughout this chapter, we shall ignore the possibility that agents might use random (mixed) strategies.) The agent's *contingent strategy* or *strategy rule* is given by the function $\sigma^i(\cdot)$. If agent i is the sole agent, he will choose $\mu^i(\theta^i)$ and $\alpha^i(\theta^i, \cdot)$ to maximize the expected value of $u_i(\cdot, \cdot, \theta^i)$, where we speak of *expected* value, because r, d, and y^i may be random. With more than one agent, an incentive scheme is a genuine game; agent i's payoff will, in general, depend, through r and d, on the strategies of others. Thus, his choice of strategy will ordinarily depend on how he believes others behave. In other words, in addition to the "objective" uncertainty associated with the possible randomness of r, d, and y^i, the agent may face "strategic" uncertainty: uncertainty about others' strategies. Notice that he would face this uncertainty even if he knew the values of others' parameters θ^{-i}. The fact that he might not know these values merely compounds his problem.

There are several alternative hypotheses (drawn from game theory) in the incentives literature about how an agent might act under strategic uncertainty. These hypotheses are embodied in alternative solution concepts. That is, a solution concept implicitly prescribes a way of resolving strategic uncertainty.

We shall discuss four often-studied solution concepts later. For the time being, we observe that for a specified solution concept, the planner's problem is to choose an incentive scheme whose equilibrium maximizes his expected payoff. We assume that the planner's preferences depend on his decision d, the vector of outcomes y, and agents' information $\theta = (\theta^1, \ldots, \theta^n)$.[6] His preferences are represented by the von Neumann-Morgenstern utility function

$$v : D \times Y \times \Theta \to \mathbf{R}$$

We can think of the planner as the Stackelberg leader in a two-move game. First, he moves by choosing an incentive scheme; then, everyone else reacts to that scheme.

Unfortunately, the preceding phrase, "choose an incentive scheme whose equilibrium maximizes," may not have a well-defined meaning. For a given incentive scheme, and relative to a specific solution concept, there may be no equilibrium, or there may be several. The former possibility poses no great conceptual difficulty; the planner can simply confine his attention to those schemes that have an equilibrium. Moreover, the latter may not be especially troubling in the case of a single agent. If an agent has multiple optimal strategies, it may not be overly heroic to suppose that he chooses the one (or among the ones) that the planner prefers. At any rate, that is what the literature, for the most part, assumes. With more than one agent, however, agents will not, in general, be indifferent among multiple equilibria. Therefore, for the planner to count on a particular equilibrium arising may be unwarranted; agents who prefer another may thwart him. The issue of multiple equilibria has not been uniformly satisfactorily resolved throughout the incentives literature for more than one agent. As we shall see below, it remains, for certain solution concepts in particular, an important difficulty.

In contrast with the optimal incentive scheme – the incentive scheme that maximizes the planner's (expected) payoff – is the *full optimum*, which consists, in addition to response and decision functions, of the strategy rules that the planner, were he permitted, would *impose* on the agents. Because in the full optimum there is no informational problem, we can take the joint message space $M^1 \times \cdots \times M^n$ to be $\Theta^1 \times \cdots \times \Theta^n$. Formally, (θ, r^*, d^*), together with functions

$$a^{*i} : \Theta^i \times R \to A^i, \quad i = 1, \ldots, n$$

is a full optimum with respect to the prior distribution $F(\theta)$ if it solves the problem

$$\max_{r(\cdot),\, d(\cdot),\, a^i(\cdot)} \quad E_\theta v(d, y, \theta)$$

subject to

$$Eu^i(d(\theta, \bar{y}), a^i(\theta^i, r(\theta)), \theta^i) \geq \bar{u}^i, \quad i = 1, \ldots, n$$

for some choice of $\bar{u}^1, \ldots, \bar{u}^n$. The $\bar{u}^i$'s can be interpreted as the "minimal expected payoffs" mentioned in the introduction.

There are two reasons, mentioned in the introduction, why an optimal incentive scheme may not be a full optimum. One is that the value of θ may not be known to the planner a priori. This is the problem of adverse selection. The other is that y^i may depend on a^i. This is moral hazard. We shall have more to say about these two problems later.

1.2   Solution concepts

In this subsection we discuss some of the more widely used solution concepts in the incentives literature. Several others will be mentioned in Sections 2 and 3. We divide solution concepts into three categories: those that can be defined without reference to the information that agents possess about one another (e.g., equilibrium in dominant and maximin strategies); those that require the vector θ of informational parameters to be drawn from a joint probability distribution (viz., Bayesian equilibrium); and those that, in effect, assume complete information (e.g., Nash equilibrium).

By far the strongest, but in several ways the least controversial, solution concept is that of equilibrium in dominant strategies. A dominant strategy is a strategy that an agent, given his information, is willing to use regardless of what he believes others know and the way he believes others behave. Formally, $(\mu^i(\theta^i), \alpha^i(\theta^i, \cdot))$ is a *dominant strategy* for agent i with information θ^i in incentive scheme $(M, \tilde{\rho}, \tilde{\delta})$ if for any choice $(m^{-i}, a^{-i}(\cdot))$ of strategies by other agents (where a^{-i} is such that $a^{-i}: R \rightarrow A^{-i}$), $(m^i, a^i(\cdot)) = (\mu^i(\theta^i), \alpha^i(\theta^i, \cdot))$ maximizes

$$(1.1) \quad Eu^i(\tilde{d}(m, \bar{y}(a(\tilde{r}(m)), \theta)), a^i(\tilde{r}(m)), \theta^i)$$

for all θ^{-i}, where the expectation is taken with respect to $\tilde{d}$, $\bar{y}$, and $\tilde{r}$. The strategy rules $\sigma = (\sigma^1, \ldots, \sigma^n)$ are in dominant strategy equilibrium if for all i and all θ^i, $\sigma^i(\theta^i) = (\mu^i(\theta^i), \alpha^i(\theta^i, \cdot))$ is a dominant strategy for agent i with information θ^i.

To suppose that if agents have dominant strategies they will play them is an appealing behavioral postulate, because it assumes very little about agents. It is a weak assumption in three senses. First, it does not specify what beliefs an agent has about others' information. Second, it does not ascribe to an agent any particular theory of how others behave (i.e., how they choose *their* strategies). Third, it does dictate how the agent resolves his strategic uncertainty: The maximaxer, the maximiner, and the Bayesian will all play their dominant strategies, if they have them.

The principal limitation of the dominant strategy solution concept for the planner (apart from its neglect of possible collusion by agents) is the difficulty of designing incentive schemes whose dominant strategy equilibria generate a satisfactory payoff for the designer. The Gibbard-Satterthwaite theorem (Gibbard, 1973; Satterthwaite, 1975) gives an indication of this difficulty. It asserts that, in the case where A and Y are null (so that an incentive scheme is given by $\delta : M \rightarrow D$), if for each i and each ordering of D there exists $\theta^i \in \Theta^i$ such that $u^i(\cdot, \theta^i)$ corresponds to that ordering, then the only incentive schemes $\delta : M \rightarrow D$ for which $\delta(M)$ contains at least three elements and a dominant strategy equilibrium exists are dictatorships, that is, schemes in which there exists an agent j such that for all $\bar{d} \in \delta(M)$ there exists $\bar{m}^j \in M^j$ with $\delta(\bar{m}^j, m^{-j}) = \bar{d}$ for all m^{-j}. Such an agent j is called a dictator because of his complete power to have his own way. If the planner's objective function v reflects the preferences of agents at all democratically, it is clear that a dictatorial incentive scheme will not go very far toward the maximization of the planner's expected payoff.

Despite the negativism of the Gibbard-Satterthwaite result, satisfactory dominant strategy incentive schemes do exist in some models. In Section 3, we shall study one such model in considerable detail.

Maximin strategies, like dominant strategies, implicitly ascribe to an agent neither a theory of what others know nor a theory of how they behave. Maximin equilibrium, however, imposes a very strong method for resolving strategic uncertainty: namely, extreme pessimism. Formally, $(\mu^i(\theta^i), \alpha^i(\theta^i, \cdot))$ is a maximin strategy for agent i with information θ^i if $(m^i, a^i(\cdot)) = (\mu^i(\theta^i), \alpha^i(\theta^i, \cdot))$ maximizes

$$(1.2) \qquad \min_{m^{-i}, a^{-i}, \theta^{-i}} Eu^i(\tilde{d}(m, \bar{y}(a(\tilde{r}(m))), \theta)), a^i(\tilde{r}(m)), \theta^i)$$

where the expectation is taken with respect to $\tilde{d}$, $\bar{y}$, and $\tilde{r}$. The strategy rule vector $\sigma(\cdot) = (\sigma^1(\cdot), \ldots, \sigma^n(\cdot))$ is a maximin equilibrium if for all i and θ^i, $\sigma^i(\theta^i)$ is a maximin strategy for agent i with information θ^i.

The shortcomings (except in two-person zero-sum games) of maximin strategies as a plausible hypothesis for strategic behavior are well known. Even accepting the maximin hypothesis, moreover, one cannot typically make very accurate predictions about the outcome of a game. This is because, in many games, virtually *any* strategy maximizes equation (1.2), so that almost anything can be an equilibrium.

In contrast with dominant and maximin strategies, the Bayesian solution concept (Harsanyi, 1967) is defined explicitly in terms of an agent's beliefs about others. Assume that each agent i believes that θ is drawn from a joint probability distribution G^i (not all agents need have the same G^i). Suppose, furthermore, that agent i believes that agent j uses the strategy rule $\bar{\sigma}^j(\cdot)$. The strategy rule vector $\bar{\sigma}(\cdot) = (\bar{\sigma}^1(\cdot), \ldots, \bar{\sigma}^n(\cdot))$ is a Bayesian equilibrium as long as for all i and θ^i, $\sigma^i(\theta^i) = \bar{\sigma}^i(\theta^i)$ maximizes

$$(1.3) \quad \int_{\theta^{-i}} Eu^i(\sigma^i(\theta^i), \bar{\sigma}^{-i}(\theta^{-i}))\, dG^i(\theta^i, \theta^{-i})$$

where $Eu^i(\sigma^i(\theta^i), \bar{\sigma}^{-i}(\theta^{-i}))$ is shorthand for agent i's expected utility when strategies are $(\sigma^i(\theta^i), \bar{\sigma}^{-i}(\theta^{-i}))$. Of course, an equilibrium may not exist in general unless agents can play random strategies, but we will not worry about this problem.

One objection to this definition of a Bayesian equilibrium is that it does not explain why agent i believes that others use the strategy rule $\bar{\sigma}^{-i}(\cdot)$. In a conventional Nash equilibrium (in a game where players know all relevant information about each other) a player can calculate other players' equilibrium strategies. In the Bayesian setting, to predict that agent j will use the strategy rule $\bar{\sigma}^j$, one must attribute to him not only probabilistic beliefs about θ but also beliefs about others' beliefs about θ, beliefs about beliefs about beliefs, etc. That is, there is an infinite and increasingly complex sequence of attributions of beliefs. Moreover, besides creating a very complicated problem for agent i, this formulation serves only to push back the unexplained hypotheses one step, from the level of behavior to the level of belief.

One case in which this complexity is avoided is when probabilistic beliefs about θ arise as the result of some common experience – say a public pronouncement about the distribution of θ.[7] In that case, everyone knows the distribution, everyone knows that everyone knows it, and so on. That is, the distribution of θ is common knowledge. Of course, that knowledge of this kind is common is by no means an innocuous assumption, but its enormously simplifying implications have led to its almost universal adoption in the literature on Bayesian incentives.

We turn finally to complete information and Nash equilibrium. The incentives literature employing Nash equilibrium has typically not *formally* modeled the information that agents have about others. That is, θ^i

is generally taken to embody only data about agent i's *own* preferences, endowment, etc. In this case a vector of strategies (not strategy rules) $(\bar{\sigma}^1(\theta^1), \ldots, \bar{\sigma}^n(\theta^n))$ is an equilibrium for agents with parameters $(\theta^1, \ldots, \theta^n)$ if for all i, $\sigma^i(\theta^i) = \bar{\sigma}^i(\theta^i)$ maximizes

$$Eu^i(\sigma^i(\theta^i), \bar{\sigma}^{-i}(\theta^{-i}))$$

where the expectation is taken with respect to $\tilde{d}$, $\tilde{y}$, and $\tilde{r}$. This approach has the defect that we can no longer speak of an equilibrium vector of strategy *rules*, contrary to our approach so far; if θ^{-i} changes, $\bar{\sigma}^i(\theta^i)$ is no longer, in general, a Nash equilibrium strategy. Thus an approach more in keeping with the rest of this chapter is to let θ^i incorporate *all* of agent i's information. In fact, we can write

$$\theta^i = (\theta^i_i, \theta^i_{-i})$$

where θ^i_i can be interpreted as agent i's information about his own preferences, etc., whereas θ^i_{-i} represents his information about others. The assumption of complete information can then be stated formally as

(1.4) $\theta^i_k = \theta^j_k$ for all i, j, and k

On the basis of equation (1.4) we can define a Nash equilibrium of strategy rules. Indeed, formulated in this way, a Nash equilibrium is merely a special case of a Bayesian equilibrium, where the "specialness" is embodied in (1.4). The reason why the literatures on Bayesian and Nash incentives have evolved separately is that work in the former area has typically assumed that θ^i's are distributed independently, whereas the latter approach, as (1.4) indicates, requires not only that the θ^i's be perfectly correlated but coincident.

It may seem strange to model behavior by a solution concept of complete information when, so often in the incentives literature, the very lack of information is the central problem. For example, in many models of public goods allocation only the absence of information about preferences of consumers for these goods potentially prevents a full optimum from being attained. One might argue that if consumers have complete information about each others' preferences, then the planner should have this knowledge too. But if so, he can simply propose the optimum *ab initio*, avoiding the design of an incentive scheme altogether.

Nonetheless, there are at least two distinct justifications for the Nash equilibrium approach. First, the approach makes sense in many situations in which the "planner" is fictitious (or a surrogate for the collection of agents themselves) and the method of making collective decisions (the incentive scheme) must be determined well in advance of the decision making itself. For example, in democratic societies, the allocation of resources to public goods is not imposed by an omniscient planner but is decided by legislative methods fixed long before people's (or their representatives') preferences for any particular public good are known. Nonetheless, by the time that representatives actually decide on a particular allocation, they may well have a good idea about what each others' preferences are or (and what will often suffice) at least what the distribution of preferences is. Thus Nash equilibrium (or one of its refinements) may not be too bad a way to model behavior.

The other justification for Nash equilibrium is quite different and relies on viewing an equilibrium as a stationary point of some kind of (usually implicit) adjustment process. The idea is that at each stage of the process, an agent either responds explicitly to the others' current strategies by modifying his own or, ignorant perhaps of what others are doing, "experiments" with his strategy and modifies it according to his experimental success or failure. In either case, strategy revision ceases (a stationary point is reached) when the current strategies form a Nash equilibrium, because only then will agents find further (unilateral) deviation undesirable. Thus Nash equilibrium is the appropriate concept to predict the outcome, even though agents may not have complete information.

Neither of these justifications is entirely satisfactory. The first rationale has the virtue of being consistent game-theoretically. Indeed, if agents do, in fact, have complete information, Nash equilibrium seems virtually the only way to model (noncooperative) behavior. It has, however, the drawback of limited applicability. There are simply many situations where supposing that agents have complete information does not make sense.

The second rationale would appear to apply to situations regardless of agents' information, but it does not cohere so well formally. On the one hand, if agents react merely to the current strategies of others, then there is a strong element of myopia in their behavior. Why do they not foresee the reactions that their own deviations induce in others? Moreover, if they are ignorant of others' preferences, they should presumably attempt to draw inferences about these from others' behavior. On the other hand, if agents merely "experiment" without directly observing the behavior of others, they may have trouble disentangling the effects of their own experiments from those of others.[8]

1.3   Direct revelation

The four solution concepts we have considered share the property that, with some qualification, the only incentive schemes a planner need consider are those where the message spaces are of the form

$$M^i = \Theta^i$$

and each agent's equilibrium message is his true parameter. That is, an agent's message is equivalent to an element θ^i of his information space, and in equilibrium he truthfully reveals his information. That one can restrict attention to message spaces of this form has been observed by many, including Harris and Townsend (1981), Gibbard (1973), and Green and Laffont (1977) and has been called the idea of direct revelation (Dasgupta, Hammond, and Maskin, 1979) or the revelation principle (Myerson, 1979).

Its explanation is straightforward. If (M, ρ, δ) is an incentive scheme and $\sigma(\cdot) = (\sigma^1(\cdot), \ldots, \sigma^n(\cdot))$, where $\sigma^j(\cdot) = (\mu^j(\cdot), \alpha^j(\cdot))$ is a corresponding equilibrium, define

$$\bar{M}^j = \Theta^j$$

$$\bar{\delta} : \bar{M} \times Y \to D$$

$$\bar{\rho} : \bar{M} \to R$$

$$\bar{\mu}^j : \Theta^j \to \bar{M}^j$$

$$\bar{\alpha}^j : \Theta^j \times R \to A^j$$

so that

$$\bar{\delta}(\theta, y) = \delta(\mu^1(\theta^1), \ldots, \mu^n(\theta^n), y)$$

$$\bar{\rho}(\theta) = \rho(\mu^1(\theta^1), \ldots, \mu^n(\theta^n))$$

$$\bar{\mu}^j(\theta^j) = \theta^j$$

$$\bar{\alpha}^j(\theta^j, r) = \alpha^j(\mu^j(\theta^j), r)$$

Then, it is immediate to verify that for dominant Bayesian and Nash strategies the strategy rule vector $(\bar{\sigma}^1, \ldots, \bar{\sigma}^n)$ is an equilibrium for the incentive scheme $(\Theta, \bar{\rho}, \bar{\delta})$. Thus, if (M, ρ, δ) is an "optimal" incentive scheme, so is $(\Theta, \bar{\rho}, \bar{\delta})$. For maximin equilibrium, this argument does not quite work, because in moving from (M, ρ, δ) to $(\Theta, \bar{\rho}, \bar{\delta})$ we change the joint strategy space and change the domain over which the minimization (1.2) is performed. Thus, although $\sigma^j(\cdot)$ may be a maximin strategy rule in the former scheme, $\bar{\sigma}^j(\cdot)$ may not be maximin in the latter. This difficulty can, to some extent, be avoided by changing the definition of a maximin equilibrium so that agents' minimizations are performed only over those strategies that could be maximin strategies for others. (For the details on this kind of *restricted* maximin equilibrium, see the work of Dasgupta, Hammond, and Maskin, 1979, pp. 207-9.)

There may also be a problem with direct revelation schemes in the case of dominant strategies. Here the problem is not that $\bar{\sigma}^j(\cdot)$ might fail to be a dominant strategy rule in $(\Theta, \bar{\rho}, \bar{\delta})$ but that even if (M, ρ, δ) has a unique equilibrium (or, alternatively, all equilibria generate the same expected payoff for the planner), $(\Theta, \bar{\rho}, \bar{\delta})$ may have multiple equilibria, some of which give the planner a lower payoff.[9]

Still, one feels intuitively that, at least in incentive problems that are sufficiently nondegenerate, the problem of multiple equilibria with dominant strategies should not be terribly severe in direct revelation schemes. This rather vague intuition can be expressed formally in several different ways. First, it can easily be shown that when agents' preference orderings are strict (i.e., when for all θ^i the indifference sets corresponding to $u^i(\cdot, \cdot, \theta^i)$ are singletons), there exists at most one dominant strategy equilibrium outcome (the equilibrium outcome consists of the planner's decision and the agents' actions) (Dasgupta, Hammond, and Maskin, 1979, p. 196) for each profile $(\theta^1, \ldots, \theta^n)$. Second, it is obvious that if, as in some problems, agents' preferences are strictly convex in their own strategies, they cannot have more than one dominant strategy. Third, suppose that changing θ^i or a^i changes agent i's preferences over D. One way of capturing the idea that the incentive scheme is not degenerate is to suppose that by varying m^i (holding $a^i(\cdot)$ and other players' strategies fixed) agent i can make the incentive scheme trace out a subset of D with the same dimension as the hyperplane tangent to a point of agent i's indifference surface in D and, furthermore, that as *other* agents' strategies vary (holding $a^i(\cdot)$ and m^i fixed) the incentive scheme traces out all of D. Formally, suppose that all spaces have suitable topologies and that the u^j's are analytic functions such that, for all θ^j, $\theta^{j\,\prime}$, a^j, and $a^{j\,\prime}$

$$u^j(\cdot, a^j, \theta^j) = u^j(\cdot, a^{j\,\prime}, \theta^{j\,\prime})$$

if and only if $a^j = a^{j\,\prime}$ and $\theta^j = \theta^{j\,\prime}$. Suppose that (Θ, ρ, δ) is a (differentiable) direct revelation scheme with a truthful dominant strategy equilibrium $\sigma(\cdot) = (\sigma^1(\cdot), \ldots, \sigma^n(\cdot))$. (By truthful, we mean that $\sigma^j(\theta^j) = (\mu^j(\theta^j), \alpha^j(\theta^j))$, where $\mu^j(\theta^j) = \theta^j$ for all j and θ^j.) Assume that y^j (differentiable) does not depend on a^j and that R is null, so that we can ignore ρ. Because δ depends on θ through ρ, σ, and y, we may write δ as a function of θ directly, where $\delta(\theta)$ is the decision if all agents use their truthful dominant strategies. For $d \in D$, $a^j \in A^j$, and θ, let $D^j(d, a^j, \theta^j)$ be the hyperplane tangent to agent j's indifference surface (for utility function $u^j(\cdot, \cdot, \theta^j)$) at (d, a^j). (That such a hyperplane exists at every point implies that indifference surfaces are not thick.) Let $C^j(\delta, \theta)$ be the linear space spanned by the derivative of $\delta(\theta)$ with respect to θ^j, and let $C^{-j}(\delta, \theta)$ be the space spanned by the derivatives of δ with respect to all θ^i's other than θ^j. Because $\sigma^j(\theta)$ is a dominant strategy for agent j with parameter θ^j,

$$C^j(\delta, \theta) \subseteq D^j(\delta(\theta), \alpha^j(\theta^j), \theta^j)$$

The result is Proposition 1.1.

Proposition 1.1: In the formulation of the preceding paragraph, if for all j and θ

$$C^j(\delta, \theta) = D^j(\delta(\theta), \alpha^j(\theta^j), \theta^j) \quad \text{and} \quad C^{-j}(\delta, \theta) = D$$

then if $(\sigma^1(\cdot), \ldots, \sigma^n(\cdot))$ is a dominant strategy equilibrium for the direct revelation incentive scheme (Θ, δ), only truthful strategies are dominant.

Remark: The condition $C^j = D^j$ amounts to requiring that, by varying m^j, agent j can trace out a subset of D with the same dimension as that of the hyperplane tanget to his indifference surface. The condition $C^{-j} = D$ means that the set of outcomes obtained by varying m^{-j} locally looks like D.

Proof: Suppose that besides $\sigma^i(\theta^i)$, $\sigma^{i\prime} = (m^{i\prime}, a^{i\prime})$ is dominant for agent i with parameter θ^i. Because the scheme is direct revelation, $m^{i\prime} = \bar{\theta}^i$ for some $\bar{\theta}^i \in \Theta^i$. Then,

$$(1.5) \qquad \frac{\partial u^i}{\partial d}(\delta(\bar{\theta}^i, \theta^{-i}), a^{i\prime}, \theta^i) \cdot \frac{\partial \delta(\bar{\theta}^i, \theta^{-i})}{\partial \theta^i} = 0 \quad \text{for all } \theta^{-i}$$

Because $\sigma^i(\bar{\theta}^i)$ is dominant for agent i with parameter $\bar{\theta}^i$,

$$(1.6) \qquad \frac{\partial u^i}{\partial d}(\delta(\bar{\theta}^i, \theta^{-i}), \alpha^i(\bar{\theta}^i), \bar{\theta}^i) \cdot \frac{\partial \delta}{\partial \theta^i}(\bar{\theta}^i, \theta^{-i}) = 0 \quad \text{for all } \theta^{-i}$$

Because $C^i(\delta, \bar{\theta}^i, \theta^{-i}) = D^i(\delta(\bar{\theta}^i, \theta^{-i}), \alpha^i(\bar{\theta}^i), \theta^i)$ by hypothesis and because of (1.5) and (1.6), the vector $\partial u^i / \partial d(\delta(\bar{\theta}^i, \theta^{-i}), a^{i\prime}, \theta^i)$ is a scalar multiple of $\partial u^i / \partial d(\delta(\bar{\theta}^i, \theta^{-i}), \alpha^i(\bar{\theta}^i), \bar{\theta}^i)$ for all θ^{-i}. For some $\bar{\theta}^{-i}$, let $\bar{d} = \delta(\bar{\theta}^i, \bar{\theta}^{-i})$. Because $C^{-i}(\delta, \bar{\theta}^i, \bar{\theta}^{-i}) = D$, $\delta(\bar{\theta}^i, \cdot)$ is (locally) onto D in a neighborhood of $\bar{\theta}^{-i}$, there exists a neighborhood N of $\bar{d}$ such that $\partial u^i / \partial d(d, \alpha^i(\bar{\theta}^i), \bar{\theta}^i)$ is a scalar multiple of $\partial u^i / \partial d(d, \alpha^{i\prime}, \theta^i)$ for all $d \in N$. Thus the ordering corresponding to $u^i(\cdot, \alpha^i(\bar{\theta}^i), \bar{\theta}^i)$ coincides with that of $u^i(\cdot, a^{i\prime}, \theta^i)$ when restricted to N. Because u^i is analytic, these orderings coincide for all of D. But then, from hypothesis,

$$(\alpha^i(\bar{\theta}^i), \bar{\theta}^i) = (a^{i\prime}, \theta^i) \quad \text{and so} \quad \bar{\theta}^i = \theta^i \qquad \text{Q.E.D.}$$

With Bayesian equilibrium, multiple equilibria do not create difficulty in converting an incentive scheme to an equivalent direct revelation scheme; the set of equilibria in the original scheme is isomorphic to that in the direct scheme. However, multiple equilibria are a more general problem for Bayesian equilibrium. Very little is known about the circumstances under which a scheme has unique equilibrium or, alternatively, all equilibrium outcomes are equivalent. Indeed, we will show in Section 3 that in a simple public goods model – much studied in the literature – there is a whole continuum of Bayesian equilibria, almost all "bad."

The issue of multiple equilibria is important too for Nash equilibrium as a solution concept. But, in this case, the existing literature has dealt with it. Usually the approach has been not to design schemes for which equilibrium is unique – indeed, with Nash equilibrium that is often impossible – but rather (e.g., Groves and Ledyard, 1977; Maskin, 1977; Hurwicz, 1979a; Schmeidler, 1980) to ensure that all Nash equilibria are equally desirable. A characterization of when such insurance is possible (in the case where the A^i's are null) is given by Maskin (1977).

1.4   Random incentive schemes

In our general incentives model we allow for the possibility that δ and α may be stochastic. There are two reasons why the planner may wish to make them stochastic.

The first is that the spaces D and R may not be convex. Randomization simply permits the planner to convexify these spaces. A recent example where this kind of randomization figures prominently is the problem of auctioning an indivisible object (Myerson, 1978; Maskin and Riley, 1980a). Here a nonconvexity is created by the constraint that the seller (planner) can assign the object to at most one bidder. (That is, D is nonconvex.) The seller may therefore wish to randomize among certain bidders to determine the winner in order to overcome the nonconvexity. Another model in which D is inherently nonconvex is the model of discrete public investment studied in Section 3 of this chapter.

The second rationale for randomization is, formally, that the constraints of the planner's maximization problem will not in general be convex. The planner maximizes subject to agents' maximizing as well. If $\bar{\sigma}^i(\theta^i)$ is a maximizing strategy for agent i, then

$$(1.7) \qquad Eu^i(\bar{\sigma}^i(\theta^i)) \geq Eu^i(m^i, a^i(\cdot))$$

for any alternative strategy choice $(m^i, a^i(\cdot))$ (where we have, for convenience, written i's utility as a function of his strategy directly and have omitted other agents' strategies). If u^i is linear in strategies, then (1.7) represents a convex constraint. But if utility is strictly concave (if the agent is risk-averse), then the set generated by (1.7) will in general not be convex (because a concave function appears on both sides of the inequality).

This argument constitutes a prima facie case for randomization when agents are risk-averse. On closer examination (Maskin, 1980*b*) it turns out that this kind of randomization is quite generally useful as a screening device in models of adverse selection, but it is desirable only under rather restrictive (and often implausible) assumptions in models of pure moral hazard.

2   The incentive literature

In this section we quickly review the incentives literature to illustrate how work in this field fits neatly into the framework of Section 1. We do not attempt, however, to survey the literature exhaustively. Our greatest emphasis is on work about implementation and resource allocation.

2.1   *Models of adverse selection*

We begin by discussing models in which adverse selection (the inability of the planner to observe agents' information) prevents the attainment of a full optimum. The simplest variety of adverse selection model is one in which agents do nothing but transmit messages. That is, A^i is null.

Pure message transmission. A substantial part of incentives theory consists of models of pure message transmission. These include the implementation, allocation mechanism, nonlinear-pricing, and auction-design literatures.

In the implementation literature, the planner represents society. His objectives are embodied in a correspondence

$$f: \Theta \to D$$

where Θ^i typically consists of the possible preference orderings over D that agent i can have. For any profile θ, $f(\theta)$ consists of the "welfare-optimal" or "best" decisions. In the notation of Section 1, the planner's objectives can be expressed as

$$v: D \times \Theta \to \mathbf{R}$$

where

$$v(d, \theta) = 1, \quad d \in f(\theta)$$

$$= 0, \quad \text{otherwise}$$

The implementation problem is to find an incentive scheme (M, δ) (we can ignore ρ) such that for each θ the set of equilibria (with respect to a given solution concept) coincides with, or is a subset of, $f(\theta)$. (See the work of Dasgupta, Hammond, and Maskin, 1979, for more detail.) If such a scheme exists, f is said to be implementable.

The implementation literature subdivides according to solution concepts. In addition to the four solution concepts discussed in Section 1, there are numerous variants.

The basic (negative) result for dominant strategies (see Section 1) is due to Gibbard (1973) and Satterthwaite (1975). Related results are due to Pattanaik (1975), Barberá (1977a), Gärdenfors (1976), Kelly (1977), and others. These results are proved for unrestricted domains. Extensions to restricted domains, showing the connection between implementability of a correspondence and the existence of a social welfare function satisfying Arrow's conditions, have been studied by Maskin (1976) and Kalai and Müller (1977). (For more on restricted domains, see the work of Pattanaik and Sengupta, 1977, Moulin, 1980b.) In particular, it is shown (Dasgupta, Hammond, and Maskin, 1979) that if the correspondence f is generated by an Arrow social welfare function (i.e., $f(\theta)$ represents the top-ranked elements in the social ordering), then it can be implemented not only in dominant strategies but in *coalitionally* dominant strategies. That is, the formation of collusive coalitions does not change the set of equilibria.

The implementability of a single-valued correspondence f in dominant strategies is equivalent to f's satisfying "independent person-by-person monotonicity." IPM asserts that if $a \in f(\theta)$ and a is strictly preferred to b under $\theta^{i\,\prime}$, then $b \notin f(\theta^{i\,\prime}, \theta^{-i})$. The conditions for implementability in coalitionally dominant strategies are stronger (independent weak monotonicity), but the two kinds of implementability are equivalent when preferences are strict (indifference is ruled out) and preferences are sufficiently "rich."[10]

There is a recent literature on dominant strategy implementation when preferences and incentive schemes are differentiable. Contributions include those of Chichilnisky and Heal (1980a, 1980b) (which also consider Nash equilibrium) and Satterthwaite and Sonnenschein (1981).

Another line consists of studying *random* incentive schemes (i.e., schemes where δ is a stochastic function of m). Gibbard (1977) has shown that by allowing the scheme to be stochastic, but otherwise preserving the hypotheses of the Gibbard-Satterthwaite theorem, one enlarges the set of implementable correspondences (here allowing for *random* correspondences) to include those that are lotteries over dictatorships and those correspondences with a range of at most two elements. For related results, see the work of Barberá (1977b).

There is practically no analysis of maximin equilibrium at the most general level of implementation theory. There is also relatively little on Bayesian equilibrium; however, see the work of Myerson (1979) and Rosenthal (1979). On the other hand, the literature on Nash equilibrium and its variants is large. Hurwicz and Schmeidler (1978) have studied the possibility of constructing incentive schemes whose Nash equilibria are Pareto-optimal when message spaces have the cardinality of preference spaces. Maskin (1977) enlarged the message spaces and showed that any correspondence that is monotonic (see Section 3.4) and satisfies a weak nonveto property[11] is Nash-implementable. In particular, the Pareto correspondence (the correspondence that selects all Pareto optima) is implementable for any domain of preferences.

There is an intimate connection between Nash and dominant strategy implementation. K. Roberts (1979a) demonstrated that with unrestricted domain, the only single-valued Nash-implementable correspondences are dictatorial (see also Pattanaik, 1976). This corresponds to the Gibbard-Satterthwaite theorem for dominant strategies. Dasgupta, Hammond, and Maskin (1979) extended this result by showing that any single-valued Nash-implementable correspondence is implementable if the domain of strategies is rich. This means that, at least for rich domains, one does not extend the set of implementable correspondences by weakening the solution concept from dominant strategies to Nash, if single-valuedness is maintained.

Much work has been done on implementation with variants of Nash equilibrium. Moulin (1979, 1980a) studied implementation by successive elimination of dominated strategies (dominance solvability). This solution concept, due to Farquharson (1969), is closely related to the notion of perfect equilibrium proposed by Selten (1975). In particular, Moulin was able to show that in contrast to the results for Nash equilibrium, a large class of single-valued correspondences are implementable even for an unrestricted domain of preferences.

Another variant of Nash equilibrium is the strong equilibrium, in which equilibrium strategies are compared not just with the deviations of single agents but with those of coalitions. Contributions to the theory of strong implementation include the work of Moulin and Peleg (1980), Maskin (1979a), and Kalai, Postlewaite, and Roberts (1977).

One difficulty with incentive schemes that implement correspondences in strong equilibrium is that they typically have many ordinary (i.e., noncooperative) Nash equilibria in addition to their strong equilibria. These Nash equilibria, moreover, may well not be elements of $f(\theta)$. That is, to adopt strong equilibrium as a solution concept is not just to allow for the collusion of coalitions but to *insist* on it; without collusion, equilibrium may not be in $f(\theta)$. To accommodate a planner's uncertainty about the collusiveness of agents, Maskin (1979*b*) proposed the concept of *double implementation*, in which the Nash and strong equilibria of an incentive scheme coincide. Because of this coincidence, it makes no difference which coalitions, if any, form; the set of equilibria is always the same.

A line of research related to implementation derives from the work of Peleg (1978*a*). For a scheme to be *consistent* with f, Peleg, in effect, required that at least one of its strong equilibria be in $f(\theta)$. If $f(\theta)$ is a subset of the strong equilibria of the scheme, then, in the terminology of Sengupta (1979), f is *partially implemented.* In addition to these articles by Peleg and Sengupta, work on consistency and partial implementation includes that of Peleg (1978*b*) and Dutta and Pattanaik (1978).

The literature on incentives in *resource allocation* closely resembles that on implementation, but it deals with more structured models. In particular, D becomes the space of possible allocations of goods across agents rather than just an abstract decision space, and the correspondence f becomes an allocation rule. Moreover, preferences are restricted. As before, the subject subdivides according to solution concept.

In his pioneering article, Hurwicz (1972) showed that in a pure exchange economy of *private* goods, no Pareto-optimal, individually rational[12] allocation rule is implementable in *dominant strategies* when the preference domains include at least the Cobb-Douglas family. This result has been extended by Satterthwaite (1976), Satterthwaite and Sonnenschein (1981), and Dasgupta, Hammond, and Maskin (1979) by dropping the hypothesis of individual rationality and substituting the conclusion that only dictatorial allocation rules are implementable.

Most work on dominant strategy allocation rules, however, concerns public goods. Indeed, most of it assumes that agents' preferences for a public good and private good take the form

(2.1) $u^i(x, t) = v^i(x) + t$

where x is the level of the public good and t is a transfer of the private good. Virtually all research has been concerned with successful allocation rules, rules that, given $v^1(\cdot), \ldots, v^n(\cdot))$, choose the public-good level to maximize

$$\sum_{i=1}^{n} v^i(x)$$

In three seminal articles, Groves (1973), Clarke (1971), and Smets (1972) independently demonstrated the existence of *successful* allocation rules that are implementable in dominant strategies. Groves showed that a successful allocation rule is implementable if its transfers take the form

$$(2.2) \quad t^i(v^1(\cdot),\ldots,v^n(\cdot)) = \sum_{j\neq i} v^j(d) + h^i(v^{-i}(\cdot))$$

where $x=d$ maximizes $\sum_{i=1}^n v^i(x)$,

$$v^{-i}(\cdot) = (v^1(\cdot),\ldots,v^{i-1}(\cdot),v^{i+1}(\cdot),\ldots,v^n(\cdot))$$

and h^i is an arbitrary function of $v^{-i}(\cdot)$. Let us call the set of successful rules whose transfers satisfy (2.2) the Groves class. Clarke (1971) exhibited the particularly interesting member of the class in which

$$h^i(v^{-i}(\cdot)) = -\sum_{j\neq i} v^j(d^i)$$

where $x=d^i$ maximizes $\sum_{j\neq i} v^j(x)$. This is often callen the "pivotal" mechanism because only agents who change the public-good level from what it would be without them get transfers (which are, in fact, negative). The second price auction of Vickrey (1961) is, in fact, the private-good analogue of this rule. Smets (1972) examined the Groves rule in which $h^i \equiv 0$.

Green and Laffont (1977) established that the Groves class coincides with the set of all implementable allocation rules when the domain of possible valuation functions $v^i(\cdot)$ is unrestricted. A monograph by Green and Laffont (1979a) provides a detailed analysis of the properties of the Groves class. Green and Laffont (1976) and Hurwicz (1975) established, in particular, that no member of the Groves class has transfers that balance (sum to zero identically). Walker (1980) generalized this result. That no member of the Groves class is immune from manipulation by coalitions has been demonstrated by Green and Laffont (1979b) and Bennett and Conn (1977).

There is a small literature on interesting restrictions of the domain of valuation functions. Groves and Loeb (1975) examined quadratic valuations and showed that, for this domain, balancing the transfers is possible. Laffont and Maskin (1980a) studied successful and implementable allocation rules when valuation functions are differentiable and are parametrized by θ^i ranging in an open interval of the real line. In this framework, the proof that the set of such allocation rules coincides with the Groves class is virtually immediate, amounting merely to integrating a partial differential equation. (Indeed, in the differentiable setting, the whole question of implementability boils down to the integrability of systems of partial differential equations.) Holmstrom (1979b) demonstrated, however, that this characterization depends crucially on the domain of θ^i being smoothly connected. He showed that without this assumption, there are successful and implementable rules outside the Groves class. Laffont and Maskin (1980a) also showed that, with differentiability, questions about transfer balance and manipulation by coalitions are easy to handle. An illustration of the power of the "differentiable approach" is given in Section 3 of this chapter.

Another line of work concerns nonsuccessful allocation rules. K. Roberts (1979) showed that when the space of valuation functions is unrestricted, any implementable rule must choose the public-good level to maximize

$$\sum_{i=1} \lambda^i v^i(x) + K(x)$$

where $\lambda^i \geqslant 0$ and K is an arbitrary function. Laffont and Maskin (1980b) placed the further restrictions on valuation functions of differentiability and concavity and showed that any member of the class of implementable and neutral (treating all public-good levels symmetrically) rules must take the public-good level to satisfy

$$h\left(\frac{dv^1}{dx}(x), \ldots, \frac{dv^n}{dx}(x) \right) = 0$$

where $h : \mathbf{R}^n \to \mathbf{R}$ is continuous and semi-strictly increasing. In Section 3 of this chapter we characterize all (piecewise differentiable) implementable allocation rules when the public-good level is restricted to the values 0 and 1 (although we allow for randomization as well).

Finally, instead of working with severely restricted preferences, Roberts and Postlewaite (1976), Hammond (1979), and Mas-Colell (1978) examined dominant strategies in economies with many agents. Roberts and Postlewaite showed that in the limit, price-taking behavior becomes a dominant strategy as a pure exchange economy grows. Hammond studied an economy with a continuum of agents and demonstrated that implementable and Pareto-optimal allocation rules must be competitive. Similarly, Mas-Colell showed that an implementable allocation rule satisfying convexity, anonymity, nondegeneracy, and neutrality properties is necessarily competitive.

The literature on maximin equilibrium and resource allocation is considerably smaller than that for dominant strategies. Dubins (1974) exhibited a balanced allocation rule that can be implemented in maximin equilibrium when utility functions take the form of equation (2.1). Green and Laffont (1979a, Chapter 7) showed that this rule is not individually rational (does not guarantee agents at least the utility of their initial endowments) and that it encounters difficulties when consumption sets are bounded from below. They constructed a generalized rule that is individually rational on average and argued that this modified Dubins rule is the static analogue of the Malinvaud-Drèze-de la Vallée

Poussin planning procedure (see the discussion of planning procedures that follows). Thomson (1979*a*) characterized all maximin implementable allocation rules when preferences are of the form (2.1) and also in the 0–1 project case.

Using the Harsanyi (1967) concept of Bayesian equilibrium (see Section 1), d'Aspremont and Gérard-Varet (1979) showed that there exist Bayesian implementable allocation rules that are successful and for which transfers balance when preferences take the form of equation (2.1) and when the joint probability distribution of valuation functions is common knowledge, with $v^i(\cdot)$ distributed independently of $v^{-i}(\cdot)$. Arrow (1979) offered a similar analysis. Laffont and Maskin (1979*a*) characterized the class of Bayesian implementable successful rules and demonstrated its close connection with the Groves class. They also extended the d'Aspremont-Gérard-Varet results to the case where the v^i's are "negatively correlated." Unfortunately, these analyses examined only "truthful" equilibria in which agents, in effect, reveal their true preferences. The possibility of untruthful equilibria was not considered. That untruthful equilibria are likely to exist in profusion is discussed in Section 3. Other work on Bayesian incentives and resource allocation includes that of Harris and Townsend (1981) and Ledyard (1977), both general discussions of the issues and concepts involved in resource allocation with incomplete information.

Groves and Ledyard (1977) inspired much of the literature on incentives and Nash equilibrium. They developed an incentive scheme that, for any number of private and public goods, and for a domain of preferences restricted little more than by the "classical" assumption of convexity, monotonicity, and continuity, has the feature that all its Nash equilibrium[13] outcomes are Pareto-efficient. (There may, however, be difficulties with the existence of equilibrium unless preferences are restricted rather more. See the work of Green and Laffont, 1979*a*, Chapter 7.) Schmeidler (1980) exhibited an incentive scheme for a pure exchange economy of private goods whose Nash equilibria coincide with the Walrasian (competitive) equilibria when preferences are classical. However, the scheme violates both individual and aggregate feasibility constraints out of equilibrium. Hurwicz (1979*a*) devised a scheme whose Nash equilibria coincide with the Lindahl equilibria of a classical economy, but again the scheme may be aggregately infeasible when in disequilibrium. These infeasibilities, moreover, are necessary; feasible implementation in Nash equilibrium of the Lindahl and Walras correspondences is impossible. The difficulty is, as shown by Postlewaite, that these correspondences are not monotonic at the boundary of the feasible set as Nash implementation requires (Maskin, 1977). However, as Hurwicz, Postlewaite, and Maskin (1979) demonstrated, the *con-strained* Walrasian and Lindahl correspondences are Nash imple-mentable (the constrained correspondences include, in addition to ordinary Walrasian and Lindahl allocations, the allocations obtained by constraining an individual's demand from exceeding the total endow-ment of the economy). Moreover, as shown by Hurwicz (1979a), the constrained Walrasian and Lindahl correspondences are the *smallest* continuous, Pareto-optimal, and indivually rational correspondences that are Nash implementable if the domain includes all classical pref-erences. That is, any other such correspondence must include all con-strained Walrasian allocations (for a private-good economy) or all con-strained Lindahl allocations (for an economy with public goods). Other work on Nash implementation in resource allocation includes that of Hurwicz (1975), Thomson (1980), Walker (1977), and Wilson (1978).

The incentive schemes mentioned so far for allocation of resources have been "one-shot" games: Agents report their messages, on the basis of which the planner chooses an allocation (although, as discussed in Section 1, Nash equilibrium is sometimes viewed as a stationary point in an adjustment process). An alternative approach, pioneered by Drèze and de la Vallée Poussin (1971), Malinvaud (1972), and Tideman (1972), is to allocate through a dynamic incentive scheme. In the three articles cited, each agent consumer reports his marginal rates of substitution between a public good and private good at each instant of time. The planner uses this information to alter the public-good level and to make transfers of private good. Over time, the allocation converges to a Pareto optimum. Moreover, along the way, the utility of each consumer con-tinually increases (i.e., the procedure is individually rational). Champ-saur (1976) showed that the class of such "MDP" procedures is "neu-tral" or "unbiased"; that is, any individually rational Pareto optimum is the limit point of a member of this class (see the work of Champsaur, Drèze, and Henry, 1977, for a comprehensive study of the stability and existence of solutions in these procedures).

One important question about MDP procedures is the incentive for truthful reporting of marginal rates of substitution. Drèze and de la Vallée Poussin (1971) showed that truthful revelation is a local maximin strategy (i.e., maximizes the minimum instantaneous payoff, the instan-taneous payoff here being the gradient of utility) and consequently also globally maximin (maximizes the minimum utility of the final allocation). They also observed that at the stopping point of a process, revelation of true marginal rates of substitution forms a Nash equi-librium. Malinvaud (1971) suggested that MDP procedures will converge even if agents "lie" along the way. Indeed, J. Roberts (1979) proved that if, at each instant, consumers report their Nash equilibrium strategies of the local revelation game (by local revelation games we mean that consumers report so as to maximize the instantaneous increase of utility), Nash equilibrium is unique, but the equilibrium strategies are untruthful except at the stopping point.[14] The procedure still converges to a Pareto optimum, although at a slower speed than under truthful revelation (see also Henry, 1977).

As discussed in Section 1, modeling consumers' behavior by Nash equilibrium implicitly entails one of two alternative assumptions. Either one assumes that consumers know one another's preferences and so can directly calculate the Nash equilibrium, or one supposes that equilibrium is itself reached through an iterative adjustment procedure. Both assumptions have unappealing features. In particular, the second leads to a double infinity – an infinity of adjustments in the local Nash game and another in the MDP procedure itself. Schoumaker (1977) and Henry (1977) attempted to disentangle this double infinity by studying discrete-time versions of the MDP procedure.

One way of avoiding both assumptions is to devise a procedure ensuring that at each instant truthful revelation is a dominant strategy for the agent. Green and Laffont (1979a) devised procedures with this incentive property, but these are not individually rational, and their transfers do not balance. Fugigaki and Sato (1981), however, exhibited a class of generalized MDP procedures for which truthful reporting is locally dominant. One member of this class, moreover, is individually rational. Laffont and Maskin (1980b) exhibited the entire class of such procedures. They also showed the close connection between the theory of dynamic procedures and the static schemes mentioned earlier.

Most of the literature on incentives in resource allocation has taken preferences to be the information that agents transmit to the planner. There is, however, a small literature in which the relevant information is endowments. This includes the work of Postlewaite (1979) (dominant strategy equilibrium), Maskin (1980a) (dominant strategy and Nash equilibrium), and Hurwicz, Maskin, and Postlewaite (1979) (Nash equilibrium, both preferences and endowments private information).

The theory of *optimal nonlinear pricing* by a monopolist who does not know the preferences of individual consumers (although he may know the distribution of preferences) is another instance of pure message transmission by agents. Here the monopolist assumes the role of planner and maximizes profit (or expected profit, if he does not know the actual distribution of preferences). An incentive scheme is a rule that on the basis of an agent's professed preferences assigns the agent a quantity of the good and a price he must pay for it. A more familiar, but entirely equivalent, formulation has the monopolist announce a schedule relating prices and quantities, with the agents then choosing their favorite points along the schedule. Contributions to this literature include those of Spence (1977), Goldman, Leland, and Sibley (1977), Harris and Raviv (1981), Maskin and Riley (1980a), K. Roberts (1979a) among numerous others. An interesting special case is where the monopolist sells a single or several indivisible items. Then the monopolist's selling scheme is an auction. In an auction, an agent's message is his bid, and the incentive scheme is a rule that assigns each agent an amount to pay and a probability of winning the item on the basis of these bids. Optimal auctions (from the monopolist's viewpoint) have been studied by Harris and Raviv (1978), Riley and Samuelson (1981), Myerson (1981), Maskin and Riley (1980b), and Holt (1980).

The value of information in models of pure information transmission has been studied by Green (1979) and Green and Stokey (1980a).[15] In this work, θ^i, agent i's information, is a signal that is correlated with the payoff-relevant state of nature. On the basis of the message the agent sends him (there is only one agent), the planner takes a decision. The planner's and agent's ultimate payoffs depend on this decision as well as on the state of nature. To place this model within our framework, we must "expect out" the state of nature – which is not observed by anyone until all actions are taken – so that objective functions do not depend on the state.

Adverse selection with "active" agents. Some incentive models of adverse selection involve agents taking actions instead of (or in addition to) sending messages. These remain essentially adverse selection models, however, because the actions are perfectly observable.

In the literature on optimal commodity taxation (Diamond and Mirrlees, 1971), for example, agents choose net trades that are perfectly observable by the planner (tax authority). In the notation of Section 1, a net trade corresponds to a^i, and $y^i = a^i$. Decisions (taxes) are a function of the y^i's alone. However, the only obstacle to the attainment of a full optimum is the planner's imperfect knowledge of agents' preferences over net trades. Indeed, we can reformulate the problem equivalently as a pure message transmission in which agents report their preferences, and the planner thereupon assigns them net trades.

The recent research on implicit contracts with asymmetric information (for example, Green, 1980; Grossman and Hart, 1981) provides another example. In these models, a worker (who may be thought of as the planner) signs a contract with a firm (the agent) that specifies his compensation for each level of employment. It is assumed that when employment decisions are to be made, only the firm knows the worker's productivity, and so he chooses the level of employment unilaterally. This procedure is, of course, equivalent to an incentive scheme in which an employment-compensation pair is assigned to each possible announcement the firm could make about the worker's productivity.

2.2 Models of moral hazard

We next turn to models in which the failure to attain a full optimum is due to the inability of the planner to observe agents' actions perfectly. Many of these fall under the rubric of the *principal-agent problem*. For instance, see the work of Ross (1973), Holmstrom (1979*b*), Guenerie and Laffont (1979), Harris and Raviv (1979), Mirrlees (1975), Shavell (1979*a*, 1979*b*), Grossman and Hart (1980), and Stiglitz (1974). In these models, the principal (planner) observes outcome y, which depends randomly on the agent's action. A "decision" often takes the form of a monetary reward. An incentive scheme assigns a reward to the agent for each possible observed outcome. The planner's payoff depends on the reward (negatively) and outcome, whereas the agent's payoff depends on the reward (positively) and his action.

In the principal-agent problem, only moral hazard creates incentive problems. There are a number of models, however, that combine moral hazard and adverse selection.

One example is the capital allocation model described in Section 1. Another is the income tax model of Mirrlees (1971). In this latter model, agents share the same preferences for consumption and leisure. They differ, however, in their (constant) marginal products for producing the consumption good. Adverse selection arises because the planner (tax authority) does not know individual agents' marginal products. There is an additional problem ("moral hazard") created by his inability to observe agents' labor-leisure choices.

A final example combining moral hazard and adverse selection is described in the "bonus" literature (Weitzman, 1976). In these models, a planner attempts to elicit statistical information from an agent by an incentive scheme depending on the agent's message and an observed outcome y that depends stochastically on θ.

3 Indivisible public projects: an extended example of incentive theory

In this section we concentrate on a single, but much-studied, problem in incentive theory: the question whether or not society ought to undertake a given public project. Within the scheme of Section 1, this is a pure informational problem; the answer depends solely on agents' preferences – there is no question of observing their behavior. Nevertheless, the problem is representative of a large chunk of the incentive literature and is thus a useful illustrative example. Our intention is to show that by assuming that the relevant functions are differentiable (or, at least, piecewise differentiable), many of the major theorems, as well as some new results, can be easily derived. For a summary of these new results, see Section 3.2.

Throughout we shall consider a model with n consumers and two goods: one public, one private. The public good can either be produced ($x=1$) or not be produced ($x=0$); that is, it is indivisible. (For a similar analysis when the possible public project levels are continuous, see the work of Laffont and Maskin, 1979a, 1979b, 1980a, 1980b; the two theories are qualitatively very similar.) However, because, as pointed out in Section 1.4, randomization may be desirable in incentive problems where the outcome space is not convex, we shall often allow x to assume any value in the interval $[0, 1]$; x is then to be interpreted as the probability that the project will be carried out. Consumers' preferences for the public good and a vector of transfers $t = (t^1, \ldots, t^n)$ of private good are assumed to be representable by utility functions of the form

(3.1) $u^i(x, t) = \theta^i x + t^i$

where θ^i lies in Θ^i, an open interval (containing zero) of the real line. If $x=0$ or 1, then equation (3.1) simply asserts that preferences are additively separable and linear in the private good. θ^i is consumer i's marginal rate of substitution or his "willingness to pay" (in terms of private good) for the public project.[16] If x can assume values strictly between 0 and 1, then (3.1) further implies that the consumer is risk-neutral in his attitude toward gambles on the level of public good. We shall assume that the functional form (3.1) is public knowledge but that the value θ^i is known, a priori, to consumer i alone.

For most of this part of the chapter, we shall work with dominant strategies (or coalitionally dominant strategies) as our solution concept. We do this not only because dominant strategies have figured most prominently in the literature to date but also because this solution concept, for a number of reasons discussed in Section 1.2, is the least controversial and the one making the weakest behavioral assumptions of those in current use.

3.1 *Definitions and summary of results*

In Section 1 we argued that, except for possible problems caused by multiple equilibria, it suffices to consider only direct revelation schemes when working with dominant strategies. Because we can show (see Theorem 3.8, *infra*) that, in our framework, multiple equilibrium outcomes cannot occur, we shall work only with such schemes.

An incentive scheme δ is a mapping,

$$\delta = (x, t^1, \ldots, t^n) : \prod_{i=1}^{n} \Theta^i \rightarrow [0, 1] \times \mathbf{R}^n$$

which associates with each n-tuple $\hat{\theta} = (\hat{\theta}^1, \ldots, \hat{\theta}^n)$ of announced preference parameters a (possibly random) public decision $x(\hat{\theta})$ and a vector $t(\hat{\theta}) = (t^1(\hat{\theta}), \ldots, t^n(\hat{\theta}))$ [17] of private-good transfers. Let $\tilde{\theta}^{-i} = (\tilde{\theta}^1, \ldots, \tilde{\theta}^{i-1}, \tilde{\theta}^{i+1}, \ldots, \tilde{\theta}^n)$ and

$$(\bar{\theta}^i, \tilde{\theta}^{-i}) = (\tilde{\theta}^1, \ldots, \tilde{\theta}^{i-1}, \bar{\theta}^i, \tilde{\theta}^{i+1}, \ldots, \tilde{\theta}^n).$$

An incentive scheme is *individually rational* if and only if

$$\theta^i x(\theta) + t^i(\theta) \geq 0 \quad \text{for all } i, \theta$$

That is, agent i, whatever the value of his preference parameter, can guarantee himself at least a zero or "status quo" payoff by announcing the truth.

An incentive scheme is *incentive-compatible in dominant strategies* (DSIC) if and only if

$$\theta^i x(\theta^i, \theta^{-i}) + t^i(\theta^i, \theta^{-i}) \geq \theta^i x(\hat{\theta}^i, \theta^{-i}) + t^i(\hat{\theta}^i, \theta^{-i})$$

for all i, θ^i, $\hat{\theta}^i$, and θ^{-i}. That is, the truth is always a dominant strategy.

Let C be a subset of $\{1, \ldots, n\}$. θ^C shall represent a vector of characteristics of members of C, whereas θ^{-C} shall be a vector for the complement of C. An incentive scheme is *incentive-compatible in coalitionally dominant strategies* (CDSIC) if for all $C \subseteq \{1, \ldots, n\}$

$$\sum_{i \in C} [\theta^i x(\theta^C, \theta^{-C}) + t^i(\theta^C, \theta^{-C})]$$
$$\geq \sum_{i \in C} [\theta^i x(\hat{\theta}^C, \theta^{-C}) + t^i(\hat{\theta}^C, \theta^{-C})]$$

for all i, θ, and $\hat{\theta}^C$. That is, the truth is a dominant strategy even for a collusive coalition.

A DSIC scheme is *feasible* if and only if

$$\sum_{i=1}^{n} t^i(\theta) \leqslant 0 \quad \text{for all } \theta$$

Feasibility ensures that the designer will not run a deficit of private good. A stronger condition still is the requirement that the budget balance. A DSIC scheme is *balanced* if and only if

$$\sum_{i=1}^{n} t^i(\theta) = 0 \quad \text{for all } \theta \in \Theta$$

If consumers' utilities are interpersonally and cardinally comparable, a common welfare objective is the maximization of the utilitarian social welfare function

$$(3.2) \quad \sum_{i=1}^{n} (\theta^i x + t^i)$$

Clearly, the maximizing choice of x is 1 if $\sum \theta^i \geqslant 0$ and 0 if $\sum \theta^i < 0$. This corresponds to the idea from cost-benefit theory that a project should be undertaken if the sum of the net benefits is positive. It is natural, therefore, to say that an incentive scheme is *successful* if and only if

$$(3.3) \quad \begin{aligned} x(\theta) &= 1, \quad \sum \theta_i \geqslant 0 \\ &= 0, \quad \sum \theta_i < 0 \end{aligned}$$

A property considerably weaker than success is the stipulation that the project be undertaken at least when everyone derives net positive benefit and that it be rejected (at least) when everyone suffers a net loss. Hence, a DSIC scheme is *weakly efficient* if and only if

$$\begin{aligned} x(\theta) &= 1, \quad \text{if} \quad \theta_i > 0 \quad \text{for all } i \\ &= 0, \quad \text{if} \quad \theta_i < 0 \quad \text{for all } i \end{aligned}$$

Finally, we shall call a scheme *fully optimal* if it is both successful and balanced. (It is fully optimal in that it maximizes (3.2) subject to the constraint of feasibility.)

The study of incentive in public-good provision has, to date, been largely concerned with successful mechanisms. We shall argue here that this emphasis has been, to some extent, misguided. But first, we begin, in Section 3.2, with success. Apart from reviewing some of the major results from the literature, we demonstrate (Theorem 3.3) that no feasible and successful incentive scheme dominates the much-studied Groves-Clarke pivotal mechanism. We then turn, in Section 3.3, to schemes that need not be successful. So that we can use calculus, we study schemes that are piecewise differentiable (more precisely, regular). We also often limit our attention to deterministic schemes (ones for which x takes on only the values 0 and 1). In the corollary to Theorem 3.7 we characterize all DSIC regular schemes. Next (Theorem 3.8), we show that equilibrium is essentially unique in such schemes. In Theorem 3.9 we characterize all deterministic DSIC schemes. Then, in Theorem 3.11, we show that a regular DSIC scheme that is weakly efficient, balanced, and symmetric (treats all agents identically) must be a positional dictatorship (i.e., there exists an integer i such that for each profile of parameters $(\theta^1, \ldots, \theta^n)$ the agent with the ith highest parameter "decides" on the project - if his parameter is nonnegative, the project is undertaken, otherwise not). Theorem 3.12 exhibits the "best" balanced DSIC scheme, the balanced scheme that maximizes the expectation of the utilitarian criterion (3.2). In Theorem 3.13 we show that the only weakly efficient, feasible, and individually rational DSIC scheme is the nth positional dictator. Finally, Theorem 3.14 establishes that no weakly efficient DSIC incentive scheme is immune to manipulation by coalitions.

Turning to Bayesian equilibrium in Section 3.4, we show that in our public project model the scheme proposed by d'Aspremont and Gérard-Varet (1979) and Arrow (1979) has a continuum of equilibria in addition to the one they proposed. We conclude in Theorems 3.16 and 3.17 by characterizing Nash-incentive-compatible schemes.

3.2 Successful DSIC incentive schemes

Theorem 3.1: Successful and feasible DSIC incentive schemes exist (Vickrey, 1961; Groves, 1973; Clarke, 1971; Smets, 1972):

Proof: Take x as in (3.3) and define

$$\bar{t}^i(\hat{\theta}) = \sum_{j \neq i} \hat{\theta}^j, \quad \text{if} \quad \sum_{k=1}^{n} \hat{\theta}^k \geqslant 0 \quad \text{and} \quad \sum_{j \neq i} \hat{\theta}^j < 0$$

$$= -\sum_{j \neq i} \hat{\theta}^j, \quad \text{if} \quad \sum_{k=1}^{n} \hat{\theta}^k < 0 \quad \text{and} \quad \sum_{j \neq i} \hat{\theta}^j > 0$$

$$= 0, \quad \text{otherwise}$$

The incentive scheme so defined is successful, feasible, and DSIC.

Q.E.D.

The scheme defined in the proof of Theorem 3.1 is called the Groves-Clarke pivotal mechanism (the term "pivotal" refers to the fact that only pivotal agents - those whose strategy changes the public decision from what it would be without them – are affected by transfers). Among feasible successful schemes, the pivotal mechanism is optimal in a sense defined by Theorem 3.3 (*infra*).

We first characterize all successful schemes.

Theorem 3.2: An incentive scheme is DSIC and successful if and only if $x(\cdot)$ satisfies (3.3) and

$$(3.4) \quad t^i(\theta) = \sum_{j \neq i} \theta^j + h^i(\theta^{-i}), \quad \text{if} \quad \sum_{i=1}^{n} \theta^i \geq 0$$

$$= h^i(\theta^{-i}), \quad \text{if} \quad \sum_{i=1}^{n} \theta^i < 0$$

where $h^i(\cdot)$ is an arbitrary function of θ^{-i}.

Proof: (See the work of Green and Laffont, 1979a, Chapter 3, and Theorem 3.9, *infra*.) The pivotal mechanism is not balanced. Some of the transfers may be strictly negative; that is, there may be a net budget surplus. A natural question, therefore, is whether or not there exist feasible and successful schemes for which the magnitude of the surplus is smaller. Although it is easy to give examples of feasible schemes yielding smaller surpluses for some values of θ, no such scheme dominates the pivotal mechanism uniformly. That is:

Theorem 3.3: There exists no feasible and successful incentive scheme (x, t) such that for all θ

$$|\Sigma t^i(\theta)| \leq |\Sigma \bar{t}^i(\theta)|$$

with strict inequality for some θ, where, as before, $\bar{t}^i$ is the pivotal mechanism's transfer to agent i.

Proof: Because the proof is long and messy, we relegate it to the Appendix.

Corollary: (See the work of Green and Laffont, 1976, 1979a, Chapter 5, and Hurwicz, 1975.) There exists no fully optimal DSIC scheme.

Proof: The Groves-Clarke mechanism is successful and feasible but not balanced; it sometimes generates a strictly positive surplus. From Theorem 3.3, there exists no successful and feasible scheme that dominates Groves-Clarke. That is, no such scheme is balanced.   Q.E.D.

The Groves-Clarke mechanism shows that success and feasibility are mutually consistent. Similarly, by taking $h^i(\theta^{-i}) \equiv 0$ in (3.4), we obtain a successful and individually rational scheme. However, feasibility, individual rationality, and success cannot be satisfied simultaneously.

Theorem 3.4: No feasible, individually rational, successful DSIC scheme exists.

Proof: Choose θ such that $\sum_{j=1}^{n} \theta^j > 0$ and such that for all i there exists $\bar{\theta}^i \in \Theta^i$ with $\bar{\theta}^i + \sum_{j \neq i} \theta^j < 0$. Suppose that $\delta = (x, t)$ is a feasible, individually rational, successful scheme. From Theorem 3.2, t^i satisfies (3.4) for some function h^i. Thus, from success, the payoff to agent i with parameter $\bar{\theta}^i$, if other agents have parameters θ^{-i}, is $h^i(\theta^{-i})$. From individual rationality,

(3.15) $h^i(\theta^{-i}) \geqslant 0$

But from feasibility and success,

$$(n-1) \sum_{i=1}^{n} \theta^i + \sum_{i=1}^{n} h^i(\theta^{-i}) \leqslant 0$$

and so

$$\sum_{i=1}^{n} h^i(\theta^{-i}) < 0$$

in contradiction to (3.15).   Q.E.D.

Theorem 3.5: No successful CDSIC scheme exists.

Proof: (See the work of Bennett and Conn, 1977, and Green and Laffont, 1979a, Chapter 5, and Theorem 3.14, *infra*.)

Because fully optimal DSIC incentive schemes do not exist, the requirement that schemes nonetheless be successful is arbitrary. After all, success pertains only to the public decision, and so to require success alone in a scheme is to ignore the welfare implications of its private transfers. A more general approach consists of characterizing the class of all DSIC incentive schemes and then optimizing whatever welfare function one might have (e.g., function (3.2)) subject to the scheme's being in this or a narrower class (e.g., the class of balanced schemes or the class of successful schemes). This is the approach we now briefly pursue. We establish a number of results characterizing DSIC incentive schemes, and, in particular (see Theorem 3.12), we consider the optimization of (3.2) subject to the scheme's being balanced.

3.3   *General DSIC incentive schemes*

An incentive scheme is differentiable if $x(\cdot)$ and $t(\cdot)$ are differentiable. For analytical simplicity, we are concerned in this section with *simple* and *regular* incentive schemes. A *simple* incentive scheme (x, t) is defined in terms of a closed set A with the property that if $\theta \in A$ and $\theta' \geqslant \theta$, then $\theta' \in A$. The scheme is simple if there exist differentiable functions x^- and x^+ such that

$$x(\theta) = x^-(\theta), \quad \theta \notin A$$
$$\quad\quad = x^+(\theta), \quad \theta \in A$$

A *regular* scheme (x, t) is a straightforward generalization of a simple scheme. Instead of the single set A, there is a collection of closed sets $A_1, \ldots, A_q$, each with the property that if $\theta \in A_j$ and $\theta' \geqslant \theta$, then $\theta \in A_j$. For each j, there is a pair of differentiable functions x_j^- and x_j^+ such that

$$x(\theta) = \sum_{j=1}^{n} x^{z(j)}(\theta)$$

where $z(j)$ is $-$ if $\theta \notin A_j$, and $z(j)$ is $+$ if $\theta \in A_j$.

Some examples of simple incentive schemes are the Groves-Clarke mechanism (see Theorem 3.1), the ith dictatorship, and the ith positional dictatorship.

Example 3.1: The ith dictatorship.

$$x(\theta) = 1, \quad \theta^i \geqslant 0$$
$$\quad\quad = 0, \quad \text{otherwise}$$
$$t^j(\theta) = h^j(\theta^{-j}) \quad \text{for all } j$$

Example 3.2: The ith positional dictatorship.

$$x(\theta) = 1, \quad \{j \mid \theta^j \geqslant 0\} \quad \text{has at least } i \text{ elements,}$$
$$\quad\quad = 0, \quad \text{otherwise}$$
$$t^j(\theta) \equiv h^j(\theta^{-j}) \quad \text{for all } j$$

An example of a regular scheme that is not simple is the random dictatorship.

Example 3.3: Random dictatorship.

$$x(\theta) = \sum_{j=1}^{n} x^k(\theta), \quad \text{where} \quad x^k(\theta) = 0, \quad \text{if} \quad \theta^k < 0$$

$$= \frac{1}{n}, \quad \text{if} \quad \theta^k \geqslant 0$$

$$t^j(\theta) = h^j(\theta^{-j}) \quad \text{for all } j$$

We shall call a public decision function $x: \prod_{i=1}^{n} \Theta^i \to [0,1]$ *implementable* if there exists a transfer rule vector t such that (x,t) is a DSIC scheme.

Lemma: A public decision function $x(\cdot)$ is implementable only if it is weakly increasing.

Proof: Let $\bar{\theta}^i$ and $\tilde{\theta}^i$ be alternative values of agent i's characteristic. If x is implementable, there exists t such that

(3.16) $\quad \bar{\theta}^i x(\bar{\theta}^i, \theta^{-i}) + t^i(\bar{\theta}^i, \theta^{-i}) \geqslant \bar{\theta}^i x(\tilde{\theta}^i, \theta^{-i}) + t^i(\tilde{\theta}^i, \theta^{-i}) \quad$ for all θ^{-i}

and

(3.17) $\quad \tilde{\theta}^i x(\tilde{\theta}^i, \theta^{-i}) + t^i(\tilde{\theta}^i, \theta^{-i}) \geqslant \tilde{\theta}^i x(\bar{\theta}^i, \theta^{-i}) + t^i(\bar{\theta}^i, \theta^{-i}) \quad$ for all θ^{-i}

Adding (3.16) to (3.17) and collecting terms, we obtain

$$(\bar{\theta}^i - \tilde{\theta}^i) x(\bar{\theta}^i, \theta^{-i}) - x(\tilde{\theta}^i, \theta^{-i})) \geqslant 0 \qquad \text{Q.E.D.}$$

We shall begin by characterizing differentiable DSIC schemes.

Theorem 3.6: A differentiable incentive scheme (x,t) is DSIC if and only if (i) x is weakly increasing and (ii)

$$t^i(\theta) = -\int_0^{\theta^i} s \frac{\partial x}{\partial \theta^i} (s, \theta^{-i})\, ds + h^i(\theta^{-i})$$

where h^i is an arbitrary piecewise differentiable function of θ^{-i}, $i = 1, \ldots, n$.

Proof: We begin with necessity. From the lemma, x must be weakly increasing. For each θ^{-i}, agent i chooses $\hat{\theta}^i$ to maximize

$$\theta^i x(\hat{\theta}^i, \theta^{-i}) + t^i(\hat{\theta}^i, \theta^{-i})$$

If the maximum is to occur at $\hat{\theta}^i = \theta^i$, we must have

$$(3.18) \quad \theta^i \frac{\partial x}{\partial \theta^i}(\theta^i, \theta^{-i}) + \frac{\partial t^i}{\partial \theta^i}(\theta^i, \theta^{-i}) = 0$$

Because (3.18) must hold for all θ, (3.18) is an identity. Thus

$$(3.19) \quad t^i(\theta) = -\int_0^{\theta^i} s \frac{\partial x}{\partial \theta^i}(s, \theta^{-i})\, ds + h^i(\theta^{-i})$$

where h^i is an arbitrary differentiable function of θ^{-i}. Thus necessity is established. For sufficiency, observe that, in view of (ii),

$$\theta^i x(\theta^i, \theta^{-i}) + t^i(\theta^i, \theta^{-i}) \geq \theta^i x(\hat{\theta}^i, \theta^{-i}) + t^i(\hat{\theta}^i, \theta^{-i}) \quad \text{for all} \quad \hat{\theta}^i, \theta^{-i}$$

if and only if

$$(3.20) \quad (\theta^i - \hat{\theta}^i) x(\hat{\theta}^i, \theta^{-i}) \leq \int_{\hat{\theta}^i}^{\theta^i} x(s, \theta^{-i})\, ds \quad \text{for all} \quad \hat{\theta}^i$$

But (3.20) holds because x is weakly increasing.   Q.E.D.

We are now ready to characterize simple DSIC incentive schemes. For simple schemes, as defined earlier, let

$$a^i(\theta^{-i}) = \min\{\theta^i \,|\, (\theta^i, \theta^{-i}) \in A\} \quad \text{(if this minimum exists)}$$

Theorem 3.7: A simple scheme is DSIC if and only if (i) x is weakly increasing and (ii)

$$t^i(\theta) = -\int_0^{\theta^i} s \frac{\partial}{\partial \theta^i} x^-(s, \theta^{-i})\, ds + h^i(\theta^{-i}), \quad \theta \notin A$$

$$= -\int_0^{\theta^i} s \frac{\partial}{\partial \theta^i} x^+(s, \theta^{-i})\, ds + h^i(\theta^{-i}) + C^i(\theta^{-i}), \quad \theta \in A$$

where h^i is an arbitrary piecewise differentiable function and

$$C^i(\theta^{-i}) = 0, \quad \text{if} \quad a^i(\theta^{-i}) \quad \text{is not defined}$$

$$= \int_0^{a^i(\theta^{-i})} (x^-(s, \theta^{-i}) - x^+(s, \theta^{-i}))\, ds, \quad \text{otherwise}$$

Proof: Suppose that the simple scheme (x, t) is DSIC. From the lemma, x must be weakly increasing. From Theorem 3.6,

$$(3.21) \quad t^i(\theta) = -\int_0^{\theta^i} s \frac{\partial x^-}{\partial \theta^i}(s, \theta^{-i})\, ds + h^i(\theta^{-i}), \quad \text{if} \quad \theta \notin A$$

$$= -\int_0^{\theta^i} s \frac{\partial x^+}{\partial \theta^i}(s, \theta^{-i})\, ds + k^i(\theta^{-i}), \quad \text{if} \quad \theta \in A$$

Now $\hat{\theta}^i x(\hat{\theta}^i, \theta^{-i}) + t^i(\hat{\theta}^i, \theta^{-i})$ is evidently continuous as a function of $\hat{\theta}^i$ for $\hat{\theta}^i < a^i(\theta^{-i})$ and for $\hat{\theta}^i > a^i(\theta^{-i})$. We claim it is continuous as well at $\hat{\theta}^i = a^i(\theta^{-i})$. If not, then $\gamma(\theta^{-i}) \neq 0$, where

$$\gamma(\theta^{-i}) = \lim_{\hat{\theta}^i \to a^i(\theta^{-i})} (\hat{\theta}^i x^-(\hat{\theta}^i, \theta^{-i}) + t^i(\hat{\theta}^i, \theta^{-i}))$$

$$- (a^i(\theta^{-i}) x^+(a^i(\theta^{-i}), \theta^{-i}) + t^i(a^i(\theta^{-i}), \theta^{-i}))$$

Suppose $\gamma(\theta^{-i}) > 0$. Then for $\theta^i = a^i(\theta^{-i})$ and $\hat{\theta}^i$ slightly less than θ^i, agent i's payoff is higher from the strategy $\hat{\theta}^i$, if his parameter is θ^i, than from announcing the truth. Similarly, if $\gamma(\theta^{-i}) < 0$, agent i's payoff is larger from $\hat{\theta}^i = a^i(\theta^{-i})$ than from $\hat{\theta}^i = \theta^i$, if θ^i is slightly less than $a^i(\theta^{-i})$. Hence, $\gamma(\theta^{-i}) = 0$, and continuity at $a^i(\theta^{-i})$ is established. But from (3.21), continuity implies

$$a^i(\theta^{-i}) x^-(a^i(\theta^{-i}), \theta^{-i}) - \int_0^{a^i(\theta^{-i})} s \frac{\partial x^-}{\partial \theta^i}(s, \theta^{-i})\, ds + h^i(\theta^{-i})$$

$$= a^i(\theta^{-i}) x^+(a^i(\theta^{-i}), \theta^{-i}) - \int_0^{a^i(\theta^{-i})} s \frac{\partial x^+}{\partial \theta^i}(s, \theta^{-i})\, ds + k^i(\theta^{-i})$$

Integrating by parts and rearranging terms, we obtain

$$k^i(\theta^{-i}) = h^i(\theta^{-i}) + \int_0^{a^i(\theta^{-i})} (x^-(s, \theta^{-i}) - x^+(x, \theta^{-i}))\, ds$$

thus establishing the necessity of (ii). For sufficiency, consider $\theta \notin A$ and $\hat{\theta}^i \geqslant a^i(\theta^{-i})$. The gain to agent i with parameter θ^i from announcing the truth rather than $\hat{\theta}^i$ is

$$(3.22) \quad \theta^i x^-(\theta) - \int_0^{\theta^i} s \frac{\partial x^-}{\partial \theta^i}(s, \theta^{-i})\, ds$$

$$- \left(\theta^i x^+(\hat{\theta}^i, \theta^{-i}) - \int_0^{\hat{\theta}^i} s \frac{\partial x^+}{\partial \theta^i}(s, \theta^{-i})\, ds + C(\theta^{-i}) \right)$$

$$= (\hat{\theta}^i - \theta^i) x^+(\hat{\theta}^i, \theta^{-i}) - \int_{\theta^i}^{a^i(\theta^{-i})} x^-(s, \theta^{-i})\, ds$$

$$- \int_{a^i(\theta^i)}^{\hat{\theta}^i} x^+(s, \theta^{-i})\, ds$$

But (3.22) is nonnegative because x is (weakly) increasing. Similarly, the gain from truth telling is nonnegative if $\theta \in A$ and $\hat{\theta}^i < a^i(\theta^{-i})$.   Q.E.D.

The generalization of Theorem 3.7 to regular incentive schemes is immediate. For all i, j, let

$$a_j^i(\theta^{-i}) = \min\{\theta^i \mid (\theta^i, \theta^{-i}) \in A_j\} \quad \text{(if this minimum exists)}$$

Corollary: A regular scheme is DSIC if and only if (i) x is weakly increasing and (ii)

$$t^i(\theta) = \sum_{j=1}^{q} \left[-\int_0^{\theta^i} \frac{\partial}{\partial \theta^i} x_j^{z(j)}(s, \theta^{-i})\, ds + h^i(\theta^{-i}) + y(j) C_j^i(\theta^{-i}) \right]$$

where h^i is an arbitrary piecewise differentiable function, $y(j) = 1$ for $\theta \in A_j$ and 0 for $\theta \notin A_j$ and

$$C_j^i(\theta^{-i}) = 0, \quad \text{if} \quad a_j^i(\theta^{-i}) \quad \text{is not defined}$$

$$= \int_0^{a_j^i(\theta^{-i})} (x_j^+(s, \theta^{-i}) - x_j^-(s, \theta^{-i}))\, ds, \quad \text{otherwise}$$

We now can demonstrate that a DSIC regular scheme has a unique equilibrium public decision for each choice of θ.

Theorem 3.8: A DSIC regular scheme (x, t) has a unique equilibrium public decision $x(\theta)$ for each choice of θ.

Proof: We shall argue for the case of simple schemes. Suppose that, for some θ and $\bar{\theta}$, $\hat{\theta} = \bar{\theta}$ is a dominant strategy equilibrium if the true parameters are θ. That is, $x(\bar{\theta})$ is an equilibrium public decision in addition to $x(\theta)$. In particular, because $\bar{\theta}^1$ is a dominant strategy for agent 1, we have

$$\theta^1 x(\theta^1, \theta^{-1}) + t^1(\theta^1, \theta^{-1}) = \theta^1 x(\bar{\theta}^1, \theta^{-1}) + t^1(\bar{\theta}^1, \theta^{-1})$$

that is,

$$(3.23) \quad \theta^1(x(\theta^1, \theta^{-1}) - x(\bar{\theta}^1, \theta^{-1})) = t^1(\bar{\theta}^1, \theta^{-1}) - t^1(\theta^1, \theta^{-1})$$

If either both (θ^1, θ^{-1}) and $(\bar{\theta}^1, \theta^{-1})$ lie in A or do not lie in A, then (3.23) becomes

$$\theta^1(x(\theta^1, \theta^{-1}) - x(\bar{\theta}^1, \theta^{-1})) = -\int_0^{\bar{\theta}^1} s \frac{\partial}{\partial \theta^1} x(s, \theta^{-1})\, ds$$

$$+ \int_0^{\theta^1} s \frac{\partial}{\partial \theta^1} x(s, \theta^{-1})\, ds$$

$$= \theta^1 x(\theta^1, \theta^{-1}) - \bar{\theta}^1 x(\bar{\theta}^1, \theta^{-1})$$

$$- \int_{\bar{\theta}^1}^{\theta^1} x(s, \theta^{-1})\, ds$$

Rearranging, we obtain

$$(3.24) \quad (\bar{\theta}^1 - \theta^1) x(\bar{\theta}^1, \theta^{-1}) = \int_{\theta^1}^{\bar{\theta}^1} x(s, \hat{\theta}^{-1})\, ds$$

Because x is weakly increasing, we conclude that

$$(3.25) \quad x(\hat{\theta}^1, \hat{\theta}^{-1}) = x(\theta^1, \theta^{-1}), \quad \text{for all } \hat{\theta}^1 \text{ between } \theta^1 \text{ and } \bar{\theta}^1.$$

If $(\theta^1, \theta^{-1}) \notin A$ but $(\bar{\theta}^1, \theta^{-1}) \in A$ (the opposite case can be argued similarly), then (3.23) becomes

$$\theta^1(x^-(\theta^1, \theta^{-1}) - x^+(\bar{\theta}^1, \theta^{-1})) = -\int_0^{\bar{\theta}^1} s \frac{\partial}{\partial \theta^1} x^+(s, \theta^{-1})\, ds$$

$$+ \int_0^{\theta^1} s \frac{\partial}{\partial \theta^1} x^-(s, \theta^{-1}) \, ds + C^1(\theta^{-1})$$

$$= -\bar{\theta}^1 x^+(\bar{\theta}^1, \theta^{-1}) + \theta^1 x^-(\theta^1, \theta^{-1})$$

$$+ \int_{a^1(\theta^{-1})}^{\bar{\theta}^1} x^+(s, \theta^{-1}) \, ds$$

$$+ \int_{\theta^1}^{a^1(\theta^{-1})} x^-(s, \theta^{-1}) \, ds$$

Rearranging, we find

$$(\bar{\theta}^1 - \theta^1) x^+(\bar{\theta}^1, \theta^{-1}) = \int_{a^1(\theta^{-1})}^{\theta^1} x^+(s, \theta^{-1}) \, ds + \int_{\theta^1}^{a^1(\theta^{-1})} x^-(s, \theta^{-1}) \, ds$$

from which we conclude, because x is weakly increasing and $x^+ \geqslant x^-$, that (3.25) again holds. Thus, in all cases (3.25) holds. Continuing iteratively for $i = 2, \ldots, n$,

$$x(\theta) = x(\bar{\theta}) \qquad \text{Q.E.D.}$$

From Theorem 3.7 we can immediately characterize those regular DSIC schemes that are *deterministic* (x can take on only the values 0 and 1). Such schemes, of course, are automatically simple.

Theorem 3.9: A regular deterministic incentive scheme is DSIC if and only if

(i) $x(\theta) = 0, \quad \theta \notin A$
        $\qquad\;\; = 1, \quad \theta \in A$

(ii) $t^i(\theta) = h^i(\theta^{-i}), \quad \theta \notin A$
        $\qquad\;\;\; = -a^i(\theta^{-i}) + h^i(\theta^{-i}), \quad \theta \in A \quad \text{and} \quad a^i(\theta^{-i}) \text{ defined}$
        $\qquad\;\;\; = h^i(\theta^{-i}), \quad \text{otherwise}$

Note that Theorem 3.2 is a special case of Theorem 3.9, in which

$$x(\theta) = 1, \quad \sum \theta^i \geqslant 0$$
$$\qquad\;\; = 0, \quad \text{otherwise}$$

Hence $a^i(\theta^{-i}) = -\sum_{j \neq i} \theta^j$. Theorem 3.9 also shows that the form of the transfers when the public decision rule is that of a dictatorship or positional dictatorship is

$$t^i(\theta) = h^i(\theta^{-i})$$

We turn next to the issue of balance.

Theorem 3.10: If a regular incentive scheme is balanced, then

$$\frac{\partial^n x_j^+}{\partial \theta^i \ldots \partial \theta^n} \equiv 0 \equiv \frac{\partial^n x_j^-}{\partial \theta^1 \ldots \partial \theta^n}, \quad j = 1, \ldots, q$$

Proof: For simplicity we shall argue for the case of simple schemes. Choose $\theta \notin A$. From balance,

$$(3.26) \qquad \sum_{t=1}^{n} t^i(\theta) \equiv 0$$

From Theorem 3.7,

$$\sum_{i=1}^{n} \left[\int_0^{\theta^i} s \frac{\partial x^-}{\partial \theta^i} (s, \theta^{-i}) \, ds + h^i(\theta^{-i}) \right] \equiv 0$$

and so

$$\sum_{i=1}^{n} \theta^i \frac{\partial^n x^-}{\partial \theta^1 \ldots \partial \theta^n} \equiv 0$$

We have, therefore,

$$\frac{\partial^n x^-}{\partial \theta^1 \ldots \partial \theta^n} \equiv 0$$

Similarly for x^+.   Q.E.D.

We observed earlier that when the public decision rule corresponds to a generalized dictatorship, the transfers take the form $t^i(\theta) = h^i(\theta^{-i})$. In particular, if $h^i(\theta^{-i}) \equiv 0$, the scheme is automatically balanced. One may ask whether or not there exist balanced deterministic DSIC schemes that are nondictatorial. The following example answers the question affirmatively.

Example 3.4: Let $n = 3$ and let $x(\theta) = 1$ for $\theta^2 + \theta^3 \geq 0$ and 0 otherwise,

$$t^1(\theta) = -\theta^2 - \theta^3, \quad \theta^2 + \theta^3 \geqslant 0$$
$$= 0, \quad \text{otherwise}$$

$$t^2(\theta) = \theta^3, \quad \theta^2 + \theta^3 \geqslant 0$$
$$= 0, \quad \text{otherwise}$$

$$t^3(\theta) = \theta^2, \quad \theta^2 + \theta^3 \geqslant 0$$
$$= 0, \quad \text{otherwise}$$

The scheme of Example 3.4 treats agent 1 asymmetrically, and with good reason: Nondictatorial, deterministic balanced schemes cannot be symmetric. We shall call an incentive scheme (x, t) symmetric if x is a symmetric function.

Theorem 3.11: A weakly efficient, symmetric, deterministic, balanced, and regular DSIC scheme must be a positional dictatorship.

Proof: See Appendix.

Theorem 3.11 applies only to deterministic schemes, and so it is natural to ask what "good," *nondeterministic* schemes that are balanced look like. By a good scheme, we mean one that maximizes the utilitarian criterion (3.2) in an expected sense, where the expectation is performed with respect to a prior distribution $F(\theta^1, \ldots, \theta^n)$. That is, we seek a balanced scheme (x, t) that maximizes

$$(3.44) \quad \int \sum_{i=1}^{n} (\theta^i x(\theta) + t^i(\theta)) \, dF(\theta)$$

Because transfers sum to zero in a balanced scheme, (3.44) becomes

$$(3.45) \quad \int \sum_{i=1}^{n} \theta^i x(\theta) \, dF(\theta)$$

From Theorem 3.10, balance implies that if x is n times differentiable (or the pointwise limit of a sequence of n-times differentiable functions), then

$$(3.46) \quad x(\theta) = \sum_{i=1}^{n} x_i(\theta^{-i})$$

It is easy to see, moreover, that (3.46) is a sufficient condition for the existence of transfers that balance. Thus, if we restrict our attention to x's that are pointwise limits of n-times differentiable functions, we seek $x_1, \ldots, x_n$ to maximize

$$(3.47) \quad \int \left(\sum_{i=1}^{n} \theta^i \right) \left(\sum_{j=1}^{n} x_j(\theta^{-j}) \right) dF(\theta)$$

such that

$$(3.48) \quad 0 \leqslant \sum x_j(\theta^{-j}) \leqslant 1$$

and

$(3.49) \quad x_j$'s are weakly increasing

Suppose that $x_2, \ldots, x_n$ have already been chosen optimally and that $E(\theta^1 | \theta^2, \ldots, \theta^n)$ (the expectation of θ^1 conditional on $\theta^2, \ldots, \theta^n$) is independent of $(\theta^2, \ldots, \theta^n)$. We must choose x_1 to maximize

$$(3.50) \quad \int (E\theta^1 + \theta^2 + \cdots + \theta^n) x_1(\theta^{-1}) \, dF^1(\theta^{-1})$$

subject to constraints (3.48) and (3.49), where F^1 is the marginal distribution of θ^{-1}. From (3.48) and (3.49), for any θ^{-1},

$$(3.51) \quad x_1(\theta^{-1}) \leqslant \lim_{\tilde{\theta}^{-1} \to \infty} x_1(\tilde{\theta}^{-1}) \leqslant 1 - \sum_{i=2}^{n} \lim_{\tilde{\theta}^{-i} \to \infty} x_i(\tilde{\theta}^{-i})$$

Take

$$\mu_i = \lim_{\tilde{\theta}^{-i} \to \infty} x_i(\tilde{\theta}^{-i})$$

From (3.50) and (3.51), the optimal choice of $x_1(\theta^{-1})$ is

$$x_1(\theta^{-1}) = 0, \quad \sum_{j=2}^{n} \theta^j < E\theta^1$$

$$= 1 - \sum_{i=2}^{n} \mu_i, \quad \sum_{j=2}^{n} \theta^j \geqslant E\theta^1$$

Thus (3.47) becomes

$$(3.52) \quad \sum_{i=1}^{n} \mu_i \operatorname{Prob}\left(\sum_{j \neq i} \theta^j \geqslant -E\theta^i \right)$$

We can therefore state Theorem 3.12.

Theorem 3.12: The balanced incentive scheme (x, t), where

$$x(\theta) = \sum_{j=1}^{n} x_j(\theta^{-j})$$

$$x_j(\theta^{-j}) = 0, \quad \sum_{i \neq j} \theta^i + E\theta^j < 0$$

$$= \mu_j, \text{ otherwise}$$

$$\sum_{j \in D} \mu_j = 1$$

$$D = \left\{ j \,\middle|\, \mathrm{Prob}\left\{ \sum_{i \neq j} \tilde{\theta}^i + E\theta^j \geq 0 \right\} \text{ is maximal} \right\}$$

maximizes (3.44) among all balanced incentive schemes for which x is the pointwise limit of a sequence of n-times differentiable functions.

Note that if F is symmetric and $E\theta^j = 0$, then x_j in Theorem 3.12 becomes

$$x_j(\theta^{-j}) = 0, \quad \sum_{i \neq j} \theta^i < 0$$

$$= \frac{1}{n}, \quad \sum_{i \neq j} \theta^i \geq 0$$

That is, the best balanced scheme has a public decision rule that is utilitarian for each of the n coalitions of $n-1$ agents, where each coalition contributes probability weight $1/n$.

It is natural to compare the welfare properties of the best balanced scheme with those of the Groves-Clarke mechanism. The former has balanced transfers but does not always take the public decision maximizing the utilitarian criterion. The latter takes the correct public decision but does not always balance the budget (although, from Theorem 3.3, no alternative feasible and successful DSIC scheme dominates it). There certainly seems to be no a priori reason to favor the Groves-Clarke mechanism. Therefore, we believe that the emphasis in the literature on successful mechanisms, ignoring welfare losses due to transfer imbalances, is somewhat misguided. Indeed, as the following example shows, the best balanced scheme can do better than the Groves-Clarke mechanism in the expected sense of (3.44).

Example 3.5: Take $n=2$ and let $F(\theta^1, \theta^2)$ be the joint uniform distribution on $[-\frac{1}{2}, \frac{1}{2}]$. That is,

$$F(\theta^1, \theta^2) = (\theta^1 + \tfrac{1}{2})(\theta^2 + \tfrac{1}{2})$$

The expected sum of utilities under the Groves-Clarke mechanism is the expected sum of utilities from the public decision

$$\int\limits_{\theta^1+\theta^2\geqslant 0} (\theta^1 + \theta^2)\, dF(\theta^1,\theta^2) = \frac{1}{6}$$

plus the expected sum of transfers

$$-\int\limits_{\substack{\theta^1+\theta^2\geqslant 0 \\ \theta^1\geqslant 0 \\ \theta^2\leqslant 0}} \theta^2\, dF(\theta^1,\theta^2) - \int\limits_{\substack{\theta^1+\theta^2\geqslant 0 \\ \theta^1\leqslant 0 \\ \theta^2\geqslant 0}} \theta^1\, dF(\theta^1,\theta^2) - \int\limits_{\substack{\theta^1+\theta^2<0 \\ \theta^1\geqslant 0 \\ \theta^2\leqslant 0}} \theta^1\, dF(\theta^1,\theta^2)$$

$$-\int\limits_{\substack{\theta^1+\theta^2<0 \\ \theta^1\leqslant 0 \\ \theta^2\geqslant 0}} \theta^2\, dF(\theta^1,\theta^2) = -\frac{1}{12}$$

That is, the expected sum of utilities is $1/12$. The expected sum under the best balanced mechanism, on the other hand, is just the expected public payoff:

$$\int\limits_{\substack{\theta^1\geqslant 0 \\ \theta^2\geqslant 0}} (\theta^1 + \theta^2)\, dF + \frac{1}{2}\int\limits_{\substack{\theta^1\geqslant 0 \\ \theta^2<0}} (\theta^1 + \theta^2)\, dF + \frac{1}{2}\int\limits_{\substack{\theta^1<0 \\ \theta^2>0}} (\theta^1 + \theta^2)\, dF = \frac{7}{48}$$

Therefore, the best balanced mechanism is better than Groves-Clarke. Of course, we have taken the extreme position of treating the budget surplus under Groves-Clarke as a total loss. Nonetheless, the example illustrates that it is unduly restrictive to consider only successful schemes.

We next turn to feasibility and individual rationality. As in the special case when x satisfies (3.3), we can readily choose t so that (x, t) is DSIC and feasible or DSIC and individually rational if x satisfies the conditions for a regular public decision rule. However, feasibility and individual rationality together cannot be satisfied by a weakly efficient DSIC scheme unless it is the nth positional dictator.

Theorem 3.13: If a weakly efficient and feasible regular DSIC scheme is individually rational, then it is the nth positional dictator.

Proof: Suppose that (x, t) satisfies the hypotheses. We shall assume for convenience that (x, t) is simple. Choose $\bar{\theta} \geqslant 0$. From weak efficiency, $\bar{\theta} \in A$. If for some i, $a^i(\bar{\theta}^{-i})$ is not defined, then choose $\bar{\theta}^i < 0$. We have

$(\tilde\theta^i, \bar\theta^{-i}) \in A$. From Theorem 3.7, agent i's payoff when the parameters are $(\tilde\theta^i, \bar\theta^{-i})$ is

$$\int_0^{\tilde\theta^i} x^+(s, \bar\theta^{-i})\, ds + h^i(\bar\theta^{-i})$$

From individual rationality,

$$h^i(\bar\theta^{-i}) \geqslant \int_{\tilde\theta^i}^0 x^+(s, \bar\theta^{-i})\, ds$$

From choice of $\tilde\theta^i$, and because $x^+(0, \bar\theta^{-i}) = 1$, $\int_{\tilde\theta^i}^0 x^+(s, \bar\theta^{-i})\, ds > 0$. Thus

(3.53) $h^i(\bar\theta^{-i}) > 0$

If, for given i, $a^i(\bar\theta^{-i})$ is defined, then from weak efficiency,

(3.54) $a^i(\bar\theta^{-i}) \leqslant 0$

For such i, choose $\hat\theta^i < a^i(\bar\theta^{-i})$. Then $(\hat\theta^i, \bar\theta^{-i}) \notin A$. Thus i's payoff when the parameters are $(\hat\theta^i, \bar\theta^{-i})$ is

$$\int_0^{\hat\theta^i} x^-(s, \bar\theta^{-i})\, ds + h^i(\bar\theta^{-i})$$

From individual rationality,

(3.55) $h^i(\bar\theta^{-i}) > \int_{\hat\theta^i}^0 x^-(s, \bar\theta^{-i})\, ds$

Therefore, because, from (3.54), $\hat\theta^i < 0$,

(3.56) $h^i(\bar\theta^{-i}) \geqslant 0$

From Theorem 3.7, i's transfer, when the parameters are $\bar\theta$ and $a^i(\bar\theta^{-i})$ is not defined, is

(3.57) $-\bar\theta^i x^+(\bar\theta) + \int_0^{\bar\theta^i} x^+(s, \bar\theta^{-i})\, ds + h^i(\bar\theta^{-i})$

From weak efficiency, $x^+(s, \bar{\theta}^{-1}) = 1$ for all $s \geqslant 0$. Thus, (3.57) reduces to

$$h^i(\bar{\theta}^{-i})$$

which is positive, from (3.53). Thus, because the sum of the transfers is nonpositive by feasibility, there must exist i for whom $a^i(\bar{\theta}^{-i})$ is defined and whose transfer, when parameters are $\bar{\theta}$, is nonpositive. That is,

$$(3.58) \quad -\bar{\theta}^i x^+(\bar{\theta}) + \int_0^{\bar{\theta}^i} x^+(s, \bar{\theta}^{-i}) \, ds + h^i(\bar{\theta}^{-i})$$

$$+ \int_0^{a^i(\bar{\theta}^{-i})} (x^{-(s, \bar{\theta}^{-i})} - x^+(s, \bar{\theta}^{-i})) \, ds + h^i(\bar{\theta}^{-i}) \leqslant 0$$

The first two terms on the left-hand side of (3.58) cancel, because $x^+(s, \theta) = 1$ for $s \geqslant 0$. Therefore, (3.58) becomes

$$(3.59) \quad h^i(\bar{\theta}^{-i}) \leqslant \int_{a^i(\bar{\theta}^{-i})}^0 (x^-(s, \bar{\theta}^{-i}) - x^+(s, \bar{\theta}^{-i})) \, ds$$

Because in (3.55) $\hat{\theta}^i < a^i(\bar{\theta}^{-i})$, (3.59) implies

$$(3.60) \quad h^i(\bar{\theta}^{-i}) \leqslant h^i(\bar{\theta}^{-i}) - \int_{a^i(\bar{\theta}^{-i})}^0 x^+(s, \bar{\theta}^{-i}) \, ds = h^i(\bar{\theta}^{-i}) + a^i(\bar{\theta}^{-i})$$

Thus, $a^i(\bar{\theta}^{-i}) \geqslant 0$, and so, from (3.54),

$$(3.61) \quad a^i(\bar{\theta}^{-i}) = 0$$

Furthermore, from feasibility, if there exists j for which $a^j(\bar{\theta}^{-j})$ is not defined, then there exists i for which (3.59) and hence (3.60) hold with strict inequality, an impossibility. Thus, (3.61) holds for all i and all $\bar{\theta} \geqslant 0$. But this implies that the incentive scheme is the nth positional dictatorship. Q.E.D.

We turn finally to the issue of coalitions. The following result generalizes Theorem 3.5.

Theorem 3.14: There exists no weakly efficient, regular CDSIC incentive scheme.

Proof: See Appendix.

3.4   *Other solution concepts*

In Subsections 3.2 and 3.3 we dealt exclusively with the solution concept of dominant strategies. In this subsection, we briefly treat Bayesian and Nash equilibria in our simple public project model.

Turning first to Bayesian equilibrium, we suppose that it is common knowledge that the θ^i's are distributed according to the (cumulative) probability distribution $F(\theta^1, \ldots, \theta^n)$. Knowing the prior F and his own parameter θ^i, agent i has beliefs given by the posterior distribution $F^i(\theta^{-i} | \theta^i)$. We shall suppose that the distribution of θ^{-i} is, in fact, independent of θ^i, so that we may write $F^i(\theta^{-i})$. (For a treatment of the dependent case, see the last section of the chapter by Laffont and Maskin, 1979a.) An incentive scheme (x, t) is *incentive-compatible in Bayesian strategies* (BSIC) if and only if

$$\int [\theta^i x(\theta^i, \theta^{-i}) + t^i(\theta^i, \theta^{-i})] \, dF^i(\theta^{-i})$$

$$\geq \int [\theta^i x(\hat{\theta}^i, \theta^{-i}) + t^i(\hat{\theta}^i, \theta^{-i})] \, dF^i(\theta^{-i})$$

for all i, θ^i, and $\hat{\theta}^i$. That is, telling the truth maximizes an agent's expected utility, given that others tell the truth.

In the corollary to Theorem 3.3 we demonstrated that there is no fully optimal DSIC scheme. One advantage that the Bayesian approach to incentive has is that full optimality is attainable.

Theorem 3.15: (See the work of Arrow, 1979, and d'Aspremont and Gérard-Varet, 1979.) There exist fully optimal BSIC incentive schemes.

Proof: The proof is by explicit example. (For a characterization of all such schemes, see the work of Laffont and Maskin, 1979a.) Take

$$(3.73) \quad t^i(\theta) = \int_{\theta^{-i}} \sum_{j \neq i} \theta^j x(\theta) \, dF^i(\theta^{-i})$$

$$- \frac{1}{n-1} \sum_{k \neq i} \int_{\theta^{-k}} \sum_{j \neq k} \theta^j x(\theta) \, dF^k(\theta^{-k})$$

where x, of course, satisfies (3.3). By construction,

$$\sum_{i=1}^{n} t^i(\theta) = 0$$

Therefore the scheme is balanced. In maximizing his expected utility, agent i can ignore the second term in (3.73) because it does not depend on θ^i. Thus agent i chooses $\hat{\theta}^i$ to maximize

$$(3.74) \quad \int \left[\theta^i x(\hat{\theta}^i, \theta^{-i}) + \int_{\theta^{-i}} \sum_{j \neq i} \theta^j x(\hat{\theta}^i, \theta^{-i}) \, dF^i(\theta^{-i}) \right] dF^i(\theta^{-i})$$

After rearrangement, (3.65) becomes

$$(3.75) \quad \int_{\theta^{-i}} \left(\sum_{j=1}^n \theta^j x(\hat{\theta}^i, \theta^{-i}) \right) dF^i(\theta^{-i})$$

But for each θ^{-i}, $\hat{\theta}^i = \theta^i$ maximizes $\sum_{j=1}^n \theta^j x(\hat{\theta}^i, \theta^{-i})$. Therefore, $\hat{\theta}^i = \theta^i$ maximizes (3.66).   Q.E.D.

We discussed some of the drawbacks of Bayesian incentive theory in Section 1. Bayesian equilibrium demands both stronger behavioral assumptions and stronger informational assumptions (most notably, the assumption that F is common knowledge) than dominant strategy equilibrium. Furthermore, as we shall now see, Bayesian incentive schemes are plagued by multiple equilibria.

Suppose that $n = 2$ and that

$$F^i(\theta^i) = 0, \quad \theta^i \leq -1$$
$$= \frac{\theta^i + 1}{2}, \quad -1 \leq \theta^i \leq 1$$
$$= 1, \quad \theta^i \geq 1$$

That is, the distribution of θ^i is uniform on the interval $[-1, 1]$. From the proof of Theorem 3.13, we know that the strategy rules $(\bar{\mu}^1(\cdot), \bar{\mu}^2(\cdot))$, where

$$\bar{\mu}^i(\theta^i) = \theta^i \quad \text{for all} \quad \theta^i$$

form a Bayesian equilibrium in the incentive scheme defined by (3.3) and (3.64). However, there is a continuum of other equilibria. For any $k \geq 1$, define

$$\mu_k^1(\theta^1) = -1, \quad k\theta^1 < -1$$
$$= k\theta^1, \quad -1 \leq k\theta^1 \leq 1$$
$$= 1, \quad k\theta^1 > 1$$

and

$$\mu_k^2(\theta^2) = \frac{1}{k} \theta^2$$

The pair (μ_k^1, μ_k^2) is an equilibrium. To see this, first consider agent 1. Agent 1 chooses $\hat{\theta}^1$ to maximize

$$\theta^1 \int\limits_{\mu_k^2(\theta^2) \geqslant -\hat{\theta}^1} dF^1(\theta^2) + \int\limits_{\theta^2 \geqslant -\hat{\theta}^1} \theta^2 \, dF^2(\theta^2)$$

$$= \theta^1 \left(1 - \left(\frac{-k\hat{\theta}^1 + 1}{2} \right) \right) + \frac{1}{4}(1 - (\hat{\theta}^1)^2)$$

The first-order condition for an interior maximum is, therefore,

$$\frac{k\theta^1}{2} - \frac{\hat{\theta}^1}{2} = 0 \quad \text{or} \quad \hat{\theta}^1 = k\theta^1$$

Thus the optimal choice of $\hat{\theta}^1$ is $k\theta^1$, if $-1 \leqslant k\theta^1 \leqslant 1$, and one of the two endpoints, otherwise. The argument is similar for agent 2.

This example is symptomatic of Bayesian equilibrium in our public project model. For continuous distributions F^i, there will, in general, be continua of equilibria.

Finally, we turn to Nash equilibrium. When Nash equilibrium is the solution concept, we can no longer take agents' strategy spaces to coincide with their parameter spaces Θ^i. This is because, as discussed in Section 1, an agent's relevant information consists not only of his own parameter but of those of others as well. We therefore define an incentive scheme $\delta = (x, t)$ on the domain

$$S^1 \times \cdots \times S^n$$

For each profile $(\theta^1, \ldots, \theta^n)$, let $NE_d(\theta^1, \ldots, \theta^n)$ be the set of Nash equilibrium outcomes for profile $(\theta^1, \ldots, \theta^n)$ in the scheme d. That is,

$$NE_d(\theta^1, \ldots, \theta^n) = \{(x(s), t(s)) \mid s \in \Pi S^i \text{ is a Nash equilibrium for } (\theta^1, \ldots, \theta^n) \text{ in the scheme } d\}$$

$NE_d(\cdot)$ is a correspondence from Θ to $[0, 1] \times \mathbf{R}^n$. We will call a correspondence $f: \Theta \rightarrow [0, 1] \times \mathbf{R}^n$ *monotonic* if, for all $(\theta^1, \ldots, \theta^n)$, $(\theta^{1\prime}, \ldots, \theta^{n\prime}) \in \Theta$, and all $(x, t) \in f(\theta^1, \ldots, \theta^n)$

$$[\forall(x', t') \forall i \quad \theta^i x + t^i \geqslant \theta^i x' + t^{i\prime} \rightarrow \theta^{i\prime} x' + t^i \geqslant \theta^{i\prime} x' + t^{i\prime}]$$
$$\rightarrow (x, t) \in f(\theta^{1\prime}, \ldots, \theta^{n\prime})$$

The following result is drawn from the work of Maskin (1977).

Theorem 3.16: For correspondence $f: \Theta \rightarrow [0, 1] \times \mathbf{R}^n$ there exists an incentive scheme d such that

(3.76) $\forall \theta \quad NE_d(\theta) = f(\theta)$

if and only if f is monotonic.

An incentive scheme d satisfying (3.76) is said to *implement f*. In our public project framework it is simple to characterize those correspondences that are implementable (monotonic):

Theorem 3.17: f is monotonic, and hence implementable, if and only if

$$(0, t) \in f(\theta^1, \ldots, \theta^n) \quad \text{implies} \quad (0, t) \in f(\theta^{1\prime}, \ldots, \theta^{n\prime})$$
$$\text{for all} \quad (\theta^{1\prime}, \ldots, \theta^{n\prime}) \leqslant (\theta^1, \ldots, \theta^n)$$

and

$$(1, t) \in f(\theta^1, \ldots, \theta^n) \quad \text{implies} \quad (1, t) \in f(\theta^{1\prime}, \ldots, \theta^{n\prime})$$
$$\text{for all} \quad (\theta^{1\prime}, \ldots, \theta^{n\prime}) \geqslant (\theta^1, \ldots, \theta^n)$$

Proof: Immediate verification. We can consider f as a welfare criterion. Theorem 3.16 shows that implementability places little restriction on welfare criteria in this framework. In particular,

$$f(\theta^1, \ldots, \theta^n) = \left\{ (x, t) \mid t = 0 \quad \text{and} \quad x = \begin{cases} 0, & \sum \theta^i < 0 \\ 1, & \sum \theta^i \geqslant 0 \end{cases} \right\}$$

is implementable. Thus, with Nash equilibrium as the solution concept, we can use the utilitarian public decision rule incentive compatibly without making any transfers at all in equilibrium.

APPENDIX

We collect here the proofs of those theorems left unproved in the text.

Theorem 3.3: There exists no feasible and successful incentive scheme (x, t) such that for all θ

$$\left| \sum t^i(\theta) \right| \leqslant \left| \sum \bar{t}^i(\theta) \right|$$

with strict inequality for some θ, where $\bar{t}^i$ is the pivotal mechanism's transfer to agent i.

Proof: We confine our attention to the case $n = 3$ and to schemes whose transfer functions are piecewise differentiable. Suppose that the scheme (x, t) uniformly dominates the Groves-Clarke mechanism, $(x, \bar{t})$. From Theorem 3.2, t^i satisfies (3.4) from some choice of $h^i(\theta^{-i})$. If θ is such that $\sum_{j \neq i} \theta^j < 0$ for all i, then because $\sum_{i=1}^{3} \bar{t}^i(\theta) = 0$, we have

(3.5) $\displaystyle\sum_{i=1}^{3} h^i(\theta^{-i}) = 0$

Thus, if the h^i's are differentiable at θ, we have

$$\frac{\partial h^1}{\partial \theta^2} = -\frac{\partial h^3}{\partial \theta^2}$$

(3.6) $$\frac{\partial h^1}{\partial \theta^3} = -\frac{\partial h^2}{\partial \theta^3}$$

$$\frac{\partial h^2}{\partial \theta^1} = -\frac{\partial h^3}{\partial \theta^1}$$

and

(3.7) $$\frac{\partial^2 h^1}{\partial \theta^2 \partial \theta^3} = \frac{\partial^2 h^2}{\partial \theta^1 \partial \theta^3} = \frac{\partial^2 h^3}{\partial \theta^1 \partial \theta^2} = 0$$

From (3.5)–(3.7), we conclude that

$$h^1(\theta^2, \theta^3) = f(\theta^2) + g(\theta^3), \quad \text{for } \theta^2 + \theta^3 < 0$$

(3.8) $$h^2(\theta^1, \theta^3) = e(\theta^1) - g(\theta^3), \quad \text{for } \theta^1 + \theta^3 < 0$$

$$h^3(\theta^1, \theta^2) = -e(\theta^1) - f(\theta^2), \quad \text{for } \theta^1 + \theta^2 < 0$$

where e, f, and g are piecewise differentiable. Similarly, because $\sum_{i=1}^{3} \bar{t}^i(\theta^{-i}) = 0$ when $\sum_{j \neq i} \theta^j \geqslant 0$ for all i, we have

$$2(\theta^1 + \theta^2 + \theta^3) + \sum_{i=1}^{3} h^i(\theta^{-i}) = 0$$

and so

$$h^1(\theta^2, \theta^3) = \tilde{f}(\theta^2) + \tilde{g}(\theta^3) - 2\theta^2, \quad \text{for } \theta^2 + \theta^3 \geqslant 0$$

(3.9) $$h^2(\theta^1, \theta^3) = \tilde{e}(\theta^1) - \tilde{g}(\theta^3) - 2\theta^3, \quad \text{for } \theta^1 + \theta^3 \geqslant 0$$

$$h^3(\theta^1, \theta^2) = -\tilde{e}^2(\theta^1) - \tilde{f}(\theta^2) - 2\theta^1, \quad \text{for } \theta^1 + \theta^2 \geqslant 0$$

Now suppose that, for some $\hat{\theta}$,

$$\left| \sum t^i(\hat{\theta}) \right| < \left| \sum \bar{t}^i(\hat{\theta}) \right|$$

Then

(3.10) $\displaystyle\sum_{i=1}^{3} \bar{h}^i(\hat{\theta}^{-i}) < \sum_{i=1}^{3} h^i(\hat{\theta}^{-i})$

where $\bar{h}^i(\theta^{-i}) = -\sum_{j \neq i} \theta^j$ for $\sum_{j \neq i} \theta^j \geqslant 0$ and 0 otherwise. Clearly, there exist i and k such that $\sum_{j \neq i} \hat{\theta}^j > 0$ and $\sum_{j \neq k} \hat{\theta}^j < 0$. In particular, assume that $\hat{\theta}^1 + \hat{\theta}^2 > 0$, $\hat{\theta}^2 + \hat{\theta}^3 < 0$, and $\hat{\theta}^1 + \hat{\theta}^3 < 0$ (the other cases can be argued similarly). Then (3.10) becomes

$$(3.11) \quad -\hat{\theta}^1 + \hat{\theta}^2 < f(\hat{\theta}^2) + g(\hat{\theta}^3) + e(\hat{\theta}^1)$$
$$- g(\hat{\theta}^3) - \bar{e}(\hat{\theta}^1) - \bar{f}(\hat{\theta}^2) - 2\hat{\theta}^2 - 2\hat{\theta}^1$$

If we take $\tilde{\theta}^1 < \hat{\theta}^1$ such that $\tilde{\theta}^1 + \hat{\theta}^2 = 0$, we have

$$(3.12) \quad \bar{h}^1(\hat{\theta}^2, \hat{\theta}^3) + \bar{h}^2(\tilde{\theta}^1, \hat{\theta}^3) + \bar{h}^3(\tilde{\theta}^1, \hat{\theta}^2)$$
$$= h^1(\hat{\theta}^2, \hat{\theta}^3) + h^2(\tilde{\theta}^1, \hat{\theta}^3) + h^3(\tilde{\theta}^1, \hat{\theta}^2)$$

Thus from (3.11) and (3.12), there exists $\bar{\theta}^1$ with $\tilde{\theta}^1 \leqslant \bar{\theta}^1 \leqslant \hat{\theta}^1$ such that

$$\frac{\partial \bar{h}^2}{\partial \theta^1}(\bar{\theta}^1, \hat{\theta}^3) + \frac{\partial \bar{h}^3}{\partial \theta^1}(\bar{\theta}^1, \hat{\theta}^2) < \frac{\partial h^2}{\partial \theta^1}(\bar{\theta}^1, \hat{\theta}^3) + \frac{\partial h^3}{\partial \theta^1}(\bar{\theta}^1, \hat{\theta}^2)$$

that is,

$$(3.13) \quad 1 < e'(\bar{\theta}^1) - \bar{e}'(\bar{\theta}^1)$$

where primes denote derivatives. Choose $\bar{\theta}^2$ and $\bar{\theta}^3$ such that

$$\bar{\theta}^2 + \bar{\theta}^3 < 0, \quad \bar{\theta}^1 + \bar{\theta}^2 < 0, \quad \text{and} \quad \bar{\theta}^1 + \bar{\theta}^3 = 0$$

Then

$$-\bar{\theta}^1 - \bar{\theta}^3 = f(\bar{\theta}^2) + g(\bar{\theta}^3) - e(\bar{\theta}^1) - f(\bar{\theta}^2) + \bar{e}(\bar{\theta}^1) - \bar{g}(\bar{\theta}^3) - 2\bar{\theta}^3$$

so that

$$(3.14) \quad -1 \leqslant -e'(\bar{\theta}^1) + \bar{e}'(\bar{\theta}^1)$$

Adding (3.13) to (3.14), we have $0 < 0$. Thus $\hat{\theta}$ cannot exist after all. Q.E.D.

Theorem 3.11: A weakly efficient, symmetric, deterministic, balanced, and regular DSIC scheme must be a positional dictatorship.

Proof: We shall argue the case $n = 3$ and suppose that the boundary of A (a deterministic scheme is simple) is piecewise differentiable. From Theorem 3.9, if (x, t) satisfies the hypotheses of the theorem, then t^i is of the form

$$(3.27) \quad t^i(\theta) = h^i(\theta^{-i}), \quad \theta \in A \quad \text{or} \quad a^i(\theta^{-i}) \quad \text{undefined}$$
$$= -a^i(\theta^{-i}) + h^i(\theta^{-i}), \quad \theta \in A \quad \text{and} \quad a^i(\theta^{-i}) \quad \text{defined}$$

We shall suppose, for convenience, that the h^i's are continuous and piecewise differentiable. It will suffice to show that, for every θ in the boundary of A and every i, $a^i(\theta^{-i})$ is either zero or undefined (if

$a^i(\theta^{-i}) = 0$ and the number of nonnegative components of θ^{-i} is k, then, from symmetry, the incentive scheme is the $(k+1)$th positional dictator).

Suppose not. Choose $\bar{\theta}$ from the boundary of A so that a^1 is differentiable in a neighborhood of $\bar{\theta}^{-1}$ and $a^1(\bar{\theta}^{-1}) \neq 0$. We may as well assume that $a^1(\bar{\theta}^{-1}) < 0$. Consider a sequence $\theta^1(n)$ converging from below to $\bar{\theta}^1$. From balance and (3.27),

$$h^1(\theta^2, \bar{\theta}^3) + h^2(\theta^1(n), \bar{\theta}^3) + h^3(\theta^1(n), \bar{\theta}^2) = 0 \quad \text{for all } n$$

Hence, by continuity,

$$\sum h^i(\bar{\theta}^{-i}) = 0$$

Thus, from balance,

$$(3.28) \quad \sum b^i(\bar{\theta}^{-i}) = 0$$

where

$$b^i(\bar{\theta}^{-i}) = a^i(\bar{\theta}^{-i}), \quad \text{if} \quad a^i(\bar{\theta}^{-i}) \quad \text{is defined}$$
$$= 0, \quad \text{otherwise}$$

We first show that a^1 must be constant in a neighborhood of $\bar{\theta}^{-1}$ (i.e., that $\partial a^1/\partial \theta^2 = \partial a^1/\partial \theta^3 = 0$ in a neighborhood of $\bar{\theta}^{-1}$). We must rule out two cases.

Case I: a^1 strictly decreasing in θ^2 but constant in θ^3 in a neighborhood N of $\bar{\theta}$.

Suppose first that a^3 is not defined in a neighborhood of $\bar{\theta}^{-3}$. Because a^1 is constant as a function of θ^3 in N, we may write a^1 as a function of θ^2 alone in this neighborhood. Hence, for all $\theta \in N$,

$$\theta \in A \quad \text{if and only if} \quad \theta^1 \geqslant a^1(\theta^2)$$

Furthermore, from (3.28),

$$b^3(a^1(\theta^2), \theta^2) = -a^1(\theta^2) - \theta^2$$

since $a^2(a^1(\theta^2), \theta^3) = \theta^2$. From arguments virtually identical with those in the proof of Theorem 3.3, we can conclude that for all $\theta \in N$,

$$h^2(\theta^1, \theta^3) = e(\theta^1) + g(\theta^3)$$
$$h^1(\theta^2, \theta^3) = f(\theta^2) - g(\theta^3)$$
$$(3.29) \quad h^3(\theta^1, \theta^2) = -e(\theta^1) - f(\theta^2), \quad \theta^1 < a^1(\theta^2)$$
$$= -e(\theta^1) - f(\theta^2) + (a^1)^{-1}(\theta^1) + a^1(\theta^2)$$
$$+ b^3(\theta^1, \theta^2), \quad \theta^1 \geqslant a^1(\theta^2)$$

where e, f, and g are continuous and piecewise differentiable. Choose $\tilde{\theta} \in N$ such that $\tilde{\theta}^1 > a^1(\tilde{\theta}^2)$ and such that e is differentiable at $\tilde{\theta}^1$, f at $\tilde{\theta}^2$, and h^2 and h^1 at $(\tilde{\theta}^1, \tilde{\theta}^2, \tilde{\theta}^1)$. By symmetry,

$$h^1(\tilde{\theta}^2, \tilde{\theta}^1) = h^3(\tilde{\theta}^3, \tilde{\theta}^2)$$

Thus

(3.30) $h^1(\tilde{\theta}^2, \tilde{\theta}^1) = h^3(\tilde{\theta}^1, \tilde{\theta}^2)$
$$= -e(\tilde{\theta}^1) - f(\tilde{\theta}^2) + (a^1)^{-1}(\tilde{\theta}^1) + a^1(\tilde{\theta}^2) + b^3(\tilde{\theta}^1, \tilde{\theta}^2)$$

If $(\tilde{\theta}^1, \tilde{\theta}^2, \tilde{\theta}^1) \in A$ (because $(\tilde{\theta}^1, \tilde{\theta}^2, \tilde{\theta}^1)$ need not be in N, we cannot infer from $\tilde{\theta}^1 > a^2(\tilde{\theta}^1)$ that $(\tilde{\theta}^1, \tilde{\theta}^2, \tilde{\theta}^1)$ is in A)

$$0 = \sum_i t^i(\tilde{\theta}^1, \tilde{\theta}^2, \tilde{\theta}^1) = -\sum a^i + \sum h^i$$

(3.31)
$$= -a^2(\tilde{\theta}^1, \tilde{\theta}^1) - 2b^3(\tilde{\theta}^1, \tilde{\theta}^2) - 2e(\tilde{\theta}^1) - 2f(\tilde{\theta}^2)$$
$$+ 2(a^1)^{-1}(\tilde{\theta}^1) + 2a^1(\tilde{\theta}^2) + 2b^3(\tilde{\theta}^1, \tilde{\theta}^2) + h^2(\tilde{\theta}^1, \tilde{\theta}^1)$$
$$= -a^2(\tilde{\theta}^1, \tilde{\theta}^1) - 2e(\tilde{\theta}^1) - 2f(\tilde{\theta}^2) + 2(a^1)^{-1}(\tilde{\theta}^1)$$
$$+ 2a^1(\tilde{\theta}^2) + h^2(\tilde{\theta}^1, \tilde{\theta}^1)$$

where we have used the fact, from symmetry, that $a^1(\tilde{\theta}^2, \tilde{\theta}^1) = b^3(\tilde{\theta}^1, \tilde{\theta}^2)$. Differentiating (3.31) by θ^2, we obtain

$$0 = -2 \frac{df}{d\theta^2}(\tilde{\theta}^2) + 2 \frac{da^1}{d\theta^2}(\tilde{\theta}^2)$$

Because a^1 is strictly decreasing in θ^2, we have

$$\frac{df}{d\theta^2}(\tilde{\theta}^2) < 0$$

If $(\tilde{\theta}^1, \tilde{\theta}^2, \tilde{\theta}^1) \notin A$, then

(3.32) $0 = \sum h^i = -2e(\tilde{\theta}^1) - 2f(\tilde{\theta}^2) + 2(a^1)^{-3}(\tilde{\theta}^1) + 2a^1(\tilde{\theta}^2)$
$$+ 2b^3(\tilde{\theta}^1, \tilde{\theta}^2) + h^2(\tilde{\theta}^1, \tilde{\theta}^1)$$

Differentiating (3.32) with respect to θ^2, we have

(3.33) $0 = -2 \frac{df}{d\theta^2}(\tilde{\theta}^2) + 2 \frac{da^1}{d\theta^2}(\tilde{\theta}^2) + 2 \frac{\partial b^3}{\partial \theta^2}(\tilde{\theta}^1, \tilde{\theta}^2)$

Because $\partial b^3 / \partial \theta^2 \leqslant 0$, we conclude that, regardless of whether or not $(\tilde{\theta}^1, \tilde{\theta}^2, \tilde{\theta}^1) \in A$,

(3.34) $\dfrac{\partial f}{\partial \theta^2}(\tilde{\theta}^2) < 0$

Now choose $\hat{\theta} \in N$ such that $\hat{\theta}^2 = \tilde{\theta}^2$, $\hat{\theta}^1 < a^2(\hat{\theta}^2)$, and such that e is differentiable at $\hat{\theta}^1$ and h^2 at $(\hat{\theta}^1, \hat{\theta}^2, \hat{\theta}^1)$. From symmetry, $h^1(\hat{\theta}^2, \hat{\theta}^1) = h^3(\hat{\theta}^1, \hat{\theta}^2) = -e(\hat{\theta}^1) - f(\hat{\theta}^2)$. If $(\hat{\theta}^1, \hat{\theta}^2, \hat{\theta}^1) \notin A$, then

(3.35) $0 = \sum h^i = h^2(\hat{\theta}^1, \hat{\theta}^1) - 2e(\hat{\theta}^1) - 2f(\hat{\theta}^2)$

Differentiating (3.35) with respect to θ^2, we obtain

$$0 = \frac{df}{d\theta^2}(\hat{\theta}^2)$$

which contradicts (3.34), as $\hat{\theta}^2 = \bar{\theta}^2$. Therefore, suppose $(\hat{\theta}^1, \hat{\theta}^2, \hat{\theta}^1) \in A$. But then,

(3.36)
$$\begin{aligned}
0 = \sum t^i &= -\sum a^i + \sum h^i \\
&= -a^1(\hat{\theta}^2, \hat{\theta}^1) - a^2(\hat{\theta}^1, \hat{\theta}^1) - a^3(\hat{\theta}^1, \hat{\theta}^2) \\
&\quad - 2e(\hat{\theta}^1) - 2f(\hat{\theta}^2) + h^2(\hat{\theta}^1, \hat{\theta}^1)
\end{aligned}$$

Differentiating (3.36) with respect to θ^2, we obtain

(3.37) $0 = -\dfrac{\partial a^1}{\partial \theta^2}(\hat{\theta}^2, \hat{\theta}^1) - \dfrac{\partial a^3}{\partial \theta^2}(\hat{\theta}^1, \hat{\theta}^2) - 2\dfrac{df}{d\theta^2}(\hat{\theta}^2)$

But $\partial a^1 / \partial \theta^2$ and $\partial a^3 / \partial \theta^2$ are nonpositive, and so, from (3.37), we infer that $df/d\theta^2(\hat{\theta}^2)$ is nonnegative, contradicting (3.34). We conclude, therefore, that Case I is impossible.

Case II: a^1 is strictly decreasing in both θ^2 and θ^3 in a neighborhood N of $\bar{\theta}$.

Consider $\theta \in N$ on the boundary of A. Then $a^1(\theta^2, \theta^3) \leq \theta^1$. If the inequality holds strictly, then for $(\tilde{\theta}^2, \tilde{\theta}^3)$ slightly less than (θ^2, θ^3),

(3.38) $(a^1(\tilde{\theta}^2, \tilde{\theta}^3), \tilde{\theta}^2, \tilde{\theta}^3) < (\theta^1, \theta^2, \theta^3)$

But $(a^1(\tilde{\theta}^2, \tilde{\theta}^3), \tilde{\theta}^2, \tilde{\theta}^3) \in A$. Thus, (3.38) contradicts the assumption that θ is on the boundary. Hence

(3.39) $a^1(\theta^2, \theta^3) = \theta^1$

If, for $\tilde{\theta}^2 < \theta^2$, $(\theta^1, \tilde{\theta}^2, \theta^3) \in A$, then as a^1 is strictly decreasing θ^2, $a^1(\tilde{\theta}^2, \theta^3) > \theta^1$. But $a^1(\tilde{\theta}^2, \theta^3) \leq \theta^1$, as $(\theta^1, \tilde{\theta}^2, \theta^3) \in A$. Therefore,

(3.40) $a^2(\theta^1, \theta^3) = \theta^2$

Similarly,

(3.41) $a^3(\theta^1, \theta^2) = \theta^3$

Hence, from (3.28) and (3.39)–(3.41),

(3.42) $\theta^1 + \theta^2 + \theta^3 = 0$

Because (3.42) holds for all boundary points in N, we conclude that the incentive scheme is locally successful. From the same argument that establishes the corollary to Theorem 3.3, we thus generate a contradiction. Case II is therefore impossible, and we have verified that in the neighborhood N of $\bar{\theta}$, $\partial a^1/\partial\theta^2 = \partial a^1/\partial\theta^3 = 0$. We can conclude that $(\partial a^i/\partial\theta^j)(\theta^{-i}) = 0$ for any $i \neq j$ and θ^{-i} for which $\partial a^i/\partial\theta^j$ is defined.

Because $a^1(\bar{\theta}^2, \bar{\theta}^3) < 0$, (3.28) implies that either $a^2(\bar{\theta}^1, \bar{\theta}^3) > 0$ or $a^3(\bar{\theta}^1, \bar{\theta}^2) > 0$. Without loss of generality, assume the former. Because $\bar{\theta}$ is on the boundary of A, either $a^2(\bar{\theta}^1, \bar{\theta}^3) = \bar{\theta}^2$ or $a^3(\bar{\theta}^1, \bar{\theta}^2) = \bar{\theta}^3$. Assume the former (if $a^3(\bar{\theta}^1, \bar{\theta}^2) = \bar{\theta}^3$, the argument is entirely analogous). Consider points of the form $(\bar{\theta}^1, \bar{\theta}^2, \theta^3)$ for $\theta^3 \geqslant \bar{\theta}^3$. Let

$$\tilde{\theta}^3 = \min\{\theta^3 \geqslant \bar{\theta}^3 \mid a^2(\bar{\theta}^1, \theta^3) \neq a^2(\bar{\theta}^1, \bar{\theta}^3)\}.$$

Because $\bar{\theta}^2 = a^2(\bar{\theta}^1, \theta^3)$ for all $\theta^3 < \tilde{\theta}^3$, $(\bar{\theta}^1, \bar{\theta}^2, \theta^3)$ is on the boundary of A for such θ^3. Therefore, $(\bar{\theta}^1, \bar{\theta}^2, \tilde{\theta}^3)$ is on the boundary of A. Thus, from (3.28),

(3.43) $a^1(\bar{\theta}^2, \tilde{\theta}^3) + a^2(\bar{\theta}^1, \tilde{\theta}^3) + a^3(\bar{\theta}^1, \bar{\theta}^2) = 0$

But from the definition of $\tilde{\theta}^3$, $a^1(\bar{\theta}^2, \tilde{\theta}^3) \leqslant a^1(\bar{\theta}^2, \bar{\theta}^3)$ and $a^2(\bar{\theta}^1, \tilde{\theta}^3) < a^2(\bar{\theta}^1, \bar{\theta}^3)$, a contradiction of (3.43). Therefore, $\tilde{\theta}^3$ does not exist, and, for all $\theta^3 \geqslant \bar{\theta}^3$, $a^2(\bar{\theta}^1, \theta^3) = \bar{\theta}^2$. Choose $\theta^3 > 0$. By similar argument, $a^2(\theta^1, \theta^3) = \bar{\theta}^2$ for all $\theta^1 \geqslant \bar{\theta}^1$. Choose $\theta^1 > 0$. Then $(\theta^1, \bar{\theta}^2, \theta^3)$ lies on the boundary of A because $\bar{\theta}^2 = a^2(\theta^1, \theta^3)$. But $(\theta^1, \bar{\theta}^2, \theta^3) > 0$, so by weak efficiency it lies in the interior of A. We conclude that $a^1(\bar{\theta}^2, \bar{\theta}^3)$ cannot differ from zero after all.   Q.E.D.

Theorem 3.14: There exists no weakly efficient, regular CDSIC incentive scheme.

Proof: Suppose that (x, t) is a weakly efficient regular CDSIC scheme. It is convenient to suppose that (x, t) is simple. For $\theta \notin A$, the payoff to the coalition of agents 1 and 2 is

(3.62) $\theta^1 x^-(\theta) - \displaystyle\int_0^{\theta^1} s\frac{\partial x^-}{\partial\theta^1}(s, \theta^{-1})\,ds + \theta^2 x^-(\theta)$

$$- \int_0^{\theta^2} s\frac{\partial x^-}{\partial\theta^2}(s, \theta^{-2})\,ds + h^1(\theta^{-1}) + h^2(\theta^{-2})$$

Given that the coalition chooses θ^1 optimally, (3.62) implies

$$(3.63) \quad \theta^2 \frac{\partial x^-}{\partial \theta^1}(\theta) - \int_0^{\theta^2} s \frac{\partial^2 x^-}{\partial \theta^1 \partial \theta^2}(s, \theta^{-2}) \, ds + \frac{\partial h^2}{\partial \theta^1}(\theta^{-2}) = 0$$

Because (3.63) holds for all θ^2 locally, we obtain

$$(3.64) \quad \frac{\partial x^-}{\partial \theta^1} = 0$$

Thus

$$(3.65) \quad \frac{\partial x^-}{\partial \theta^j} = 0 \quad \text{for all } j$$

For $\theta \in A$, the coalition of agents 1 and 2 has payoff

$$(3.66) \quad (\theta^1 + \theta^2) x^+(\theta) - \int_0^{\theta^1} s \frac{\partial x^+}{\partial \theta^1}(s, \theta^{-1}) \, ds - \int_0^{\theta^2} s \frac{\partial x^+}{\partial \theta^2}(s, \theta^{-2}) \, ds$$

$$+ \int_0^{a^1(\theta^{-1})} (x^-(s, \theta^{-1}) - x^+(s, \theta^{-1})) \, ds$$

$$+ \int_0^{a^2(\theta^{-2})} (x^-(s, \theta^{-2}) - x^+(s, \theta^{-2})) \, ds$$

$$+ h^1(\theta^{-1}) + h^2(\theta^{-2})$$

If a^2 is differentiable as a function of θ^1, optimal choice of θ^1 in (3.66) implies

$$(3.67) \quad \theta^2 \frac{\partial x^+}{\partial \theta^1} = \int_0^{\theta^2} s \frac{\partial^2 x^+}{\partial \theta^1 \partial \theta^2}(s, \theta^{-2}) \, ds + (x^-(a^2(\theta^{-2}), \theta^{-2})$$

$$- x^+(a^2(\theta^{-2}), \theta^{-2})) \frac{\partial a^2}{\partial \theta^1}(\theta^{-2}) + \frac{\partial h^2}{\partial \theta^1}(\theta^{-2})$$

$$= 0$$

Because (3.67) holds locally for all θ^2,

$$\frac{\partial x^+}{\partial \theta^1} = 0$$

Therefore,

(3.68) $\quad \dfrac{\partial x^+}{\partial \theta^i} = 0 \quad$ for all i

From weak efficiency, (3.65) and (3.68) imply that $x^- \equiv 0$ and $x^+ \equiv 1$. That is, the scheme is simple. Choose θ on the boundary of A. Then $\theta^i = a^i(\theta^{-i})$ for some i. Suppose, without loss of generality, that $\theta^1 = a^1(\theta^{-1})$. Then, for $\hat\theta^1 < a^1(\theta^{-1})$, the payoff to a coalition of 1 and 2 for parameters $(\hat\theta^1, \theta^{-1})$ is

(3.69) $\quad h^1(\theta^{-1}) + h^2(\hat\theta^1, \theta^{-1-2})$

Because θ^2 is chosen optimally,

$$\frac{\partial h^1}{\partial \theta^2}(\theta^{-1}) = 0$$

For $\hat\theta^1 \geqslant a^1(\theta^2, \theta^3)$, the payoff to the coalition is

$$\hat\theta^1 + \theta^2 - a^1(\theta^{-1}) - a^2(\hat\theta^1, \theta^{-1-2}) + h^1(\theta^{-1}) + h^2(\hat\theta^1, \theta^{-1-2})$$

Optimal choice of θ^2 implies

(3.70) $\quad -\dfrac{\partial a^1}{\partial \theta^2} + \dfrac{\partial h^1}{\partial \theta^2} = 0$

Thus, from (3.60) and (3.61),

$$\frac{\partial a^1}{\partial \theta^2}(\theta^{-1}) = 0$$

Similarly,

$$\frac{\partial a^1}{\partial \theta^j}(\theta^{-1}) = 0 \quad \text{for all} \quad j \neq 1$$

That is, a^1 is locally constant. Now consider $\hat\theta^1$ slightly less than θ^1. Because it is optimal for the coalition of 1 and 2 to play truthful strategies, we have, when parameters are θ,

$$\theta^1 + \theta^2 - a^1(\theta^{-1}) - a^2(\theta^{-2}) + h^1(\theta^{-1}) + h^2(\theta^{-2})$$
$$\geqslant h^1(\theta^{-1}) + h^2(\hat\theta^1, \theta^{-1-2})$$

Therefore,

(3.71) $\quad \theta^2 - a^2(\theta^{-2}) + h^2(\theta^{-2}) \geqslant h^2(\hat\theta^1, \theta^{-1-2})$

Similarly, if the true parameters are $(\hat{\theta}^1, \theta^{-1})$, $h^1(\theta^{-1}) + h^2(\hat{\theta}^1, \theta^{-1-2}) \geq \hat{\theta}^1 + \theta^2 - \theta^1 - a^2(\theta^{-2}) + h^1(\theta^{-1}) + h^2(\theta^{-2})$, so that

$$(3.72) \quad h^2(\hat{\theta}^1, \theta^{-1-2}) \geq \theta^2 + (\hat{\theta}^1 - \theta^1) - a^2(\theta^{-2}) + h^2(\theta^{-2})$$

Inequalities (3.71) and (3.72) together imply that

$$\theta^2 - a^2(\theta^{-2}) \geq h^2(\hat{\theta}^1, \theta^{-1-2}) - h^2(\theta^{-2}) \geq \theta^2 + (\hat{\theta}^1 - \theta^1) - a^2(\theta^{-2})$$

which is impossible, because the middle expression does not depend on θ^2. Thus the scheme cannot be CDSIC after all.   Q.E.D.

NOTES

1 There are many other synonyms as well.
2 The term "members of society" may be misleading. Incentives theory applies to many purely "private" situations as well (e.g., the employer-employee relationship).
3 Like "planner" and "agent," "incentive scheme" goes under a variety of different names, depending on the area of application. For example, the term "contract" is often used in work on insurance, whereas "mechanism" applies in the allocation literature, and "voting scheme" or "game form" applies in the social choice context.
4 An incentive scheme is, in effect, a promise by the planner to react in a specified way to what agents do or reveal. The literature does not generally consider how the promise is enforced.
5 For an alternative model that is, in fact, somewhat more general, see the work of Myerson (1980).
6 It may seem peculiar that θ should enter the planner's payoff function, because it was assumed to be unobservable. We have included θ to allow, for example, the planner's objective function to be a social welfare function whose arguments are individual agents' utilities. Of course, if θ is unobservable, the planner can only maximize the expectation of his payoff with respect to θ.
7 In principle, each individual could attach a different subjective distribution to θ, and these distributions could jointly be common knowledge.
8 However, some recent progress in laying the theoretical foundations of "experimental" Nash equilibrium has been made by Levine (1981).
9 An example of this possibility is provided in Dasgupta and associates (1979, p. 195).
10 A domain of preferences Θ^i is "rich" if and only if for all $\theta_1, \theta_2 \in \Theta^i$ and all $d_1, d_2 \in D$ for which d_1 is preferred (strictly preferred) to d_2 under θ_1 implies that d_1 is preferred (strictly preferred) to d_2 under θ_1, there exists θ_3 such that for all c and $j = 1, 2$, d_j is preferred to c under θ_3, if d_j is preferred to c under θ_j.
11 The nonveto property requires that if all agents, except possibly one, prefer d to all other decisions, then $d \in f(\theta)$.
12 An allocation rule is individually rational if it assigns allocations that all agents prefer to their initial endowments.

13 Actually, the strong equilibria coincide with the Nash equilibria in Schmeidler's scheme, as in the work on double implementation.

14 Hurwicz (1972) and J. Roberts (1979) have shown that truthful behavior cannot constitute a global Nash equilibrium. However, Champsaur and Laroque (1980) have demonstrated that if the procedure is truncated at time T, then the global Nash equilibrium allocations converge to Lindahl equilibria as T tends to infinity. Truchon (1980) has shown that by introducing thresholds in the adjustment of public goods, a large class of *global* Nash equilibria leads to individually rational Pareto-optimal outcomes.

15 Green and Stokey (1980*b*) considered a similar model; but where the planner cannot commit himself to a scheme in advance. Their paper, therefore, does not fit within our framework.

16 We assume here either that the project is costless or that θ^i is the consumer's willingness to pay *net* of his share of the cost (the rule for dividing the costs is taken to be exogenous).

17 We have not allowed for random transfers because the space of transfers is convex and consumers are risk-neutral with respect to the private good. Thus, according to the reasoning of Section 1.4, there is no need to randomize transfers.

REFERENCES

Arrow, K. J. 1951. *Social Choice and Individual Values.* Cowles Foundation Monograph 12.

Arrow, K. J. 1979. "The Property Rights Doctrine and Demand Revelation under Incomplete Information" in *Economics and Human Welfare,* edited by M. Boskin, New York: Academic Press.

Barberá, S. 1977. "Manipulation of Social Decision Functions." *Journal of Economic Theory* 15:266–78.

Barberá, S. 1977*b*. "Manipulation of Voting Schemes that Do Not Leave too Much to Chance." *Econometrica,* 15:1573–88.

Bennett, E., and Conn, D. 1977. "The Group Incentive Properties of Mechanisms for the Provision of Public Goods." *Public Choice* 24-2:95–102.

Champsaur, P. 1976. "Neutrality of Planning Procedures in an Economy with Public Goods." *Review of Economic Studies* 43:293–300.

Champsaur, P., Drèze, J., and Henry, C. 1977. "Stability Theorems with Economic Applications." *Econometrica* 45:273–94.

Champsaur, P., and Laroque, G. 1980. "Strategic Behavior in Decentralized Planning Procedures." Unpublished mimeograph.

Chichilnisky, G., and Heal, G. 1980*a*. "Public Decision Rules Implementable by Non-cooperative Games: A Characterization." Unpublished mimeograph.

Chichilnisky, G., and Heal, G. 1980*b*. "Games to Prevent Free Riding: Existence and Construction." Unpublished mimeograph.

Clarke, E. 1971. "Multipart Pricing of Public Goods." *Public Choice* 8:19–33.

Dasgupta, P., Hammond, P., and Maskin, E. 1979. "The Implementation of Social Choice Rules," *Review of Economic Studies* 46:185–216.

d'Aspremont, C., and Gérard-Varet, L. 1979. "Incentives and Incomplete Information." *Journal of Public Economics* 11:25–45.

Diamond, P., and Mirrlees, J. 1971. "Optimal Taxation and Public Production, I." *American Economic Review* 61:261–78.

Drèze, J., and de la Vallée Poussin, D. 1971. "A Tâtonnement Process for Public Goods." *Review of Economic Studies* 38:133-50.

Dubins, L. 1974. "Group Decision Devices." Unpublished mimeograph.

Dutta, B., and Pattanaik, P. K. 1978. "On Nicely Consistent Voting Systems." *Econometrica* 46:163-70.

Farquharson, R. 1969. *Theory of Voting,* New Haven: Yale University Press.

Ferejohn, J., Grether, D., and McKelvey, R. 1980. "Implementation of Democratic Social Choice Functions." Unpublished mimeograph.

Fugigaki, Y., and Sato, K. 1981. "Incentives in the Generalized MDP Procedure for the Provision of Public Goods." *Review of Economic Studies* 48:473-86.

Gärdenfors, P. 1976. "Manipulation of Social Choice Functions." *Journal of Economic Theory* 13:217-28.

Gibbard, A. 1973. "Manipulation of Voting Schemes: A General Result." *Econometrica* 41:587-602.

Gibbard, A. 1977. "Manipulation of Schemes that Mix Voting with Chance." *Econometrica* 45:665-82.

Goldman, S., Leland, H., and Sibley, D. 1977. "Optimal Nonuniform Prices." Unpublished mimeograph.

Green, J. 1979. "Statistical Decision Theory Requiring Incentives for Information Transfer." Unpublished mimeograph.

Green, J. 1980. "Wage-Employment Contracts." Unpublished mimeograph.

Green, J., and Laffont, J. J. 1976. "Révélation des Préférences pour les Biens Publics." *Cahiers du Séminaire d'Econométrie.*

Green, J., and Laffont, J. J. 1977. "Characterization of Satisfactory Mechanisms for the Revelation of Preferences for Public Goods." *Econometrica* 45:427-38.

Green, J., and Laffont, J. J. 1979a. *Incentives in Public Decision-Making.* Amsterdam: North-Holland.

Green, J., and Laffont, J. J. 1979b. "On Coalition Incentive Compatibility." *Review of Economic Studies* 46:243-254.

Green, J., and Stokey, N. 1980a. "The Value of Social Information in the Delegation Problem." Unpublished mimeograph.

Green, J., and Stokey, N. 1980b. "A Two-Person Game of Information Transmission." Unpublished mimeograph.

Grossman, S., and Hart, O. 1980. "An Analysis of the Principal-Agent Problem." Unpublished mimeograph.

Grossman, S., and Hart, O. 1981. "Implicit Contracts, Moral Hazard, and Unemployment." *American Economic Review,* 71:301-7.

Groves, T. 1973. "Incentives in Teams." *Econometrica* 41:617-31.

Groves, T., and Ledyard, J. 1977. "Optimal Allocation of Public Goods: A Solution to the Free Rider Problem." *Econometrica* 45:783-810.

Groves, T., and Loeb, M. 1975. "Incentives and Public Inputs." *Journal of Public Economics* 4:311-26.

Guenerie, R., and Laffont, J. J. 1979. "Regulating a Monopolist." Unpublished mimeograph.

Hammond, P. 1979. "Straightforward Individual Incentive Compatibility in Large Economies." *Review of Economic Studies* 46:63-82.

Harris, M., and Raviv, A. 1978. "Allocation Mechanisms and the Design of Auctions." Unpublished mimeograph.

Harris, M., and Raviv, A. 1979. "Optimal Incentive Contracts with Imperfect Information." *Journal of Economic Theory* 20:231–59.

Harris, M., and Raviv, A. 1981. "A Theory of Monopoly Pricing Schemes with Demand Uncertainty." *American Economic Review* 71:347–69.

Harris, M., and Townsend, R. 1981. "Resource Allocation under Asymmetric Information." *Econometrica* 49:33–64.

Harsanyi, J. 1967. "Games with Incomplete Information Played by 'Bayesian' Players." *Management Science: Theory* 14:159–82, 320–34, 486–502.

Henry, C. 1977. "The Free Rider Problem in the MDP Procedure," unpublished mimeograph.

Holmstrom, B. 1979a. "Groves Schemes on Restricted Domains." *Econometrica*, 47:1137–1144.

Holmstrom, B. 1979b. "Moral Hazard and Observability." *Bell Journal of Economics* 10:74–91.

Holt, C. 1980. "Competitive Bidding for Contracts under Alternative Auction Procedures." *Journal of Political Economy* 88:433–45.

Hurwicz, L. 1972. "On Informationally Decentralized Systems." In: *Decision and Organization,* edited by C. B. McGuire and R. Radner, Amsterdam: North-Holland.

Hurwicz, L. 1975. "On the Existence of Allocation Systems whose Manipulative Nash Equilibria are Pareto Optimal." Unpublished mimeograph.

Hurwicz, L. 1979a. "Outcome Functions Yielding Walrasian and Lindahl Allocations at Nash Equilibrium Points." *Review of Economic Studies* 46:217–25.

Hurwicz, L. 1979b. "On Allocations Attainable through Nash Equilibria." *Journal of Economic Theory* 21:140–65.

Hurwicz, L., Postlewaite, A., and Maskin, E. 1979. "Feasible Implementation of Social Choice Correspondences by Nash Equilibria." Unpublished mimeograph.

Hurwicz, L., and Schmeidler, D. 1978. "Outcome Functions which Guarantee the Existence and Pareto Optimality of Nash Equilibria." *Econometrica* 46:1447–74.

Hurwicz, L., and Shapiro, L. 1978. "Incentive Structures Maximizing Residual Gain under Incomplete Information." *Bell Journal of Economics* 9:180–91.

Kalai, E., and Müller, E. 1977. "Characterization of Domains Admitting Nondictatorial Social Welfare Functions and Non Manipulatible Voting Procedures." *Journal of Economic Theory* 16:456–69.

Kalai, E., Postlewaite, A., and Roberts, J. 1977. "A Group Incentive Compatible Mechanism Yielding Core Allocations." Unpublished mimeograph.

Kelly, J. 1977. "Strategy-Proofness and Social Choice Functions without Single-valuedness." *Econometrica* 45:439–46.

Laffont, J. J., and Maskin, E. 1979a. "A Differential Approach to Expected Utility Maximizing Mechanisms." In: *Aggregation and Revelation of Preferences,* edited by J. J. Laffont, pp. 289–308. Amsterdam: North-Holland.

Laffont, J. J., and Maskin, E. 1979b. "On the Difficulty of Attaining Distributional Goals with Imperfect Information." *Scandinavian Journal of Economics* 81:227–37.

Laffont, J. J., and Maskin, E. 1980*a*. "A Differential Approach to Dominant Strategy Mechanisms." *Econometrica* 48:1507–20.

Laffont, J. J., and Maskin, E. 1980*b*. "Nash and Dominant Strategy Impenetration in Economic Environments." Unpublished mimeograph.

Laffont, J. J., and Maskin, E. 1980*c*. "A Characterization of SLIIC Planning Procedures with Public Goods." Unpublished mimeograph.

Ledyard, J. 1977. "Incentive Compatibility and Incomplete Information." Unpublished mimeograph.

Levine, D. 1981. *The Enforcement of Collusion in Oligopoly,* unpublished MIT Ph.D. dissertation.

Malinvaud, E. 1971. "A Planning Approach to the Public Good Production." *Swedish Journal of Economics* 73:96–112.

Malinvaud, E. 1972. "Prices for Individual Consumption, Quantity Indicators for Collective Consumption." *Review of Economic Studies* 39:385–405.

Marschak, J., and Radner, R. 1972. *Economic Theory of Teams.* Cowles Foundation Monograph 22.

Mas-Colell, A. 1978. "An Axiomatic Approach to the Efficiency of Noncooperative Equilibrium in Economics with a Continuum of Traders." Unpublished mimeograph.

Maskin, E. 1976. "Social Welfare Functions on Restricted Domains." Unpublished mimeograph.

Maskin, E. 1977. "Nash Equilibrium and Welfare Optimality." Unpublished mimeograph.

Maskin, E. 1979*a*. "Implementation and Strong Nash Equilibrium." In: *Aggregation and Revelation of Preferences,* edited by J. J. Laffont, pp. 433–49, Amsterdam: North-Holland.

Maskin, E. 1979*b*. "Incentive Schemes Immune to Group Manipulation." Unpublished mimeograph.

Maskin, E. 1980*a*. "On First Best Taxation." In *Income Distribution: the Limits to Redistribution,* edited by D. Collard, R. Lecomber, and M. Slater, pp. 9–22. Bristol: Scientechnica.

Maskin, E. 1980*b*. "Randomization in Incentive Problems." Unpublished mimeograph.

Maskin, E. and Riley, J. 1980*a*. "Monopoly Selling Strategies when Information is Incomplete, Price Discrimination, and Bundling." Unpublished mimeograph.

Maskin, E., and Riley, J. 1980*b*. "Auctioning an Indivisible Object." Unpublished mimeograph.

Mirrlees, J. 1971. "An Exploration in the Theory of Optimum Income Taxes." *Review of Economic Studies,* 38:175–208.

Mirrlees, J. 1975. "The Theory of Moral Hazard and Unobservable Behaviour —Part I" Unpublished mimeograph.

Moulin, H. 1979. "Prudence versus Sophistication in Voting Strategy." Unpublished mimeograph.

Moulin, H. 1980*a*. "Implementing Efficient, Anonymous, and Neutral Social Choice Functions." *Journal of Mathematical Economics* 7:249–69.

Moulin, H. 1980*b*. "On Strategy Proofness and Single Peakedness." *Public Choice* 35:437–55.

Moulin, H., and Peleg, B. 1980. "Stability and Implementation of Effectivity Functions." Unpublished mimeograph.

Myerson, R. 1979. "Incentive Compatibility and the Bargaining Problem." *Econometrica* 47:61-73.

Myerson, R. 1981*a*. "Optimal Coordination Mechanisms in Principal Agent Problems." Unpublished mimeograph.

Myerson, R. 1981*b*. "Optimal Auction Design." *Mathematics of Operations Research* 6:58-73.

Pattanaik, P. K. 1975. "Strategic Voting without Collusion under Binary and Democratic Group Decision Rules." *Review of Economic Studies* 42:93-104.

Pattanaik, P. K. 1976. "Counter-threats and Strategic Manipulation under Voting Schemes." *Review of Economic Studies* 43:11-18.

Pattanaik, P. K., and Sengupta, M. 1977. "Restricted Preferences and the Strategy-Proofness of a Class of Group Decision Rules," unpublished mimeograph.

Peleg, B. 1978*a*. "Consistent Voting Systems." *Econometrica* 46:153-61.

Peleg, B. 1978*b*. "Representation of Simple Games by Social Choice Functions." *International Journal of Game Theory* 7:81-94.

Postlewaite, A. 1979. "Manipulation via Endowments." *Review of Economic Studies* 44:255-62.

Radner, R. 1980. "Monitoring Cooperative Agreements in a Repeated Principal-Agent Relationship." Unpublished mimeograph.

Riley, J., and Samuelson, W. 1981. "Optimal Auctions." Unpublished mimeograph.

Roberts, J. 1979. "Incentives in Planning Procedures for the Provision of Public Goods." *Review of Economic Studies* 55:283-92.

Roberts, J., and Postlewaite, A. 1976. "The Incentives for Price-taking Behavior in Large Exchange Economies." *Econometrica* 44:115-28.

Roberts, K. 1979*a*. "The Characterization of Implementable Rules." In: *Aggregation and Revelation of Preferences,* edited by J. J. Laffont, pp. 321-48. Amsterdam: North-Holland.

Roberts, K. 1979*b*. "Welfare Considerations of Nonlinear Pricing," *Economic Journal* 89:66-83.

Rosenthal, R. 1979. "Arbitration of Two-part Disputes under Uncertainty." *Review of Economic Studies* 45:595-604.

Ross, S. 1973. "The Economic Theory of Agency: The Principal's Problem." *American Economic Review* 63:134-9.

Rubinstein, A., and Yaari, M. 1980. "Repeated Insurance Contracts and Moral Hazard," unpublished mimeograph.

Satterthwaite, M. 1975. "Strategy-Proofness and Arrow's Conditions: Existence and Correspondence Theorems for Voting Procedures and Social Welfare Functions." *Journal of Economic Theory* 10:187-217.

Satterthwaite, M. 1976. "Straightforward Allocation Mechanisms." Unpublished mimeograph.

Satterthwaite, M., and Sonnenschein, H. 1981. "Strategy Proof Allocation Mechanisms." *Review of Economic Studies* 48:587-98.

Schmeidler, D. 1980. "Walrasian Analysis via Strategic Outcome Functions," *Econometrica* 48:1585-94.

Schoumaker, F. 1977. "Best Reply Strategies in the Champsaur, Drèze and Henry Procedure." Unpublished mimeograph.

Selten, R. 1975. "Reexamination of the Perfectness Concept for Equilibrium

Points in Extensive Games." *International Journal of Game Theory* 4:25-55.

Sengupta, M. 1979. "Implementable Social Choice Rules: Characterization and Correspondence Theorems under Strong Nash Equilibrium." Unpublished mimeograph.

Shavell, S. 1979a. "On Moral Hazard and Insurance." *Quarterly Journal of Economics* 93:541-62.

Shavell, S. 1979b. "Risk Sharing and Incentives in the Principal and Agent Relationship." *Bell Journal of Economics* 10:55-73.

Smets, H. 1972. "Le Principe de la Compensation Réciproque: Un Instrument Economique pour la Solution de Certains Problèmes de Pollution Transfrontière." Paris: O.C.D.E., Direction de l'Environment.

Spence, M. 1977. "Nonlinear Prices and Welfare." *Journal of Public Economics.*

Stiglitz, J. 1974. "Incentives and Risk Sharing in Sharecropping." *Review of Economic Studies* 61:219-56.

Thomson, W. 1979. "Maximin Strategies and the Elicitation of Preferences." In: *Aggregation and Revelation of Preferences,* edited by J. J. Laffont, pp. 245-68. Amsterdam: North-Holland.

Thomson, W. 1980. "On the Manipulability of Resource Allocation Mechanisms." Unpublished mimeograph.

Tideman, N. 1972. "The Efficient Provision of Public Goods." In: *Public Prices for Public Products,* edited by S. Mushkin, Washington: The Urban Institute.

Truchon, M. 1980. "Implementation of Pareto Optima with the MDP Procedure when Consumers are Non-Myopic." Unpublished mimeograph.

Vickrey, W. 1961. "Counterspeculation, Auctions, and Competitive Sealed Tenders." *Journal of Finance* 16:1-17.

Walker, M. 1977. "An Informationally Efficient Auctioneerless Mechanism for Attaining Lindahl Allocations." Unpublished mimeograph.

Walker, M. 1980. "On the Impossibility of a Dominant Strategy Mechanism to Optimally Decide Public Questions." *Econometrica* 48:1521-40.

Weitzman, M. 1976. "The New Soviet Incentive Model." *Bell Journal of Economics* 7:251-7.

Wilson, R. 1978. "Competitive Exchange." *Econometrica* 46:577-85.

PART II

INFORMATION AND THE
MARKET MECHANISM

CHAPTER 3

The role of private information in markets and other organizations

Roy Radner

Introduction

The notion that competitive markets facilitate the efficient production and allocation of resources in a decentralized manner, that is, without a complete exchange of information among economic agents, is an old one, going back at least to the "socialist controversy" and perhaps to Adam Smith. Phrasing this "conventional wisdom" in this way emphasizes the premise that economic agents come to markets with diverse information that is not publicly available, or at least only at substantial cost. The mention of *information* implies the prior existence of *uncertainty* about something, whether that uncertainty be probabilistic or not. I suppose it was to be expected that a rigorous and systematic examination of the conventional wisdom had to await the elaboration of a systematic and rigorous theory of competitive equilibrium under *certainty*, a process that culminated in the work of Arrow and Debreu.

Although the Arrow–Debreu model was originally put forward for the case of certainty, an ingenious device enabled the theory to be reinterpreted to cover the case of a market in which all relevant future information was to be publicly available, and one could extend to this case, in a natural way, the theorems on the existence and optimality of competitive equilibrium in the case of certainty. Subsequent research, however, has shown that in many cases the presence of *private information*

I have benefitted from the comments of S. J. Grossman, L. Hurwicz, C. V. Kuh, R. W. Rosenthal, and M. Rothschild on earlier drafts of this chapter.

can prevent a competitive equilibrium from being efficient (given the structure of information), and can even prevent the existence of an equilibrium. This chapter summarizes recent results on two topics in this area: (1) rational expectations equilibrium and the information revealed by prices, and (2) principal–agent and other profit-sharing relationships.

The Arrow–Debreu theory of competitive equilibrium under uncertainty extended the analysis of markets under certainty to the case in which there exists a complete set of contracts for delivery of any commodity contingent on the occurrence of any future event (Arrow, 1953; Debreu, 1953, 1959; Baudier, 1954). At its face value, this theory appeared to take account only of information that would become publicly available in the future, because the verification of the performance of a contract would require that all concerned parties (including those responsible for enforcement) be able to verify the occurrence or nonoccurrence of the relevant event. It was later pointed out that the Arrow–Debreu model could be reinterpreted to cover the case of informational differences among agents, provided that the following three conditions (among others) were satisfied:

1 *Exogenous information:* The structure of information is given in advance, and the information is about exogenous events.
2 *No moral hazard:* The performance of a contract for contingent delivery can be verified.
3 *Unsophisticated demand:* No economic agent takes advantage of his knowledge of the equations of equilibrium to make inferences about other agents' information from the realized values of equilibrium prices.

In this extension of the Arrow–Debreu model one can apply the standard theorems on the existence and optimality of competitive equilibrium. In particular, optimality is defined relative to the available sets of strategies, which are constrained by the respective informational limitations of the agents. In such a theory, there is no role for money and liquidity. All contracts may be thought of as negotiated at the beginning of time, and from then on all actions are determined by the equilibrium strategies. These strategies may, of course, take account of the new information as it becomes available. The present value of each firm is known with certainty at the beginning of time, so there is no role for an active market in the shares of firms.

In contrast to this theoretical picture, the economic facts of life are that there are both spot markets and futures markets at every date, but the futures markets are not complete in the Arrow-Debreu sense. There are also contracts for delivery contingent on events that are not purely exogenous. I shall call the first of these phenomena *sequential markets,* and the second, *moral hazard.*

The incompleteness of futures markets and the concomitant sequential nature of markets are often explained by the importance of transaction costs. But even without appealing to transaction costs, one is led to an explicit consideration of sequential markets by a careful critique of the extended Arrow–Debreu model with private information. To the extent that contracts involving moral hazard are excluded, contracts for delivery at some future date, contingent on future events about which there will be only private information, will not appear in an equilibrium of the current market. When the future date arrives, however, and agents observe those private events, their occurrence will affect supply and demand at that date and there will typically be an incentive to reopen markets. In other words, sequential markets are a natural consequence of the existence of private information.

A further implication of the incompleteness of the futures markets is that, at any date, an economic agent (consumer or firm) will typically be unable to realize on the current set of markets the full potential value of his future economic wealth. Each agent will therefore be faced by a *sequence of budget constraints,* rather than a single overall budget constraint as in the Arrow–Debreu model.

What notion of economic rationality is appropriate to a theory of sequential markets? Observe that, given the behavior of economic agents and any particular definition of equilibrium in a sequence of markets, the equilibrium prices in successive markets will be functions, directly or indirectly, of the history of exogenous events (call this history the *state of nature*). In the language of the econometricians, this functional dependence is expressed by the reduced form of the equilibrium equation system. If, as I shall suppose here, the economic agents have probability beliefs (possibly different) about the alternative states of nature, then, given the reduced form, the successive prices will be random variables in the technical (as well as common sense) meaning of the term, namely, functions on a common probability space. I shall say that the agents have *consistent expectations* if they agree on the reduced-form price equations. Note that, because agents may have different probability beliefs about the alternative states of nature, they may have consistent expectations and yet not agree about the joint probability distribution of future prices.

Given an agent's probability beliefs about the states of nature and a particular system of reduced-form price equations, the prices can enter the agent's economic calculations in two ways. First, the prices will enter his successive budget constraints in the usual way. At each date an agent's decision problem will be formally similar to the corresponding decision problem at the beginning of time in the Arrow–Debreu model, but the indirect expected utility of a portfolio of assets at any date will depend on the joint probability distribution of future prices and the state of nature.

Second, because the successive prices are functions of the state of nature, they will reveal information about the state of nature and that information may be useful to an economic agent. In other words, for a given agent at a specified date, the conditional distribution of the state of nature and future prices, *given current and past prices* and the agent's current and past nonprice information, may be different from the corresponding conditional distribution given only the agent's nonprice information. In particular, a current price may reveal to some agents useful information that has been observed by other agents. To the extent that agents use such information, I shall say that they *learn from prices*.

A *rational expectations equilibrium* in a sequence of markets is a set of consistent price expectations (i.e., a system of reduced-form price equations) such that, if agents learn all they can from prices and calculate their excess demands accordingly, then the prices forecast by the reduced form will clear the markets at each date in each state of nature. The consideration of learning from prices introduces some novel and difficult problems in equilibrium theory, many of them still unsolved. In the first part of this chapter, I shall sketch some of these problems and describe the results of some current research on them. In particular, one can show that the existence and efficiency of equilibrium are not to be taken for granted, even under the most standard textbook conditions, and that the understanding of adjustment and stability presents challenges beyond those encountered in the case of certainty.

In a sense, the theory of rational expectations equilibrium carries the spirit of the Arrow–Debreu model about as far as it can go in dealing with private information without explicit consideration of contracts with moral hazard, and without abandoning the hypothesis of thoroughgoing rationality. Early systematic theoretical studies of contracts with moral hazard were particularly concerned with markets for insurance and for medical care. More recently, this subject has received attention in connection with taxation, sharecropping, labor contracts, the law of torts, and the so-called principle-agent model. A conceptually related topic is the study of mechanisms for the decentralized allocation of resources, as in the incentive-compatibility (or incompatibility) of competitive and Lindahl equilibria, in the design of incentives in teams, and more generally in the design of games whose Nash equilibria (or other "solutions") implement some social or group goal.

If a noncontractual relationship involving moral hazard is modeled as a noncooperative game, the Nash equilibria of the game are typically not efficient, that is, not Pareto optimal. In the second part of this chapter I shall sketch how the inefficiencies of such equilibria, which we may think of as *short-run* equilibria, may be remedied if the concerned parties (e.g., traders) enter into long-run relationships in which apparent departures from efficient behavior are punished only when they are serious enough to appear "statistically significant." Technically, this involves an extension of known results in the theory of repeated games (supergames) to the case of games with imperfect information, in which it is shown that efficient outcomes can be realized in the long run (on the average) by means of sequential strategies that form a noncooperative equilibrium of the supergame. Because of this last feature, efficient behavior can be made self-enforcing, that is, without reliance on contracts that are enforceable by outside parties. Thus, apparently cooperative behavior is sustained by an underlying (sequential) noncooperative equilibrium, by means that are generally ignored in the standard theory of competitive markets.

References to the literature and to related topics not treated in this chapter are gathered in bibliographic notes at the end of each section.

1   Rational expectations equilibrium

Instead of beginning my systematic discussion of rational expectations equilibrium with a general definition in a general model, I prefer to introduce the main ideas in the context of a very simple example. Following an extended discussion of this example, I shall briefly sketch the nature of other models and the results that have been obtained for them.

The Grossman model

In this example, there is a single asset traded at each date, and each trader's demand for the asset at any date is a linear function both of the current price and of the trader's forecast of the future "value" of the asset. It will help preserve the simplicity of the example if we suppose that the future value will be its consumption value, as in the case of wine laid down for future consumption, and not its price on some future spot market. (I shall take up the second case later.)

A trader's forecast of the future value of the asset depends, in turn, both on his nonprice information (determined exogenously) and on the current price. The possible dependence of his forecast on the current price is motivated by his realization that, in equilibrium, the market price would (in principle) depend jointly on the nonprice information of all the traders, and hence might reveal to any one trader something about other traders' nonprice information.

By assuming that all of the random variables in question are Gaussian, one can confine one's attention to linear forecast functions. (Linear models of this type have been studied extensively by Sanford Grossman and others, as well as in the macroeconomic literature on rational expectations. I shall therefore call this the Grossman model.)

Consider then I traders in successive markets for a single commodity; the markets will be dated $t = 1, 2, \ldots$, ad infinitum. The eventual value of a unit of commodity bought at date t will be some exogenous random variable r_t. Let f_{it} denote trader i's exogenous information signal at t, and p_t the price of the commodity at t; F_{it} will denote the sigma field generated by the current and past information signals, $\{f_{im} : m \leqslant t\}$, and P_t will denote the sigma field generated by the current and past prices, $\{p_m : m \leqslant t\}$. Define $\tilde{r}_{it}$ to be i's forecast of r_t, given F_{it} and P_t, and assume that i's excess demand at t is the linear function

(1.1) $\delta \tilde{r}_{it} - \delta' p_t$,   where $\delta, \delta' > 0$

Imagine that, in addition to any possibly negative excess demand by the traders who are explicitly described above, there is an exogenous supply, e_t, which is a random variable. The total excess supply at date t is therefore

(1.2) $e_t + \alpha p_t - \delta \sum_i \tilde{r}_{it}$,   where $\alpha \equiv I\delta'$

Assume further that, for all i and t,

(1.3) $f_{it} = r_t + y_{it}$,

that the random variables $e_t, r_t, y_{1t}, \ldots, y_{It}$ are all Gaussian and mutually independent (among themselves and through time), and that the successive $(I + 2)$-tuples $(e_t, r_t, y_{1t}, \ldots, y_{It})$ are identically distributed. (One may interpret f_{it} as a "measure" of r_t based on i's nonprice information, and y_{it} as the measurement error.) To simplify the exposition and without serious loss of generality, I assume that all of the above random variables have mean zero; define

(1.4) $\epsilon = Ee_t^2,$ $\rho = Er_t^2,$ $\eta_i = Ey_{it}^2$

Suppose that agent i's forecast function is

(1.5) $\tilde{r}_{it} = b_i p_t + c_i f_{it},$ $i = 1, \ldots, I$

At each date at which the forecast functions (1.5) are used, the market clearing price will be

(1.6) $\quad p_t = \dfrac{\delta \sum_i c_i f_{it} - e_t}{\alpha - \delta \sum_i b_i}$

Call this a *temporary expectations equilibrium* (TEE). Equation (1.6) brings out the dependence of price on the exogenous random variables and nonprice information. The conditional expectation of r_t given p_t and f_{jt} is

(1.7) $\quad E\{r_t | p_t, f_{jt}\} = b_j' p_t + c_j' f_{jt},$

where

(1.8) $\quad c_j' = \left(\dfrac{1}{\Delta_j}\right) \rho \delta^2 \left(\dfrac{\sum_i c_i^2 \eta_i}{I^2} + \dfrac{\mu}{\delta^2} - \dfrac{\bar{c} c_j \eta_j}{I}\right),$

$\quad b_j' = \left(\dfrac{1}{\Delta_j}\right) (\delta' - \delta \bar{b}) \delta \rho \eta_j \left(\bar{c} - \dfrac{c_j}{I}\right),$

$\quad \Delta_j = \delta^2 \Bigg[\bar{c} \rho \eta_j \left(\bar{c} - \dfrac{2 c_j}{I}\right)$

$\quad\quad\quad + (p + \eta_j) \left(\dfrac{\sum_i c_i^2 \eta_i}{I^2} + \dfrac{\mu}{\delta}\right) - \dfrac{c_j^2 \eta_j^2}{I^2} \Bigg],$

$\quad \bar{b} = \dfrac{1}{I} \sum_i b_i, \quad\quad \bar{c} = \dfrac{1}{I} \sum_i c_i, \quad\quad \mu = \dfrac{\epsilon}{I^2}.$

Note that each c_j' is a ratio of quadratic functions of all the coefficients c_i, and each b_j is a function of both sets of coefficients.

A *rational expectations equilibrium* (REE) is a temporary expectations equilibrium in which the forecast functions (1.5) are correct, that is in which, for each j, $b_j = b_j'$ and $c_j = c_j'$. Thus an REE is characterized by the conditions:

(1.9) $\quad p_t = \dfrac{\delta \sum_i c_i^* f_{it} - e_t}{\alpha - \delta \sum_i b_i^*},$

(1.10) $\quad E\{r_t | F_{it}, P_t\} = b_i^* p_t + c_i^* f_{it}.$

In spite of the apparent simplicity of the model just presented, a complete analysis of the solutions of equations (1.9) and (1.10) does not to my knowledge yet exist. One can show that a solution exists, however, and more is known about some special cases. For example, one can show that if the number of traders is large enough and if the error variances, η_i, are sufficiently similar, then the solution is unique. Another well-understood case, which I shall discuss below, is one in which there are two groups of traders, *informed* and *uninformed*. The informed traders have identical nonprice information (not necessarily complete), and the uninformed traders have *no* nonprice information (the variance of error is infinite). Again, in this case equilibrium exists and is unique.

I might also point out that, in the limiting case of the model in which the variance of the exogenous supply is zero, there exists no REE as defined above.

The Futia model

In many, if not most, important speculative markets, the eventual value of an asset is its price on some future market or markets. C. Futia has given an analysis of REE in such a sequence of markets, in the context of a linear-Gaussian model similar to the one just discussed. Consideration of Futia's model will also provide a convenient framework for the introduction of some additional concepts that have been useful in the study of REEs. I shall give here a very brief account of the model and some of Futia's results.

Consider a doubly infinite sequence of dates, t, with a market for a single commodity at each date, and let p_t denote the price of the commodity at date t. Each trader has a (random) nonnegative endowment of the commodity at each date; let e_t denote the total endowment at t. Each trader i also observes at each date some information signal, f_{it}, a random vector.

I shall assume that the sequences (e_t) and (f_{it}) are stationary and Gaussian. For each trader i, let F_{it} denote the sigma field generated by the random vector $\{f_{im} : m \leqslant t\}$, and let F_t denote the sigma field obtained by pooling the sigma fields F_{it}, $i = 1, \ldots, I$. Since it is natural to suppose that each trader can observe his own endowment, it is equally natural to assume that, for every t, e_t is measurable with respect to F_t. Finally, let P_t denote the sigma field generated by the current and past prices, namely $\{p_m : m \leqslant t\}$.

I shall consider prices that form a stationary sequence of Gaussian random variables. Trader i's conditional expectation of p_{t+1} given his information at date t (including his past and current information signals, and the past and current prices) is

(1.11) $\bar{p}_{it} = E\{p_{t+1} | F_{it}, P_t\}.$

Assume that the total excess supply at date t is linear:

(1.12) $\alpha p_t - \sum_i \tilde{p}_{it} + e_t,$

where α is a parameter that is strictly greater than I. A (stationary) rational expectations equilibrium is a stationary price sequence such that excess supply at every date is (almost surely) zero.

A useful auxilliary equilibrium concept is that of a *full communication equilibrium* (FCE) in which, at every date, each trader has the pooled information F_t. One can show that in this model there exists a unique FCE, say $\hat{p} = (\hat{p}_t)$. Call the FCE *informative* if, for every i and t,

(1.13) $E\{\hat{p}_{t+1} | F_{it}, P_t\} = E\{\hat{p}_{t+1} | F_t\}.$

If $p^* = (p_t^*)$ is a rational expectations equilibrium, call p^* *symmetric* if, for every i, j, and t, traders i and j would (almost surely) make the same conditional forecast of p_{t+1}^*; in other words, $\tilde{p}_{it}^* = \tilde{p}_{jt}^*$.

Theorem 1.1. There exists a *symmetric* rational expectations equilibrium if and only if the corresponding full communication equilibrium is informative; in this case the two equilibria are equal.

Since the condition (1.13) is well defined for any price sequence, it also makes sense to ask whether an REE is informative. By definition, however, an informative REE is symmetric; hence, by Theorem 1.1, an REE is informative if and only if it is the FCE. I should emphasize that in an informative equilibrium the market price alone need not reveal all traders' nonprice information, or even be a sufficient statistic for that information. Nevertheless, an informative equilibrium enables each trader to make as good a conditional prediction of the next period's price as if he had the pooled information of all traders.

Theorem 1.1 does not exclude the possibility of the existence of non-symmetric REEs even when symmetric ones do not exist. The next theorem shows that, even in the special case of a linear model with Gaussian random variables, the situation in which the environment-information space is infinite is quite different from the one in which it is finite. In particular, it is not the case that the existence of REEs is generic.

Before stating the next theorem, I shall describe more precisely the underlying probability space and the family of stochastic processes that will be considered. Let ϵ_{tj} be a family of independent Gaussian (normal) random variables, each with zero mean and unit variance, where $j = 1, \ldots, J$, and $-\infty < t < \infty$, and let ϵ_t denote the J-dimensional vector with coordinates ϵ_{tj}. Let H be the family of all random variables of the form

(1.14) $\sum_t \alpha_t \cdot \epsilon_t,$

where (α_t) is a doubly infinite sequence of J-dimensional vectors whose lengths are square summable. Note that such a random variable is Gaussian, with zero mean and variance equal to

$$\sum_t \alpha_t \cdot \alpha_t$$

For a random variable h in H given by (1.14), define the shift of h, denoted by Th, by

(1.15) $Th = \sum_t \alpha_t \cdot \epsilon_{t-1}.$

A sequence (h_t) of random variables in H will be called *stationary* if there is a random variable h in H such that $h_t = T^t h$, for all t. A sequence of random vectors with coordinates in H will be called stationary if it is stationary coordinate by coordinate. We may take the underlying probability space to be the space S of sequences (ϵ_t). It is to be understood that all random variables considered in this model are in H.

The space H of random variables can be identified with the space of square-summable sequences (α_t), and hence is a Hilbert space. Furthermore, every stationary sequence of random variables in H is generated by shifting a single random variable in H. Finally, it can be shown that every closed subspace of H can be identified with the sigma field generated by some collection of random variables in H. These considerations lead to a natural topology on the set of models just described. With this topology we have Theorem 1.2.

Theorem 1.2. The set of models with no REE and the set of models with only asymmetric REEs each have a nonempty interior, provided $J>1$.

Finally, I should point out that the same methods of analysis can be applied to the case in which price information is used only with a lag.

Adjustment toward rational expectations equilibrium

The definition of rational expectations equilibrium presented in the previous section postulates behavior that makes heavy demands on the rationality of the economic agents, insofar as it requires them not only to make the usual expected utility calculations in the standard model of a market with uncertainty, but also to have a correct model of the joint distribution of equilibrium prices, their own initial information, and the eventual values of the assets in which they are trading – their "market models." In a theory of adjustment toward a rational expectations equilibrium, what are the appropriate assumptions about the agent's rationality during the "learning" process? As agents revise their market models, the true market model changes in a way that, in principle, depends on the revision rules of all of the agents. Thus, a theory of thoroughgoing rationality would seem to point to a treatment of the learning and adjustment process as a sequential game with incomplete and imperfect information.

In my opinion, such an approach would be unrealistic and contrary to the spirit of a process of adjustment and learning. A more realistic alternative would envisage some form of bounded rationality during the adjustment process, which, if stable, would converge to a fully rational equilibrium. I shall sketch here two closely related processes of this type, in the context of the linear model of Equations (1.1)–(1.8).

First, if we define the adjustment process by the difference equation

$$(1.16) \quad c_j(n + 1) = c_j'(n), \qquad b_j(n + 1) = b_j'(n),$$
$$j = 1, \ldots, I,$$
$$n = 1, 2, \ldots, \text{ ad infinitum.}$$

(cf. Equation (1.8)), then any limit of this sequence is an REE. One can show that the system (1.16) may be locally stable or unstable, depending on the parameters. Roughly speaking, the system may be unstable if, in the REE, the coefficients b_i^* of current price are "too large" compared to the coefficients c_i^* of current nonprice information. This can occur, for example, if the variance ϵ of the exogenous supply is sufficiently small.

The difference Equation (1.16) approximately represents a situation in which agents revise their forecast coefficients infrequently, but only on the basis of experience since the last revision. The following difference equation represents a situation in which, at each revision, agents average over all of their previous experience:

$$(1.17) \quad c_j(n + 1) = \left(\frac{1}{n + 1}\right)[c_j'(n) + c_j(n) + \cdots + c_j(1)],$$

and similarly for $b_j(n+1)$. One can show that, at least for certain special cases, Equation (1.17) is stable when (1.16) is not.

A more satisfactory theory of adjustment would take account of the fact that agents must revise their forecast functions after only a finite number of periods, so that their successive coefficients constitute a stochastic process rather than a deterministic one as in Equations (1.16) or (1.17). For example, consider the process in which, after each date, each agent i uses ordinary least squares to estimate new forecast (regression) coefficients from all of the previous observations (f_{it}, p_t, r_t). For the purposes of this section, I shall call this the ordinary least squares process (OLS).

Unfortunately, the OLS process leads to highly nonlinear stochastic difference equations, whose asymptotic behavior has not yet been analyzed at even the low level of generality of the present model. However M. Bray (1980) has succeeded in demonstrating the stability of the OLS process in a simpler example. Suppose that there are two sets of traders, the "informed" denoted by N, and the "uninformed" denoted by U. All informed traders have the same nonprice information,

(1.18) $f_{it} = r_t + y_t \equiv f_t,$ i in N,

whereas the uninformed traders have no nonprice information,

(1.19) $f_{it} = $ constant, i in U.

Assume that the random variables r_t, y_t, and e_t are independent and Gaussian, and that the successive triples (r_t, y_t, e_t) are identically distributed, with mean zero and respective variances ρ, η, and ϵ. Assume, finally, that the structure of information is common knowledge.

An implication of the last assumption is that the informed traders can infer that, in a TEE, the price p_t can depend only on the current and past nonprice signals f_t (which are known to all informed traders), and hence provides no information about r_t not already revealed by f_t. So an informed trader can do no better than to use the forecast function

(1.20) $\bar{r}_{it} = E\{r_t | f_t\} = \left(\dfrac{\rho}{\rho + \eta} \right) f_t,$ i in N.

The uninformed traders' forecast functions must at most depend on prices, and in an REE will depend on current price. Thus, suppose that the uninformed traders' forecast functions are

(1.21) $\bar{r}_{it} = b_{it} p_t,$ i in U.

It is straightforward to verify that the equation for a TEE corresponding to Equation (1.6) is

(1.22) $p_t = \dfrac{\delta N(\rho/\rho_U + \eta) f_t - e_t}{\alpha - \delta \sum_{i \in U} b_{it}},$

where $N = \#N$ is the number of informed traders. Given the TEE (1.22), the true regression of r_t on p_t is

(1.23) $E(r_t | p_t) = b_t' p_t,$

where

$$(1.24) \quad b_t' = k\left[\frac{\delta'}{(1-\nu)\delta} - \bar{b}_t\right],$$

$$\bar{b}_t = \frac{\sum_{i\in U} b_{it}}{I - N},$$

$$\nu = \frac{N}{I},$$

$$k = \frac{\nu(1-\nu)\delta^2\rho^2}{\nu^2\delta^2\rho^2 + \mu(\rho+\eta)}.$$

(These equations correspond to Equations (1.7) and (1.8).) Note that ν is the fraction of informed traders.

From Equation (1.24) we see that in an REE the coefficients b_{it} will be the same for all uninformed traders, say b^*, where b^* is the (unique) solution of

$$b^* = k\frac{\delta'}{(1-\nu)\delta} - b^*,$$

or

$$(1.25) \quad b^* = \frac{k\delta'}{(1+k)(1-\nu)\delta}.$$

In this example, the OLS adjustment process is defined as follows. The initial coefficients (b_{il}) for the uninformed traders are given a priori. At each date $t \geq 1$ the price is determined by the TEE Equation (1.22), and at each date $t+1$ the coefficient $b_{i,t+1}$ is the ordinary least squares estimate of b in the equation $r = bp$, fitted to the data points $(p_1, r_1), \ldots, (p_t, r_t)$, that is,

$$(1.26) \quad b_{i,t+1} = \frac{\sum_{n=1}^{t} r_n p_n}{\sum_{n=1}^{t} p_n^2}, \quad t > 1.$$

Note that for $t > 1$, all uninformed traders will have the same coefficients b_{it}.

Theorem 1.3. For the OLS adjustment process defined by (1.22) and (1.26),

$$\lim_{t\to\infty} b_{it} = b^*, \quad \text{almost surely.}$$

(For a proof of Theorem 1.3, see [Bray, 1980].) Bray also considers the case in which f_t and e_t are negatively correlated. In this case the parameter corresponding to k in (1.24) may be negative. An REE exists only if $k \neq -1$, and the convergence of the OLS process has been proved only for $k > -1$. It is conjectured, but not yet proved, that the OLS process is unstable for $k < -1$.

It is of interest to compare the asymptotic properties of the OLS process in the present example ($k > 0$) with those of the deterministic process corresponding to (1.16). Here it is easy to see from (1.24) that the latter is stable if and only if $k < 1$. On the other hand, the deterministic process corresponding to Equation (1.17) is stable for all $k > 0$. In some sense, the OLS process is a stochastic analogue of this second deterministic process.

The assumption that the structure of information is common knowledge plays an important role in achieving the simplicity of the Bray model. Without this knowledge the informed traders would not be justified in forecasting r_t from f_t alone, that is, in ignoring current price, at least when the market is not in an REE. The effect of abandoning this assumption would be to make the OLS process multidimensional rather than one-dimensional.

Because of the extreme simplicity of the model, it would be imprudent to conclude from Bray's result that the OLS process is stable in more general contexts. Nevertheless, her proof provides for the first time a method that shows promise of being applicable to the study of the OLS process in more complicated linear models.

Bibliographic notes to section 1

Section 1 is largely based on Radner (1982), where the reader will find a fuller account of the subject and its history. The term "rational expectations equilibrium" has been used here to describe a market equilibrium in which traders use equilibrium market prices to make inferences about the environment. The same term is often used to describe equilibria in a sequence of markets under uncertainty in which the traders correctly anticipate the stochastic process of equilibrium prices. (This latter phenomenon, as well as learning from prices, is represented in the Futia model.) The term REE has also been used in connection with other concepts of equilibrium that involve some notion of expectations.

A formal analysis of a model in which traders learn from prices was introduced in Radner (1967), and independently in Lucas (1972) and Green (1973). The idea was further elaborated by Grossman in his Ph.D. dissertation (1975) and in subsequent papers (Grossman, 1979). The first two models discussed in this section are suggested by the papers of Grossman. The results on existence for the Grossman model alluded to here have been obtained by Hellwig (1980) and by this author (unpublished).

Existence of REE in nonlinear versions of the Grossman model is not assured even with strong regularity conditions. A REE is called *revealing* if the mapping from the traders' pooled information to equilibrium prices is one-to-one. Radner (1979) showed that, under certain smoothness and other regularity conditions, existence of a revealing REE is generic if the set, S, of states of the environment and traders' pooled information is finite. Allen (1982) generalized this by giving conditions for generic existence of a revealing REE if the dimension of S is less than the dimension of the price space. Grossman and others have studied cases in which the REE price is a sufficient statistic for the payoff-relevant state of the environment (see Grossman, 1979). A further extension of this idea is represented by Futia's concept of an informative REE. The discussion of the aforementioned Futia model is based on Futia (1981). The problem of determining general conditions for the existence or nonexistence of nonrevealing REEs remains to be fully explored.

Grossman and Stiglitz (1980) have studied examples of markets in which traders may change their nonprice information by expending resources.

The above material on adjustment to an REE is based on Bray (1980) and on unpublished material by this author. For other references to the subject, see Bray (1980) and Blume, Bray, and Easley (1982).

The literature on REE usually uses a definition that is different in a subtle but important way from the one used in this section. Thus, in the Grossman model described, in the limiting case in which the variance of the exogenous supply is zero there exists no REE as defined here, but there does exist one in the more usual sense. These conceptual problems have been discussed by Beja (1976), Hellwig (1980), and Radner (1982).

Limitations on space do not permit description of the important series of papers by Jordan on endogenous expectations, REE, and the "efficient markets hypothesis." For references to these and other papers on REE, see Radner (1982), and Jordan and Radner (1982).

2   Decentralization and moral hazard

A *decentralized* organization will be defined here as one with more than one decision maker, in which different decision makers are responsible for different decision variables and make those decisions on the basis of different information, and in which the outcome to the organization depends jointly on the several decisions and on some stochastic environmental variables. For a given system of rewards to the decision makers – whom I shall call the *members* of the organization – one can regard the situation as a several-person game, and one might expect the resulting combination of decision rules to form a noncooperative Nash equilibrium of that game.

The class of relationships I have in mind – under the rubric *organizations* – includes both market and nonmarket relationships, for example, a firm, managers in a firm, managers and workers, suppliers and customers (clients), a bureaucracy, and so forth.

If the organization is short-lived or if the members are short-sighted, Nash equilibria of the corresponding game will typically be inefficient in the sense that some other combination of decision rules would give each member a higher level of expected utility. This will typically be the case even if the designer of the organization has some freedom to choose the system of rewards. On the other hand, if the organization is *long-lived* and if *the members can monitor the information signals and decisions of the other members ex post,* then the members may have an opportunity to use *self-enforcing* rules of behavior that sustain efficient decision rules. Formally, this means that there may be Nash equilibria of the "long-run game" that result in efficient decision-making. In particular, in the theory of repeated games, the situation in which the decision situation is repeated infinitely often, with perfect monitoring of all random variables and decisions after each repetition, has been studied in some detail. Thus, in the situation of perfect ex post monitoring one might say that the theory of repeated games has explained rigorously how long-term relationships can sustain self-enforcing, efficient behavior.

Unfortunately, the *same circumstances that lead to the decentralization of information and decision-making usually make perfect ex post monitoring of information and decisions impractical.* Is the theory of repeated games then powerless to demonstrate the efficiency of long-term relationships in just those circumstances in which decentralization is most likely to occur? In fact, in this Section I shall sketch how some well-known powerful tools of probability theory can be applied to extend the theory of repeated games to the case of imperfect monitoring. I should add that in this case, as well as in the case of perfect monitoring, the assumption that the members do not discount the future (or do not discount it too heavily) plays an important role. In other words, not only must the organization be "long-lived," but the members must not be "short-sighted."

The next subsection will present a special model of a decentralized organization in which, in each period, each member's action is measured by a single number, interpreted as "effort," and the outcome of the members' decisions is also measured by a single number, interpreted as "output." I call this a *decentralized enterprise.* In order to focus on the problems caused by lack of ex post monitoring, I make the extreme assumption that after each period the output is to be shared among the members as a function only of the magnitude of the output. Thus, each member receives a reward that is a function of the output that period, and the sum of the rewards must not exceed the output. Each member prefers more reward to less, and less effort to more.

It can be shown that, in general, for no combination of reward functions is the corresponding short-term Nash equilibrium of decision functions efficient; I shall not give the details here. What I will do here, however, is sketch how long-term relationships, that is, Nash equilibria of the infinitely repeated game, can sustain efficient decision-making.

Closely related to the above model is the principal-agent model, in which one of the members (the principal) takes no decision that directly affects the output of the enterprise, but does control the reward functions for himself and the other members (the agents). In fact, the principal-agent models that have been studied thus far assume that either there is only one agent or each agent has an individual output that can be monitored. One can obtain for the principal-agent model results that are analogous to those for the decentralized enterprise (see Radner, 1981a).

A model of a decentralized enterprise

As I said, in order to have a reasonably precise discussion of efficiency and inefficiency in decentralized organizations, it is useful to conduct the discussion in the context of one or more well-defined models of organization. I shall discuss here an organization that I called above a decentralized enterprise. This organization has the underlying information- and decision-theoretic structure of a *team* (see Marschak and Radner [1972]), but with members who have *conflicting interests.*

Each member, i, of the enterprise has an *action variable, A_i,* under his control. The *output, C,* of the enterprise depends both on the joint action, $A = (A_1, \ldots, A_I)$ of the members and on some random variable, X, the (payoff-relevant) state of *environment.* Thus

(2.1) $\quad C = G(A, X)$

To fix the ideas, think of the output of the enterprise as measured in dollars. This output is available to be shared among the members of the enterprise.

Before deciding on his action, each member has available to him (through direct observation and/or communication) some *information signal, Y_i*. I shall say that the organization is (informationally) *decentralized* if not all the members have the same information. A member's action is determined as a function of his information signal, according to his *decision function, D_i*:

(2.2) $A_i = D_i(Y_i)$

The output of the enterprise is to be shared among the members as a function of the output alone. This models the extreme situation in which the information signal and action of one member are not – or need not be – observable by all of the other members. Thus, to every member there will correspond a reward function, R_i, that determines his reward, W_i, as a function of the enterprise output:

(2.3) $W_i = R_i(C)$

The joint reward function, $R = (R_1, \ldots, R_I)$, must have the feasibility property that, for every output, the sum of the rewards to the members does not exceed the output:

(2.4) $R_1(C) + \cdots + R_I(C) \leqslant C$

The joint probability distribution of the environment and the information signals is given and known to the members. In particular, at this point in the discussion I shall assume that the choice of information signals for the enterprise has already been made. On the other hand, still to be determined is the pair consisting of a joint decision function and a joint reward function; I shall call such a pair, (R, D), an *arrangement*. Every arrangement induces a corresponding probability distribution of actions $(A_1, \ldots, A_I)$ and rewards $(W_1, \ldots, W_I)$, which are the variables of interest to the members.

I shall suppose here that member i's utility is a function of his own reward and action, and that this function is additively separable in these two variables so that his net utility is the difference between a utility of reward, $P_i(W_i)$, and a disutility of action, $Q_i(A_i)$:

(2.5) $U_i = P_i(W_i) - Q_i(A_i)$.

Furthermore, each member judges an arrangement according to the corresponding *expected utility* that it produces for him.

In what follows, I shall assume that a member's action is a real variable, that his utility of reward is strictly increasing in reward, and that his disutility of action is strictly increasing in action. Thus, the member's action may be interpreted as an amount of effort. I shall also assume that the output function is strictly increasing in each member's action, for every state of the environment. Finally, unless otherwise noted, I shall suppose that there are at least two members.

Short- and long-term arrangements

The situation that I have just described can be envisaged as being repeated a number of times. In this case, one would have to specify the probability law of the environment and information signals over time. For example, successive realizations of this vector of random variables might be statistically independent and identically distributed, which is the case that I shall consider here. (This assumption does not, of course, preclude the statistical dependence of the environment and the information signals at any one time period.)

I shall call a particular arrangement in any one period a *short-term arrangement*. Short-term arrangements can be made to vary from one time period to the next as a function of the information available to the several members of the enterprise. At the beginning of a given period, for any one member, this information will consist of the past values of his own information signals, his own actions, and the enterprise outputs. A rule that determines how the short-term arrangements change over time as a function of this information will be called a *long-term arrangement*.

I now want to distinguish *efficient* from *equilibrium* short-term arrangements. I shall take as the definition of efficiency the concept of Pareto-optimality. Thus an arrangement is *efficient* if no other arrangement yields every member at least as great an expected (one-period) utility and yields at least one member strictly greater expected utility.

A short-term arrangement will be called an equilibrium if, given the joint reward function, the joint decision function constitutes a (noncooperative) Nash equilibrium of the game in which: (1) The players are the members; (2) Each member's set of pure strategies is his set of decision functions; and (3) Each member's payoff is his expected utility, that is, his expected utility of reward less his expected disutility of effort. Recall that in this context a joint decision function is a Nash equilibrium if no member can increase his expected utility by unilaterally changing his own decision function.

The concept of Nash equilibrium provides a natural theory of the behavior of the members if they are motivated solely by "self-interest" and *if there is no mechanism available whereby the members can commit themselves in advance to use a particular joint decision function.* In other words, a Nash equilibrium is "self-enforcing." The case for a Nash equilibrium is even stronger if it is unique, for then every member can predict what the equilibrium is, without any prior communication. I shall not discuss here the difficult questions of determining conditions for the existence and uniqueness of (short-term) equilibria. Indeed, in what follows it is to be understood (unless otherwise noted) that there exist equilibria in pure strategies.

One can show that, *typically,* an equilibrium short-term arrangement *cannot* be efficient (although there are special cases in which it can).

Roughly speaking, what prevents an equilibrium from being efficient is the fact that each member's effort produces a "positive externality" by increasing the output available to be shared by others, provided that the joint reward function gives other members some positive share of that increase. In computing his best response to the other members' decision functions, however, any one member does not take account of that externality in his own expected utility. (This is the familiar "free rider" problem.) I have no space here to give an adequate treatment of this matter, which in any case only provides the motive for asking whether long-term arrangements can be used to remedy any inefficiency that exists.

Long-term arrangements

Suppose now that the short-term game is repeated a number of times (finite or infinite). The resulting sequential game will be called the *supergame,* and the original game will be called the *one-period game.* In the supergame, each player is allowed to make his decision in each period depend on the history of what he has observed up to the time of decision. This information history consists of his past and current information signals, the past total outputs (but not the current one), and, of course, his past decisions. His entire sequence of decision rules is called his *sequential strategy.* The space of sequential strategies for any one member is thus immensely larger than his space of decision functions in the one-period game, if the length of the supergame (the number of repetitions) is at all large.

For the present discussion, I shall focus on the case in which the length of the supergame is infinite, and the utility to each player is the long-run average of his one-period expected utilities.

I shall define an *equilibrium long-term arrangement* to be a Nash equilibrium of the supergame in which either the reward function is fixed or it is controlled in a well-defined way by the actions of the players. I shall say that an equilibrium long-term arrangement *sustains* a particular short-term arrangement, say S, if, when the strategies in the long-term arrangement are carried out, the long-run average expected utility to the players equals their respective one-period expected utilities under *S*.

Recall that equilibrium short-term arrangements are typically not efficient. Recall, too, that I am assuming that – even ex post – members never learn directly the actual information signals or decisions of the other members (although the members' information signals may be correlated). How, then, in the absence of direct monitoring, could the members sustain an efficient short-term arrangement by a long-term arrangement?

A clue to an answer lies in that, if the members of the enterprise use the same joint decision function every period, and if the underlying stochastic process of information signals and the payoff-relevant state of the environment is stationary, then the stochastic process of outputs will also be stationary. Hence, if this stochastic process is actually sensitive to changes in each member's decision functions, then the members might hope to detect, by appropriate statistical methods, continued departures from the desired joint decision function. Of course, statistical methods are not certain, so there would be some chance that, on the one hand, defections would go undetected and, on the other hand, the members would be misled into reacting to apparent defections that in fact did not occur. Furthermore, the detection of "cheating" by statistical methods takes time. For any given level or mode of cheating, the smaller one tries to make the probabilities of the two types of error, the longer is the time required to reduce the probabilities of the two errors to any desired levels. Indeed, the dilemma that the members face is more subtle and more difficult than the usual one in hypothesis testing, because each member has available a large set of sequential strategies for cheating, and his incentive to cheat depends not only on the probability of eventual detection, but also on whether he can increase his long-run average expected utility.

Thus, it is not a priori obvious that the members of the decentralized enterprise can sustain an efficient short-term equilibrium combination of sequential strategies even when the stochastic process of exogenous random variables is stationary. Nevertheless, one can show that under suitable conditions it is possible to sustain some efficient short-term arrangements by equilibrium long-term arrangements. Roughly speaking, for every efficient short-term arrangement *that is more efficient than some equilibrium short-term arrangement,* there are Nash equilibria of the supergame that give each player a long-run average expected utility that is equal to his one-period expected utility under the short-term arrangements.

In what follows I shall sketch the nature of some long-term arrangements that can sustain efficiency. (Such arrangements are not unique.) The technical details are somewhat formidable, although the methods are familiar in modern probability theory, and I shall leave the exposition of those details to another occasion. Also, I shall not attempt to describe the various assumptions used in the argument, which are primarily in the nature of regularity conditions. I shall limit this discussion to the case in which the successive realizations of the exogenous random variables are statistically independent and identically distributed. I should emphasize that this does not preclude the mutual dependence of the information signals and the payoff-relevant state of the environment at any one period.

Suppose, then, that the members of the enterprise wish to attain, in long-run average expected utility, the expected one-period utility that is yielded by some efficient short-term arrangement, say $\hat{S} = (\hat{R}, \hat{D})$, which is more efficient than a short-term equilibrium arrangement, S^*. It is to be understood that the (joint) reward function $\hat{R}$ corresponding to the short-term arrangement $\hat{S}$ either is the same as in S^* or it cannot be implemented without the unanimous agreement of the members.

If the members implement the arrangement $\hat{S}$ for the first t periods, then the corresponding outputs will be independent and identically distributed, with common expected value, say $\hat{c}$. Let $\bar{C}_t$ denote the *average* realized output over the first t periods; in the same circumstances, the expected value of $\bar{C}_t$ would also be $\hat{c}$, and its variance would be proportional to $1/t$. Indeed, if the arrangement $\hat{S}$ were implemented in all periods, then $\bar{C}_t$ would converge to $\hat{c}$ almost surely, by the strong law of large numbers.

On the other hand, if one or more members do not use the decision functions that correspond to $\hat{S}$, and the distribution of output is sufficiently sensitive to their decisions, then the expected value of $\bar{C}_t$ will be something other than $\hat{c}$. In particular, if some members "cheat" by providing less effort than the arrangement $\hat{S}$ calls for, then the expected value of $\bar{C}_t$ will be less than $\hat{c}$.

These considerations suggest a family of "trigger strategies." Let (b_t) be some sequence of positive numbers, and let N be the first period, if any, at which average realized output, $\bar{C}_t$, reaches or falls below $(\hat{c} - b_t)$; if this last event never happens, then we shall assign N the value infinity. Note that N is a random variable, whose realized value is either a positive integer or infinity. Call the sequence (b_t) the *stopping boundary,* and N the *stopping time.* Given the stopping boundary (b_t), the corresponding combination of trigger strategies is defined as follows: Each member implements the arrangement $\hat{S}$ through period N; thereafter each member implements S^*, that is, enforces the corresponding reward function and uses the corresponding decision function. Call this sequential strategy combination $L(b_t)$.

Following R. Aumann, one may call strategies of the type $L(b_t)$ *grim*, because the short-run equilibrium arrangement is used forever after period N. It turns out that with grim strategies one can only *approximately* sustain efficiency by a long-term arrangement, in the following sense. For any positive number epsilon, an *epsilon-equilibrium* of a game is a combination of strategies such that no one player can increase his expected utility by more than epsilon by unilaterally changing his strategy. One can show that, for any (strictly) positive epsilon, there is a strategy combination $L(b_t)$ such that: (1) $L(b_t)$ is an epsilon-equilibrium of the supergame; and (2) $L(b_t)$ yields each member a long-run average expected utility within epsilon of his expected one-period utility under the short-term arrangement $\hat{S}$.

In order to exactly sustain efficiency with an exact equilibrium of the supergame, one can use strategies that are "rehabilitating." However, because the grim strategies are simpler, I shall discuss them first.

Roughly speaking, in order for the first condition above (epsilon-equilibrium) to be satisfied, it must not be possible for any member to accumulate too much extra expected utility by cheating before the other members switch to the arrangement S^*. One can show that for this condition to be satisfied, it is sufficient to choose the stopping boundary so that the sequence (b_t) converges to zero. (The proof uses the martingale systems theorem.) I should emphasize that this condition on the stopping boundary is sufficient to make *any* sequential cheating strategy "unprofitable" in the long run; in particular, the members are not constrained to cheating by constant amounts.

One can show that in order for the second condition to be satisfied the probability of the stopping time being finite must be small. Roughly speaking, this is so because, if the members follow the strategy combination $L(b_t)$, the arrangement $\hat{S}$ will last through the stopping time, and then will be followed by the arrangement S^* (forever). Therefore, the second condition is in potential conflict with the first, because if the stopping boundary converges to zero too quickly, the stopping time will have too large a probability of being finite. For example, if b_t is proportional to $1/t$, then the stopping time will be finite with probability one. One can show that it is possible to satisfy both conditions however. For example, one can take

$$(2.6) \quad b_t = k \left(\frac{\log \log t}{t} \right)^{1/2},$$

where k is a sufficiently large positive number. In other words, the first condition is satisfied for *any* positive *k*, and the larger *k* is, the closer is each member's long-run average expected utility to his expected one-period utility under the short-term arrangement $\hat{S}$. (The constant *k* must be at least greater than $\sqrt{2}$ times the standard deviation of one-period output.)

I want to make two observations about this particular solution to our problem. First, there are other stopping boundaries that work. Any sequence that converges to zero no faster than Equation (2.6) can be used to construct a stopping boundary. Nevertheless, the choice of the stopping boundary is somewhat delicate.

Second, in order to calculate an appropriate long-term arrangement, it is necessary to know the probability distribution of output under the target desired arrangement $\hat{S}$, or at least the mean and variance of that distribution.

One can achieve an exact Nash equilibrium of the supergame and attain a long-run average expected utility for each member that exactly equals his expected utility under the efficient short-term arrangement $\hat{S}$ by resorting to "rehabilitating" strategies of the following type. Let (ϵ_n) be a sequence of strictly positive numbers converging monotonically to zero. The history of the enterprise will be characterized by a finite or infinite sequence of "epochs," each epoch in turn being divided into an initial "cooperative" phase and a subsequent "noncooperative" phase. The first cooperative phase starts at period 1. For $n = 1, 2, \ldots,$ the *n*th cooperative phase ends when the average performance for the first *t* periods of that phase reaches or falls below $(\hat{c} - b_t)$. The length of the *n*th noncooperative phase is calculated to be long enough so that at the end of the *n*th epoch each member's average expected utility over the *entire history up to that point* does not exceed his one-period short-term equilibrium expected utility plus ϵ_n.

In summary, the last result shows how to sustain by an equilibrium long-term arrangement any efficient short-term arrangement that (weakly) dominates a short-term equilibrium arrangement. Using this result, one can show that any short-term arrangement that dominates a convex combination of equilibrium short-term arrangements can also be sustained by a long-term equilibrium arrangement. The typical multiplicity of equilibrium long-term arrangements leaves open the problem of predicting which one will actually obtain.

Bibliographic notes to section 2

The material in this section is based on Radner (1982b), where a precise theorem on efficient equilibrium long-term arrangements is proved.

That paper also contains information about the set of equilibria in the supergame, but not a complete characterization. The result is also extended to the case in which after each one-period game each player can only observe his own realized utility (rather than a commonly observed consequence, as in the case treated here). Analogous results for epsilon-equilibria of repeated games for the principal-agent relationship were presented in Radner (1981a). Rubinstein (1979a) and Rubinstein and Yaari (1980) have analyzed repeated principal-agent-type relationships in the same spirit.

For material on infinite supergames with perfect monitoring, see Rubinstein (1979b) and the references cited therein. Applications to the theory of altruism have been given by Kurz (1978), and to the theory of oligopoly by Radner (1980).

For other aspects of the design of incentives in economic organizations, see Hurwicz (1972, 1979). The particular problem addressed in this paper was inspired in part by Groves (1973).

REFERENCES

Allen, B. 1982. Strict rational expectations equilibria with diffuseness. Dept. of Economics, Univ. of Pennsylvania (to appear in *J. of Econ. Theory*).
Arrow, K. J. 1953. Le rôle de valeurs boursières pour la répartition la meilleure des risques. *Econométrie:* 41–48. Paris: C.N.R.S.
Baudier, E. 1954. L'introduction du temps dans la théorie de l'équilibre général. *Les Cahiers Economiques:* 9–16.
Beja, A. 1976. The limited information efficiency of market processes. Working Paper no. 43, Research Program in Finance, Univ. of Calif. Berkeley.
Blume, L. E., Bray, M. M., and Easley, D. 1982. Introduction to the stability of rational expectations equilibrium (to appear in *J. of Econ. Theory*).
Bray, M. 1980. Learning, estimation, and the stability of rational expectations, Graduate School of Business, Stanford Univ. (to appear in *J. of Econ. Theory*).
Debreu, G. 1953. Une économie de l'incertain. Paris: Elecricité de France, mimeo.
Debreu, G. 1959. *Theory of Value*. New York: Wiley. Reprinted, New Haven: Yale University Press, 1971.
Futia, C. 1981. Rational expectations in stationary linear models. *Econometrica* 49: 171–192.
Green, J. R. 1973. Information, efficiency, and equilibrium. Discussion Paper 284. Harvard Institute of Economic Research, Harvard Univ.
Grossman, S. J. 1975. The existence of futures markets, noisy rational expectations, and informational externalities, Ph.D. dissertation, Dept. of Economics, Univ. of Chicago.
Grossman, S. J. 1981. An introduction to the theory of rational expectations under asymmetric information. *Rev. of Econ. Studies* 48: 541–559.
Grossman, S. J. and Stiglitz, J. E. 1980. On the impossibility of informationally efficient markets. *Amer. Econ. Rev.* 70: 393–408.

Groves, T. 1973. Incentives in teams. *Econometrica* 41: 617–631.

Hellwig, M. F. 1980. On the aggregation of information in capital markets. *J. of Econ. Theory* 22: 477–498.

Hurwicz, L. 1972. On informationally decentralized systems. Ch. 14 of C. B. McGuire and R. Radner, eds., *Decision and organization.* Amsterdam: North-Holland.

Hurwicz, L. 1979. On the interaction between information and incentives in organizations. In K. Krittendorff, ed., *Communication and control in society.* New York: Gordon and Breach, pp. 123–147.

Jordan, J. S. and Radner, R. 1982. Rational expectations in microeconomics models: an overview (to appear in *J. of Econ. Theory*).

Kurz, M. 1978. Altruism as an outcome of social interaction. *Amer. Econ. Rev.* 68: 216–222.

Lucas, R. E. 1972. Expectations and the neutrality of money. *J. of Econ. Theory* 4: 103–124.

Marschak, J. and Radner, R. 1972. *Economic Theory of Teams.* New Haven: Yale University Press.

Radner, R. 1967. Equilibre des marchés à terme et au comptant en cas d'incertitude. *Cahiers d'Econométrie* 4: 35–52. C.N.R.S., Paris.

Radner, R. 1979. Rational expectations equilibrium: generic existence and the information revealed by prices. *Econometrica* 47: 655–678.

Radner, R. 1980. Collusive behavior in noncooperative epsilon-equilibria of oligopolies with long but finite lives. *J. of Econ. Theory* 22: 136–154.

Radner, R. 1981a. Monitoring cooperative agreements in a repeated principal-agent relationship. *Econometrica* 49: 1121–1148.

Radner, R. 1981b. Optimal equilibria in a class of repeated partnership games with imperfect monitoring. Bell Laboratories, Murray Hill, N.J. (To appear in *Rev. of Econ. Stud.*)

Radner, R. 1982. Equilibrium under uncertainty. Ch. 20 of K. J. Arrow, and M. D. Intriligator, eds., *Handbook of mathematical economics,* vol. 2, Amsterdam: North-Holland.

Rubinstein, A. 1979a. Offenses that may have been committed by accident – an optimal policy of retribution. In S. J. Brams, A. Schotter, and G. Schwödiauer, eds., *Applied Game Theory,* Würzburg: Physica-Verlag.

Rubinstein, A. 1979b. Equilibrium in supergames with the overtaking criterion. *J. of Econ. Theory* 21: 1–9.

Rubinstein, A. and Yaari, M. E. 1980. Repeated insurance contracts and moral hazard. Res. Mem. no. 37, Center for Res. in Math. Econ. and Game Th., Hebrew University, Jerusalem. (To appear in *J. of Econ. Theory.*)

PART III

NON-WALRASIAN ECONOMICS

CHAPTER 4

Developments in non-Walrasian economics
and the microeconomic foundations
of macroeconomics

Jean-Pascal Benassy

After the seminal contributions of Clower (1965) and Leijonhufvud (1968),[1] there has been a considerable renewal of interest in non-Walrasian economics as a way to provide rigorous microfoundations to macroeconomics. The basic idea behind all the models in this area is that prices may not clear the markets at all times, and thus that adjustments can, at least partially, be carried out through quantities. Such a theme is evidently at the heart of Keynesian economics, as Clower and Leijonhufvud pointed out. Further progress in the domain has in a large proportion been made along two lines.

The first is the construction of general microeconomic models abandoning the assumption of competitive equilibrium on all markets. A first category of these models assumes some degree of price rigidity and studies the associated quantity adjustments: Glustoff (1968); Drèze (1975); Benassy (1975a, 1975b, 1977); Younès (1975); Grandmont–Laroque (1976); Malinvaud–Younès (1978); Böhm–Levine (1979); and Heller–Starr (1979). A second category addresses the problem of noncompetitive price formation: Negishi (1961, 1972); Benassy (1976); and Hahn (1978). As we shall see in Section 1.5, these two types of models can actually be synthesized.

The second line of research consists of constructing specific aggregated models to study macroeconomic themes such as unemployment or inflation: Solow–Stiglitz (1968); Younès (1970); Barro–Grossman (1971,

I wish to thank T. Negishi for his comments.

1974, 1976); Grossman (1971); Benassy (1973, 1974, 1978a, 1978b); Malinvaud (1977); Negishi (1978, 1979); Hildenbrand–Hildenbrand (1978); Dixit (1978); and Muellbauer–Portes (1978).

In this chapter we shall not make a survey of the field, but rather give an outlook on these two lines of work: The first section will present a number of non-Walrasian equilibrium concepts in microeconomic models, and the second section will study the role of expectations in a simple macromodel of unemployment.

1   Non-Walrasian equilibrium concepts

One of the purposes for constructing new concepts of non-Walrasian equilibrium is to bridge the gap with Keynesian models. These usually are, at least implicitly, temporary equilibrium models with some degree of price rigidity, where quantity adjustments thus replace price adjustments to some extent: The most common IS-LM model assumes the interest rate flexible, but the price and wage level given. Other models will differ in that they assume the price level flexible, either adjusting competitively, or, in a more truly Keynesian vein, determined in a pattern of monopolistic competition.

In order to accommodate these different formulations, we shall present successively two concepts: A concept of fix-price equilibrium (Section 1.3), in some ways the polar case of the general equilibrium concept, and a concept of temporary equilibrium with price makers (Section 1.5), which allows flexible prices to be determined by agents internal to the economy. The role of expectations in these temporary equilibria is shown in Section 1.4. Before studying the concepts themselves, we shall present a typical Walrasian model (Section 1.1) in order to emphasize better the specificities of non-Walrasian economics, and describe the common institutional framework of our models (Section 1.2).

1.1   A typical Walrasian equilibrium model

The exchange economy considered will have r goods, indexed by $h = 1, \ldots, r$, and n consumers-traders, indexed by $i = 1, \ldots, n$. Agent i has a bundle of initial resources represented by a vector $e_i \in R_+^r$, carries net trades represented by a vector $z_i \in R^r$ with components z_{ih} satisfying $e_i + z_i \geq 0$, and has a utility function over these trades $U_i(z_i)$, which we shall assume to be strictly concave. For each price vector $p \in R_+^r$, agent i determines his vector of net demands by maximizing utility subject to the budget constraint, that is,

Maximize $U_i(z_i)$ s.t.

$$e_i + z_i \geqslant 0$$
$$pz_i = 0$$

One obtains in this way a net demand function $z_i(p)$, with components $z_{ih}(p)$ for each good. We should point out that this demand function is *notional*, in the terminology of Clower (1965), that is, constructed under the assumption that any desired trade can be carried out. A Walrasian equilibrium price vector p^* will be determined by the condition that net excess demand be zero for all goods:

$$\sum_{i=1}^{n} z_{ih}(p^*) = 0 \quad h = 1, \ldots, r$$

Concavity assumptions on preferences are sufficient here to guarantee the existence of such an equilibrium.

1.2   *Non-Walrasian models: The institutional setting*

In Walrasian analysis, a transactor is assumed to be able to reach any trade on his budget line. One does not need to specify which markets (in the sense of the Walrasian trading posts) are open or how exchange is organized on each market. In non-Walrasian analysis, where quantity constraints may be present, these problems become important and we turn to them now.

1.2.1   *A monetary economy*

In all that follows, we shall work in a *monetary economy,* money being a numeraire, a medium of exchange, and a store of value. Thus let r be nonmonetary goods, indexed by $h = 1, \ldots, r$, plus money. Let p_h be the money price of good h. Money being the medium of exchange, there will be r trading posts, or markets, on which each of these goods will be exchanged against money. z_{ih} will thus represent the intensity of the trade of good h against money, the monetary counterpart being $p_h z_{ih}$. Aggregating all these partial trades, one obtains a budget constraint similar to the traditional one, $pz_i + M_i = \bar{M}_i$, where $\bar{M}_i$ is the initial money holding of agent i, and M_i his final money holding.

We should emphasize that we do not mean that the monetary transaction structure is necessary for quantity constraints analysis as has been wrongly understood by a few authors,[2] but rather that the following analysis is the one relevant to a monetary economy. Non-Walrasian analysis can be applied to barter or other frameworks, at the price of a different and somewhat heavier formalization (Bennassy, 1975a).

1.2.2   *Demands, transactions, and rationing schemes*

We must now make an important distinction, which by nature is not made in equilibrium models, that between *demands* and *transactions*.

Transactions, that is, purchases and sales, are the exchanges actually carried on a market. They must balance as an identity on each market, that is, calling z_{ih}^* the transaction of agent i on market h:

$$\sum_{i=1}^{n} z_{ih}^* \equiv 0 \quad \text{for all } h$$

Demands and supplies on the contrary are tentative trades, signals transmitted to the market before exchange takes place. So if we denote by $\tilde{z}_{ih}$ the net effective demand of agent i on market h, we may have

$$\sum_{i=1}^{n} \tilde{z}_{ih} \neq 0$$

Each market has a particular organization, which converts possibly inconsistent demands and supplies into consistent transactions. This will be represented through a *rationing scheme,* that is, a set of n functions:

$$z_{ih}^* = F_{ih}(\tilde{z}_{1h}, \ldots, \tilde{z}_{nh}) \quad i = 1, \ldots, n \quad \text{such that}$$

$$\sum_{i=1}^{n} F_{ih}(\tilde{z}_{1h}, \ldots, \tilde{z}_{nh}) = 0 \quad \text{for all} \quad \tilde{z}_{1h}, \ldots, \tilde{z}_{nh}$$

We shall actually rewrite these functions under the form

$$z_{ih}^* = F_{ih}(\tilde{z}_{ih}, \tilde{Z}_{ih})$$

with $\tilde{Z}_{ih} = \{\tilde{z}_{1h}, \ldots, \tilde{z}_{i-1,h}, \tilde{z}_{i+1,h}, \ldots, \tilde{z}_{nh}\}$.

We shall assume throughout that the rationing schemes have the following properties:

(i) F_{ih} is continuous in its arguments, nondecreasing in $\tilde{z}_{ih}$.

(ii) $z_{ih}^* \cdot \tilde{z}_{ih} \geqslant 0$, $|z_{ih}^*| \leqslant |\tilde{z}_{ih}|$.

This last property is generally known as *voluntary exchange.*

Another often made assumption, but which we shall not need in the sequel, is that of the "short-side rule," according to which traders on the short side[3] realize their desired trades:

(iii) $\quad \left(\sum_{j=1}^{n} \tilde{z}_{jh}\right) \cdot \tilde{z}_{ih} \leqslant 0 \Rightarrow z_{ih}^* = \tilde{z}_{ih}$

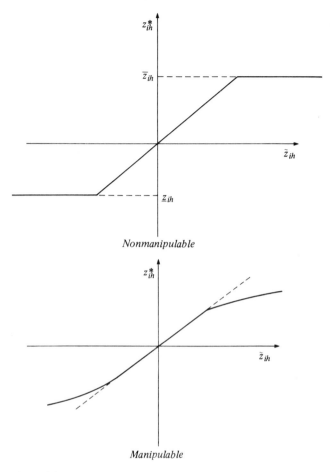

Figure 4.1

Examples of rationing schemes are numerous: uniform rationing, proportional rationing, queueing, priority systems, and so forth. To each of these will be associated a particular set of functions F_{ih}.

1.2.3   Manipulation, quantity signals

We introduce here a classification that will appear important in what follows – that between *manipulable* and *nonmanipulable* rationing schemes. The difference is clearly seen in Figure 4.1, where we plot the relation between z_{ih}^* and $\tilde{z}_{ih}$ with $\tilde{Z}_{ih}$ being held constant. A scheme is nonmanipulable if each trader faces upper and lower bounds in his trades, which he cannot manipulate. A scheme is manipulable if a trader can, even if he is rationed, increase his transaction by increasing his demand. The queueing process is nonmanipulable; the proportional rationing scheme is manipulable. Mathematically, we shall say that a rationing scheme is nonmanipulable if:

$$F_{ih}(\tilde{z}_{ih}, \tilde{Z}_{ih}) = \frac{\min[\tilde{z}_{ih}, \bar{G}_{ih}(\tilde{Z}_{ih})] \quad \text{if} \quad \tilde{z}_{ih} \geqslant 0}{\max[\tilde{z}_{ih}, \underline{G}_{ih}(\tilde{Z}_{ih})] \quad \text{if} \quad \tilde{z}_{ih} \leqslant 0}$$

where:

$$\bar{G}_{ih}(\tilde{Z}_{ih}) = \max\{\varsigma \mid F_{ih}(\varsigma, \tilde{Z}_{ih}) = \varsigma\}$$

$$\underline{G}_{ih}(\tilde{Z}_{ih}) = \min\{\varsigma \mid F_{ih}(\varsigma, \tilde{Z}_{ih}) = \varsigma\}$$

Otherwise the scheme is manipulable. Manipulable schemes usually lead to a process of overbidding that may prevent the existence of an equilibrium (Benassy, 1977a). In what follows we shall thus concentrate on nonmanipulable schemes, which can be represented shortly as:

$$z_{ih}^* = \frac{\min(\tilde{z}_{ih}, \bar{z}_{ih}) \quad \tilde{z}_{ih} \geqslant 0}{\max(\tilde{z}_{ih}, \underline{z}_{ih}) \quad \tilde{z}_{ih} \leqslant 0}$$

or $z_{ih}^* = \min[\bar{z}_{ih}, \max(\tilde{z}_{ih}, \underline{z}_{ih})]$ with $\bar{z}_{ih} = \bar{G}_{ih}(\tilde{Z}_{ih})$, $\underline{z}_{ih} = \underline{G}_{ih}(\tilde{Z}_{ih})$. $\bar{z}_{ih}$ and $\underline{z}_{ih}$ will be called the *perceived constraints*.

1.3   Fix-price equilibria[4]

We shall first study the polar case of Walrasian analysis by assuming that all prices are given in the period of analysis, a formalization of Hicks's fix-price method (Hicks, 1965).

1.3.1   Markets and agents

We shall thus have a monetary exchange economy with r markets $(h = 1, \ldots, r)$. The price p_h on each market will be given. There will be n agents $(i = 1, \ldots, n)$. Agent i has an initial endowment of goods $e_i \in R_+^r$, of money $\bar{M}_i \geqslant 0$. He has an indirect utility function $V_i(z_i, M_i, \sigma_i)$, where $\sigma_i = \{p, \bar{z}_i, \underline{z}_i\}$ is the set of price and quantity signals received by i. The derivation of V_i from more basic data will be seen in the next section. We shall assume that V_i is strictly concave in z_i and concave in M_i.

The fix-price equilibrium concept will involve three types of quantities: effective demands $(\tilde{z}_{ih})$, transactions (z_{ih}^*), and perceived constraints $(\bar{z}_{ih}, \underline{z}_{ih})$. We have already seen how transactions and perceived constraints were derived from effective demands:

$$z_{ih}^* = F_{ih}(\tilde{z}_{ih}, \tilde{Z}_{ih})$$
$$\bar{z}_{ih} = \bar{G}_{ih}(\tilde{Z}_{ih})$$
$$\underline{z}_{ih} = \underline{G}_{ih}(\tilde{Z}_{ih})$$

We will now study the determination of effective demands themselves.

1.3.2   *Effective demands*

Consider a trader i facing a price vector p and vectors of quantity constraints $\bar{z}_i$ and $\underline{z}_i$. He will choose the vector of effective demands so as to yield the best transaction possible. Let us call $\zeta_i^*(p, \bar{z}_i, \underline{z}_i)$ this best transaction. It will be the solution to the following program:

> Maximize $\quad V_i(z_i, M_i, \sigma_i) \quad$ s.t.
> $e_i + z_i \geqslant 0 \quad M_i \geqslant 0$
> $pz_i + M_i = \bar{M}_i$
> $\underline{z}_{ih} \leqslant z_{ih} \leqslant \bar{z}_{ih} \quad h = 1, \ldots, r$

However, we are interested here in effective demands. The transaction z_{ih} resulting from effective demand $\tilde{z}_{ih}$ on market h is

$$z_{ih} = \min[\bar{z}_{ih}, \max(\tilde{z}_{ih}, \underline{z}_{ih})]$$

The vector of effective demands will be chosen so as to yield the best possible transaction, that is, it will be the solution of the following program:

> Maximize $\quad V_i(z_i, M_i, \sigma_i) \quad$ s.t.
> $e_i + z_i \geqslant 0 \quad M_i \geqslant 0$
> $pz_i + M_i = \bar{M}_i$
> $z_{ih} = \min[\bar{z}_{ih}, \max(\tilde{z}_{ih}, \underline{z}_{ih})] \quad h = 1, \ldots, r$

Unfortunately, even with V_i strictly concave in z_i, the set of solutions of the above program is generally multivalued. Rather than to work with a correspondence, we shall make a selection in the solution set and define an effective demand function. Formally, the effective demand function on market h, which we shall denote functionally $\tilde{\zeta}_{ih}(p, \bar{z}_i, \underline{z}_i)$, will be the hth component of the vector solution of the following program:

> Maximize $\quad V_i(z_i, M_i, \sigma_i) \quad$ s.t.
> $pz_i + M_i = \bar{M}_i$
> $e_i + z_i \geqslant 0 \quad M_i \geqslant 0$
> $\underline{z}_{ik} \leqslant z_{ik} \leqslant \bar{z}_{ik} \quad$ for all $\quad k \neq h$

In words, effective demand corresponds to the utility maximizing trade, taking into account perceived constraints on the *other* markets. It is easily shown that under strict concavity this function belongs to the above correspondence. Without strict concavity, one should revert to the more general definition (Benassy, 1977a).

1.3.3   *Fix-price equilibrium*

We are now ready to define a fix-price equilibrium (or K-equilibrium) associated to a price vector p as a set of effective demands, transactions, and perceived constraints such that

(1) $z_{ih}^* = F_{ih}(\tilde{z}_{ih}, \tilde{Z}_{ih})$ for all i, h

(2) $\tilde{z}_{ih} = \bar{G}_{ih}(\tilde{Z}_{ih})$ for all i, h

$\quad\quad \underline{z}_{ih} = \underline{G}_{ih}(\tilde{Z}_{ih})$

(3) $\tilde{z}_{ih} = \tilde{\zeta}_{ih}(p, \tilde{z}_i, \underline{z}_i)$ for all i, h

(4) $z_{ih}^* = \zeta_{ih}^*(p, \tilde{z}_i, \underline{z}_i)$ for all i, h

Note that condition (4) is redundant in view of the definition of effective demand. It is included here as a reminder. Existence of a fix-price equilibrium is easily proved under strict concavity of V_i in z_i.

   If the rationing scheme on market h satisfies the short-side rule, then agents on only one side of the market will perceive binding constraints, a property central to Drèze's (1975) concept.

1.4   *Temporary Keynesian equilibrium*[5]

In the previous sections we assumed that each agent was endowed with an indirect utility function $V_i(z_i, M_i, \sigma_i)$, having only current trades, money holdings, and signals as arguments. We shall now show how this can be derived from a multiperiod optimization program taking expectations about future prices and quantities into account. Accordingly, the current equilibrium will have the character of a temporary equilibrium. The construction will at the same time provide a formalization of money's role as a store of value in situations of possible disequilibrium.

1.4.1   *Markets and agents*

We shall consider here a two-period exchange economy. (The argument would extend without problem to any finite number of periods.) In the first period there are markets for r_1 nonmonetary goods; in the second period, for r_2. Money is assumed to be the only store of value between the two periods.

There are n traders, indexed by $i=1,\ldots,n$. Trader i has initial endowments $e_{i1} \in R^{r_1}_+$ and $e_{i2} \in R^{r_2}_+$ in the first and second period, respectively. His net trades $z_{i1} \in R^{r_1}$ and $z_{i2} \in R^{r_2}$ must satisfy

$$e_{i1} + z_{i1} \geqslant 0 \qquad e_{i2} + z_{i2} \geqslant 0$$

At the outset of the first period, agent i has an initial quantity of money $\bar{M}_i$. He will transfer to the second period a quantity M_i given by

$$p_1 z_{i1} + M_i = \bar{M}_i.$$

Transactions of the second period will have to satisfy

$$p_2 z_{i2} \leqslant M_i.$$

We shall assume that each agent ranks his possible transaction streams (current and expected) according to a utility function $U_i(z_{i1}, z_{i2})$. Finally, each agent holds expectations about the price and quantity signals he will face in the second period, which we shall denote σ_{i2}:

$$\sigma_{i2} = \{p_2, \bar{z}_{i2}, \underline{z}_{i2}\}$$

We shall assume that expected price-quantity signals depend upon current signals σ_{i1} (and past signals, which are a datum here), so that we shall write $\sigma_{i2} = \psi_i(\sigma_{i1})$.

1.4.2   The indirect utility of money

Assume that agent i has traded z_{i1} in the first period and transferred a quantity of money M_i. With given price-quantity expectations σ_{i2}, his expected transaction vector in the second period should be the one maximizing his utility, subject to the budget constraint and all quantity constraints, that is, it should be the solution of

$$\text{Maximize} \quad U_i(z_{i1}, z_{i2}) \quad \text{s.t.}$$
$$p_2 z_{i2} \leqslant M_i$$
$$e_{i2} + z_{i2} \geqslant 0$$
$$\underline{z}_{i2} \leqslant z_{i2} \leqslant \bar{z}_{i2}$$

Let us write the vector solution of this program as $Z^*_{i2}(z_{i1}, M_i, \sigma_{i2})$. Now we can rewrite the level of utility, as expected from the first period, as

$$U_i[z_{i1}, Z^*_{i2}(z_{i1}, M_i, \sigma_{i2})] = U^*_i(z_{i1}, M_i, \sigma_{i2})$$
$$= U^*_i[z_{i1}, M_i, \psi_i(\sigma_{i1})] = V_i(z_{i1}, M_i, \sigma_{i1})$$

This indirect utility function now has current trades and money holdings as arguments. It also depends upon current price and quantity signals, through their influence on expected price and quantity constraints.

1.4.3   *Temporary fix-price equilibrium*

We can now suppress the index 1 of the current period. We thus have current fix-price markets. There are n traders indexed by $i=1,\ldots,n$. Each has an endowment $(e_i, \bar{M}_i)$ and an indirect utility function $V_i(z_i, M_i, \sigma_i)$. The structure is thus exactly the same as that of Section 1.3. The existence of an equilibrium can be proved, provided the function U_i is strictly concave in its arguments.

1.5   *Temporary equilibrium with price makers*[6]

Obviously, fix-price models are only a first step, and we must now study models where at least some prices are flexible. Besides "auctioneer" mechanisms, two types of price making arrangements can be envisioned: The price may be set unilaterally by price makers on one side of the market, or it may be bargained between the two sides. In order to avoid game-theoretic complications, we shall study only the first arrangement.

In such a setting, price makers change the price so as to "manipulate" the quantity constraints they face. An equilibrium will be reached when price makers are satisfied with the price-quantity combination they have obtained. Price makers behave thus very much like imperfect competitors, and the concept of equilibrium we will have is in line with that in the pioneering article of Negishi (1961). It generalizes Negishi's concept in allowing some markets to have rigid prices, while others adjust in this imperfectly competitive manner.

1.5.1   *Perceived demand curves*

Our economy will consist as before of exchangers, indexed by $i=1,\ldots,n$; trader i has endowments $(e_i, \bar{M}_i)$ and a utility function $V_i(z_i, M_i, \sigma_i)$. We shall assume that agent i controls the prices of goods $h \in H_i$, with

$$H_i \cap H_j = \{\varnothing\} \quad i \neq j$$

There may be a set of goods H_o whose prices are fixed (and thus controlled by no one). We shall call p_i the subvector of prices controlled by agent i.

Each price making agent has a perceived demand curve [resp. supply curve] relating the maximum quantities he can sell [resp. buy] to the price he sets. We shall denote them with the usual sign convention:

$$\underline{Z}_{ih}(p_i \mid \sigma_i) \quad \text{for the perceived demand curve}$$

$$\bar{Z}_{ih}(p_i \mid \sigma_i) \quad \text{for the perceived supply curve}$$

Perceived demand and supply curves must be consistent with the signals received in the sense that if trader i has observed a signal $\sigma_i = \{\bar{p}, \bar{z}_i, \underline{z}_i\}$, we must have

$$\bar{Z}_{ih}(\bar{p}_i \mid \bar{p}, \bar{z}_i, \underline{z}_i) = \bar{z}_{ih}$$

$$\underline{Z}_{ih}(\bar{p}_i \mid \bar{p}, \bar{z}_i, \underline{z}_i) = \underline{z}_{ih}$$

that is, the perceived curves must "go through" the observed point.

1.5.2 *Price making*

A price maker will choose a price vector so as to maximize his utility subject to the trades that he perceives as possible. Assume that he receives price and quantity signals $\sigma_i = \{\bar{p}, \bar{z}_i, \underline{z}_i\}$. He will choose his vector of prices p_i so as to

$$\text{Maximize} \quad V_i(z_i, M_i, \sigma_i) \quad \text{s.t.}$$

$$p z_i + M_i = \bar{M}_i$$

$$e_i + z_i \geq 0 \quad M_i \geq 0$$

$$p_h = \bar{p}_h \quad \underline{z}_{ih} \leq z_{ih} \leq \bar{z}_{ih} \quad h \notin H_i$$

$$\underline{Z}_{ih}(p_i, \sigma_i) \leq z_{ih} \leq \bar{Z}_{ih}(p_i, \sigma_i) \quad h \in H_i$$

We shall denote the optimal price functionally as:

$$\mathcal{P}_i^*(\sigma_i) = \mathcal{P}_i^*(\bar{p}, \bar{z}_i, \underline{z}_i)$$

1.5.3 *Equilibrium with price makers*

Intuitively, one can define an equilibrium with price makers as a fix-price equilibrium such that no price maker has any incentive to change his prices. We shall formalize this in the following definition.

An equilibrium with price makers is defined by a price vector p^*, net trades z_i^*, effective demands $\tilde{z}_i$, perceived constraints $\bar{z}_i$ and $\underline{z}_i$, such that:

(1) (z_i^*), $(\tilde{z}_i)$, $(\bar{z}_i, \underline{z}_i)$ are a fix-price equilibrium with respect to p^*,

(2) $p_i^* = \mathcal{P}_i^*(p^*, \bar{z}_i, \underline{z}_i)$.

The temporary equilibrium so obtained will depend upon the values of prices that are fixed. The existence of such an equilibrium can be proved only if the functions $\mathcal{P}_i^*$ satisfy some boundedness assumptions. These may be jeopardized by some patterns of expectation formation, a difficulty already known in studies of competitive temporary equilibrium (Grandmont, 1974).

2   Unemployment and expectations

We want to construct here a simple macromodel using the methods described above, and notably the concept of fix-price equilibrium, to study the problem of the nature of unemployment. There is already a fairly developed body of literature along this line, consisting mainly of the seminal work of Barro-Grossman (1971, 1976) and its different adaptations: Benassy (1974, 1978a); Malinvaud (1977); Hildenbrand–Hildenbrand (1978); and Muellbauer–Portes (1978).

Our emphasis here will be on showing in a very explicit manner the effects of expectations on the current equilibrium and the nature of unemployment.[7] We shall see in particular that the traditional association between the type of unemployment (classical or Keynesian in Malinvaud's terminology) and specific patterns of current excess demands and supplies is not valid anymore, an issue somewhat overlooked in other works.

Our exposition will proceed as follows. We shall first construct a simple fix-price model adapted from Barro–Grossman, where firms do not hold any stocks (Section 2.1). Equilibria and types of unemployment will be described in this simple model (Section 2.2). We shall then extend the model by allowing the firm to hold some stocks (Section 2.3). The different types of equilibria will be studied for this model (Section 2.4) and their relation to the firm's expectations described (Section 2.5).

2.1   *The model without stocks: presentation*

2.1.1   *Markets and agents*

We shall consider here a simple monetary economy. There are three representative economic agents: household, firm, and government, and three economic goods, output, labor, and money. Accordingly, there are two current markets: one on which output is exchanged against money at the price p and one on which labor is exchanged against money at the wage w. The household demands output and supplies labor, the firm demands labor and supplies output, the government demands some output. On each market, transactions realized are assumed to be the minimum of supply and demand. In what follows we shall be interested in the determinants of the current level of employment l^* and output sales y^*. First, however, we shall describe in more detail the agents and their behavior.

2.1.2 The firm

The representative firm has a short-run production function:

$$q = F(l)$$

with the traditional properties:

$$F(0) = 0 \qquad F'(l) > 0 \qquad F''(l) < 0$$

With no inventories, production will be equal to sales y in equilibrium. The firm attempts to maximize profits $\pi = py - wl$ under the constraint $y \leqslant q$. These profits are entirely distributed to the household; household's income in real terms will thus be equal to y.

2.1.3 The household

The household will be assumed to have a fixed supply of labor l_0. Its effective demand for goods will be described through a consumption function

$$\tilde{c} = C(y, \bar{M}, p, \tau)$$

where $\bar{M}$ is the initial holding of money of the household, and τ the tax rate at which his income is taxed. We shall assume $0 < C_y' < 1$, $C_{\bar{M}}' > 0$, $C_p' < 0$, and $C'_\tau < 0$. This consumption function is derived through the maximization of an indirect utility function subject to the budget constraint under a given income y:

$$\text{Maximize} \quad V(c, M, p, y) \quad \text{s.t.}$$
$$pc + M = \bar{M} + (1 - \tau)y$$

The indirect utility function itself comes from an intertemporal utility maximization program, as seen in Section 1.4, where expected future incomes and prices depend upon the current ones.

As an example, we shall sometimes use the indirect utility function:

$$\alpha \log c + (1 - \alpha) \log M/p$$

yielding a linear consumption function:

$$\tilde{c} = \alpha[(\bar{M}/p) + (1 - \tau)y]$$

2.1.4   Government

The government taxes income at the rate τ, and expresses an effective demand for output equal to $\tilde{g}$. Actual purchases will be noted g^*.

2.1.5   Effective demand for labor

An important element in determining whether unemployment is of classical or Keynesian type is the form of the effective demand for labor. Let us call $\bar{y}$ the quantity constraint on sales that the firm faces ($\bar{y}$ is actually equal to $\tilde{c} + \tilde{g}$, that is, the total demand for output). Then the effective demand for labor $\tilde{l}^d$ will be given by the following program:

$$\text{Maximize}\quad py - wl$$
$$y \leqslant q = F(l)$$
$$y \leqslant \bar{y} = \tilde{c} + \tilde{g}$$

which yields:

$$\tilde{l}^d = \min\{F'^{-1}(w/p), F^{-1}(\bar{y})\}$$

We see that the demand for labor has a dual nature: classical if the firm is not constrained on the goods market, Keynesian if it is.

2.2   The different regions

Anticipating what follows, we shall see that there are in this simple model three types of fix-price equilibria, according to the values of the parameters p, w, $\bar{M}$, $\tilde{g}$, and τ:

> classical unemployment, with excess supply of labor and excess demand of goods,[8]
> Keynesian unemployment, with excess supply of labor and goods,
> repressed inflation with excess demand of labor and goods.

Because of the absence of stocks the fourth possibility (excess supply of goods, excess demand of labor) reduces to a degenerate case, at the limit between the two last ones. Also we should note that the association of excess demand [resp. supply] of goods to classical [resp. Keynesian] unemployment is valid only in this simplified model.

We shall now try to determine the level of employment and production in each of these cases, then determine for which values of the parameters they are relevant.

2.2.1 *Keynesian unemployment*

This case corresponds to the traditional situation of excess supply on the two markets. Sales and income y will be equal to the aggregate demand for goods, that is, be the solution of:

$$y = \tilde{c} + \tilde{g} = C(y, \bar{M}, p, \tau) + \tilde{g}$$

Let us call $y_k(\bar{M}, p, \tilde{g}, \tau)$ the solution to this equation:

$$y^* = y_k(\bar{M}, p, \tilde{g}, \tau)$$

This is a traditional Keynesian multiplier formula with:

$$\frac{\partial y^*}{\partial \tilde{g}} = \frac{1}{1 - C_y'} > 1$$

Employment l^* is equal to $F^{-1}(y_k)$ and consumption c^* to $y_k - \tilde{g}$. We can remark that consumption is an increasing function of $\tilde{g}$ as:

$$\frac{\partial c^*}{\partial \tilde{g}} = \frac{\partial y_k}{\partial \tilde{g}} - 1 = \frac{C_y'}{1 - C_y'}$$

For example, if $\tilde{c} = \alpha[(\bar{M}/p) + (1 - \tau)y]$:

$$y_k = \frac{1}{1 - \alpha(1 - \tau)} \left[\frac{\alpha \bar{M}}{p} + \tilde{g} \right] \quad \text{and}$$

$$c^* = \frac{1}{1 - \alpha(1 - \tau)} \left[\frac{\alpha \bar{M}}{p} + \alpha(1 - \tau)\tilde{g} \right]$$

2.2.2 *Classical unemployment*

As hinted earlier, this is the case of excess supply on the labor market, excess demand on the goods market. The firm is thus on the short side of both markets, and will be able to realize its unconstrained neoclassical employment-production plan. The corresponding values of employment and sales l^* and y^*, will thus be:

$$l^* = F'^{-1}(w/p)$$

$$y^* = F[F'^{-1}(w/p)]$$

Because consumption and government purchases add up to production, private consumption (assuming government has priority in the allocation of goods) will be given by

$$c^* = y^* - \min(y^*, \tilde{g})$$

We see here that private consumption is inversely related to government purchases.

The reason why unemployment will be called classical is quite clear, as there is excess supply of labor and the demand for labor has the classical form. An increase in prices or a decrease in wages would reduce the level of unemployment. Increasing government spending would have no effect however but to reduce private consumption and increase the excess demand for goods.

2.2.3   *Repressed inflation*

We are here in a situation of excess demand on the two markets. Because the household is on the short side on the labor market, the level of employment will be equal to the inelastic labor supply l_0. Accordingly, production and sales will be equal to full-employment production $F(l_0)$

$$l^* = l_0$$

$$y^* = y_0 = F(l_0)$$

Assuming again that government is served in priority on the goods market, private consumption is equal to

$$c^* = y_0 - \min(y_0, \bar{g})$$

and thus varies inversely with government demand.

2.2.4   *Determination of the regime*

In the three combinations of excess demands and supplies cited above, we determined the expression of the employment level l^* and sales y^*. There remains now for us to determine for which values of the parameters we shall be in any of these three cases.[9]

In equilibrium, the transactions of each agent are the "best" with respect to his criterion, taking account of all the constraints he faces. (This property was seen above in Section 1.3.) In particular, the transactions of the firm should maximize its profits, subject to all constraints. This means that l^*, y^*, and q^* are solutions of:

Maximize $py - wl$

$y \leqslant q = F(l)$

$l \leqslant l_0$

$y \leqslant \bar{y} = \tilde{c} + \tilde{g}$

But, because $\tilde{c} = C(y, \bar{M}, p, \tau)$, $y \leqslant \tilde{c} + \tilde{g}$ is equivalent to

$$y \leqslant y_k(\bar{M}, p, \tilde{g}, \tau),$$

so that the above program can be rewritten as:

Maximize $\quad py - wl$

$y \leqslant q = F(l)$

$l \leqslant l_0$

$y \leqslant y_k$

with the solution:

$$l^* = \min\{F^{-1}(y_k), F'^{-1}(w/p), l_0\}$$

$$y^* = \min\{y_k, F[F'^{-1}(w/p)], F(l_0)\}$$

Here we see that the rigid relation between employment and sales, due to the absence of stocks, prevents the firm from being constrained on both markets and thus suppresses the potential "fourth case," in which the firm would be on the "long side" of both markets. Rewriting one of the two above switching conditions in function of the exogenous variables of the model, we obtain:

$$y^* = \min\{y_k(\bar{M}, p, g, \tau), F[F'^{-1}(w/p)], y_0\}$$

We can classify the regions according to the values of two fundamental parameters: the real wage w/p and the Keynesian level of income $y_k(\bar{M}, p, g, \tau)$ (Figure 4.2). Their equilibrium values are, respectively, $F'(l_0)$ and y_0.

A few points are of particular interest: Point W is of course the short-run Walrasian equilibrium, and the points on the boundary between the Keynesian and the classical regions correspond to the textbook Keynesian model, in which prices "clear" the goods market.

These regions can alternatively be depicted in the price-wage space, holding $\bar{M}$, $\tilde{g}$ and τ constant (p^* and w^* are the short-run equilibrium price and wage) (Figure 4.3).

2.3   Stocks and expectations

To the very simplified model considered above, we shall now add the possibility of holding inventories for the firm. We shall also consider how expectations influence current equilibrium. Quite a number of results will be drawn from this exercise:

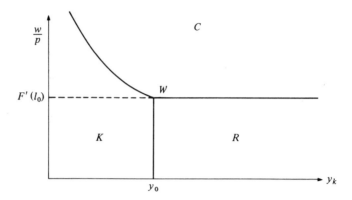

Figure 4.2

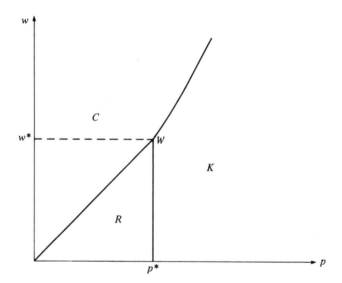

Figure 4.3

First, we shall see that the occurrence of full employment or of classical or Keynesian unemployment, does not depend only upon current or expected prices, but also upon quantity expectations.

Second, our model will exhibit the fourth region of excess demand for labor – excess supply of goods.

Third, we will see that the types of unemployment (classical, Keynesian) do not coincide necessarily with specific combinations of current excess demands and supplies. For example, classical unemployment may occur with either excess demand or excess supply of goods.

2.3.1   The model

We shall thus extend the horizon of the firm to an additional period. Current period quantities will have a subindex 1, future period quantities a subindex 2. To simplify, consumer and government will be taken the same as in the previous model: The household will have a supply of labor l_0 and a consumption function:

$$\tilde{c}_1 = C(y_1, \bar{M}, p, \tau)$$

y_1 now being current period income.

Government will tax income at the rate τ and express an effective demand for goods $\tilde{g}$.

2.3.2   The firm

The firm is assumed to have the same production function in the two periods:

$$q_1 = F(l_1) \qquad q_2 = F(l_2)$$

We shall assume that goods not sold in the first period can be stored costlessly until the second period. Thus, calling I the level of inventories, y_1 and y_2 the sales in the first and second period, we will have:

$$y_1 + I = q_1 \quad I \geqslant 0$$

$$y_2 \leqslant q_2 + I$$

which can be also written:

$$y_1 \leqslant q_1$$

$$y_1 + y_2 \leqslant q_1 + q_2$$

The firm must form some *expectations* about future prices and quantity constraints. Because we want to concentrate on only one expectational variable, we shall assume:

that future price and wage are expected to be the same as the current ones (p and w),

that no constraint on the labor market is expected,

that a constraint $\bar{y}_2$ on the future goods market is expected. This constraint, which represents the expected level of demand, will be the expectation variable we shall use as a parameter.

The firm is assumed to maximize the sum of current and expected profits,[10] that is, to maximize: $\pi_1 + \pi_2 = py_1 - wl_1 + py_2 - wl_2$.

2.3.3   *The effective demand for labor*

The form of the effective demand for labor by the firm will be important in determining whether one is in a situation of Keynesian or classical unemployment. The effective demand for labor is obtained through maximization of the objective function of the firm, subject to quantity constraints on markets other than the current labor market, that is, it is given by:

$$\text{Maximize} \quad py_1 - wl_1 + py_2 - wl_2 \quad \text{s.t.}$$
$$q_1 = F(l_1) \qquad q_2 = F(l_2)$$
$$y_1 \leqslant q_1$$
$$y_1 + y_2 \leqslant q_1 + q_2$$
$$y_1 \leqslant \bar{y}_1$$
$$y_2 \leqslant \bar{y}_2$$

yielding

$$\tilde{l}_1^d = \min\left\{ F'^{-1}\left(\frac{w}{p}\right), F^{-1}\left[\max\left(\bar{y}_1, \frac{\bar{y}_1 + \bar{y}_2}{2}\right)\right]\right\}$$

We recognize immediately a classical and a Keynesian demand. The last one now depends not only on current effective demand $\bar{y}_1$, but also on expected future demand $\bar{y}_2$. We see that in the event of a binding current constraint on sales $\bar{y}_1$, the producer may want to produce beyond $\bar{y}_1$, piling up inventories for later sales. We can remark also that for the demand for labor to have the Keynesian form, *both* constraints $\bar{y}_1$ and $\bar{y}_2$ must be binding.

2.4   *The different regions*

We shall now determine the level of employment and income, according to the pattern of excess demand or supply on the labor and goods markets. Whenever unemployment is present, we shall pay particular attention to its nature (classical or Keynesian).

2.4.1   *Excess supply on both markets*

In this case, output sales will be equal to the aggregate demand for goods

$$y_1 = \tilde{c} + \tilde{g} = C(y_1, \bar{M}, p, \tau) + \tilde{g}$$

which yields the equilibrium income

$$y_1^* = y_k(\bar{M}, p, \tilde{g}, \tau)$$

Income is thus given by a multiplier formula, as in the model above. Employment l_1^* is equal to the effective demand for labor, which, since $\bar{y}_1 = y_k$, yields:

$$l_1 = \min\left\{ F'^{-1}\left(\frac{w}{p}\right), F^{-1}\left[\max\left(y_k, \frac{y_k + \bar{y}_2}{2}\right)\right]\right\}$$

We see that this expression differs somewhat from the expression in the stockless model, that is, $F^{-1}(y_k)$:

First, for an optimistic $\bar{y}_2$, employment may be pushed to $F'^{-1}(w/p)$. Unemployment is thus classical, and Keynesian measures will have no effect on employment even though we are in the region of general excess supply.

Second, even when employment has a Keynesian value, it may be bigger than the employment necessary to produce for current demand. In such a case the employment multiplier will also be smaller as part of the unsold goods is absorbed into inventories.

To summarize, the excess supply region will be separated into two subregions; in both, income will be given by a Keynesian multiplier formula. However, in one (noted K)[11] unemployment will be Keynesian, while in the other (noted CK) it will be classical.

2.4.2   *Excess supply of goods, excess demand for labor*

Because there is an excess supply of goods, the level of income is again given through a multiplier formula

$$y_1^* = y_k$$

Because there is excess demand for labor, employment is determined by the inelastic supply

$$l_1^* = l_0$$

Note that this situation did not exist, except as a limiting case, in the stockless model. For it to happen here, we must have an effective demand for labor higher than l_0, even though current demand y_k is smaller than y_0. This thus implies optimistic expectations (specifically $\bar{y}_2 > y_0$), so that the firm will be led to hire all labor force and pile up inventories for future sales. We shall denote this region FK because there is full employment with income determined in a Keynesian manner.

2.4.3   *Excess demand for goods, excess supply of labor*

With excess demand for goods, the demand for labor has the classical form, and employment is equal to this demand

$$l_1^* = F'^{-1}(w/p)$$

Sales of goods are equal to production

$$y_1^* = F[F'^{-1}(w/p)].$$

This region is thus characterized by classical unemployment and will be denoted C.

2.4.4   *Excess demand on both markets*

Here employment is equal to the inelastic supply

$$l_1^* = l_0$$

Sales are blocked by full employment production

$$y_1^* = y_0$$

We shall denote this region R (for repressed inflation) as in the stockless model.

2.5   *The complete picture*

There remains now for us to determine for which values of the parameters p, w, $\bar{M}$, $\tilde{g}$, τ, $\bar{y}_2$ we shall have each of the above possibilities. We know that current employment l_1^*, sales y_1^* and production q_1^* will be solutions of the optimization program of the firm taking into account all quantity constraints, that is, they will be solution of:

$$\text{Maximize} \quad py_1 - wl_1 + py_2 - wl_2 \quad \text{s.t.}$$
$$q_1 = F(l_1) \qquad q_2 = F(l_2)$$
$$y_1 \leqslant q_1$$
$$y_1 + y_2 \leqslant q_1 + q_2$$
$$y_1 \leqslant \bar{y}_1 = \tilde{c}_1 + \tilde{g}$$
$$y_2 \leqslant \bar{y}_2$$
$$l_1 \leqslant l_0$$

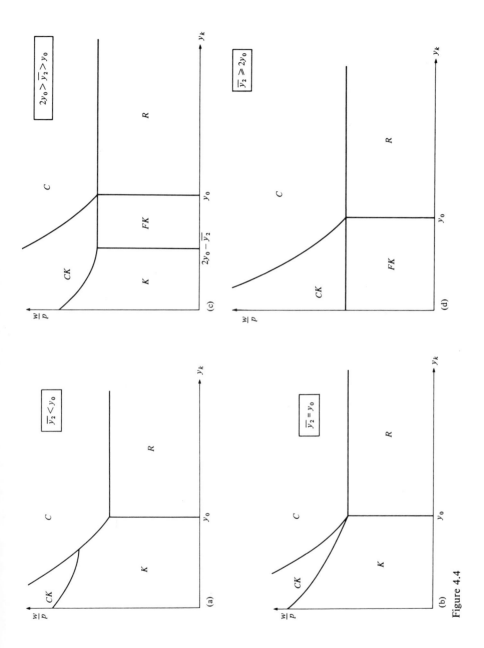

Figure 4.4

The constraint $y_1 \leqslant \bar{y}_1$ can be as above replaced by $y_1 \leqslant y_k(M, p, \bar{g}, \tau)$ and the program then yields:

$$y_1^* = \min\left\{y_0, F\left[F'^{-1}\left(\frac{w}{p}\right)\right], y_k\right\}$$

$$q_1^* = \min\left\{y_0, F\left[F'^{-1}\left(\frac{w}{p}\right)\right], \max\left[y_k, \frac{y_k + \bar{y}_2}{2}\right]\right\}$$

$$l_1^* = \min\left\{l_0, F'^{-1}\left(\frac{w}{p}\right), F^{-1}\left[\max\left(y_k, \frac{y_k + \bar{y}_2}{2}\right)\right]\right\}$$

As for the stockless model, the different regions have been drawn in a $(w/p, y_k)$ plane, for different values of $\bar{y}_2$ (Figure 4.4).

NOTES

1 Early contributions in a similar direction are found in B. Hansen (1951), Patinkin (1956).
2 Drazen (1980) is a recent and conspicuous example.
3 That is, demanders if there is excess supply, suppliers if there is excess demand.
4 The material in this section is borrowed from Benassy (1975b, 1977). Numerous alternative formalizations of fix-price equilibria have been given, starting with the seminal paper of Drèze (1975). Let us quote also Younès (1975), Böhm–Levine (1979), Heller–Starr (1979). For concepts in nonmonetary economies, see Benassy (1975a), Malinvaud–Younès (1978).
5 This section is based on Benassy (1975b).
6 This section is based on Benassy (1976).
7 A similar question is addressed, though in a different way, by Neary–Stiglitz (1980).
8 Actually one should say "demand-determined transactions" instead of excess supply, and "supply-determined transactions" instead of excess demand.
9 The method we use here was suggested by P. Michel (1980).
10 The assumptions of a zero rate of discount, as well as a zero rate of depreciation of inventories are made only to yield simple calculations.
11 The notations refer to Figure 4.4.

REFERENCES

Abramowitz, M., ed. (1959). *The allocation of economic resources.* Stanford University Press.
Arrow, K. J. (1959). Towards a theory of price adjustment. In Abramowitz, ed, *The allocation of economic resources.* Stanford University Press.
Arrow, K. J. and Hahn, F. H. (1971). *General competitive analysis.* San Francisco: Holden-Day.

Barro, R. J. and Grossman, H. I. (1971). A general disequilibrium model of income and employment. *American Economic Review* 61: 82-93.

Barro, R. J. and Grossman, H. I. (1974). Suppressed inflation and the supply multiplier. *Review of Economic Studies* 41: 87-104.

Barro, R. J. and Grossman, H. I. (1976). *Money, employment and inflation.* Cambridge University Press.

Benassy, J. P. (1973). Disequilibrium theory, Ph.D. dissertation, University of California, Berkeley. Hungarian translation in *Szygma* (1974).

Benassy, J. P. (1974). Théorie néokeynésienne du déséquilibre dans une économie monétaire. *Cahiers du Séminaire d'Econométrie* 17: 81-113.

Benassy, J. P. (1975a). Disequilibrium exchange in barter and monetary economies. *Economic Inquiry* 13: 131-156.

Benassy, J. P. (1975b). Neo-Keynesian disequilibrium theory in a monetary economy. *Review of Economic Studies* 42: 503-523.

Benassy, J. P. (1976). The disequilibrium approach to monopolistic price setting and general monopolistic equilibrium. *Review of Economic Studies* 43: 69-81.

Benassy, J. P. (1977). On quantity signals and the foundations of effective demand theory. *The Scandinavian Journal of Economics* 79: 147-168.

Benassy, J. P. (1978a). A Neokeynesian model of price and quantity determination in disequilibrium. In G. Schwödiauer, ed., *Equilibrium and disequilibrium in economic theory,* Proceedings of a Conference in Vienna, June 1974. Boston: D. Reidel.

Benassy, J. P. (1978b). Cost and demand inflation revisited: A neo-Keynesian approach. *Economie Appliquée* 31: 113-133.

Böhm, V. and Levine, J. P. (1979). Temporary equilibria with quantity rationing. *Review of Economic Studies* 46: 361-377.

Bushaw, D. W. and Clower, R. (1957). *Introduction to mathematical economics.* Homewood, Ill.: Richard D. Irwin.

Clower, R. W. (1965). The Keynesian counterrevolution: a theoretical appraisal. In F. H. Hahn and F. P. R. Brechling, eds., *The theory of interest rates.* London: Macmillan.

Clower, R. W. (1967). A reconsideration of the microfoundations of monetary theory. *Western Economic Journal* 6: 1-9.

Debreu, G. (1959). *Theory of value,* New York: Wiley.

Dixit, A. (1978). The balance of payments in a model of temporary equilibrium with rationing. *Review of Economic Studies* 45: 393-404.

Drazen, A. (1980). Recent developments in macroeconomic disequilibrium theory. *Econometrica* 48: 283-306.

Drèze, J. (1975). Existence of an equilibrium under price rigidity and quantity rationing. *International Economic Review* 16: 301-320.

Glustoff, E. (1968). On the existence of a Keynesian equilibrium. *Review of Economic Studies* 35: 327-334.

Grandmont, J. M. (1974). On the short run equilibrium in a monetary economy. In J. Drèze, ed., *Allocation under uncertainty, equilibrium, and optimality.* London: Macmillan.

Grandmont, J. M. (1977). Temporary general equilibrium theory. *Econometrica* 45: 535-572.

Grandmont, J. M. and Laroque, G. (1976). On Keynesian temporary equilibria. *Review of Economic Studies* 43: 53-67.

Grandmont, J. M., Laroque, G. and Younès, Y. (1978). Equilibrium with quantity rationing and recontracting. *Journal of Economic Theory* 19: 84–102.

Hahn, F. H. (1978). On Non-Walrasian equilibria. *Review of Economic Studies* 45: 1–17.

Hahn, F. H. and Negishi, T. (1962). A theorem of non-tâtonnement stability. *Econometrica* 30: 463–469.

Hansen, Bent (1951). *A study in the theory of inflation*. London: Allen and Unwin.

Heller, W. P. and Starr, R. M. (1979). Unemployment equilibrium with myopic complete information. *Review of Economic Studies* 46: 339–359.

Hicks, J. (1965). *Capital and growth*. Oxford University Press.

Hildenbrand, K. and Hildenbrand, W. (1978). On Keynesian equilibria with unemployment and quantity rationing. *Journal of Economic Theory* 18: 255–277.

Keynes, J. M. (1936). *The general theory of money, interest and employment*. New York: Harcourt Brace.

Leijonhufvud, A. (1968). *On Keynesian economics and the economics of Keynes*. Oxford University Press.

Malinvaud, E. (1977). *The theory of unemployment reconsidered*. Oxford: Blackwell.

Malinvaud, E. and Younès, Y. (1978). Une nouvelle formulation générale pour l'étude des fondements microéconomiques de la macroéconomie. *Cahiers du Séminaire d'Econométrie*.

Michel, P. (1980). Keynesian equilibrium and fix-price equilibria. Warwick Discussion Paper, February.

Muellbauer, J. and Portes, R. (1978). Macroeconomic models with quantity rationing. *Economic Journal* 88: 788–821.

Neary, P. and Stiglitz, J. (1980). Towards a reconstruction of Keynesian economics: expectations and constrained equilibria.

Negishi, T. (1961). Monopolistic competition and general equilibrium. *Review of Economic Studies* 28: 196–201.

Negishi, T. (1972). *General equilibrium theory and international trade*. Amsterdam: North Holland.

Negishi, T. (1978). Existence of an under employment equilibrium. In G. Schwödiauer, ed., *Equilibrium and disequilibrium in economic theory*. Boston: Reidel.

Negishi, T. (1979). *Microeconomic foundations of Keynesian macroeconomics*. Amsterdam: North-Holland.

Patinkin, D. (1956, 2nd ed. 1965). *Money, interest and prices*. New York: Harper and Row.

Solow, R. M. and Stiglitz, J. (1968). Output, employment and wages in the short run. *Quarterly Journal of Economics,* November.

Younès, Y. (1970). Sur les notions d'équilibre et de déséquilibre utilisées dans les modèles décrivant l'évolution d'une économie capitaliste. CEPREMAP.

Younès, Y. (1975). On the role of money in the process of exchange and the existence of a non-Walrasian equilibrium. *Review of Economic Studies* 42: 489–501.

CHAPTER 5

On equilibria with rationing

Yves Younès

The literature about the so-called equilibria with rationing is one attempt (among many) to tackle questions that arise at levels that can be categorized for analytical convenience.

On one hand, there has been some discomfort with the way in which competitive Walrasian equilibrium is formulated classically. The classical definition does not depict any relations among economic units and, consequently, there is an unknown of the system (the equilibrium price vector) that is not chosen by any agent. Alternatively, one of the first proofs of the existence of a competitive Walrasian Equilibrium (Arrow and Debreu, 1954) reduces an economy with m agents to a game in normal form with $m+1$ agents, the last one of which is the auctioneer whose role is to choose the price vector. This provides a centralized version of Walrasian competitive equilibria (WCE). Clearly, the theorem regarding the equivalence of the core and the set of Walrasian equilibria in large economies gives a decentralized version of Walras's notion.

On the other hand, there has been a gap between macroeconomics and microeconomics. Whereas, given the assumption of competition, it was assumed in microeconomic theory that individuals act only on the basis of price, it is supposed in macroeconomic Keynesian theory that agents take into account quantity constraints.

More precisely, it is possible to connect the recent development of the formalized theory of equilibrium with rationing with four anterior trends of analysis.

I benefited from remarks by Y. Balasko, P. Champsaur, G. Laroque, H. Moulin, M. Quinzi and particularly J. M. Grandmont. I am responsible for errors.

147

The first connection is well known and goes back to Keynes. In a nutshell, Clower (1965) and Leijohnufvud (1977) emphasize the necessity of taking into account the way in which transactions are made and the difficulty of getting an equilibrium price vector in a decentralized way.

The second one seems to be largely unknown although it is a natural development of Keynesian thinking. I refer to the works of economists who tried to give foundations to French Planning (see, for instance, Massé, 1965). French Planning – a kind of decentralized planning – is usually defined as a "generalized market study." It is argued that the price mechanism is often ineffective even when markets exist and that there is no spontaneous way of coordinating agents' plans when there is no market, for instance, in the case of almost all future goods. Note that the method consists first of all in providing a set of compatible trades between sectors that they are, in principle, interested to take into account as a basis for their computations. It is not known whether the trades are not too much aggregated to be useful, even for big firms.

The third trend is that of decentralized processes (mechanisms) particularly as they were introduced by Hurwicz (1959). In his paper, Hurwicz defines decentralization from the point of view of information only for so called concrete processes for which the set of messages is a subset of the power set of acts. These processes are interesting because if acts are conceived as contracts, a message is a set of contract proposals.[1] In particular Hurwicz defines the greed process for which each agent sends all contract proposals that are better than the allocation he thinks he can get. There is an identity shared between the set of equilibria of the greed process and the set of Pareto optima.

The fourth connection is that of nontâtonnement processes as they were formulated by Hahn and Negishi (1962) and Uzawa (1962). In these papers, it is assumed that agents exchange at some unique price vector that is not necessarily Walrasian. Also they assumed that the result is any Pareto optimal point relative to the budget constraint at the given price vector.[2] As for the greed process, there is no way for an agent to refuse a Pareto-optimal point (under budgetary constraint at a given price vector).

More precisely, let us assume an exchange economy with two goods and two agents. W is the initial endowment in an Edgeworth box. The slope Wp is the given price ratio.

If people refuse an allocation only in the case in which they can simultaneously increase their utility, any point of the segment (A, B) would be an equilibrium.

If we consider that good 2 is money, Figure 5.1 shows a buyers' market and we are accustomed to thinking that in a buyers' market, buyers

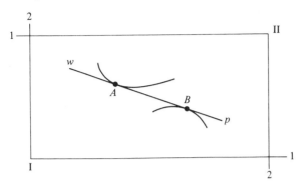

Figure 5.1

are stronger than sellers, and thus only point A is an equilibrium. It is possible to capture this idea by adding to the above axiom another one stating that no agent in a large competitive economy can be constrained to trade more than he wants. This idea can be formulated by saying that each agent maximizes his utility under the trade constraints or by some similar device. Thus, an allocation is an equilibrium if it satisfies two axioms.

Axiom 1: It is impossible to find another allocation (satisfying inter alia the price constraints) that gives more utility to all traders: It is efficient in the set delimited inter alia by the price constraints.

Axiom 2: At this allocation, no agent can increase his utility by trading less.

Remark: If we take into account only the second axiom, zero trade would always be an equilibrium. When there are more than two goods, we are constrained to define how the trades are made in order to write down these two axioms precisely (on these points see Younès (1970(b)). Consider for instance a model with three goods (labor, a produced good, and money) and two kinds of agents (firms and consumers). Assume also that the price vector ($\bar{p}$) is given. If we say that each of the first two goods can be exchanged only for money, there will exist allocations (if $\bar{p}$ is chosen adequately) that would be equilibria in this setup, but that would not be if it was possible to exchange labor for the produced good directly. In this connection, the central concept is that of type of transaction or direction of trades that specify the goods which can enter in a trade. The two axioms are then defined relative to the set of allowable types of transaction.

In order to justify the content of this chapter, I shall give here a partial bibliography. Concerning the situations in which people can trade at only one price vector and also the formal side of the general theory, the initial papers are those by Drèze (1975), Benassy (1975(a), 1975(b)), and Younès (1970(b), 1975). For the aggregated model with three goods (money, labor, and a produced good) and the different regimes associated with varied price vectors, see Barro and Grossman (1971), Malinvaud (1977), and Younès (1970(a)). In Malinvaud and Younès (1978), it is shown that the two axioms when people can trade at any price vector result in Walrasian competitive equilibria. Champsaur (1979) proved that when there are public goods, these same two axioms result in only Lindahl equilibria.

Gandmont, Laroque, and Younès (1978) showed that it is possible to give foundations to the second axiom in terms of the bargaining set concept in large economies. Laroque (1978) proved theorems concerning comparative statics, using Drèze's framework.

A part of Grandmont's survey (1977) is devoted to this theory (in the case people can trade at only one price vector) and Sylvestre (1981) compares different approaches when the price vector is given. Finally, see the book by Negishi (1979).

In the first section of this chapter, we will define a concept of equilibrium based on the two axioms and examine its relations with the notion of competitive Walrasian equilibrium and that of Lindahl equilibrium when there are public goods. In the second section, the basic ideas will be cast in the framework of a process or mechanism. In this perspective, we will try to give a definition of decentralization from the point of view of decision.

1   Concepts and equivalence theorems

We shall consider three points in this section. First, we shall argue in an exchange economy, initially not taking into account the precise way transactions are made. Later, we will consider a simple economy with public goods. Generally, we shall argue from an aggregative point of view, that is, we shall assume that each agent trades with the set of all other agents.

Let us consider an exchange economy with r goods $h=1,\ldots,r$ and m consumers $i=1,\ldots,m$. We note $u_i(x_i)$ the continuous and strictly quasi-concave[3] and increasing utility function of consumer i defined on his convex consumption set $X_i \subset \mathbf{R}^r$. We define $U_i(z_i)=u_i(w_i+z_i)$ where $z_i \equiv x_i - w_i$ ($w_i \in \mathring{X}_i$ is the initial endowment of i).

1.1 *No privileged means of exchange*

When we want to introduce only the requirement that prices are not totally flexible and assume that all goods can be exchanged for all goods, it is simpler to assume that an act is a net trade z. We define then $\bar{B}_i \equiv \{ z_i \in \mathbf{R}^r \mid w_i + z_i \equiv x_i \in X_i \}$. A net trade z_i is possible for i if $z_i \in \bar{B}_i \cdot z = [z_1, \ldots, z_m]$ is balanced if $\sum_i^m z_i = 0$.

Let us note $\bar{\bar{Z}}$ the set of normalized allowable directions of trade in $\mathbf{R}^r$, defined in such a way that Z and $-Z$ are identified. Then the set of allowable trades is $\bar{\bar{Z}} = \{ \bar{\bar{z}} \in \mathbf{R}^r \mid \exists \lambda \in \mathbf{R} \text{ and } \bar{\bar{z}} \in \bar{\bar{Z}} \text{ such that } \bar{\bar{z}} = \lambda \bar{\bar{z}} \}$. We assume that $\bar{\bar{Z}}$ is closed. We also assume essentially that if z^1 and $z^2 \in \bar{\bar{Z}}$ are such that sign $z_h^1 = $ sign z_h^2 for each h then $\mu z^1 + (1-\mu) z^2 \in \bar{\bar{Z}}$ for each $\mu \in [0, 1]$.

Example: Let us assume that P is the set of price vectors such that $p_r = 1$ and $\underline{p}_h \leqslant p_h \leqslant \bar{p}_h$ for $h \neq r$ ($0 \leqslant \underline{p}_h \leqslant \bar{p}_h$). Then $\bar{\bar{Z}} = \{ \bar{\bar{z}} \in \mathbf{R}^r \mid \exists p \in P \text{ such that } p\bar{\bar{z}} = 0 \}$. $\bar{\bar{Z}}$ satisfies the above assumption. Let us take z^1 and $z^2 \in \bar{\bar{Z}}$ with sign $z_h^1 = $ sign z_h^2 for each h.

Then there exist p^1 and $p^2 \in P$ such that $p^1 z^1 = p^2 z^2 = 0$. Let us consider $z^3 = \mu z^1 + (1-\mu) z^2$ where $\mu \in [0, 1]$. We have $\mu p^1 z^1 + (1-\mu) p^2 z^2 \equiv \mu \sum_h p_h^1 z_h^1 + (1-\mu) \sum_h p_h^2 z_h^2 = 0$. Let us define

$$p_h^3 = \left(\frac{\mu z_h^1}{\mu z_h^1 + (1-\mu) z_h^2} \right) p_h^1 + \left(\frac{(1-\mu) z_h^2}{\mu z_h^1 + (1-\mu) z_h^2} \right) p_h^2$$

for $h \neq r$. Then $p^3 \in P$ and $p^3 z^3 = 0$ (Figure 5.2).

A feasible trade $z = [z_1, \ldots, z_m]$ is then balanced, possible for each i, and $z_i \in \bar{\bar{Z}}$ for each i.

In order to construct a notion of optimality, let us first argue in the classical case where all trades are allowable. Let us consider a feasible trade $z^1 = [z_1^1, \ldots, z_m^1]$. One can say that it cannot be improved by an exchange of order k, if for each subset of k agents there is no other feasible trade $z^2 = [z_1^2, \ldots, z_m^2]$ such that $z_i^2 = z_i^1$ for $m - k$ agents and $U_i(z_i^2) > U_i(z_i^1)$ for each i such that $z_i^1 \neq z_i^2$. Thus, a Pareto-optimal trade cannot be improved by an exchange of any order (complete multilateralism is possible). Let us now show that any feasible trade z can be canonically split in pairwise trades, each agent i trading at most with two other agents (see Malinvaud and Younès, 1978).

Let us define:

$$z_{12} = z_1; \qquad z_2 = -z_{12} + z_{23}; \qquad z_3 = -z_{23} + z_{34}; \cdots$$

$$z_{m-1} = -z_{m-2, m-1} + z_{m-1, m} \quad \text{and} \quad z_m = -z_{m-1, m}$$

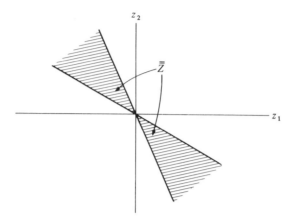

Figure 5.2

It is clear that this construction can be used to define an efficient trade of order k (which cannot be improved by any exchange of order k). We call it the canonical splitting. When $\bar{\bar{Z}}$ is different from $\mathbf{R}^r$, we have only to consider the net trades which belong to $\bar{\bar{Z}}$.

Let us now define what we mean by a myopic voluntary exchange of order $l \geq 1$. For $l = 1$, we shall say that a possible m-uple $z^1 = [z_1^1, \ldots, z_m^1]$ is myopically rational of order 1 if for each i, z_i^1 maximizes $U_i(z)$ in the set $I(z_i^1) = \{z \in \bar{B}_i \mid \lambda_i z_i^1 = z \text{ for } \lambda_i \in [0, 1]\}$.

Definition: A feasible m-uple $z^1 = [z_1^1, \ldots, z_m^1]$ is myopically rational of order l relative to $\bar{\bar{Z}}$ if for each subset of l agents (without loss of generality, we can renumber agents assuming that they are the l first agents) there is no other *possible* and allowable $z^2 = [z_1^2, \ldots, z_m^2]$ with:

1 $z_1^2 = \bar{z}_1^1 + \bar{z}_{12}$ where $\bar{z}_{12} \in \bar{\bar{Z}}$ and $\bar{z}_1^1 \in I(z_1^1)$; $z_2^2 = \bar{z}_2^1 - \bar{z}_{12} + \bar{z}_{23}$ where $\bar{z}_{23} \in \bar{\bar{Z}}$ and $\bar{z}_2^1 \in I(z_2^1), \ldots, z_l^2 = \bar{z}_l^{-1} - z_{l-1,l}$ where $\bar{z}_l^1 \in I(z_l^1)$, and $z_i^2 = \bar{z}_i^1$ for $i > l$
2 For each i, $U_i(z_i^2) \geq U_i(z_i^1)$ with strict inequality for each i such that either $z_i^1 \neq z_i^2$ or $z_i^1 \neq \bar{z}_i^1$

We emphasize that now z^2 is not necessarily balanced and that if z^1 is myopically rational of order l ($\leq m$), is is also myopically rational of order $1 \leq l' < l$. Moreover, if a feasible z^1 is myopically rational of order l, it is efficient of order l.

Before defining a concept that formulates precisely, in some way, our two axioms, we will remark that z^1 is myopically rational of order $l > 1$ if no one has an interest either in breaking a previous contract or in making a new contract after eventually breaking a previous contract.

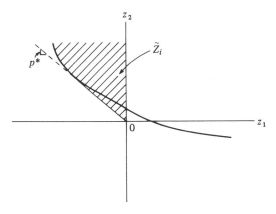

Figure 5.3

Definition: Given $\bar{\bar{Z}}$, an m-uple $z^* = [z_1^*, \ldots, z_m^*]$ is a strong non-cooperative equilibrium (SNCE) of order l relative to $\bar{\bar{Z}}$ iff:

1 z^* is feasible relative to $\bar{\bar{Z}}$.
2 z^* is myopically rational of order l relative to $\bar{\bar{Z}}$.

Remark: For $l=1$, $[0, \ldots, 0]$ is an SNCE for any economy.

We shall now consider only an SNCE of maximal order, m. We notice that an SNCE of order m is a feasible z^* such that there is no balanced and allowable $\tilde{z}$ such that $U_i(\bar{z}_i^* + \tilde{z}_i) \geqslant U_i(z_i^*)$ for any i and strict inequality for any i such that either $\bar{z}_i^* \neq z_i^*$ or $\bar{z}_i^* + \tilde{z}_i \neq z_i^*$ where $\bar{z}_i^* \in I(z_i^*)$ and $\bar{z}_i^* + \tilde{z}_i \in \bar{B}_i$.

Proposition 1.1: Under our assumptions and if $\bar{\bar{Z}} = \mathbf{R}^l$ (all prices are possible a priori), for any economy, there is identity between the set of SNCE and the set of Walrasian competitive equilibria (WCE).

(i) Let us consider a WCE $[p^{**}, z^{**}]$. We shall prove that z^{**} is an SNCE. Clearly z^{**} is myopically rational of order 1. Assume that z^{**} is not myopically rational of order $m > 1$. We could get for each i, $p^* z_i \geqslant 0$ with strict inequality for at least one i. But this is impossible because $\sum_i \tilde{z}_i = 0$.

(ii) Let us consider an SNCE z^*. We shall prove that there exists $p^* \geqslant 0$ such that (p^*, z^*) is a WCE.

We define $\tilde{Z}_i = \{ \tilde{z}_i \in \mathbf{R}^l \mid \exists \lambda_i \in [0, 1]$ such that $U_i(\lambda_i z_i^* + \tilde{z}_i) > U_i(z_i^*)$ and $\lambda_i z_i^* + \tilde{z}_i \in \bar{B}_i \}$ (see Figure 5.3). $\tilde{Z}_i$ is convex and so is $\tilde{\bar{Z}} = \sum_i \tilde{Z}_i$. As z^* is an SNCE, 0 does not belong to $\tilde{\bar{Z}}$. By a separation theorem, there is then p^* such that $p^* \tilde{\bar{z}} \geqslant 0$ for each $\tilde{\bar{z}} \in \tilde{\bar{Z}}$. As $\tilde{\bar{Z}}$ contains the positive cone

$\tilde{Z}_i$ we have that $p^* \geq 0$. But $\sum_i z_i^* = 0$ belongs to the closure of $\tilde{Z}$. Thus, by independence of the sets $\tilde{Z}_i$, this entails that 0 and z_i^* minimizes $p^* \tilde{z}_i$ in $\tilde{Z}_i$. Thus, that $p^* z_i^* = 0$ and that z_i^* minimizes $p^* z_i$ in

$$Z^{z_i} = \{ z_i \in \bar{B}_i \mid U_i(z_i) \geq U_i(z_i^*) \}$$

As $w_i \in \mathring{X}_i$, this entails that (p^*, z^*) is a WCE.

Remark: For any $\tilde{\tilde{Z}}$ satisfying our assumptions, and to any z^* which is an SNCE of order m relative to $\tilde{\tilde{Z}}$, the same kind of proof can be used to show that it is possible to associate $p^* \geq 0$ such that:

(a) For each i, $p^* z_i^* = 0$. This means that all trades are made at the same implicit vector price (law of one price).

(b) For each i, z_i^* minimizes $p^* z_i$ in $\tilde{\tilde{Z}} \cap Z_i^{z_i^*}$ where

$$Z_i^{z_i^*} = \{ z \in \bar{B}_i \mid U_i(z_i) \geq U_i(z_i^*) \}$$

(see Figure 5.4).

1.2   *Restrictions on trades*

Let us now be more precise about the way trades are made. In the following, T is a fixed set of normalized directions in $\mathbf{R}^r$, with $\sum_h^r |t_h| = 1$ and such that t is identified with $-t$. An act for i is a measure a_i with a finite support on T, and results are linked to acts by the following relation:

$$x_h = w_h + \int_T t_h \, da(t) \quad \text{or} \quad x = w + \int_T t \, da(t)$$

The set of possible acts for i is:

$$B_i = \left\{ a \mid w_i + \int_T t \, da(t) \equiv x_i \in X \right\}$$

We define

$$\mathcal{U}_i(a_i) \equiv u_i \left\{ w_i + \int_T t \, da(t) \right\} \quad \text{for} \quad a_i \in B_i$$

An m-uple of acts $a = \{ a_i, \ldots, a_m \}$ is balanced if $\sum_i a_i = 0$. An m-uple of acts $a = \{ a_i, \ldots, a_m \}$ is feasible if it is balanced and for each i, $a_i \in B_i$. In this framework, each agent makes profitable proposals of acts to be matched by other agents, that is, the set of messages is included in the

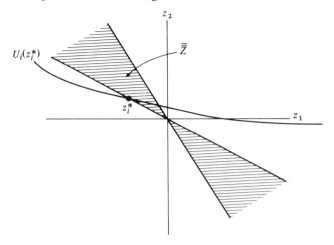

Figure 5.4

power set of acts. But additional proposals are made for each direction separately. Actually, this is in accord with the logic of the formalism, because otherwise we would violate the assumption that T is given. For instance, let us assume that $r=3$ and that the first two goods can only be exchanged separately with the last one. Thus, $T=\{(t_1^1,0,t_3^1); (0,t_2^2,t_3^2)\}$. If we assumed that agent i has the possibility to make a proposal simultaneously for all $t \in T$, this would imply that he can actually directly exchange good 1 with good 2 and thus that T also includes: $t^3=(t_1^3,t_2^3,0)$ with $t_1^3=t_1^1 t_3^2$ and $t_2^3=-t_2^2 t_3^1$.

The formalism leads to a specific notion of optimality. In order to define it, we take into account the way in which transactions are made only *marginally*, that is, for deviations with respect to a feasible $a=[a_1,\ldots,a_m]$.

Let us first define for any a_i^1:

$$I(a_i^1) = \{a_i \in B_i \,|\, \exists \lambda_i : T \to [0,1] \text{ such that } a_i = \lambda_i \cdot a_i^1\}$$

Definition: A feasible m-uple $a^1=[a_1^1,\ldots,a_m^1]$ is efficient of order g ($g \geqslant 1$) relatively to T if for each subset of l agents ($l \leqslant g$) (we take the first l ones), there is no feasible $a^2=[a_1^2,\ldots,a_m^2]$ with $a_i^2=a_i^1$ for $i>l$, such that:

(1) $\mathcal{U}_i(a_i^2) > \mathcal{U}_i(a_i^1)$ for $i=1,\ldots,l$

(2) $a_1^2 = \bar{a}_1^1 + \sum_{\nu}^{n_1} \delta(t_{12}^\nu)$

where $\bar{a}_1^1 \in I(a_1^1)$ and for each ν, $\delta(t_{12}^\nu)$ is a measure concentrated on $t_{12}^\nu \in T$ such that $\bar{a}_1^1 + \delta(t_{12}^\nu)$ is possible and better, for 1, than a_1^1

$$a_2^2 = \bar{a}_2^1 - \sum_\nu^{n_1} \delta(t_{12}^\nu) + \sum_\nu^{n_2} \delta(t_{23}^\nu)$$

where $\bar{a}_2^1 \in I(a_2^1)$ and for each $\delta(t_{23}^\nu)$ is a measure concentrated on t_{23}^ν such that $-\sum_\nu^{n_1} \delta(t_{12}^\nu) + \bar{a}_2^1 + \delta(t_{23}^\nu)$ is possible and better, for 2, than a_2^2

$$a_l^2 = \bar{a}_l^1 - \sum_\nu^{n_{l-1}} \delta(t_{l-1,l}^\nu) \quad \text{with} \quad \bar{a}_l^1 \in I(a_l^1)$$

Remark 1: Thus we take into account the fact that T is given by requiring not only that $\mathcal{U}_i(a_i^2) > \mathcal{U}_i(a_i^1)$ for $i = 1, \ldots, l$, but also that each agent i is interested in making a new proposal separately in each direction.

Remark 2: If T contains all directions in $\mathbf{R}^r$, then by canonical decomposition, a m-uple a^1 that is efficient of order m is Pareto optimal.

The notion of an SNCE relative to T is constructed in the same way.

Definition: A feasible m-uple $a^1 = [a_1^1, \ldots, a_m^1]$ is myopically rational of order l relative to T if for each subset of l agents (we take the first l agents) there is no other set of possible measures

$$[a_1^1, \ldots, a_1^{n_1}; a_2^1, \ldots, a_2^{n_2}; \ldots; a_{l-1}^1, \ldots, a_{l-1}^{n_l-1}; a_l]$$

such that

1. $a_1^\nu = \bar{a}_1^\nu + \delta(t_{12}^\nu)$ where $\bar{a}_1^\nu \in I(a_1^1)$ and $\delta(t_{12}^\nu)$ is a measure concentrated on $t_{12}^\nu \in T$ for $\nu = 1, \ldots, n_1$.

$$a_2^\nu = \bar{a}_2^\nu - \sum_\nu^{n_1} \delta(t_{12}^\nu) + \delta(t_{23}^\nu)$$

where $\bar{a}_2^\nu \in I(a_2^1)$ and $\delta(t_{23}^\nu)$ is a measure concentrated on $t_{23}^\nu \in T$ for $\nu = 1, \ldots, n_2$.

$$\vdots$$
$$a_l = \bar{a}_l - \sum_\nu^{n_{l-1}} \delta(t_{l-1,l}^\nu) \quad \text{with} \quad \bar{a}_l \in I(a_l^1).$$

2. For each $i = 1, \ldots, l$ and each $\nu = 1, \ldots, n_i$: $\mathcal{U}_i(a_i^\nu) \geqslant \mathcal{U}_i(a_i^1)$ with strict inequality if either $a_i^1 \neq \bar{a}_i^\nu$ or $\nexists t_{i-1,i}^\nu$ such that

$$-\delta(t_{i-1,i}^\nu) + \delta(t_{i,i+1}^\nu) = 0.$$

Definition: Given T, a feasible m-uple $a^* = [a_1^*, \ldots, a_m^*]$ is an SNCE of order l relative to T if it is myopically rational of order l relative to T.

Proposition 1.2: If the utility functions u_i are continuous, strictly quasi-concave and increasing, the consumption sets X_i are convex and $w_i \in \mathring{X}_i$ for each i, then for any finite T there is an SNCE of order l for any l with $1 \leqslant l \leqslant m$. For the proof, see for instance Malinvaud and Younès (1977).

For a T not necessarily finite, a convergence argument can be used to prove existence (at least in the case in which T contains only t's with two nonzero entries).

Remark: For $l=1$, $[0, \ldots, 0]$ is an SNCE for any economy. Thus, grossly speaking, an SNCE of order 1 is a kind of noncooperative equilibrium (Nash).

Proposition 1.3: For any exchange economy satisfying the assumptions of the above proposition, there is "identity" between the set of Walrasian competitive equilibria and the set of SNCE of order m relative to T containing all t such that $\sum_h |t_h| = 1$ (t being identified with $-t$). T is Walrasian.

This means that to any Walrasian competitive equilibrium $[x^*, p^*]$, we can associate a SNCE a^* such that for each i: $w_i + \int_T da_i^*(t)t = x_i^*$, and that to any SNCE a^* we can associate (x^*, p^*) which is a WCE with $x_i^* = w_i + \int_T da_i^*(t)t$. First, we note that as $w_i \in \mathring{X}_i$ for each i, a pair (x^*, p^*) such that for each i, x^* minimizes p^*x among the x such that $u_i(x) \geqslant u_i(x_i^*)$ and with $p^*w_i = p^*x_i^*$ (or $pz_i^* = 0$) for each i is a WCE. Second, by the splitting of $z = [z_1, \ldots, z_m]$ with $\sum_i z_i = 0$ in bilateral z_{ij}, we can associate to any z with $\sum_i z_i = 0$ a set of acts $a = [a_i, \ldots, a_m]$ with $\sum_i a_i = 0$ by putting $\delta(t^{ij}) \cdot t^{ij} = z_{ij}$ where $\delta(t^{ij})$ is a measure concentrated on t^{ij}. Third, we note that, when T is Walrasian, an m-uple $a^1 = [a_1^1, \ldots, a_m^1]$ that is efficient of order m is Pareto optimal. Let us define $z_i^1 = \int_T t\, da_i^1(t)$ for each i and let us assume that $z^1 = [z_1^1, \ldots, z_m^1]$ is not Pareto optimal. There is then $z^2 = [z_1^2, \ldots, z_m^2]$ with $\sum_i z_i^2 = 0$ such that $u_i(w_i + z_i^2) > u_i(w_i + z_i^1)$ for each i.

We split z^2 in bilateral trades and we define $\delta(t^{ij})t^{ij} = z_{ij}^2$. By putting $\bar{a}_i^1 = 0 \in I(a_i^1)$ for each i, we get a contradiction.

(i) If a^* is an SNCE, then there exists p^* such that (z^*, p^*) is a competitive equilibrium where $z_i^* = \int_T t\, da_i^*(t)$. As a^* is myopically rational of order m relatively to T, which is Walrasian, for any $z = (z_1, \ldots, z_m)$ with $\sum_i z_i = 0$, we cannot have (by canonical splitting) for any i:

$$\mathfrak{U}_i\left(\int_T t\, da_i^*(t) \right) \leqslant \mathfrak{U}_i\left(\int_T t\, da_i(t) + z_i \right)$$

for any $a_i = \lambda_i a_i^*$, $\int_T t\,da_i(t) + z_i + w_i \in X_i$, with strict inequality for any i such $a_i \neq a_i^*$ or $z_i \neq 0$. Let us note Z^{z_i} the convex sets in $\mathbf{R}^r$ such that $U_i(z_i) > U_i(z_i^*)$, $z_i + w_i \in X_i$ for each i.

Let us define

$$\tilde{Z}_i = \left\{ \tilde{z}_i \in \mathbf{R}^r \mid \exists \lambda_i : T \to [0,1] \text{ such that } a_i = \lambda_i a_i^* \right.$$

$$\left. U_i\left(\int_T t\,da_i(t) + \tilde{z}_i \right) > U_i(z_i^*) \right\}$$

This set is convex and thus $\tilde{Z} = \Sigma_i \tilde{Z}_i$ is convex. By assumption $0 \notin \tilde{Z}$. There is thus $p^* \neq 0$ such that $p^* \tilde{z} \geq 0$ for any $\tilde{z} \in \tilde{Z}$. For each i, z_i^* and 0 belong to the closure of $\tilde{Z}_i$ and by independence we get that 0 and z_i^* minimizes $p^* \cdot z$ in $\tilde{Z}_i$. This entails that z_i^* minimizes $p^* z_i$ in Z^{z_i} and that $p^* z_i^* = 0$.

This also entails that $p^* t = 0$ for any t such that there exists i with[4] $a_i^*(t) \neq 0$.

(ii) Let us consider a WCE (p^*, z^*). By canonical splitting we associate an SNCE a^* with[5] $z_i^* = \int_T t\,da_i^*(t)$ and $p^* t = 0$ for any t such that there exists i with $a_i^*(t) \neq 0$. Clearly a^* is myopically rational of order 1. Assume that a^* is not myopically rational of order $m > 1$. We would get for each i, $p^* z_i \geq 0$ with strict inequality for at least one i. But this is impossible because $\Sigma_i z_i = 0$.

Definition: Given an SNCE $a^* = [a_1^*, \ldots, a_m^*]$ of order m relative to T, we shall say that agent l is rationed at t^1 if there is a subset (eventually empty) of the set of agents (we take the first $(l-1)$ agents) and a set of possible measures $[a_1^1, \ldots, a_1^{n_1}; \ldots; a_{l-1}^1, \ldots, a_{l-1}^{n_{l-1}}]$, such that

1. $a_1^\nu = \bar{a}_1^\nu + \delta(t_{12}^\nu)$ where $\bar{a}_1^\nu \in I(a_1^*)$ and $\delta(t_{12}^\nu)$ is a measure concentrated on $t_{12}^\nu \in T$ for $\nu = 1, \ldots, n_1$

$$\vdots$$

$$a_{l-1}^\nu = \bar{a}_{l-1}^\nu - \sum_\nu^{n_{l-2}} \delta(t_{l-2,l-1}^\nu) + \delta(t_{l-1,l}^\nu)$$

where $\bar{a}_{l-1}^\nu \in I(a_{l-1}^*)$ and $\delta(t_{l-1,l}^\nu)$ is a measure concentrated on $t_{l-1,l}^\nu \in T$ for $\nu = 1, \ldots, n_{l-1}$

$$a_l = \bar{a}_l - \sum_\nu^{n_{l-1}} \delta(t_{l-1,l}^\nu) + \delta(t^1)$$

where $\bar{a}_l \in I(a_l^*)$ and $\delta(t^1)$ is a nonzero measure concentrated on $\delta(t^1)$

(with sign $\delta(t^1) = \text{sign } a_i^*(t^1)$ because a_i^* is myopically rational of order 1).

2. For $i = 1, \ldots, l-1$ and each $\nu = 1, \ldots, n_i$: $\mathfrak{U}_i(a_i^\nu) \geqslant \mathfrak{U}_i(a_i^1)$ with strict inequality if either $a_i^1 \neq a_i^\nu$ or $\exists t_{i-1,i}$ such that $-\delta(t_{i-1,i}^\nu) + (t_{i,i+1}^\nu) = 0$. Moreover $\mathfrak{U}(a_l) > \mathfrak{U}(a_l^*)$.

Remark: Let us consider an SNCE a^* relative to a Walrasian T. Then for each $t \in T$ such that $p^* \cdot t \neq 0$, there exists an agent i who is rationed at t. This kind of stability condition is sometimes used in problems of adverse selection with asymmetrical information.

Definition: We shall say that T defines a pure monetary economy if there is one good (let us say good r) such that any $t \in T$ contains only two nonzero entries among which is the last one. Let us note T_h (for $h \neq r$) the set of t's for which the hth entry is nonzero. For a pure monetary economy for each $h \neq r$, $T_h \neq \emptyset$. We shall normalize each t by putting $t_h = 1$ for each $t \in T^h$, $\forall h$. It is then possible to assimilate p_h to the $t \in T_h$ such that $t \cdot p = 0$ and write $p_h \in T_h$.

In our language, this is the setup used by Drèze (1975). He requires that for each $t \in T_h$, $t_r = -p_h$ where $p_h \in [\underline{p}_h, \bar{p}_h]$. He assumes a priori that at an equilibrium allocation z^1, all agents have to trade at the same p_h for each h, and that $p_h = \bar{p}_h$ if there is a buyer of good h who would like to buy more at z_i^1 (he is rationed for good h), and that $p_h = \bar{p}_h$ if there is seller of good h who is rationed for good h at z_i^1.

By using an argument similar to that of Proposition 1.3, it is possible to get the same result without assuming that, a priori, all agents trade at the same price vector.

More precisely, to any SNCE $a^* = [a_1^*, \ldots, a_m^*]$ of order m relative to a T, which defines a pure monetary economy with $p_h \in [\underline{p}_h, \bar{p}_h]$ for any $h \neq r$, we can associate $p^* \geqslant 0$ such that

(i) $p^* t = 0$ for any $t \in T$ such that there is i with $a_i^*(t) \neq 0$ (law of one price).

(ii) If an agent i is rationed at $p_h^* \in T_h$ with $\delta(p_h^*) > 0$ (he would like to buy more), then $p_h^* \geqslant p_h$ for any $p_h \in T_h$. Conversely, if there is an agent i who is rationed at $p_h^* \in T_h$ with $\delta(p_h^*) < 0$ (he would like to sell more) then $p_h^* \leqslant p_h$ for any $p_h \leqslant T_h$.

Note that the assumption that each p_h can vary on an interval (a convex set) is essential not only formally for separating some set from 0 in $\mathbf{R}^l$ but also fundamentally. Assume an economy with three consumers and two goods (the last one being called money) for which only two prices p^1 and p^2 $(p^2 > p^1)$ are available. Then it is possible to choose utility functions and endowments such that there is an SNCE implying that consumer 1 buys at p^1 and consumer 2 buys at p^2 from consumer 3. This is not possible if all prices between p^1 and p^2 are allowable, because consumer 3 would make a sale proposal at a price p^3 with $p^1 < p^3 < p^2$ (eventually reducing his trade at p^1), a proposal matched by a proposal from agent 2 (eventually reducing his trade at p^2).

1.3   Public goods

Now, we would like to show in a framework slightly different from the one used by Champsaur (1979) that there is identity between the set of Lindahl equilibria (LE) and the set of SNCE, for economies with public goods. We shall define a public good as a good which can be consumed at the level $x_i \leqslant x$ by every consumer i if quantity x is available. In order to simplify, we shall assume $x_i = x \, \forall i$. We shall assume that there are two goods in the economy: good 1, which is a public good, and good 2, which is a private good. There is a zero quantity of public good which is initially available. w_i is the vector of initial allocations of consumer i $(i = 1, \ldots, m)$. There is one firm (agent 0) which transforms private good into public good according to a linear production function. It costs $1/b$ units of private good to produce one unit of public good.

We treat the firm in the same way as consumers. Its initial allocation is $(0, 0)$ and it tries to maximize its quantity of private good which is not used to produce public good. Thus $U_o(z_o) = z_{o2} + (1/b)z_{o1}$. This supposes that $z_{o2} \geqslant 0$ and $z_{o1} \leqslant 0$.

We define:

$$B_i = \{ z_i \in \mathbf{R}^2 \, | \, z_i + w_i \geqslant 0 \} \quad \text{for} \quad i = 1,, \ldots, m$$

$$B_o = \{ z_o \in \mathbf{R}^2 \, | \, z_{o2} + (1/b)z_{o1} \geqslant 0 \}$$

We assume that profits in good 2 are not distributed. Because at equilibrium profits are zero, this is not a bad assumption.

A trade $z = [z_0, z_1, \ldots, z_m]$ is feasible if it is possible: $z_i \in B_i$, $i = 0, \ldots, m$ and balanced $z_{i1} + z_{01} = 0$ for $i = 1, \ldots, m$ and $\sum_0^m z_{i2} = 0$.

Definition: An $m+1$-uple $z^* = [z_1^*, \ldots, z_m^*]$ is an SNCE for this economy if:

(i) It is feasible.

(ii) It is myopically rational of order $m+1$, that is, there is no balanced $\bar{z} = [\bar{z}_0, \ldots, \bar{z}_m]$ such that for each i: $\exists \lambda_i \in [0, 1]$ with $\lambda_i z_i^* + \bar{z}_i \in B_i$ and $U_i(\lambda_i z_i^* + \bar{z}_i) \geqslant U_i(z_i^*)$ with strict inequality for any i such that either $\bar{z}_i \neq 0$ or $\lambda_i \neq 1$.

Remark: This formulation does not seem well suited for an economy with public goods. But the profound reason for this feeling is that we argue in an aggregative frame in which each agent trades with the set of all other agents. The disaggregative version would be the following if we know that each consumer i $(i=1,\ldots,m)$ trades only with the firm in this simple model.

First define an act of the firm: It is $z_{0.}=[z_0^1,\ldots,z_0^m]$ where z_0^i is the trade between 0 and $i\neq 0$. Moreover, $B_{0.}=\{z_{0.}\in\mathbf{R}^{2m}\mid\Sigma_{j=1}^2 z_{02}^j=z_{02}$ and $\forall j:-z_{01}^j\leqslant-z_{01};\ (z_{01},z_{02})\in B_0\}$

Definition: $z_.^*=[z_{0.}^*,z_{1.}^*,\ldots,z_{m.}^*]$ is an SNCE if:

(i) It is feasible, that is, $z_{0.}^*\in B_{0.}$; $z_i^*\in B_i$, $i=1,\ldots,m$ and $z_0^{*i}=-z_i^*$ for $i=1,\ldots,m$.

(ii) There is no $\tilde{z}$ such that $\tilde{z}_0^i=-\tilde{z}_i$ for $i=1,\ldots,m$ and $\forall i\neq 0$: $\lambda_i z_i^*+\tilde{z}_i\in B_i$, $U_i(\lambda_i z_i^*+\tilde{z}_i)\geqslant U_i(z_i^*)$; with strict inequality if $\lambda_i\neq 0$ or $\tilde{z}_1\neq 0$.

$$[\lambda_0^1 z_0^{*1}+\tilde{z}_0^1,\ldots,\lambda_0^m z_0^{*m}+\tilde{z}_0^m]\in B_0$$

where $\lambda_0^i\in[0,1]$ and

$$\sum_{i=1}^m[\lambda_0^1 z_{02}^{*i}+\tilde{z}_{02}^i]+\frac{1}{b}\min\{\lambda_0^i z_{01}^{*i}+\tilde{z}_{01}^i\}\geqslant\sum_{i=1}^m z_{02}^{*i}+\frac{1}{b}z_{01}^*$$

with strict inequality if either $\lambda_0^i\neq 0$ for some i or $\tilde{z}_0^i\neq 0$ for some i.

Clearly, if $z_.^*$ is an SNCE, we have $z_{01}^{*i}=z_{01}^*$ $\forall i\neq 0$. Let us now return to the aggregation version.

Definition: A couple $[z^*,p^*]$ is a Lindahl equilibrium where $p^*=[p_{i1}^*,\ldots,p_{m1}^*;p_2^*]$ and $z^*=[z_1^*;z_{02}^*,\ldots,z_{m2}^*]$ if:

(i) it is feasible.

(ii) $z_i^*=[z_1^*,z_{i2}^*]$ minimizes $[p_{i1}^*,p_2^*]z_i$ in $B_i\cap\{z\mid U_i(z)\geqslant U_i(z_i^*)\}$ for $i=1,\ldots,m$.

(iii) $\Sigma_{i=1}^m(p_{i1}^*)/p_2^*=1/b$.

Proposition 1.4: If for $i=1,\ldots,m$, we have $w_{i2}>0$ and U_i is continuous, strictly quasi-concave, and increasing, then z^* is an SNCE of order $m+1$ if and only if $\exists p^*$ such that $[z^*,p^*]$ is an LE.

We consider, for each i, the following convex set in $\mathbf{R}^2$

$$\tilde{Z}_i=\{\tilde{z}_i=[\tilde{z}_{i1},\tilde{z}_{i2}]\mid\exists\lambda_i\in[0,1]\quad\text{such that}$$
$$U_i[\lambda_i z_i^*+\tilde{z}_i]>U_i(z_i^*)\quad\text{and}\quad\lambda_i z_i^*+\tilde{z}_i\in B_i\}$$

We consider in $\mathbf{R}^{m+1}$ the following set.

$$\tilde{Z} = \{\tilde{z} \in \mathbf{R}^{m+1} \mid \tilde{z}_{i1} = \tilde{z}_{i1} + \tilde{z}_{01} \quad \text{for} \quad i = 1, \ldots, m \quad \text{and}$$

$$\tilde{z}_2 = \sum_{i=0}^{i=m} \tilde{z}_{i2} \quad \text{for} \quad \tilde{z}_i \in \tilde{Z}_i\}$$

This is a convex set. By assumption, $0 \notin \tilde{Z}$. There then exists $p^* = [p_1^*, \ldots, p_{m1}^*; p_2^*]$ such that $p^*\tilde{z} \geq 0$ for each $\tilde{z} \in \tilde{Z}$. The argument is then the same as for Proposition 1.1.

Thus, when all directions of trade are possible, the same agents' behavior results that in the case with private goods, agents exchange at only one price and in the case with public goods agents exchange at different prices. This is due to the way in which we formulate agents' trade proposals, under the name of myopically rational behavior. Assume three consumers and two goods in an exchange economy. Let us consider a state of the economy for which agent 1 buys good 1 from agents 2 and 3, but that he buys at an implicit price higher from agent 3. Agent 1 will always make proposals to trade at an intermediate price in order to decrease his trade at the higher price (private good), and agent 2 will agree to sell good 1 at a price that is higher. If all prices are possible, this process will continue until agents exchange at only one price for private goods, because a quantity of private goods that is used for a trade cannot be used for another trade. This is not the case for a public good sold by a firm, and the same behavior does not lead to the law of one price. All this seems rational, and one does not yet understand the term "myopically." Actually, this behavior is myopic and is more fully rational only in large economies in which each agent is small and has many competitors. This is so because agents in making new trade proposals do not take into account the fact that if other agents match them, they may very well break their previous contracts. This is not the case, for instance, in an exchange economy with two goods, the first one initially owned by one agent (the monopolist) and the second one distributed among many small agents. Let us consider the classical monopoly situation in this example. The monopolist will not act myopically and will not make new trade proposals at a smaller price because he knows that small agents would then break some contracts at the previous higher price. See Figure 5.5 for an example of this idea: an Edgeworth box with two consumers and two goods.

w is the point of initial endowment, wO_{II} is the competitive offer-demand curve of consumer II. All points right of wO_{II} are not myopically rational (of order 1) from the point of view of consumer II. Curves I–I′ and II–II′ are the indifference curves through x. Actually x is an

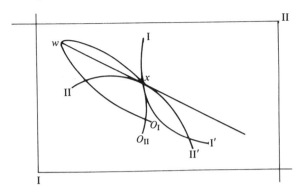

Figure 5.5

equilibrium point for a monopoly situation in which consumer I would act as a monopolist. But the trade $z_1 = x_1 - w_1$ and $z_2 = x_2 - w_2$ is not an SNCE. Let us assume that acts are net trades. There is a trade z^1 that ameliorates simultaneously the situation of agents 1 and 2. Note, however, that agent 1 will lose ultimately because such a trade is necessarily on the right of wO_{II} and thus not myopically rational of order 1 for agent 2 and ultimately agent 1 will be on the left of curve I-I'. One might say that the messages are such that agent 1 does not know this. In any case, to make things clearer, it is better to argue on a basis of a decentralized mechanism the set of equilibria of which coincides with the set of SNCE. In the next section, we shall define a concrete decentralized process directly inspired from the above ideas.

2   Decentralized processes

In this section, we would like first to discuss what one could mean by decentralization in allocation processes or mechanisms.

2.1   *Decentralization of decision*

In order to introduce definitions, let us write down some intuitive ideas about the concepts of market and decentralization.

At the roots of the notion of market (in a capitalist as well as in a planned economy) there is the notion of contract, taken from the legal point of view. It is possible to class the terms of any contract in four groups:

the names of the agents who participate to the contract (in general two agents)
the quality and the quantity of each good exchanged according to the contract

the relative price of these goods
the date and location at which these goods have to be delivered.

In this perspective, there is strictly no market element in a planned economy if the Central Planning Bureau determines all the terms of the contracts between any two economic units. For instance, in the Soviet Union before the reforms even the names of the co-contractors of each big firm were determined by the economic hierarchy above the firm. Thus the extent of the market is large if no term of an eventual contract between any couple of economic units if fixed by one privileged unit or a group of privileged units.

This point of view leads us, naturally, to some idea of decentralization. We may mean two different things by decentralization. First, we refer to "cospecialization of initial information and decision" (Radner). In this perspective, on the one hand it is possible to pair the decisions agent i has to make and this information about his set of possible decisions and his objective function, given the action of other agents; on the other hand, agent i is the only agent to have this information. Thus, initially, information is not centralized. Second, we mean that there is no center at the level of the working of the system. This means on the one hand that there is no privileged unit such that all information transfers are made between this privileged unit and each other unit of the periphery (that there is no information exchange between the units of the periphery); on the other hand, that there is no privileged unit that determines the contractual relationships between the units of the periphery given the messages of others (market).

We should now try to formulate precisely these ideas in the framework of a typical process or mechanism. Clearly, in order to do this we would have to devise a framework in which the messages between each pair of agents can be pictured, along with acts involving each pair of agents (contracts). That is, we should reason in a disaggregative frame. In this section, however, our objective is limited. We want only to show one consequence of some requirements of decentralization of decision. Thus, it would not be damaging to reason in an aggregative framework.

As usual, in order to define an allocation process or a mechanism, we have to define the underlying economy.

There are m agents $i=1, \ldots, m$ whose finite set of indices is I. Each agent i is defined by some characteristics $c_i \in C$. For each c, there is a possible set of results $X(c)$. For each c, there is an objective function $u(c): X(c) \to \mathbf{R}$. A result $x = (x_1, \ldots, x_m)$ is possible if $x_i \in X(c_i)$ for each i. A result $x = (x_1, \ldots, x_m)$ is balanced if $F(c_1, \ldots, c_m, x) = 0 \in \mathbf{R}^r$.

We assume that $X(c): C \to \mathbf{R}^r$. A result x is feasible if it is possible and balanced.

Let us assume that there is cospecialization of action and initial information. Given a class or set of economies, we define as usually an informationally decentralized mechanism for this class.[6] For each economy, it is a 5-uple $\{A, M, g, f_I, \psi_I\}$ where:

A is the set of acts α. $g: A \rightarrow \mathbf{R}^r$ is a function that associates to each $\alpha \in A$ a result x.[7] Thus, given an economy $[I, \mathcal{E}]$ an I-uple of acts $[\alpha_1, \ldots, \alpha_m]$ is possible if for each i: $g(\alpha_i) \in X(c_i)$ and it is balanced if $F[c_1, \ldots, c_m;$ $g(\alpha_1), \ldots, g(\alpha_m)] = 0$. We assume that A is a subset of a vector space containing its 0 and that it would be equivalent to write for a balanced I-uple of acts that $\sum_{i \in I} \alpha_i = 0_A$.

M is the space of messages μ for each $i \in I (\forall I)$.

Given I, f_I is the response function which associates to each $[c_i, \mu_{)i(}]$ a message μ (where $\mu_{)i(} = [\mu_1, \ldots, \mu_{i-1}, \mu_{i+1}, \ldots, \mu_m]$). If $\mu_i = f_I(c_i, \mu_{)i(})$, then $\mu_i = f_I(c_i, \mu'_{)i(})$ where $\mu'_{)i(}$ is a permutation of c_i.

Given I, ψ_I is the outcome application with associates to each $[\mu_1, \ldots, \mu_m]$ a nonempty set of $[\alpha_1, \ldots, \alpha_m]$. Assume that $[\alpha_1, \ldots, \alpha_m] \in \psi_I[\mu_1, \ldots, \mu_m]$. If $[\mu_1, \ldots, \mu_m]'$ is a permutation of $[\mu_1, \ldots, \mu_m]$, then $[\alpha_1, \ldots, \alpha_m]' \in \psi_I([\mu_1, \ldots, \mu_m]')$ where $[\alpha_1, \ldots, \alpha_m]'$ is the result of the same permutation. We make the following fundamental assumption for any $c \in C$, $0_A \in \{\alpha \in A \mid g(\alpha) \in X(c)\}$.

This means that any agent (whatever his characteristics) always has the possibility of not participating in the economy; If he chooses act 0, the set of feasible acts remaining for the other agents is the same as if he did not exist.

Moreover, we define $U(c, \alpha) \equiv u[c, g(\alpha)]$ when $g(\alpha) \in X(c)$.

Definition: A mechanism is concrete if (a) $M \subset \mathcal{P}(A)$ the set of subsets of A; (b) for each I, $\psi_I(\mu_1, \ldots, \mu_m)$ is such that for each $i \in I$, $\alpha_i \in \mu_i$. This definition is derived with modification, from a definition of Hurwicz (1959).

Definition: A mechanism is semi-concrete if (a) each μ is a couple $[\hat{\mu}, \hat{\hat{\mu}}]$ where $\hat{\mu} \in P(A)$; (b) for each I, $\psi_I(\mu, \ldots, \mu_m)$ is such that for each i: $\alpha_i \in \hat{\mu}_i$.

Definition: A mechanism is balanced if for each I:

$$\sum_{i \in I} \alpha_i = 0 \quad \text{for} \quad \alpha \in \psi_I(\mu, \ldots, \mu_m) \quad \forall(\mu, \ldots, \mu_m)$$

At this point, we shall be interested only in feasible mechanisms. Given an informationally decentralized mechanism, we would like to define simply a minimal requirement for calling it decentralized from the point of view of decision. As a first step, it would be legitimate to concentrate on the triple outcome function – space of messages – space of acts – and try to define a requirement for potentially decisionally decentralized mechanisms (assuming that the response function is the result of some rational behavior).

Let us first tackle the particular case of a semi-concrete balanced mechanism. Intuitively, we can think of the acts of i as contracts with the rest of the economy[8] and messages as constituted partly of contract proposals, and thus such a process is decisionally decentralized if the space of contract proposals is not too small, and is rich enough.

Definition: A process is (potentially) totally decentralized if: (a) for each $c \in C$: for any $x \in X(c)$, there is α such that $x = g(\alpha)$; (b) its associated semi-concrete process is such that $\hat{\mu}$ is any subset of $\mathcal{P}(A)$ containing 0. Let us consider an informationally decentralized process $\{A, M, g, f_I, \psi_I\}$. We shall argue for a fixed I; we can restrict ourselves to $M(I)$ where $M(I) = M$.

Then we define

$$A_I^i(\bar{\mu}) = \{\alpha \in A \mid \alpha \in \psi^i(\bar{\mu}_i, \mu_{I-\{i\}}) \quad \text{for some} \quad \mu_{I-\{i\}}\}$$

$A_I^i(\bar{\mu})$ is thus a function from $M(I)$ into $\mathcal{P}(A)$. We define $\tilde{M}(I) = \{[\mu, A_I^i(\mu)] \mid \mu \in M(I)\}$. The function $A_I(\mu)$ which associates to each $\mu \in M(I)$ the couple $[\mu, A_I^i(\mu)]$ is thus a bijection: $M(I) \to \tilde{M}(I)$. Given I, we then define the semi-concrete process $[A, \tilde{M}(I), g, \tilde{f}_I, \tilde{\psi}_I]$.

$$\tilde{f}_I(\tilde{\mu}, \ldots, \tilde{\mu}_{i-1}, \tilde{\mu}_{i+1}, \ldots, \tilde{\mu}_m, c)$$
$$= A_I \circ f_I(A_I^{-1}(\tilde{\mu}_1), \ldots, A_I^{-1}(\mu_{i-1}), A_I^{-1}(\mu_{i+1}), \ldots, A_I^{-1}(\tilde{\mu}_m), c)$$

$$\text{and} \quad \tilde{\psi}_I(\tilde{\mu}_1, \ldots, \tilde{\mu}_m) = \psi_I[A_I^{-1}(\tilde{\mu}_1), \ldots, A_I^{-1}(\tilde{\mu}_m)]$$

Then, we say that $\{A, M, g, f_I, \psi_I\}$ is decisionally decentralized if for each I its isomorphic semi-concrete process is also decentralized from the point of view of decision.

Remark: Obviously, along this line of thought, we can choose other definitions. A weaker requirement for a decisionally decentralized process would be that the outcome function is individually rational in the sense that for each c_i: for each $\mu_{)i(}$, there is μ_i such that

$$\inf_{a_i \in \psi^i[\mu_i, \mu_{)i(}]} U_i \; [a_i] \geq U_i(0).$$

Alternatively, for each $\mu_{)i(}$, there is μ_i such that $\psi^i[\mu_i, \mu_{)i(}] = \{0\}$, or $\{0\}$ belongs to the projection of $\mathcal{P}(A)$ on M.

We shall say that a set of acts $A^1 \subset A$ is better for i than a set $A^2 \subset A$ if for each $a^1 \in A^1$, we have $U_i(a^1) \geq U_i(a^2)$ for any $a^2 \in A^2$ and if either there is a point $\bar{a} \in A^1$ such that $U_i(\bar{a}) > U_i(a^2)$ for any $a^2 \in A^2$ or there is a point $\bar{\bar{a}}$ in A^2 such that $U_i(\bar{\bar{a}}) < U_i(a^1)$ for any $a^1 \in A^1$.

Definition: For each I, $\mu_i = f(c_i; \mu_{)i(})$ is Nash if for each c_i and each $\mu_{)i(}$ there is no other μ_i^1 such that $\psi(\mu_{)i(}, \mu_i^1)$ is better for i than $\psi(\mu_{)i(}, \mu_i)$.

In order to define an equilibrium of a process, we reason usually in the space of messages.

Definition: $\mu^* = [\mu_1^*, \dots, \mu_m^*]$ is an equilibrium of the process $[A, M, g, f_I, \psi_I]$ played for I if for each $i \in I$

$$\mu_i^* = f[c_i; \mu_{)i(}^*]$$

We would like to give a weaker definition in the space of acts.

Definition: $A^* = [A_1^*, \dots, A_m^*]$ where $A_i^* \subset A$ for each i is a weak equilibrium of the process if there exists $\mu^0 = [\mu_1^0, \dots, \mu_m^0]$ such that

1 $A^* = \psi(\mu^0)$.
2 For each $t = 1, 2, \dots, A^* = \psi(\mu^t)$ where μ^t is defined recursively from μ^{t-1} by $\mu_i^t = f(c_i; \mu_{)i(}^{t-1})$.

Remarks: A process has a response function which is Nash if and only if its trivially isomorphic semi-concrete process has a response function which is Nash. $[\mu_1^*, \dots, \mu_m^*]$ is an equilibrium of a process if and only if $[A_I(\mu_1^*), \dots, A_I(\mu_m^*)]$ is an equilibrium of its associated semi-concrete process. A process is balanced if and only if its associated semi-concrete process is.

These definitions imply that for a balanced semi-concrete decentralized process, the response function of which is Nash, $[(\{0\}, \hat{\mu}), \dots, (\{0\}, \hat{\mu})]$ is an equilibrium for any I. Thus, any balanced decentralized process the response function of which is Nash has an equilibrium, the only result of which is no participation for any agent. The consequence is the following: If we want to devise decentralized (in our sense) processes (concrete or not) the set of equilibria of which is not unusual, we have to give to the agents a less conservative (myopic) behavior than that implied by Nash. That is, we either have to give them the possibility of detecting further opportunities of trade, or we need to introduce some further degree of "cooperation".

In this perspective, we slightly extend the concept of Nash response function, without requiring that it should be strong.

Definition: A response function is (short-term) quasi-rational if for any c_i and $\mu_{)i(}$, $\mu_i = f(c_i, \mu_{)i(})$ is such that there is no μ_i^1 such that

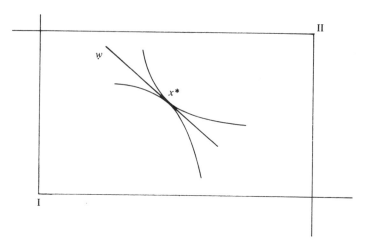

Figure 5.6

either $\psi(\mu_{)i(}, \mu_i^1)$ is better than $\psi(\mu_{)i(}, \mu_i)$ for i;
or $\psi(\mu_{)i(}, \mu_i) = \psi(\mu_{)i(}, \mu_i^1)$ and for each $\mu_{)i(}^2$, $\psi(\mu_{)i(}^2, \mu_i^1)$ is either equal to or
  better than $\psi(\mu_{)i(}^2, \mu_i)$.

With this definition, a quasi-rational totally decentralized process does not necessarily imply that $[\{0\}, \ldots, \{0\}]$ is always an equilibrium.

There is no (potentially) totally decentralized process the response function of which is quasi-rational and which gives as equilibria exactly the set of WCE, for any I, however.

Consider an exchange economy with two agents and two goods (see Figure 5.6). Consider a point x^* which is a Pareto optimum and individually rational but not a WCE. Assume that agent 2 chooses a menage μ such that $\tilde{\mu}$ is the set of acts which give 0 or which imply a set of allocations which give a utility equal to or better than x^*. The response of agent 1 necessarily implies that he proposes 0 and a subset of the set of x which implies a utility level at least equal to x^*. Because this is the same for agent 2, we see that x^* is an equilibrium in the weak sense.

It is possible to construct an example along the same lines with three agents and three goods.

It is then possible to ask for a weaker requirement. A process would be (potentially) decentralized if for each c_i, and each $\mu_i \in M$, there is μ_i^1 such that

$$\psi(\mu_{)i(}; \mu_i^1) = \psi(\mu_{)i(}; \mu_i) \cap \{\alpha \mid U_i(\alpha) \geq U_i(0)\}$$

In this perspective, there is no loss of generality in assuming that each agent i, in order to protect himself, will choose only messages μ such that for any $\mu_{)i(}$, $\psi(\mu_{)i(}, \mu)$ contains only acts at least as useful as 0.

The so-called competitive process and the mechanism we shall propose, which is actually a simple extension of the competitive process in order to take into account the possibility of rationing due to the lack of flexibility of prices, are decentralized in the above sense. But in a finite economy, their response functions are not quasi-rational. A conjecture then is that there is no decentralized and quasi-rational process of which the set of equilibria coincides with the set of WCE.

2.2   *A concrete decentralized mechanism*

We would now like to present a concrete decentralized mechanism (SNCP) the set of equilibria of which is identical with the set of SNCE of order m. We shall reason in an exchange economy and choose net trades as acts. In order to allow direct comparison with other processes, we shall stress on the aggregative version of it.

Let us begin with the disaggregative version. In the following, we shall use the term myopically rational for myopically rational of order 1, and in order to simplify notation we shall assume that all directions are possible.

Let us recall that we define:

$$B_i = \{z_i \in \mathbf{R}^r \mid z_i + w_i \in X_i\} \quad \text{for} \quad i = 1, \ldots, m$$

and

$$B_{i.} = \{z_{i.} = [z_{i1}, \ldots, z_{im}] \mid z_i \in B_i\}$$

We note $Z_t^{j.}$ the message of j and $Z_{t+1}^{i.}$ the message of i, in response to messages of agents $j \neq i$.

$Z_{t+1}^{i.} = \{z_{i.} \in B_{i.} \mid$ there is $z_{i.}^1 \in B_{i.}$, which is myopically rational and one $j_1 \neq i : U_i(\sum_j z_{ij}^1) \geqslant U_i(\sum_j \bar{z}_{ij})$ for any $\bar{z}_{i.} \in \bar{Z}_t^{i.}$ and $-z_{ij}^1$ is the ith element of $z_{j.} \in Z_t^{j.}$ for $j \neq j_1$ such that $z_{i.} = \lambda_{i.} z_{i.}^1\}$ where $\bar{Z}_t^{i.} = \{z_{i.} \in B_{i.} \mid -z_{ij}$ is the jth element of some $z_{j.} \in Z_t^{j.}$ for each $j \neq i\}$ and $\lambda_{ij} \in [0, 1]$.

We now have to define the outcome function that associates to each m-uple of sets of proposals a set of plans:

$$Y_t^i = \psi(Z_t^{1.}, \ldots, Z_t^{m.}) \equiv Y^i(Z_t)$$

Given the fact that we describe the nonaggregative version of the SNCP, we have two possibilities. We can assume that each agent i considers that he is free to choose any contract in the set of proposals sent to him by j, without regard to the other contracts made by j with other agents. Then, in a sense, the outcome function would be strictly decentralized; but, at least outside equilibrium, the result would not be possible for each j (though balanced). Alternatively, we can assume that given the messages, the relationships between agents are rich enough for warranting that each for each i, $z_{i.} \in Z_t^{i.}$ is treated as a totality. Then the result would be not only balanced, but also always possible. We shall describe the last possibility in more detail.

Definition: The set of plans Y_t^i associated with $Z_t = [z_t^{1.}, \ldots, z_t^{m.}]$ is defined by $Y_t = \psi(Z_t) \equiv Y'(Z_t)$ where $Y'(Z_t) = \{y_. = [y_{1.}, \ldots, y_m] \mid y_{i.} \in Z_t^{i.};$ $y_{ij} = -y_{ji} \forall i$ and j and there is no $z_.^1$ with $z_{i.}^1 \in Z_t^{i.}$, $z_{ij}^1 = -z_{ij}^1 \forall i$ and j such that $z_{ij}^1 = \lambda_{ij} y_{ij}$, where $\lambda_{ij} \geqslant 1$ for each (i,j) with strict inequality for at least one $(i,j)\}$.

Definition: An equilibrium of the SNC process is a 3-uple $[Z^{*.}, \bar{Z}^{*.}, Y^{*.}]$ such that:

1. For each i: $Z^{*i.} = \{z_{i.} \in B_{i.} \mid$ there is $z_i^1 \in B_{i.}$, which is myopically rational and one $j_1 \neq i$: $U_i(\sum_j z_{ij}^1) \geqslant U_i(\sum_j \bar{z}_{ij})$ for any $\bar{z}_{i.} \in \bar{Z}^{*i.}$ and $-z_{ij}^1$ is the ith element of $z_{j.} \in Z^{*j.}$ for $j \neq j_1$ such that $z_{i.} = \lambda_{i.} z_{i.}^1\}$ where $\bar{Z}^{*i.} = \{z_{i.} \in B_{i.} \mid -z_{ij}$ is the ith element of some $z_{j.} \in Z^{*j.}$ for each $j \neq i\}$
   2. $Y^{*.} = \psi(Z^{*1.}, \ldots, Z^{*m.})\}$

Let us now describe the aggregative version: $Z_{t+1}^i = \{z_i \in B_i \mid$ there is $z_i^1 \in B_i$, which is myopically rational with $U_i(z_i^1) \geqslant U_i(\bar{z}_i)$ for any $\bar{z}_i \in \bar{Z}_t^i$ and $z_i = \lambda z_i^1$, $\lambda \in (0,1)\}$. $\bar{Z}_t^i = \{z_i \in B_i \mid z_i = -\sum_{j \neq i} z_j,$ where $z_j \in Z_t^j, j \neq i\}$. $Y_t = \psi(Z_t)$, where $Z_t = [Z_t^1, \ldots, Z_t^m]$, is defined as $Y_t = \{y = [y_1, \ldots, y_m] \mid y_i \in Z_t^i$ and $\sum_i y_i = 0$ and there is no z^1 with $z_i^1 \in Z_t^i$, $\sum_i z_i^1 = 0$, $z_i^1 = \lambda_i y_i$ with $\lambda_i \geqslant 1$ for each i and strict inequality for at least one $i\}$.

Definition: An equilibrium of the aggregative version of the SNCP is a 3-uple: $[Z^*, \bar{Z}^*, Y^*]$ such that:

1. For each i: $Z^{*i} = \{z_i \in B_i \mid$ there is $z_i^1 \in B_i$ which is myopically rational with $U_i(z_i^1) \geqslant U_i(\bar{z}_i)$ for any $\bar{z}_i \in \bar{Z}^{*i}$ and $z_i = \lambda z_i^1$, $\lambda \in [0,1]\}$, where $\bar{Z}^{*i} = \{z_i \in B_i \mid z_i = -\sum_{j \neq i} z_j$ with $z_j \in Z^{*j}, j \neq i\}$.
   2. $Y^* = \psi(Z^*)$.

Proposition 2: There is identity between the set of equilibria of the aggregative SNCP and the set of SNCE of order m for any exchange economy which satisfies the assumptions of the first section.

The proof of this proposition is omitted here. Figure 5.7 indicates the nature of equilibrium messages when $\bar{Z}$ is Walrasian. x^* is a WCE. wO_I and wO_{II} are the offer-demand curves of agent 1 and agent 2, respectively. The intersection of Z^{*1} and Z^{*2} is the segment $[w, x^*]$ and $\psi(Z^{*1}, Z^{*2}) = x^*$.

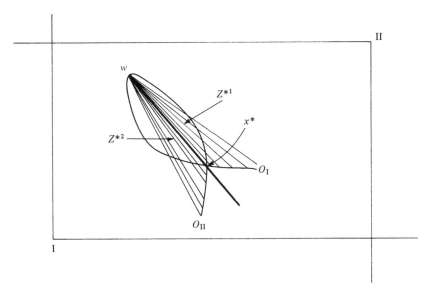

Figure 5.7

Naturally, the SNCP is not quasi-rational in a finite economy. Let us go back to Figure 5.5. Given the message z^2 (defined by wxO_{II}), agent 1 will be motivated to cheat because the message associated with an offer-demand curve that intersects wxO_{II} at x is better for agent 2 than the message specified by the response function of the SNC process.

It is not surprising that there are totally decentralized and quasi-rational processes, of which the set of equilibria coincides with the set of WCE when the number of agents is infinite.

Let us consider the following disaggregative process that stipulates that each agent i proposes to each agent j either point O (no trade) or some points, given the proposals of agents different from i and j. This mechanism incorporates a kind of bargaining or threat move reminiscent of that of the core, but in a setup different from that of the characteristic form and which clearly specifies the information exchanges.

$$Z_{t+1}^i = \{ z_i \in B_i \mid \exists \text{ one } j_1 \neq i : U_i(\sum_j z_{ij}) \geq U_i(\sum_j \bar{z}_{ij})$$

for any $\bar{z}_i \in \bar{Z}_t^i$ and z_{ij} is the ith element of $z_j \in Z_t^j$ for $j \neq j_1\}$ where $\bar{Z}_t^i = \{ z_i \in B_i \mid -z_{ij}$ is either the jth element of some $z_j \in Z_t^j$ for each $j \neq i$ or $0\}$.

$$\psi(z_i) = \text{either} \quad \{ y = [y_1, \ldots, y_m] \mid y_i \in Z_t^i, y_{ij} = -y_{ji} \; \forall (i,j)\}$$

if this set is nonempty or $y = 0$.

A WCE is always an equilibrium of this process. When one replicates the economy and the number of agents in each type tends to infinity, the set of equilibria of this process tends to coincide with the set of WCE.

NOTES

1 Moreover, the outcome function of concrete processes is a box less black than that of abstract processes.
2 In the two last chapters of Arrow and Hahn (1971), the relation between the first and last trends of thought are made clear.
3 It is easy to reformulate the notion of equilibrium when u_i is only quasi-concave.
4 As a_i^* is taken as a measure of finite support, we can argue for each t in the support of a_i^* and not only for almost any t in this support.
5 We note that for each i, $a_i^*(t) \neq 0$ for at most two t's.
6 To make it simple, we define mechanisms without institutional agents.
7 It can be assumed that for each c: for any $x \in X(c)$, there is α such that $x = g(\alpha)$.
8 This is because we consider only aggregative mechanisms.

REFERENCES

Arrow, K., and Debreu, G. Existence of equilibrium for a competitive economy. *Econometrica,* 1954: 265–290.
Arrow, K., and Hahn, F. *General competitive analysis.* San Francisco: Holden Day, 1971.
Benassy, J. P. Neo-Keynesian disequilibrium theory in a monetary economy. *Review of Economic Studies,* 1975: 503–523.
Benassy, J. P. Disequilibrium exchange in barter and monetary economies. *Economic Inquiry,* 1975(b): 131–156.
Barro, R. J. and Grossman, H. I. A general disequilibrium model of income and employment. *American Economic Review,* 1971: 82–93.
Champsaur, H. Financement volontaire d'un bien public et équilibre avec rationnement. *Cahiers du Séminaire d'Econométrie,* 1979.
Clower, R. The Keynesian counterrevolution: a theoretical appraisal. In *The theory of interest rates,* ed. F. H. Hahn and F. P. R. Brechling. London: MacMillan, 1965.
Drèze, T. Existence of an equilibrium under price rigidity and quantity rationing. *International Economic Review,* 1975: 301–320.
Grandmont, J. M. Temporary general equilibrium theory. *Econometrica,* 1977: 535–572.
Grandmont, J. M., Laroque, G. and Younès, Y. Equilibrium with quantity rationing and recontracting. *Journal of Economic Theory,* 1978: 84–102.
Hahn, F. and Negishi, T. A theorem on non-tâtonnement stability. *Econometrica,* 1962: 463–469.
Hurwicz, L. Optimality and informational efficiency in resource allocation processes. In *Mathematical methods in the social sciences,* ed. Arrow, Karlin, and Suppes. Stanford University Press, 1959.

Laroque, G. The fixed price equilibria: some results in local comparative statics. *Econometrica,* 1978.

Leijonhufvud, A. *On Keynesian economics and the economics of Keynes.* Oxford University Press, 1977.

Malinvaud, E. *The theory of unemployment reconsidered.* Oxford: Basil Blackwell, 1977.

Malinvaud, E. and Younès, Y. Une nouvelle formulation générale pour l'étude des fondements microéconomiques de la macroéconomie. *Cahiers du Séminaire d'Econométrie,* 1978.

Massé, P. *Le plan ou l'anti-hasard.* Paris: Gallimard, 1965.

Negishi, T. *Microeconomic foundations of Keynesian macroeconomics.* Amsterdam: North Holland, 1979.

Sylvestre, J. Fixprice analysis in exchange economies. Barcelona. 1981.

Uzawa, H. On the stability of Edgeworth's barter process. *International Economic Review,* 1962: 218–232.

Younès, Y. Sur les notions d'équilibre et de déséquilibre utilisées dans les modèles décrivant l'évolution d'une économie capitaliste, unpublished, CEPREMAP, 1970(a).

Younès, Y. Sur une notion d'équilibre utilisable dans le cas où les agents ne sont pas assurés de la compatibilité de leurs plans; unpublished. *Séminaire d'Econométrie de MM,* Roy et Malinvaud, 1970(b).

Younès, Y. On the role of money in the process of exchange and the existence of a non-Walrasian equilibrium. *Review of economic studies,* 1975: 489–501.

CHAPTER 6

Repeated games: an overview of the zero-sum case

Jean–François Mertens

In repeated games, crucial points in the modeling deal with information: To what extent do the players know exactly what game they are playing, including the others' utilities, and to what extent are they informed of all pure strategy choices after every stage of the game?

When such full information is not assumed, one is led to the so-called games with incomplete information:

1 There are several possible games (i.e., states of nature, or types of the several players), one of which is chosen in the beginning according to some known probability distribution. Players may have some private partial information about this choice, for instance, their own type.

2 After every stage of the game, every player gets some signal, which may depend on the state of nature, the actions of all players at this stage, and the player receiving it.

I will deal mainly with the two-player zero-sum case. The zero-sum case, among others, is needed to set the limitations in the general case – such as the minimum amount an individually rational player would accept, or, more generally, the characteristic function.

For instance, let us take a situation where three states of nature, L, M, R, are chosen with probability 1/3 each, no player getting any prior information:

$$\text{payoffs} \quad \overset{L}{\begin{pmatrix} 0 & 0 \\ 0 & 4 \end{pmatrix}} \quad \overset{M}{\begin{pmatrix} 0 & -2 \\ 2 & 0 \end{pmatrix}} \quad \overset{R}{\begin{pmatrix} 0 & 0 \\ -4 & -2 \end{pmatrix}}$$

$$\text{signals} \quad \begin{pmatrix} NR & L \\ P & Q \end{pmatrix} \quad \begin{pmatrix} NR & NL \\ P & Q \end{pmatrix} \quad \begin{pmatrix} R & NL \\ P & Q \end{pmatrix}$$

Note that the signals are the same for both players and inform them at least of each other's pure strategy choices.

Recall also that the state of nature is chosen once and for all at the beginning of the game and that the only pieces of information received by the players during the course of the game are their signals.

Let us first see if we can solve this game on the boundary of the simplex $\{(P_L, P_M, P_R)\}$.

Obviously, $\quad V_L = V_M = V_R = 0$

$$P_R = 0 \text{ gives the game } \Gamma_{NR}: \begin{pmatrix} 0 & -1, \to 0^* \\ 1 & 2 \end{pmatrix} \text{ with value } 1$$

where by "$\to 0^*$" we mean that as soon as this box is played, the game moves to an absorbing state with value 0.

$$P_L = 0 \text{ gives } \Gamma_{NL}: \begin{pmatrix} 0, \to 0^* & -1 \\ -1 & -1 \end{pmatrix} \text{ with value } -1$$

Thus the real game can also be described by

$$\begin{pmatrix} 0, & \overset{\frac{2}{3}}{\nearrow} \Gamma_{NR} & -\frac{2}{3}, & \overset{\frac{2}{3}}{\nearrow} \Gamma_{NL} \\ & \underset{\frac{1}{3}}{\searrow} \Gamma_R & & \underset{\frac{1}{3}}{\searrow} \Gamma_L \\ -\frac{1}{3}, & \to \text{same} & \frac{1}{3}, & \to \text{same} \end{pmatrix}$$

or shorter, given the preceding results:

$$\frac{2}{3}\begin{pmatrix} 1^* & -1^* \\ -1 & 1 \end{pmatrix}$$

This game is called "The Big Match" (Blackwell and Ferguson, 1968). It is a game where each player has full information about the current state of nature and the other's pure strategy choices, but a new state of nature is chosen at every stage, according to some lottery that may depend on the current state and on both players' actions in the current stage.

Shapley introduced such games in 1953 under the name "Stochastic Games." Further, this one has the property that all states of nature but one are absorbing, in the sense that once reached, they are never more left. Stochastic games with this property are called "Games with Absorbing States." The foregoing reduction of some games with incomplete information to games with absorbing states is due to Kohlberg and Zamir (1974). It applies, by induction on the number of states of nature, whenever

1. The players have no prior information on the state of nature (in general, prior information may be represented by a partition (for every player) of the set of states of nature)
2. The signals are the same to both players
3. The signals tell the players at least each other's pure strategy choices

Several other classes of games of incomplete information are solved (with solutions that are, in some sense, more interesting than the foregoing one from the point of view of the use of information), namely:

1. The case where one player is initially fully informed about the state of nature (Aumann and Maschler, 1967, 1968; Kohlberg, 1975a)
2. The case where the signals do not depend on the state of nature (Mertens and Zamir, 1971/72 in special case, Mertens 1971/72)

But here we want to continue with our example: We reduced the problem to the solution of stochastic games, but we have not yet described their solution.

Shapley, in his 1953 article, showed the existence of a value $v_\lambda(z)$ for discounted stochastic games (i.e., with payoff function $\lambda \sum_{i \geqslant 0} (1-\lambda)^i x_i$, when x_i is the payoff at stage i) (z is initial state) ($0 \leqslant \lambda \leqslant 1$).

His argument was basically a contraction argument. This argument was later extended, starting with the work of Maitra and Parthasarathy, to infinite state and action spaces. Basically, what is required is the following:

For any function $x(z)$ on the state space, denote by γ_x the game with payoff function $\lambda h_1 + (1-\lambda)x(z_2)$, where h_1 is the payoff in stage 1 and z_2 the state chosen at the end of stage 1; one needs each of these games to have a value, say $v(x)$, and the mapping $x \to v(x)$ maps some Banach space of bounded measurable functions into itself. The mapping being contracting, the existence of a fixed point follows.

Later, it was observed that an adaptation of Nash's argument for the existence of equilibria in n-person games also yielded the existence of (stationary) Nash equilibria in n-person discounted stochastic games:

If $x_i(z)$ denotes the payoff corresponding to the equilibrium, $\sigma_i(z)$ the corresponding strategies (i: player), they form a fixed point of the following correspondence:

$$\Gamma(x, \sigma) = \{ \tilde{x}, \tilde{\sigma} \colon \text{in game } \gamma_x, \ \tilde{x}(z) \text{ is the payoff to all players}$$
$$\text{if they use strategy } \sigma \text{ and } \tilde{\sigma}_i \text{ is a best reply to } \sigma \text{ of}$$
$$\text{player } i \}$$

In the zero-sum case, Bewley and Kohlberg proved, in a series of papers (1976a, 1976b, 1978), first that v_λ and σ_λ have convergent expansions (around zero) in a fractional power of λ, then that the same holds true for v_n, up to terms of the order $(1/n)\log n$.

The first part applies in the non-zero-sum case as well, yielding the existence of vectors $x_\lambda, \sigma_\lambda$ describing stationary equilibria and having a convergent expansion in fractional powers of λ.

Indeed, the condition for $x_\lambda, \sigma_\lambda$ to be a fixed point of our correspondence $\Gamma(x, \sigma)$ can be written explicitly as a finite list of polynomial equalities and inequalities in λ and the coordinates of x and σ.

Therefore, by eliminating variables, one can express a solution as a piecewise algebraic function of λ, each "piece" being delimited by the condition that a finite number of polynomials in λ is positive. Because every polynomial has only finitely many roots, the interval $(0, 1]$ is covered by a finite number of intervals, in each of which the solution is some given algebraic function in λ. In particular, one of these intervals is adjacent to zero, and because algebraic functions of λ have convergent expansions in fractional powers of λ, the result follows.

For "the big match," one checks immediately that $v_\lambda = v_n = 0$ identically; so convergence is no problem.

But we are chiefly interested in long games, and less on strategies depending on a specific discount factor or a specific number of stages in the game.

So we want to know (in the two-person zero-sum case) whether or not the infinite game has a value v_∞, in the sense that both players will have strategies such that, in any sufficiently long finite game, their guaranteed payoff will be close to v_∞. One may add the requirement that the guaranteed payoff in the infinite game, that is

$$E\left(\liminf_{n \to \infty} \frac{1}{n} \sum_{i \leq n} x_i\right)$$

be also close to v_∞. Gilette (1957) showed the existence of v_∞ in the case of perfect information and in the so-called irreducible case.

In 1968, Blackwell and Ferguson showed that our preceding example

$$\begin{pmatrix} 1^* & -1^* \\ -1 & 1 \end{pmatrix}$$

which they called "the big match," had a value 0 (so that this is also the value of the game with incomplete information we started with).

An optimal strategy of player II is obviously to play at every stage independently $(1/2, 1/2)$. It is easy to see that player I has no optimal strategy: Let i_0 be the first time player I would play Top with positive probability if player II has always played Left before, and let player II play Left up to i_0, Right at i_0, and $1/2, 1/2$ after.

It can further be seen that player I has no ϵ-optimal strategy with finite memory – in the sense that at every stage he would use a probability distribution depending only on his current state of memory and his current information to choose a new state of memory and a pure strategy. Any such strategy is defeated by a strategy of player II consisting of first playing independently $(\delta, 1-\delta)$ up to some sufficiently large time N, then always playing L.

Blackwell and Ferguson nevertheless gave a very easy ϵ-optimal strategy for player I: If K_n denotes his total payoff up to stage n, and N some large number, let player I play Top at stage n with probability $(N+K_n)^{-2}$. They also gave another ϵ-optimal strategy. They only showed that their strategies were good in the infinite game, but it can be checked that they are good in all sufficiently long finite games too.

Kohlberg, in 1974, extended their second strategy to all stochastic games with absorbing states, thereby solving completely the class of games with incomplete information described earlier.

In 1979, Neyman and I developed a strategy roughly similar to the first strategy of Blackwell and Ferguson, to cover all stochastic games. The proof, which was rather painful, and used heavily the finiteness assumption on the state of space, came out at the end of 1979 as a CORE discussion paper.

Independently, Monash developed a quite complex strategy in order to show a (somewhat weaker) version of the result: It is not claimed that this strategy is good, neither in the infinite game nor in all sufficiently long finite games, but only that, if the opponent uses the same infinite game strategy in every finite game, then for sufficiently long games (this depending on the opponent's strategy) player I will get close to the value.

Finally, very recently, Neyman and I reworked our previous proof and slightly reformulated the strategy. In this way we got an extremely simple and transparent proof of the fact that stochastic games have a value, without any finiteness assumptions, neither on the state space nor on the action sets, under the following conditions:

1   Payoffs are uniformly bounded
2   The values v_λ of the discounted games exist
3   $\forall \epsilon < 1 \; \exists \lambda_i$ decreasing to zero, $\lambda_{i+1} \geqslant \epsilon \lambda_i$

$$\sum \| v_{\lambda_{i+1}} - v_{\lambda_i} \| < \infty$$

It is an immediate consequence of the Bewley–Kohlberg result that these assumptions are always satisfied in the finite case.

The strategy involved is the following: Denote by A four times the largest absolute payoff, and fix some small $\epsilon > 0$.

Choose a decreasing integrable function $\lambda(s)$ with values in $(0, 1]$ and a positive integer-valued function $L(s)$, both defined on R_+, such that, for all $|\theta| \leqslant A$, and every state z,

$$\frac{L(s)}{s} \to 0 \quad \text{and} \quad \frac{\lambda(s + \theta L(s))}{\lambda(s)} \to 1 \quad \text{when} \quad s \to \infty$$

$$|v_z(\lambda(s + \theta L(s))) - v_z(\lambda(s))| \leqslant \frac{\epsilon}{10} L(s)\lambda(s)$$

[For instance, $L(s) = 1$ and $\lambda(s) = 1/(s \ln^2(s))$ would do for all stochastic games with finite state and action sets.] In the general case, condition 3 ensures the possibility of such choices of λ and L. Denote $\lim_{\lambda \to 0} v_\lambda$ by v_∞.

For some M sufficiently large, define inductively

$$s_0 = M, \qquad \lambda_k = \lambda(s_k), \qquad L_k = L(s_k)$$

$$B_0 = 1, \qquad B_{k+1} = B_k + L_k$$

$$s_{k+1} = \max\left[M, s_k + \sum_{B_k \leqslant i < B_{k+1}} (x_i - v_\infty(z_{B_{k+1}}) + \epsilon/2) \right]$$

where x_i and z_i denote payoff and state at stage i. The strategy is to start playing from time B_k up to time B_{k+1} an $[(\epsilon/10)L_k\lambda_k]$-optimal strategy in the λ_k-discounted game.

REFERENCES

Aumann, R. J. and Maschler, M. 1967. "Repeated Games with Incomplete Information: A Survey of Recent Results." ACDA/ST-116, Ch. III, pp. 287–403.

Aumann, R. J., and Maschler, M. 1968. "Repeated Games of Incomplete Information: The Zero-Sum Extensive Case." ACDA/ST-143, Ch. II, pp. 25–108.

Bewley, T. and Kohlberg, E. 1976a. "The Asymptotic Theory of Stochastic Games." *Mathematics of Operations Research* 1:197–208.

Bewley, T. and Kohlberg, E. 1976b. "The Asymptotic Solution of a Recursion Equation Occurring in Stochastic Games." *Mathematics of Operations Research* 1:321–36.

Bewley, T. and Kohlberg, E. 1978. "On Stochastic Games with Stationary Optimal Strategies." *Mathematics of Operations Research* 3:104–25.

Blackwell, D. and Ferguson, T. S. 1968. "The Big Match." *Annals of Mathematical Statistics* 39:159–63.

Federgruen, A. 1978. "On N-Person Stochastic Games with Denumerable State Space." *Advances in Applied Probability* 10:452–71.

Gilette, D. 1957. "Stochastic Games with Zero Stop Probabilities." In: *Contributions to the Theory of Games, Vol. III,* edited by M. Dresher, A. W. Tucker, and P. Wolfe, pp. 179–87. Princeton: Princeton University Press.

Kohlberg, E. 1974. "Repeated Games with Absorbing States." *Annals of Statistics* 2:724–38.

Kohlberg, E. 1975*a*. "Optimal Strategies in Repeated Games with Incomplete Information." *International Journal of Game Theory* 4:7–24.

Kohlberg, E. 1975*b*. "The Information Revealed in Infinitely Repeated Games of Incomplete Information." *International Journal of Game Theory* 4:57–9.

Kohlberg, E. and Zamir, S. 1974. "Repeated Games of Incomplete Information: The Symmetric Case." *Annals of Statistics* 2:1040–1.

Maitra, A. and Parthasarathy, T. 1970. "On Stochastic Games." *Journal of Optimization Theory and Applications* 5:289–300.

Mayberry, J. P. 1967. "Discounted Repeated Games with Incomplete Information." ACDA/ST-116, Ch. V, pp. 435–61.

Megiddo, N. 1980. "On Repeated Games with Incomplete Information Played by Non-Bayesian Players." *International Journal of Game Theory* 9: 157–67.

Mertens, J.-F. 1971/72. "The Value of Two-Person Zero-Sum Repeated Games: The Extensive Case." *International Journal of Game Theory* 1:217–27.

Mertens, J.-F. 1973. "A Note on 'The Value of Two-Person Zero-Sum Repeated Games: The Extensive Case.'" *International Journal of Game Theory* 2:231–4.

Mertens, J.-F. and Neyman, A. 1979. "Stochastic Games." CORE discussion paper 8001, Université Catholique de Louvain.

Mertens, J.-F. and Neyman, A. 1980. "Stochastic Games." Report 22/80, The Institute for Advanced Studies, The Hebrew University of Jerusalem.

Mertens, J.-F. and Zamir, S. 1971/72. "The Value of Two-Person Zero-Sum Repeated Games with Lack of Information on Both Sides." *International Journal of Game Theory* 1:39–64.

Mertens, J.-F. and Zamir, S. 1976*a*. "On a Repeated Game without a Recursive Structure." *International Journal of Game Theory* 5:173–82.

Mertens, J.-F. and Zamir, S. 1976*b*. "The Normal Distribution and Repeated Games." *International Journal of Game Theory* 5:187–97.

Mertens, J.-F. and Zamir, S. 1977*a*. "The Maximal Variation of a Bounded Martingale." *Israel Journal of Mathematics* 27:252–76.

Mertens, J.-F. and Zamir, S. 1977*b*. "Minmax and Maxmin of Repeated Games with Incomplete Information." CORE discussion paper 7742, Université Catholique de Louvain (forthcoming in *International Journal of Game Theory*).

Monash, C. A. 1980. "Stochastic Games: The Minmax Theorem." Unpublished reprint.

Parthasarathy, T. 1973. "Discounted, Positive, and Noncooperative Stochastic Games." *International Journal of Game Theory* 2:25–37.

Ponssard, J.-P. 1975*a*. "Zero-Sum Games with 'Almost' Perfect Information." *Management Science* 21:794–805.

Ponssard, J.-P. 1975*b*. "A Note on the L–P Formulation of Zero-Sum Sequential Games with Incomplete Information." *International Journal of Game Theory* 4:1–5.

Ponssard, J.-P. 1976. "On the Subject of Non Optimal Play in Zero-Sum Extensive Games: 'The Trap Phenomenon.'" *International Journal of Game Theory* 5:107–15.

Ponssard, J.-P. and Sorin, S. 1979*a*. "The L–P Formulation of Finite Zero-Sum Games with Incomplete Information." Ecole Polytechnique, Laboratoire d'Econemétrie, No. A195 0179.

Ponssard, J.-P. and Sorin, S. 1979*b*. "Some Results on Zero-Sum Games with Incomplete Information: The Dependent Case." Ecole Polytechnique, Laboratoire d'Econométrie, No. A196 0179.

Ponssard, J.-P. and Sorin, S. 1979*c*. "Optimal Behavioral Strategies in 0-Sum Games with Almost Perfect Information." Ecole Polytechnique, Laboratoire d'Econométrie, No. A197 0179.

Ponssard, J.-P. and Zamir, S. 1973. "Zero-Sum Sequential Games with Incomplete Information." *International Journal of Game Theory* 2:99–107.

Rogers, P. D. 1969. "Non-Zero Stochastic Games." Ph.D. thesis, University of California, Berkeley.

Shapley, L. S. 1953. "Stochastic Games." *Proceedings of the National Academy of Sciences of the U.S.A.* 39:1095–1100.

Sobel, M. 1971. "Non Cooperative Stochastic Games." *Annals of Mathematical Statistics* 42:1930–5.

Stearns, R. E. (1967). "A Formal Information Concept for Games with Incomplete Information." ACDA/ST–116, Ch. IV, pp. 405–33.

Zamir, S. 1971/72. "On the Relation between Finitely and Infinitely Repeated Games with Incomplete Information." *International Journal of Game Theory* 1:179–98.

Zamir, S. 1973*a*. "On Repeated Games with General Information Function." *International Journal of Game Theory* 2:215–29.

Zamir, S. 1973*b*. "On the Notion of Value for Games with Infinitely Many Stages." *Annals of Statistics* 1:791–6.

PART V

TOPICS IN COMPETITIVE ANALYSIS

CHAPTER 7

The Cournotian foundations of Walrasian equilibrium theory: an exposition of recent theory

Andreu Mas-Colell

1   Introduction

It is well known that the modern versions of Walrasian economics
(Debreu (1959); Arrow and Hahn (1971)) leave unexplained a key ingre-
dient of the theory, namely the hypothesis that prices are quoted and
taken as given by economic agents. In this exposition we shall attempt,
via the extensive analysis of two models, to give an account of the
efforts of the last decade to develop the classical work of Cournot (1838)
into a full-fledged general equilibrium theory that provides an endogenous explanation of price taking (we will say much less about price quoting). Specific references will be given as we go along. For a gathering of
relevant articles see the issue of the *Journal of Economic Theory* (1980)
on noncooperative approaches to the theory of perfect competition.

The starting point of the research is the (informal) hypothesis that
economic agents interact noncooperatively through given institutions.
Those being essential, it cannot be expected that the same level of institutional parsimoniousness as in Walrasian theory can be reached.
Because, as a consequence, all-encompassing models are bound to be
cumbersome, the research has proceeded by focusing on particular, pro-

This is an extended version of a lecture delivered at the Aix-en-Provence
4th World Congress of the Econometric Society in September 1980. I
am indebted for support to National Science Foundation Grant SOC78-
09934X and to the Instituto de Mathematica Pura e Aplicada at Rio de
Janeiro.

183

totypical ones. This we shall do also. We will review two models. The first (Section 2), in the line initiated by Shubik (1973) and Shapley and Shubik (1977), is a model of exchange where all agents are treated symmetrically, that is, have, in principle, the same strategic position. The second (Section 3), in the line initiated by Gabszewicz and Vial (1972), Hart (1974a), and Novshek and Sonnenschein (1978), is a model of firms that face a sector of passively adjusting consumers but interact strategically among themselves.

Noncooperation means that agents take as given the strategies (in our case, in a strict Cournotian tradition, those are quantities) of the other agents. Obviously, this is a hypothesis that demands justification. We shall not, however, be concerned with it here on the grounds that it is plausible if individual agents are relatively small and the Cournotian explanation of price-taking equilibrium runs precisely in terms of the negligibility of single traders. There are noncooperative models where price taking holds at equilibrium irrespective of the number of agents (see, for example, Dubey (1981), Simon (1981), and, in a more normative spirit, Schmeidler (1980)). For these "Bertrandian" models the above specification of the noncooperation hypothesis can be questioned.

Before the development of the noncooperative approach, the body of economic theory was not at all empty of theoretical explanations for Walrasian equilibria. One had core theory and the core equivalence theorems (of Edgeworth, Debreu, Scarf, Aumann, Hildenbrand, and many others; see Hildenbrand (1974) for an almost definitive account), which were devised for precisely this purpose. We may be excused if we refer to Mas–Colell (1982) for a comparison of approaches and an argument that their differences are only a matter of degree and not of fundamental characteristics. Another, and more recent, important line of work, which we shall also not survey, is the theory of perfect competition put forward by Ostroy (1980) and Makowski (1980).

A serious limitation of our survey is that to keep things manageable we consider only the convex case. This means that in Section 3 we leave out some of the deepest research in the area, namely the work of Novshek and Sonnenschein (1978) on noncooperative Cournotian equilibrium with set-up costs for firms, by far the most relevant case. We may refer to Mas–Colell (1981) for an analysis of this case that ties in well with the results of Section 3. See also H. Sonnenschein, Chapter 8 in this book.

In tune with the work we review, we take the point of view that the appropriated solution concept for an economy $\mathcal{E}_n$ with a finite number of agents (say n) is the Cournot noncooperative equilibrium. Then, if we look at an economy with a continuum of agents (see Aumann, 1964) as

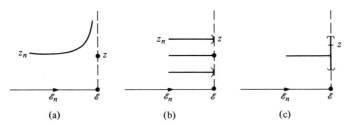

(a)   (b)   (c)

Figure 7.1

an idealization, that is, a model for an economy with many relatively small participants (i.e., large n), the central analytical question becomes to what extent the set of Walrasian equilibria of the continuum economy is also an "idealization" of the set of noncooperative equilibria of the large economies of which the continuum is a model. In other words, to what extent, if the finite economy $\mathcal{E}_n$ is close to the continuum $\mathcal{E}$ (in sequence terms, if $\mathcal{E}_n \to \mathcal{E}$), the set of Cournot equilibria of $\mathcal{E}_n$ and the set of Walrasian equilibria of $\mathcal{E}$ are similar.

A situation where it would be fully justified to call Walrasian theory the limit (as the economy grows large) of Cournotian theory would be one where for $\mathcal{E}_n \to \mathcal{E}$ the following three desiderata are satisfied (precise mathematical definitions will come in due course):

(i) If z_n symbolizes a Cournot equilibrium for $\mathcal{E}_n$, then z_n should be bounded uniformly on n (in our models this is always equivalent to z_n having a convergent subsequence), that is, "escapes to infinity" do not arise.

(ii) If $z_n \to z$ and z_n is a Cournot equilibrium for $\mathcal{E}_n$, then z is a Walrasian equilibrium of the continuum economy $\mathcal{E}$.

(iii) If z is a Walrasian equilibrium of $\mathcal{E}$, then $z_n \to z$, for a sequence z_n of Cournot equilibria for $\mathcal{E}_n$.

Mathematically, (ii) is a closed graph property, (i) and (ii) yield upper hemicontinuity of the equilibrium correspondence, and (iii) gives lower hemicontinuity. Failures of (i), (ii), and (iii) are symbolically illustrated in Figures 7.1(a), (b), (c), respectively.

Roughly speaking, a failure of (i) or (ii) indicates that the Walrasian solutions (i.e., prices are quoted and taken as given) miss some possible noncooperative equilibria. Typically, those are not going to be satisfactory from the welfare theoretic point of view, and so one may be led astray by disregarding them. A failure of (iii) indicates that some Walrasian equilibria of the continuum model have no predictive value whatsoever or, as Novshek and Sonnenschein put it, that they are merely artifacts of the continuum specification.

We shall organize the presentation of Sections 2 and 3 around theorems giving sufficient conditions for (i), (ii), and (iii) to be satisfied. As it is usual in economic theory, a good deal of the interest of the results is the light thrown on new varieties of competitive failures. In this line, a tentative conclusion of our examination is that nonpathological failures of (ii) are quite possible. In contrast, the failures of (iii) tend to be more degenerate.

All the proofs are gathered in Section 4.

2   A symmetric model of competitive exchange

The model we shall discuss in this section belongs to the class introduced by Shubik (1973) and Shapley and Shubik (1977). It has been extensively developed by, among others, Dubey and Shubik (1977), Shapley (1976), Dubey and Shapley (1977), Pazner and Schmeidler (1976), Postlewaite and Schmeidler (1978), and Jaynes, Okuno, and Schmeidler (1978). A general axiomatic analysis was attempted in Dubey, Mas-Colell, and Shubik (1980). The particular variant we will analyze was briefly described as an example in the last reference. It differs from other variants in not striving for a strict game theoretic formulation. Thus, as an instance, the outcomes of our trade mechanism are ill defined outside of equilibrium. This could be repaired (in fact, our model is similar to the one of Jaynes, Okuno, and Schmeidler (1978) supplemented by an unlimited amount of credit), but from the standpoint of the objectives of this paper, nothing essential would be gained by doing so.

2.1   Description of an exchange economy

We begin by a brief description of the familiar concept of an exchange economy. To stick to the general equilibrium tradition (as exemplified in Debreu (1959) or Arrow and Hahn (1971)) we do not include the institutional arrangements for trade in the concept. Those will be introduced separately in the next subsection.

There are $l \geq 1$ commodities. The set of commodities will sometimes be denoted L. The characteristics of a *trader* are: (i) the *consumption set*, which for the sake of simplicity we take to be $R_+^l = \{v \in R^l : v \geq 0\}$; (ii) the *preference relation* $\gtrsim$ on R_+^l which we take to be complete, transitive, continuous, strictly monotone (i.e., $v > v'$ implies $v \succ v'$) and convex (i.e., if $v \gtrsim v'$, then $\alpha v + (1-\alpha)v' \gtrsim v'$ for all $0 \leq \alpha \leq 1$); (iii) the *endowments* ω, which for the sake of simplicity we take $\omega \gg 0$.

To save on notation and technicalities we shall restrict our attention to a universe with a finite number of preference-endowment pairs $P=\{(\succsim_h,\omega_h)\}_{h=1}^m$.

Let I be a finite indexing set to be thought of as the set of trader's names. An *exchange economy* is then simply a map $\mathcal{E}:I\rightarrow P$. The characteristics of trader i are represented by $\mathcal{E}(i)$ and denoted $(\succsim_i,\omega_i)$.

A net trader is a function $x:I\rightarrow R^l$ such that $\sum_{i\in I}x(i)\leqslant 0$. We also denote $x(i)$ by x_i. A net trader is (privately) *feasible* if $x_i+\omega_i\geqslant 0$ for all i. The interpretation is that x is an exchange among traders, trader i supplying $\max\{0,-x_i^j\}$ and getting $\max\{0,x_i^j\}$ of commodity j.

2.2   Trade and Cournot-Nash equilibria

Consider a fixed reference economy $\mathcal{E}:I\rightarrow P$.

Trade takes place in l trading posts or markets, one for each commodity. There is an extra commodity called numeraire and denoted m. It does not enter the utility functions, but it mediates trade, that is, in every market the exchange is of the good against the numeraire. The best interpretation of m is as a promise to pay note. Indeed, in principle, agents can pledge to trade any amount of numeraire they wish, but we impose as an equilibrium condition that no agent should be left with a net debit position.

The mechanics of trade are easily explained. Take agent i. For each market j, he must decide on a quantity of commodity j to offer $y_i^j\geqslant 0$, for short an *offer*, and a bid of numeraire $m_i^j\geqslant 0$. So, for each i we have a $2l$ vector of bids and offers $(m_i,y_i)\in R_+^{2l}$. Economywide, this yields two functions, $m:I\rightarrow R_+^l$, $y:I\rightarrow R_+^l$. The clearing rules in each market depend only on the bids and offers for that market. Specifically, given $m^j:I\rightarrow R_+$, $y^j:I\rightarrow R_+$, the aggregate bids and offers are $z^j=\sum_i m_i^j$, $z^{l+j}=\sum_i y_i^j$. Then, trader i gets a net amount $(z^{l+j}/z^j)m_i^j-y_i^j$ of the good j in exchange for a net amount $(z^j/z^{l+j})y_i^j-m_i^j$ of numeraire (by convention we put $0/0=0$ and $\infty\cdot 0=0$). The ratio z^j/z^{l+j} can be interpreted as a clearing price. Note the distinctly Cournotian quantity-setting flavor of this execution rule. We say that (m,y) is feasible for $i\in I$ if (i) the *budget constraint* is satisfied, that is to say, the total amount of numeraire bid by i in the different markets is not greater than the total amount of numeraire received in exchange for the offers, that is, $\sum_j m_i^j\leqslant\sum_j(z^j/z^{l+j})y_i^j$; and (ii) the offers are not greater than the initial endowments, that is, $y_i^j\leqslant\omega_i^j$ for all j. If (m,y) is feasible for i, we let $x_i[m,y]$ be the induced net trade of i. Note that

$$\sum_j(z^j/z^{l+j})x_i^j[m,y]\leqslant 0.$$

By (m, y) being *feasible*, we mean that it is feasible for each $i \in I$. The corresponding net trade function is $x[m, y] : I \to R^l$.

Observe that, in the spirit of an anonymity postulate for markets, nothing prevents agents from entering both sides of the same market, that is, from making both an offer and a bid. On the other hand, there is no possible gain in so doing. Indeed, let (m, y) be feasible and suppose that (m', y') differs from (m, y) only in that for some i and j, (m_i^j, y_i^j) has been replaced by $[m_i^j + \lambda, y_i^j + (z^{l+j}/z^j)\lambda]$ for some $\lambda \geq 0$, then we clearly have $x[m, y] = x[m', y']$. So, for each i and j the same net trade is obtained with a whole one-dimensional family of bids and offers pairs. Because, furthermore, which particular one is chosen does not affect the net trade of the other agents or of any other market, there is no conceptual loss if we always choose the representative (m_i^j, y_i^j) having $m_i^j y_i^j = 0$ (which obviously always exists). So, from now on, it is a maintained hypothesis that bids and offers $(m_i, y_i) \in R_+^{2l}$ satisfy the complementarity condition $m_i y_i = 0$. Note that even then net trades do not uniquely determine bids and offers. There is still one degree of freedom left. If (m, y) is feasible and $\lambda > 0$, then $x[m, y] = x[\lambda m, y]$.

Definition 1. A feasible $(m, y) : I \to R^{2l}$ is a *Cournot-Nash (CN) equilibrium* if for every $i \in I$, there is no (m', y') such that (m', y') is feasible for i, $x_i[m', y'] + \omega_i \succ_i x_i[m, y] + \omega_i$ and $m_{i'} = m_{i'}$, $y_{i'} = y_{i'}$ for all $i' \neq i$. We call $x[m, y]$ a *Cournot-Nash net trade*.

Given a feasible (m, y) it will be instructive to investigate the shape of the budget set $B_i(m, y) \subset R^l$ of agent i, that is, $B_i(m, y) = \{x_i[m', y'] : (m', y')$ is feasible for i and $m_{i'} = m_{i'}$, $y_{i'} = y_{i'}$ for all $i' \neq i\}$. Put $\bar{m} = \sum_{i' \neq i} m_{i'}$, $\bar{y} = \sum_{i' \neq i} y_{i'}$ and assume that $\bar{m} \gg 0$ and $\bar{y} \gg 0$. Suppose that $x_i \in B_i(m, y)$. Then $-\omega_i \leq x_i \leq \bar{y}$. Further, if $x_i^j \leq 0$, the negative of the receipts from sales in market j is $[\bar{m}^j/(\bar{y}^j - x_i^j)]x_i^j$ and if $x_i^j > 0$, then denoting by v the numeraire outlays incurred we have $[(\bar{m}^j + v)/\bar{y}^j]x_i^j = v$, or $v = [\bar{m}^j/(\bar{y}^j - x_i^j)]x_i^j$. Therefore,

$$g(x_i) \equiv \sum_j \frac{\bar{m}^j}{\bar{y}^j - x_i^j} x_i^j \leq 0.$$

The converse clearly also holds, so $B_i(m, y) = \{x_i : -\omega_i \leq x_i \leq \bar{y},$ $g(x_i) \leq 0\}$. Because the function g is convex, the budget set is convex and closed. It is represented in Figure 7.2. If $\bar{m}^j = 0$ and $\bar{y}^j = 0$ for some j, then with the convention $0/0 = 0$, the above expression for $B_i(m, y)$ remains correct. The case where for some j, $\bar{m}^j > 0$, $\bar{y}^j = 0$ or $\bar{y}^j > 0$, $\bar{m}^j = 0$, we shall not need to worry about. It obviously cannot arise at equilibrium.

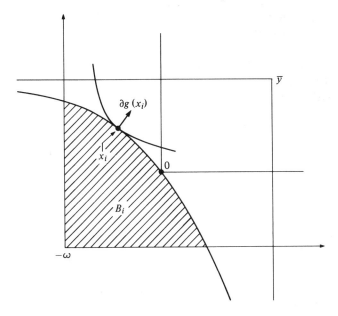

Figure 7.2

Because the budget sets are so well-behaved, it would not be surprising if an interesting existence theorem were available. We say interesting because the trivial null net trade (i.e., $m \equiv 0$, $y \equiv 0$) is always a CN equilibrium. On the other hand, if, for example, all agents are identical, then the sensible outcome is precisely no trade. What this means is that the search for interesting existence results must involve some minimal condition on the diversity of agents' characteristics. Such results are available for analogous models (Shapley and Shubik (1977), Dubey and Shubik (1977)), and without any doubt they can also be obtained for the present one. But the whole issue becomes delicate and is far from our main focus on limiting convergence properties. Thus, while we will have things to say about existence near the limit (Theorem 2), we shall not provide a general treatment.

For the asymptotic analysis, it is important to know that the equilibrium net trade of an agent cannot be arbitrarily large (so the situation depicted in Figure 7.1(a) can be ruled out).

Proposition 1. There is a $k > 0$ (depending only on P) such that if (m, y) is a CN equilibrium for an economy $\mathcal{E} : I \rightarrow P$, then $|x_i^j[m, y]| \leqslant k$ for all i and j.

Let (m, y) be a CN equilibrium for $\mathcal{E} : I \to P$. Because of the strict monotonicity of preferences, the situation where for some j, $\sum_j m_i^j = 0$ and $\sum_i y_i^j > 0$ or $\sum_i m_i^j > 0$ and $\sum_i y_i^j = 0$ cannot arise. On the other hand, $\sum_i m_i^j = 0$ and $\sum_i y_i^j = 0$ is entirely possible. In this case, we say that the market j is *inactive*. In fact, in this trading model the inactivity of any set of markets at equilibrium can be prescribed a priori. To see this, take an arbitrary set of markets and close them (i.e., eliminate them from the model). Find an equilibrium for the set of remaining markets. Then the equilibrium net trade will still be an equilibrium if the markets of the first set are reopened. Although trade is now possible in principle, no single agent has any incentive to make any bids or offers in those markets and therefore they remain inactive.

2.3   *Limit economies: Cournot–Nash and Walrasian equilibria*

An economy with a *continuum of agents* can be modeled as in Section 2.1. We only need to interpret I as the interval $[0, 1]$ and systematically replace $\sum$ by $\int$. Of course, familiar technical measurability requirements must also be imposed. We should also, where appropriate, read "almost all" for "all."

Similarly, the notion of a Cournot–Nash equilibrium pair of (measurable) bids and offers functions $(m, y) : I \to R_+^{2l}$ and of a corresponding Cournot–Nash net trade $x[m, y] : I \to R^l$ still makes sense. What is the shape of a typical budget set $B_i(m, y)$, $i \in I$? For a CN equilibrium (m, y), let $A \subset L$ be the set of active markets, that is, $j \in A$ if and only if $z^j = \int m^j > 0$ and $z^{l+j} = \int y^j > 0$ (equivalently, $j \in A$ if and only if $\int |x^j[m, y]| > 0$). Then,

$$B_i(m, y) = \{ x_i \in R^l : -\omega_i \leqslant x_i, \sum_{j \in A} \frac{z^j}{z^{l+j}} x_i^j \leqslant 0$$
$$\text{and} \quad x^j = 0 \quad \text{for} \quad j \notin A \}.$$

Remember that now z^j and z^{l+j} have the interpretations of averages. Since the value of an integral does not depend on the value of the integrand on a set of measure zero, z^j and z^{l+j} do not depend on the bids and offers of a particular agent. Therefore, what the expression for $B_i(m, y)$ tells us is that at a CN equilibrium every agent faces the same market constraints: trade is not possible in inactive markets, while in active markets trade is possible (in an amount limited only by the availability of commodities to supply) at the fixed trade ratio z^j/z^{l+j}.

If at a CN equilibrium (m, y) every market is active, then $B_i(m, y)$ is a familiar Walrasian budget set and the CN net trade is a Walrasian net trade. If the set of active markets A is smaller than L, then we can still say that the CN net trade is Walrasian with respect to A if by this we mean that in the definition of Walrasian equilibrium we take the markets in $L \setminus A$ to be closed.

Definition 2: Given the economy $\mathcal{E} : [0, 1] \to P$, a feasible net trade function $x : [0, 1] \to R^l$ is Walrasian with respect to $A \subset L$ if $x_i^j = 0$ for $j \notin A$ and all $i \in [0, 1]$, and if for each $j \in A$ there is $p^j \geqslant 0$ such that, for all $i \in [0, 1]$, $x_i + \omega_i$ is $\succsim_i$ maximal on $\{ v + \omega_i : \sum_{j \in A} p^j v^j \leqslant 0, \ v^j = 0$ for $j \in A \}$.

Then every CN equilibrium net trade is Walrasian with respect to its set of active markets. Conversely, it is trivially verified that a net trade that is Walrasian with respect to some $A \subset L$ can be sustained as a CN net trade. Observe that at a Walrasian equilibrium it is entirely possible for a market to be open but not active. But at an open market there must be a price quoted. If the market is active, we can identify the price with a certain ratio of supply and demand. If the market is not active, this is not so and we must be implicitly resorting to some institutional device for price quoting.

If all markets are open, then we have the usual notion of Walrasian equilibrium to which the familiar Pareto optimality properties apply.

2.4   *Large finite economies; sequences and convergence*

We have seen in the previous section that in a limit economy the CN net trades are precisely the same as the net trades that are Walrasian in a generalized sense which allows for closed markets. We are, however, interested in the continuum set-up and corresponding results only to the extent that they are a model for large finite economies. What we want is that if a finite economy is near the limit, its equilibrium set be similar to the equilibrium set of the limit. To formulate this property requires a notion of "nearness" for economies and net trade functions, or, more directly, a notion of convergence of finite economies and their net trades to limit economies and net trades. This we proceed to provide in this section.

Consider a sequence of finite economies $\mathcal{E}_n : I_n \to P$ with $\#(I_n) = n$ and a continuum economy $\mathcal{E} : I \to P$, $I = [0, 1]$. Dealing as we are with a finite number of types, the meaning of $\mathcal{E}_n \to \mathcal{E}$ is straightforward. We say that $\mathcal{E}_n \to \mathcal{E}$ if for each type h the fraction of agents of type h in economy $\mathcal{E}_n$ converges to the corresponding fraction in $\mathcal{E}$, or

$$(1/n) \# \{ i : \mathcal{E}_n(i) = (\succsim_h, \omega_h) \} \to \lambda(\mathcal{E}^{-1}(\succsim_h, \omega_h)),$$

where λ denotes Lebesgue measure.

Now let $x_n : I_n \rightarrow R^l$, $x : I \rightarrow R^l$ be net trades for $\mathcal{E}_n$, $\mathcal{E}$, respectively. In the sequel we will need only to consider CN equilibrium net trades. To attach a meaning to $x_n \rightarrow x$ take first the simplest case where x_n, x are symmetric, that is, net trades are the same for agents of the same type. Then we require that for every h, $x_{nh} \rightarrow x_h$ where x_{nh}, x_h denote the net trade of agents of type h in the economies $\mathcal{E}_n$, $\mathcal{E}$. If x_n, x are not symmetric, matters become slightly more delicate, but they can be handled by standard techniques. What one does is take measures μ_{nh}, μ_h, on R^l, which (up to a multiple) stand for the distribution over net trades of the traders of type h in the economies $\mathcal{E}_n$, $\mathcal{E}$, and require that, for all h, $\mu_{nh} \rightarrow \mu_h$ in the sense of the weak convergence for measures. More precisely, μ_{nh} is defined by letting, for any $B \subset R^l$,

$$\mu_{nh}(B) = (1/n)\#\{i \in I_{nh} : x_n(i) \in B\},$$

where $I_{nh} \subset I_n$ are the agents of type h. The measure μ_h is defined similarly. For "$\mu_n \rightarrow \mu$ weakly," it is meant that for every continuous bounded function $f : R^l \rightarrow R$ we have $\int f d\mu_n \rightarrow \int f d\mu$. See Hildenbrand (1974) for this.

2.5   The limit of a sequence of CN equilibria

Let $\mathcal{E}_n : I_n \rightarrow P$, $\#I_n = n$, be a sequence of finite economies converging, in the sense of the previous section, to a limit $\mathcal{E}$. Suppose that $x_n : I_n \rightarrow P$ are CN net trades for $\mathcal{E}_n$. By Proposition 1 we know that for all n and $i \in I_n$, $x_n(i) \in K = \{v \in R^l : \|v\| \leqslant k\}$, that is, independently of n and i net trades belong to a fixed bounded subset of R^l. The "escape to infinity" situation of Figure 7.1(a) cannot arise. This has an economic interpretation. It says that in this model it is guaranteed that if traders become relatively small in terms of initial endowments and if there is no singularity in their preferences (i.e., there are many traders of each possible characteristic), then the potential gains from trade of individual agents are limited. We cannot have the paradox where by treating similar agents dissimilarly some individual agents turn out at equilibrium to be relatively large in terms of their net trades.

So, let's assume that $x_n \rightarrow x$ where $x : I \rightarrow K$. What are the properties of x? Since at the limit every CN net trade is Walrasian with respect to some $A \subset L$, it is natural to expect that this will also be the case for x. The next theorem establishes this. Analogous results have been proved in the references at the beginning of Section 2.

Theorem 1. Let $\mathcal{E}_n \rightarrow \mathcal{E}$ and $x_n : I_n \rightarrow R^l$ be a sequence of CN equilibrium for $\mathcal{E}_n$. Then:

(i) x_n has a subsequence converging to some $x: I \rightarrow K$;

(ii) If $x_n \rightarrow x$, then x is Walrasian with respect to $A = \{j \in L : \int |x^j| > 0\}$.

Theorem 1 provides a (limited) justification for a "Cournot conjecture" on the Pareto optimality of noncooperative equilibria of economies with relatively small individual agents. If at the limit x all markets are active, then we indeed have a Walrasian fully (Pareto) optimal equilibrium, but, in general, we are only permitted to claim optimality with respect to reallocations of commodities with active markets. As has been pointed out in Sections 2.3 and 2.4, there is nothing pathological about this. Failures such as the ones illustrated in Figure 7.1(b), where the limit of a sequence of CN equilibria is not fully Walrasian, or even Pareto optimal, are entirely possible. Within the present model competitive forces are too weak to activate markets that should be active for optimality (in fact, to activate markets at all). The reason is that to start trading in an inactive market a minimum of cooperation among at least two agents (a buyer and a seller) is necessary, but the Cournot-Nash concept does not capture, in this model, such cooperation.

The proof of Theorem 1 does not depend in any essential way on the finiteness of P. A "compactness" property would do. As previously asserted, part (i) follows from Proposition 1 (the proof of which is somewhat technical). Part (ii) is intuitive and the proof is straightforward.

2.6   *Approximating Walrasian by Cournot-Nash equilibria*

We now investigate our problem in the other direction: Given a fully (i.e., all markets are open) Walrasian net trade $x: I \rightarrow R^l$ for a continuum economy $\mathcal{E}$ and given a sequence of approximating finite economies $\mathcal{E}_n \rightarrow \mathcal{E}$, can we find a sequence $x_n \rightarrow x$ such that (except perhaps for at most a finite number of terms of the sequence) x_n is a CN net trade for $\mathcal{E}_n$? With this generality a positive answer cannot be expected. If, to begin with, x is a Walrasian equilibrium only by coincidence and a small perturbation of the data of the economy makes it disappear, then there is no reason why it should be preserved as a CN equilibrium when the economy is perturbed from the continuum to a finite but large approximation. In addition, the nonrobustness of a coincidental Walrasian equilibrium makes it a doubtful theoretical solution concept for what are, inherently, imprecise models of the economy.

This suggests that the whole question should be placed in, or restricted to, a framework of regular economies, that is, of economies $\mathcal{E}$ having a set of (Walrasian) equilibria persistent under perturbations. The theory of regular economies, initiated by Debreu (1970), has since been extensively developed. See Dierker (1977) for a survey.

It will be convenient (but, we wish to emphasize, far from necessary) to impose smoothness conditions on preferences. Specifically, we will, for the rest of this section, assume that for every type h, $\succsim_h$ is representable by a C^2 utility function $u_h: R_+^l \to R$ with no critical point. Also, the indifference surfaces of $\succsim_h$ have everywhere nonzero curvature. Given our convexity hypothesis on $\succsim_h$, this is a kind of differentiable strict convexity, and it is equivalent (see Debreu (1972)) to the condition that for all $x \in R_+^l$

$$\begin{vmatrix} \partial^2 u(x) & \partial u(x) \\ (\partial u(x))^T & 0 \end{vmatrix} \neq 0$$

Let $p \in R_{++}^{l-1}$. We interpret p as prices for the first $l-1$ commodities relative to the lth. That is to say, we normalize the price of the lth commodity to be 1. Then, for each type h, an *excess demand function* $\hat{f}_h: R_{++}^l \to R^l$ is defined by letting $\hat{f}_h(p) + \omega_h$ maximize $\succsim_h$ on

$$\left\{ v \in R_+^l : \sum_{j=1}^{l-1} p^j(x^j - \omega_h^j) + (v^l - \omega_h^l) \leq 0 \right\}.$$

It is, of course, well known that $\hat{f}_h$ is C^2 whenever $\hat{f}_h(p) + \omega_h \gg 0$ (see Debreu (1972)). Define $d_h(p)$ (resp. $s_h(p)$) by $d_h^j(p) = \max\{0, \hat{f}_h^j(p)\}$ (resp. $s_h^j(p) = -\min\{0, \hat{f}_h^j(p)\}$). Of course, $\hat{f}_h(p) = d_h(p) - s_h(p)$. The symbols d and s stand for demand and supply.

In the economy $\mathcal{E}$ we have the corresponding aggregate functions $\hat{f}, d$, and s, that is, if we let θ^h be the fraction of agents of type h, then $\hat{f} = \sum_h \theta^h \hat{f}_h$ and similarly for d and s. We let $f: R_{++}^{l-1} \to R^{l-1}$ be defined by deleting the last coordinate from $\hat{f}$. Note that $\hat{f}^l(p) = -p \cdot f(p)$.

Let x be a fully Walrasian equilibrium net trade for $\mathcal{E}$. Then, by definition, there is p such that for any i if h is the type of i, then $x_i = \hat{f}_h(p)$. So, x is symmetric and there is a one-to-one correspondence between equilibrium net trades and equilibrium prices, that is, vectors p such that $\hat{f}(p) = 0$. By the strict monotonicity hypothesis on preferences $p \gg 0$ is guaranteed.

It will be convenient that at the equilibrium p under consideration the three functions $\hat{f}_h, d_h, s_h$ be C^1. This will be so if the following condition is satisfied, (H) for all h and j, $0 \neq \hat{f}_h^j(p) > -\omega_h^j$.

Definition 3. A Walrasian net trade $x: I \to R^l$ for $\mathcal{E}$ with corresponding $p \in R_{++}^{l-1}$ is *regular* if:
   (i) condition (H) holds; and
   (ii) rank $Df(p) = l-1$.
   Condition (ii) is the standard regularity assumption for exchange

economies (see Dierker (1977) survey). Condition (i) is specific to our problem and it is imposed merely for convenience of the proof technique; it is not essential. Regularity of the equilibria is not a restrictive hypothesis. Typically, it will be satisfied, in the sense that except for a "negligible" set of economies every Walrasian equilibrium of an economy will be regular (see Debreu (1970) and Dierker (1977)).

Theorem 2. Let $\mathcal{E}:[0,1] \to P$ be a continuum economy and $x:[0,1] \to R^l$ a regular (fully) Walrasian equilibrium. Suppose that $\mathcal{E}_n \to \mathcal{E}$. Then there is N and a sequence $x_n : I_n \to R^l$, $n > N$, of CN net trade equilibria for $\mathcal{E}_n$ such that $x_n \to x$. Further, every x_n is symmetric and, up to differences in a finite number of entries, the sequence is unique.

Theorem 2 is quite satisfactory. Note that, in particular, if we admit the existence of Walrasian equilibrium at the limit, it yields an existence result of CN equilibria for large, but finite, economies. The interpretation of the theorem is clear. In the trade model under consideration, failures of the type illustrated in Figure 7.1(c) can arise only in degenerate (nonregular) cases. Thus, typically, every Walrasian equilibrium represents a noncooperative Cournot–Nash equilibrium of the finite but large economy of which the continuum is a model.

Theorem 2 has been stated for Walrasian equilibria with a full set of open markets, but it is obvious that mutatis mutandis it applies to any Walrasian equilibria. In addition, condition (H) implies that at the considered equilibrium every open market is active. This is a side effect of the convenience hypothesis (H) and it is not an essential part of the definition of regularity. As a final observation we note that the proof of Theorem 2 we shall give does not depend in any essential way on the finiteness of P. The theorem remains true for "compact" P.

3   A model of competition among firms

In this section we present and analyze a model that is much closer to the original partial equilibrium example of Cournot than the one in Section 2. Here we will have firms and consumers. The first are strategically active via quantity competition, while the second adapt passively along a kind of general equilibrium demand curve. The model originates in Gabszewicz and Vial (1972), Hart (1979), Roberts and Sonneschein (1977), and Novshek and Sonnenschein (1978). For simplicity, we consider only the convex production case. Our treatment of it owes much to a paper by Roberts (1980). For an analysis of the nonconvex case see Novshek and Sonnenschein (1978) and Mas–Colell (1981).

3.1   *Description of the economy*

There are *l* commodities. An economy is composed of a consumption and a production sector. The strategically active agents are the producing firms (finite in number). The consumption sector is to be thought as a continuum of consumers that adapt passively to the production decisions of the firms. We will describe it first.

Formally, the consumption sector is defined by a *consumption-feasible set of aggregate productions* $J \subset R^l$ and a set-valued mapping $P: J \to R^l$ which to each $z \in J$ assigns a nonempty set of possible equilibrium prices $P(z)$. The correspondence P is to be interpreted as a general equilibrium analogue of the familiar partial equilibrium inverse demand function (an early precedent is the concept of "total demand curve" of I. Pierce (1952–53)). More specifically, let there be a population of consumers characterized by preferences, endowments, and shareholdings (as in Debreu (1959) or Arrow and Hahn (1971)). Suppose that every consumer has a uniform-across-firms share of profits. Then the profit income of every consumer depends only on the aggregate net production z and on the prevalent price vector p. So, given z we have a well-defined Walrasian general equilibrium system for which the set of equilibrium prices is $P(z)$. Of course, $P(z) = \emptyset$ is possible. The region J is precisely the set of those z for which $P(z) \neq \emptyset$. The hypothesis of uniformity over firms of profit shares of each consumer is implicit in our analysis because we take equilibrium prices to depend on aggregate production. The more general case would require a more disaggregated domain for P. There is no essential difficulty involved in allowing for it, but in this exposition we wish to keep things as simple as possible. For illustrative purposes we will next give two examples of consumption sectors.

Example 1. There are two commodities. If we assume that all consumers are identical, share equally in profits (or losses), have initial endowments $(2, 2)$, and convex, monotone preferences $\succsim$ on R_+^2, then

$$J = R_+^2 - \{(2, 2)\} \quad \text{and} \quad P(z) = \{p \in R_+^2 : pz' \succsim pz \text{ for all } z' \succsim z\}.$$

Example 2. There are two commodities and two classes of consumers (of equal weight), owners and nonowners. Owners have initial endowments $(0, a)$, consumption set R_+^2, share in profits (or losses) equally, and care only about commodity 2 which we shall choose as numeraire with price fixed at 1. Nonowners do not receive profits. For the purposes at hand it suffices to describe them by their aggregate continuous excess demand function $\varphi: R_{++}^2 \to R^2$. We do not require that nonowners be identical. Therefore, by the known characterization results for excess demand

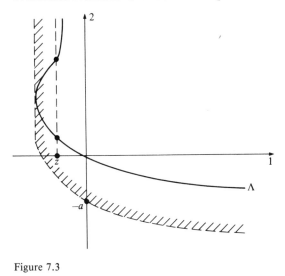

Figure 7.3

functions (see Shafer and Sonnenschein (1982)), φ is essentially unrestricted. See Figure 7.3, in which we represent the offer curve $\Lambda = \varphi(R_{++}^2)$. For this consumption sector we have

$$J = \varphi(R_{++}^2) + (\{0\} \times [-a, \infty))$$

and $P(z) = \{(q, 1) : z - \varphi(q, 1) = (0, \lambda)\}$, $z \in J$. It is worth noting that in contrast to Example 1, the region J and the correspondence P are not specially well behaved. Thus, for example, in Figure 7.1 to the production z there correspond two price equilibria. Observe also that $P(z)$ does not depend on z^2, the amount of the numeraire commodity.

As for the *production sector* we assume that there is a finite number of types of production sets $Y_1, \ldots, Y_m \subset R^l$. Each Y_h is closed, convex, bounded above, and satisfies $Y_h \cap R_+^l = \{0\}$. We let $\mathbf{Y} = \{Y_1, \ldots, Y_m\}$ and $\hat{Y} = $ convex hull $\bigcup_h Y_h$. A production sector is then a map $Y : I \to \mathbf{Y}$ where I is a finite indexing set. A *production* is a function $y : I \to R^l$. A production is *feasible* if $y(i) \in Y(i)$ for all $i \in I$. We let $\bar{Y} = [1/\#(I)] \sum_{i \in I} Y(i)$ and $\bar{y} = [1/\#(I)] \sum_{i \in I} y(i)$. Note that $\bar{Y} \subset \hat{Y}$. As in Section 2, little in our analysis depends on the finiteness (rather than "compactness") of $\mathbf{Y}$.

An economy $\mathcal{E}$ is then defined to be the pair $P : J \to R^l$, $Y : I \to \mathbf{Y}$. A production $y : I \to R^l$ is *attainable* if it is feasible and, also, consumption feasible, that is, $\bar{y} \in J$. An *attainable state* of the economy is a pair (y, p) where y is an attainable production and $p \in P(\bar{y})$. Note that we are measuring magnitudes in per-firm terms.

3.2   *Cournot–Nash equilibrium*

To develop a notion of noncooperative equilibrium for the economies under consideration we will now have to take a major leap and postulate that the behavior of the strategic players, that is, the firms, is directed by the profit maximization motive. There are at least two serious conceptual problems associated with this. The first is the justification of the profit objective itself (why not utility or surplus or sales maximization?). The second is how to evaluate profits. Even if a numeraire has been chosen, the price equilibrium correspondence may be multivalued for some $\bar{y}$ and so, profits not unambiguously determined. We comment on these two difficulties in turn.

In the case of large economies (i.e., for economies near the continuum of firms limit), the profit maximization objective has been investigated and justified as being susceptible of conveying the exact or approximate unanimous approval of owners. See Hart (1979b), Novshek and Sonnenschein (1978), and also, Makowski (1980b). To the extent that we concern ourselves only with limiting properties, those are comforting results. It is somewhat surprising, however, that no careful investigation of this basic aspect of a theory of monopolistic competition seems to be available for the general case. We may mention here that the justification of the profit motive is intimately related to guaranteeing the invariance of results with respect to the choice of numeraire, a property that any minimally satisfactory theory should possess.

We feel that the problem is important enough for us to wish to make sure that at the very least there is a consistent scenario in which profit maximization is fully justified. The following will do: One commodity is the numeraire with price fixed at 1. Think of it as a Hicksian composite commodity available in an extensive "outside world." Agents have preferences, endowments, and shareholdings. However, we impose the restriction that agents with positive share ownership in firms care only about the numeraire commodity (which is therefore endogenously determined). Perhaps they live in the outside world. Then, of course, utility maximization on the part of owners resolves in profit maximization on the part of firms. Observe that this interpretation moves the model in the direction of partial equilibrium, but not so much as to lose any of the essential general equilibrium complexities. In particular, income effects are present and J and P can still be quite complicated. In fact, Example 2 (and every example from now on) belongs to the variety discussed in this paragraph.

There remains the second problem. Even if a natural numeraire exists and prices are normalized with respect to it, the set $P(z)$ may not be a

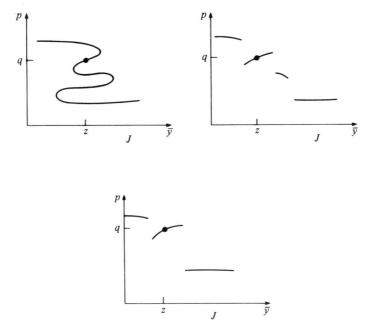

Figure 7.4

singleton (see Figures 7.4 and 7.9). To have a prevailing (i.e., "historic-ally given") z and $q \in P(z)$ will not help because profit maximization will involve the consideration of hypothetical z'. However, for z' near z, it is natural to require that the price prediction be determined, if at all possible, by continuity from q (see Figure 7.4). As it turns out, this is all that will be needed for our (large economies) results. Therefore, even if this is a serious conceptual problem, it has no drastic consequences for our analysis and we will formally proceed along the standard lines by assuming that there is an a priori given selection $p : J \rightarrow R^l$ from P, that is, $p(z) \in P(z)$, which associates to every consumption feasible produc-tion z a predicted price vector. The selection p substitutes for the incom-pleteness (in the sense of being unable to always provide a concrete pre-diction in the form, perhaps, of a random variable) of the theory, in this case, Walrasian exchange, underlying the generation of P. In Figures 7.4(b) and (c) we have two different selections from the P of Figure 7.4(a). Note that both of them are maximally continuous through the point (z, q).

The definition of a Cournot–Nash production should now be self-explanatory.

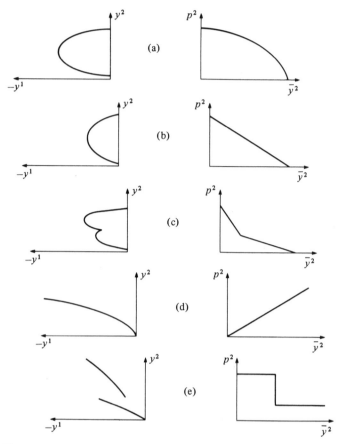

Figure 7.5

Definition 4. Given the production sector $Y : I \rightarrow \mathbf{Y}$, the attainable production $y : I \rightarrow R^l$ is a Cournot–Nash (CN) equilibrium with respect to the selection $p : J \rightarrow R^l$ if for all $i \in I$ we have $p(\bar{y})y_i \geqslant p(\bar{y}')y_i'$ for all attainable $y' : I \rightarrow R^l$ such that $y_{i'}' = y_{i'}$ for $i' \neq i$.

In other words, each firm maximizes profits given the production of the remaining firms. Observe that the isoprofit surfaces of a firm i can be determined from the aggregate production of the remaining firms. Figure 7.5 illustrates several possibilities for the zero isoprofit line of a firm. (The remaining are obtained by horizontal displacement. We implicitly take $p^1 = 1$ and assume that p^2 depends only on $\bar{y}^2$; because the production of the other firms is fixed, we may as well suppose that there is no other firm.)

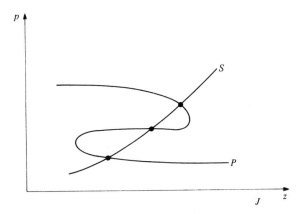

Figure 7.6

3.3   *Continuum economies and Walrasian equilibrium*

An economy with a continuum of firms is defined exactly as in Section 3.1 except that we interpret I as $[0,1]$ (and "all" as "almost all"), replace the sums by integrals, and require all functions to be measurable.

An attainable state (y, p) will be called Walrasian if all firms maximize profits taking q as given, that is, $y(i)$ solves the problem "Max qz subject to $z \in Y(i)$." For reasons of symmetry we give a formal definition in terms of demand and supply. For each type of production set Y_h let θ^h be the fraction of firms having this production set. For each $q \in R_+^l$ let $S_h(q)$ be the set of maximizers of qz on Y_h; $S_h(q)$ is convex (possibly empty). Let $S(q) = \sum_h \theta^h S_h(q)$. Then, $S(q)$ is the aggregate Walrasian supply set corresponding to q. If $z \in S(q)$ we can find $y: I \to R^l$ such that $\bar{y} = z$ and $y(i)$ is profit maximizing for each $i \in I$. Therefore, the following definition makes sense.

Definition 5. The $(z, p) \in J \times R^l$ is a Walrasian equilibrium of the economy specified by $P: J \to R^l$ and $Y: [0, 1] \to \mathbf{Y}$ if:
   (i) $p \in P(z)$, and (ii) $z \in S(p)$.
In other words, (z, p) is a common point of the graph of the supply and demand correspondences. See Figure 7.6 where there are three Walrasian equilibria.

3.4   *Large finite economies; sequences and convergences*

Given a continuum economy $\mathcal{E}$, we wish to attach a meaning to $\mathcal{E}_n \to \mathcal{E}$ where $\mathcal{E}_n$ are economies with a finite number of firms. For the sake of expositional simplicity we limit ourselves drastically and take the consumption sector to be the same (in per-firm terms) for all $\mathcal{E}_n$, $\mathcal{E}$. Then, given the corresponding production sectors $Y_n : I_n \to \mathbf{Y}$, we say that $Y_n \to Y$ if, for every h, $\theta_n^h \to \theta^h$ where $\theta_n^h = [1/\#(I_n)]\#\{i : Y(i) = Y_h\}$ and analogously for θ^h. Similarly to Section 2, if $y_n : I_n \to R^l$, $y : [0, 1] \to R^l$ are productions, we say that $y_n \to y$ if for each h we have $\mu_{nh} \to \mu_h$ weakly, where μ_{nh} is the measure in R^l defined by

$$\mu_{nh}(B) = \frac{1}{\#(I_n)} \#\{i \in I_n : Y(i) = Y_h \text{ and } y_n(i) \in B\}.$$

A word on relative sizes as $n \to \infty$ may be useful. Implicitly, we always take single consumers to be of negligible size relative to the dimension of a single firm (measured somewhat coarsely by, say, the capacity production). This remains unaltered for all $\mathcal{E}_n$ (and also for $\mathcal{E}$), and it is the justification for the passive reactive behavior of consumers. What becomes smaller as $n \to \infty$ is the size of a single firm relative to the size of the entire economy. For example, if to begin with we have a set of firms and a continuum of consumers, we can obtain a sequence of economies converging to a limit with a continuum of firms in the sense of this section if we replicate pari passu *both* the set of firms and of consumers.

3.5   The limit of a sequence of CN equilibria

Let $\mathcal{E}_n \to \mathcal{E}$ and $y_n : I_n \to R^l$ be a sequence of CN productions for $\mathcal{E}_n$. Example 3 shows that even if J is bounded below (as it should be), y_n may not be bounded above.

Example 3. There are two commodities and only one firm type with a production set as in Figure 7.7. Note that although total output is bounded, input productivity is always positive. The set J is $R_+^2 - (1, 0)$ and $P(z) = (0, 1)$ for $z^2 \leqslant 1 + z^1$ or $z^1 \geqslant 0$, and

$$P(z) = \{(0, 1), (-[(1 + z^1)/z^1], 1)\}$$

otherwise. Thus, P is compatible with the following specification of the consumption sector. There are owners and nonowners. Owners share equally in profits, have no endowments, and only care about commodity 2. Nonowners are endowed (in mean) with one unit of commodity 1 and have L-shaped indifference curves.

The economies $\mathcal{E}_n$ differ only in the number of firms, which is n in economy $\mathcal{E}_n$. We claim that a CN equilibrium $y_n : I_n \to R^l$ is given by letting $y_n(i) = 0$ for $i \neq 1$ and $y_n(1) = (-n, a_n)$ where a_n is the maximal

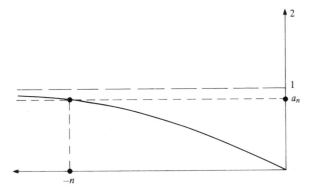

Figure 7.7

feasible production with input requirement n. Of course, y_n is not bounded. It is trivial to verify that it is an equilibrium. The key observation is that $\bar{y}_n$ is at the boundary of J.

There are two avenues to correct the situation of Example 3. One would be to investigate and impose appropriate boundary conditions on P. This would take us too far afield, and, besides, it is not clear what they would be (the boundedness of prices away from zero and infinity would do for this example but not for Example 4). The second one that, out of expediency, we shall follow is to require $\hat{Y} \subset J$. Because $\bar{Y}_n \subset \hat{Y}$, this implies that any feasible production is attainable. In other words, the consumption sector is very extensive relative to the production sector. Of course, if J is bounded below, then $\hat{Y} \subset J$ implies that each Y_h is bounded above and below. Therefore, if y_n is a sequence of CN equilibria, it is necessarily bounded and has a convergent subsequence (see proof of Theorem 1).

Theorem 3, which is easy, gives sufficient conditions for the limit of a sequence of CN equilibria to be Walrasian and therefore Pareto optimal.

Theorem 3. Suppose that $\hat{Y} \subset J$ and $P : J \to R^l$ is a continuous function. If $\mathcal{E}_n \to \mathcal{E}$, y_n is a CN production for $\mathcal{E}_n$ and $y_n \to y$, then y is a Walrasian production for $\mathcal{E}$.

Results along the lines of Theorem 3 have been provided by Gabszewicz and Vial (1972), Novshek and Sonnenschein (1978), Hart (1979), and Roberts (1980). Example 4 shows that the condition $\hat{Y} \subset J$ cannot be dispensed with, although it is far from necessary (boundary conditions on P should do). It is a variation of Example 3 and both are inspired by examples of Novshek and Sonnenschein (1979). The key requirement of the theorem, however, is that P be a continuous function. Examples 5

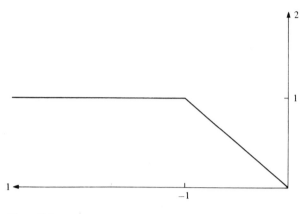

Figure 7.8

and 6 illustrate and discuss the economic significance of typical situations where y fails to be Walrasian (and Pareto optimal) on account of P not being a *globally* continuous function. They are, respectively, variations of examples due to K. Roberts (1980) and O. Hart (1980). In different ways their papers were first in putting a strong emphasis on the continuity condition.

Example 4. The consumption side is as in Example 3. There is again one type of firm with a production set as in Figure 7.8. In the economy $\mathcal{E}_n$ there are $2n$ firms. Let $y_n : I_n \to R^2$ be given by $y_n(i) = (-1, 1)$ for $1 \leqslant i \leqslant n$ and $y_n(i) = 0$ for $n < i \leqslant 2n$. Then y_n is bounded and does in fact converge to $y : [0, 1] \to R^2$ defined by $y(i) = (-1, 1)$ for $1 \leqslant i \leqslant \frac{1}{2}$, $y(i) = 0$ for $i > \frac{1}{2}$. It is trivial to verify that, as in the previous example, y_n is a CN equilibrium. However, y is not a Walrasian equilibrium for the limit economy since at prices $(0, 1)$ total mean Walrasian supply must be 1 rather than $\frac{1}{2}$.

Example 5. There are two commodities. The first is the numeraire. There is one type of firm with production set $Y = \{v \in R^2 : -2 \leqslant v^1 \leqslant 0, 0 \leqslant v^2 \leqslant -2v^1, v^2 \leqslant 2\}$; see Figure 7.9. There are two types of consumers, owners and nonowners. Owners have initial endowments $(3, 0)$ and care only about the numeraire commodity. Nonowners have preferences and endowments (only of numeraire) that when combined display the offer curve Λ of Figure 7.10(a). Then, $J = \Lambda + R_+^2 - \{(3, 0)\}$ and $P(z) = \{(1, q) : p \in \xi(z^2)\}$, $\xi(z^2) = [2, \infty)$ for $z^2 = 0$, $\xi(z^2) = \{2\}$ for $z^2 < 1$, $\xi(z^2) = [1, 2]$ for $z^2 = 1$, $\xi(z^2) = \{1/z^2\}$ for $z^2 > 1$. See Figure 7.10(b). Economy $\mathcal{E}_n$ has n firms. The Walrasian production vector of the limit

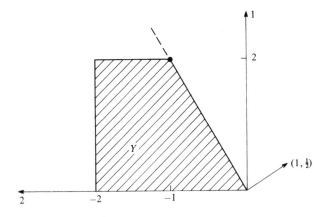

Figure 7.9

economy is $(-1, 2)$ with associated prices $(1, \frac{1}{2})$ and zero profits (see Figure 7.10(b)). The CN equilibria of $\mathcal{E}_n$ depend on which price q we select from $\xi(1)$. Suppose that $q \geqslant 3/2$. Then in the economy $\mathcal{E}_n$ it constitutes a CN equilibrium for each firm to produce $(-\frac{1}{2}, 1)$, so we have a sequence of CN equilibria that does not converge to Walrasian equilibrium. If $q < 3/2$, then a CN equilibrium for $\mathcal{E}_n$ does not exist. Nevertheless, the qualitative characteristic of the example remains. Irrespective of the value selected from $\xi(1)$, there is always a sequence of approximate CN equilibria that remains bounded away from the Walrasian production.

Of course, the problem is the lack of a continuous selection from P. The example as described is nongeneric (i.e., a convenient perturbation will yield a P that is a continuous function), but this has merely been a matter of convenience of exposition. Figures 7.10(c) and (d) hint at how the example can be modified to get a robust one.

Example 6. There are three commodities. The third is the numeraire. There are two types of production sets (they are represented in Figure 7.11):

$$Y_1 = \{v \in R^3 : v^2 = 0, \ -2 \leqslant v^3 \leqslant 0, \ v^1 \leqslant 1, \ 0 \leqslant v^1 \leqslant -(5/6)v^3\}$$

$$Y_2 = \{v \in R^3 : v^1 = 0, \ -2 \leqslant v^3 \leqslant 0, \ v^2 \leqslant 1, \ 0 \leqslant v^2 \leqslant -(5/6)v^3\}$$

Let $J = \{z \in R^3 : 0 \leqslant z^1 \leqslant 1, \ 0 \leqslant z^2 \leqslant 1, \ z^3 \geqslant -5\}$ and note that $Y_1 + Y_2 \in J$. The price correspondence is given by $P(z) = \{(1, 2, 1)\}$ if $z^2 < z^1$, $P(z) = \{(2, 1, 1)\}$ if $z^1 < z^2$, $P(z) = \{(2-\alpha, 1+\alpha, 1) : 0 \leqslant \alpha \leqslant 1\}$ if $z^1 = z^2$. This P correspondence could be derived, for example, from a consumption

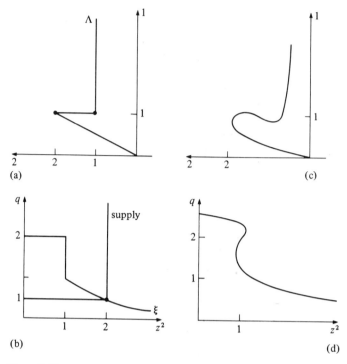

Figure 7.10

sector with two equal-weight consumer types. The first has utility function $u_1(z) = \min\{z^1 + 2z^2,\ 2z^1 + z^2\} + z^3$, endowment vector $(0,0,5)$ and consumption set R_+^3. He receives no profits. The second has utility function $u_2(z) = z^3$, endowment vector $(0,0,5)$, consumption set R_+^3 and he receives all profits.

The economy $\mathcal{E}_n$ is formed by n firms of each type. Then the unique Walrasian equilibrium production vector is $(1, 1, -12/5)$, which is sustainable by the price vector $(1.5, 1.5, 1)$. However, irrespective of the particular selection chosen from P, we have that $(0, 0, 0)$ is a CN equilibrium for $\mathcal{E}_n$ because if $z^2 = 0$ and $z^1 > 0$, then the ruling price vector is $(1, 2, 1)$ and profits for Y_1 are negative, symmetrically for Y_2. Note that there is no continuous selection from P. The example can be easily improved. Suppose that with reference to the consumption sector just described, we let the utility function of the first consumer be of the form $u_1(z) = v(z^1, z^2) + z^3$ where $v(z^1, z^2)$ is linear homogeneous and the unit isoquant of $v(z^1, z^2)$ coincides with the unit isoquant of $\min\{z^1 + 2z^2, 2z^1 + z^2\}$ except that the corner has been smoothed out.

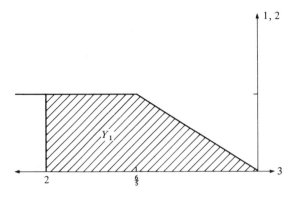

Figure 7.11

Then $P(z)$ will be a continuous function everywhere except at the origin. Nevertheless, the origin will still be a CN equilibrium for all n. Thus, there is nothing basically pathological about this example.

The economic meaning of this example (due to O. Hart (1980)) is obvious enough. If two commodities are complementary, some coordination in their production may be needed in order to guarantee optimality.

There is a parallel between the failure in this example and the failure in the models of Section 2. There we saw that the CN equilibrium notion did not embody the cooperation between buyers and sellers needed to activate a market. This same kind of degenerate failure does not happen in the model of this section: If given the trades in all other markets a particular market should be activated, it will. But it is quite possible, as this example illustrates, that the profitability of activating a market depends on some other markets being active. Thus, optimality may require a simultaneous move by several producers to activate several markets. This kind of coordination (involving, roughly speaking, more than two agents) is not captured in this model by the CN concept. Summing up: In the present model agents cooperate more than in the model in Section 1, and therefore the extreme failures of that model are avoided. In turn, to avoid the failures of the present one, it is necessary to bring more cooperation directly or indirectly among agents. For an examination of this issue from the point of the core, see Mas–Colell (1982).

3.6   *Approximating Walrasian by Cournot–Nash equilibria*

Here the problem converse to the one studied in the previous subsection takes the following form. Given $\mathcal{E}_n \to \mathcal{E}$ and a Walrasian equilibrium (y, q) for the limit economy $\mathcal{E}$, is there a price selection $p : J \to R^l$ (i.e.,

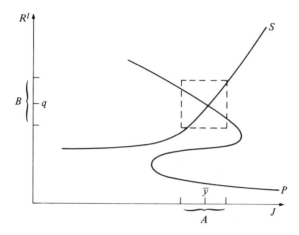

Figure 7.12

$p(z) \in P(z)$ for all $z \in J$) and a sequence $y_n \to y$ such that y_n is a CN production for $\mathcal{E}_n$ with respect to p?

Because for a sensible analysis the limit equilibrium we are starting with should not be just a fluke, we have to proceed as in Section 2 and develop a concept of regular Walrasian equilibrium. First, however, we will introduce two crucial conditions. Once they are available it will be entirely obvious how to formulate the hypothesis of regularity.

Condition U. Let $(y, q) \in J \times R^l$ be a Walrasian equilibrium for $\mathcal{E}$. We say that (y, q) satisfies Condition U (for unique value) if there are open (rel. to R^l) sets $A \subset J$, $B \subset R^l$ with $\bar{y} \in A$ and $q \in B$ such that (see Figure 7.12):

    (i)   The graph of P restricted to $A \times B$ is the graph of a C^2 function $p: A \to R^l$;
   (ii) The supply correspondence S is a C^1 function on B.

Condition U says that in a neighborhood of the Walrasian equilibrium, supply must be a C^1 function of prices and that the requirement of continuity uniquely determines a local selection from P which, furthermore, is C^2. In both cases differentiability is not of the essence but continuity is.

Let (y, q) be a Walrasian equilibrium satisfying Condition U. Take $B' \subset B$ such that $S(B') \subset A$. To define regularity it is natural to look at the C^1 map $G(v) = p(S(v)) - p$ from B into R^l. Of course, $G(q) = 0$ and any zero of G is a Walrasian equilibrium price vector. We say that (y, q) is a *Regular Walrasian Equilibrium* if condition U is satisfied and rank $DG(\bar{q}) = l$. This definition is due to K. Roberts (1980). If our P and

S correspondences derive from a general equilibrium economy with smooth aggregate excess demand, then the usual notion of regularity (maximal rank of the Jacobian matrix of excess demand at equilibrium prices) translates into the condition: $\text{rank} \, DG(\bar{q}) = l$. Thus, it is to be noted that our regularity concept here is stronger because of the first part of Condition U, which is not implied by the usual notion (the second part would, of course, be automatically satisfied). Nevertheless, this stronger concept of regular economy can still be proved to be generic in the appropriate sense.

The following theorem is due to K. Roberts (1980).

Theorem 4. Let each Y_h be bounded below. Suppose that $\mathcal{E}_n \to \mathcal{E}$ and (y, q) is a regular Walrasian equilibrium for $\mathcal{E}$. Then there is a price selection $p : J \to R^l$ continuous at $\bar{y}$ and with $p(\bar{y}) = q$, a $N > 0$ and a sequence $y_n \to y$, $n > N$, such that y_n is a CN production for $\mathcal{E}_n$ with respect to $p(\cdot)$. As with Theorem 2 we could also assert that each such y_n is symmetric (i.e., identical firms carry out identical productions).

Example 7 shows that the boundedness below of Y_h cannot be dispensed with. Examples 8 and 9 do the same for the first part of Condition U (whose importance was already perceived in a related context by Roberts and Postlewaite (1974)). Example 10 takes care of the second part. As we describe them, we shall comment on their economic significance (or lack of it). A feature common to all of them is worth noting. Every example takes place in an economy where Theorem 3 also fails. Although this is not absolutely general, it is not coincidental either. Indeed, suppose that the Walrasian equilibrium of the limit is unique. If there are forces that prevent it from being approachable by CN equilibria (failure to Theorem 4), then every convergent sequence of CN equilibria will have to converge to a non-Walrasian limit (failure to Theorem 3). Example 7 is due to Novshek and Sonnenschein (1979). Example 8 has been used in a related context by Makowski (1980) and Mas–Colell (1981).

As with Theorem 2, Theorem 4 contains an existence result. This is noteworthy since, in contrast to the model in Section 1, there is no expectation that an equilibrium will exist in an arbitrary finite economy. Nevertheless, Theorem 4 guarantees that if a finite economy is near enough a continuum economy exhibiting at least one regular Walrasian equilibrium, then a CN equilibrium will exist.

Example 7. Take the economy of Example 3. At the Walrasian equilibrium of $\mathcal{E}$ the (mean) input use $-\bar{y}^1$ is less than 1. See Figure 7.13. If y_n is a CN production for $\mathcal{E}_n$, then $-\bar{y}_n^1 = -1$, because otherwise it would

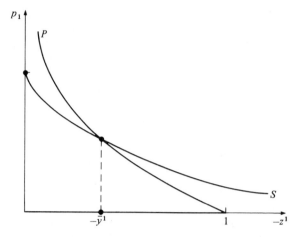

Figure 7.13

always pay any firm to exhaust input availability, bringing its price down to zero. So, the Walrasian equilibrium cannot be approached. It is clear from Figure 7.13 that the equilibrium is regular. What goes wrong is that Y is not bounded. This example looks very pathological. It should help emphasize a point already made in Section 3.4 that the refined way to proceed would be to exploit boundary conditions on P. For Theorem 4 the boundedness away from zero and infinity of the values of $P(z)$ would do.

Example 8. This example illustrates the inadequacy of the model specification of this section for market situations where the strategically active agents do not face a passively adapting group (and, by continuity, where this adapting group is thin). The market in question will be one for a purely intermediate good.

There are three commodities and two types of production sets:

$$Y_1 = \{v \in R^3 : v^2 \leqslant -v^1, \ v^1 \leqslant 0, \ v^3 \leqslant 0\}$$
$$Y_2 = \{v \in R^3 : v^3 \leqslant -v^2, \ v^2 \leqslant 0, \ v^1 \leqslant 0\}$$

Agents care only about commodity 3, which is taken to be the numeraire. There is no need to distinguish among owners and nonowners. Each agent has endowments $(1,0,0)$. Note that commodity 2 is purely intermediate. Then $J = \{v : v^1 \geqslant -1, \ v^2 \geqslant 0, \ v^3 \geqslant 0\}$ and $P(z) = \{(1,0,1)\}$ for $v^2 > 0$, $P(z) = \{(1,q,1) : q \in R_+\}$ for $v^2 = 0$. The Walrasian equilibrium aggregate production is $\bar{y} = (-1,0,1)$ and the Walrasian price vector is $\bar{p} = (1,1,1)$. Now let $\mathcal{E}_n \to \mathcal{E}$, where $\mathcal{E}_n$ is obtained by replication. Suppose that y_n is a CN equilibrium for $\mathcal{E}_n$. Then $\bar{y}_n^2 = 0$ because $\bar{y}_n^2 < 0$ is incompatible with $\bar{y}_n \in J$ and if $\bar{y}_n^2 > 0$, then the firms of type 1 would make losses. If $\bar{y}_n^3 > 0$, then some firm of type 2 is consuming a nonzero amount of good 2. Because someone is producing it, its price cannot be zero, but by contracting consumption by ϵ the firm can make the price of good 2 fall to zero and so increase its profits. Therefore, at a CN equilibrium $\bar{y}_n^3 = 0$, and we conclude that $\bar{y}$ cannot be approached. Clearly, if we introduce a bit of curvature in the boundary of Y_1, Y_2 and also bound below both sets, the nonapproachability of $\bar{y}$ remains. Thus, the source of the problem is the inexistence of a continuous selection of P through $(\bar{p}, \bar{y})$, that is, the failure of part (i) of Condition U.

Example 9. Example 8 illustrated how extreme complementarities in aggregate production led to the failure of the first part of Condition U and of Theorem 4. This example will do the same for complementarities in consumption. Both examples should serve to emphasize the point already hinted at in the discussion of Example 6, namely, that a strict individualistic viewpoint is ill-suited to analyze economic situations with extreme forms of complementarities.

The economy is the same as in Example 6. Suppose that some price selection is given and that as $n \to \infty$, the Walrasian equilibrium can be approximated by a sequence of CN equilibria. Let z_n be the corresponding CN aggregate productions. Then $z_n \to (1, 1, -(12/5))$. So, eventually $z_n^1 > 0$ and $z_n^2 > 0$. Therefore, $z_n^1 = z_n^2$ because at a CN equilibrium the profits of every firm must be nonnegative. But we claim that a situation where $z_n^1 = z_n^2$ cannot be in equilibrium. Indeed, whichever $p \in P(z_n)$ has been selected we have that either $p^1 < 2$ or $p^2 < 2$. Let $p^1 < 2$. Take any firm producing a positive amount of the first good and decrease production by ϵ. The price of the first commodity will then be 2 and profits will increase. Hence, no such sequence of CN equilibria exists. Observe that the features of the example remain if we give some curvature to the boundary of the production set. What fails is the existence of a continuous selection from P in a neighborhood of the Walrasian productions. It should be noted that the failure of the example is more degenerate (i.e., less generic) than the failure of Example 6. Here the situation can be remedied by smoothing out the corners of the indifference curves in a neighborhood of the Walrasian equilibrium. There the example remains as long as preferences are kept homothetic.

Example 10. This example will illustrate the need of the second part of Condition U. We have $l = 2$ with the first commodity being the numeraire. There is only one type of production set $Y = \{v \in R^2 : v^2 \leqslant 3,$

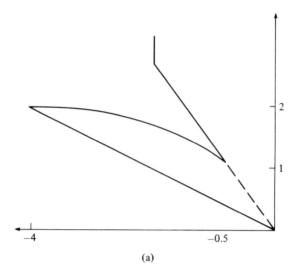

(a)

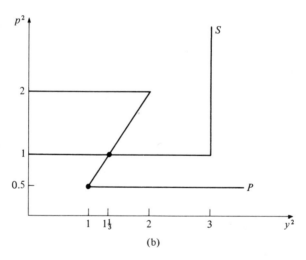

(b)

Figure 7.14

$v^2 \leqslant -v^1$, $-3 \leqslant v^1 \leqslant 0\}$. As usual the consumption sector is formed by owners (who have endowments and care only about the numeraire) and nonowners. These have the excess demand function indicated in Figure 7.14(a), which generates the P correspondence of Figure 7.14(b). The Walrasian equilibrium has a production vector $\bar{y} = (-1 - \frac{1}{3}, 1 + \frac{1}{3})$ and price vector $(1, 1)$. By replication one obtains the sequence $\mathcal{E}_n$. Suppose that y_n is a sequence of CN equilibria with respect to a selection $p(\ )$ which is continuous at $\bar{y}$ and has $p(\bar{y}) = (1,1)$. Given the P under consideration, this implies that $p(\ )$ is increasing in a neighborhood of $\bar{y}$. Suppose that $\bar{y}_n \rightarrow \bar{y}$. Then $\bar{y}_n \neq 0$ and therefore $p(\bar{y}_n) \geq 1$ (firms cannot make losses at the CN equilibrium). But then any firm not producing at capacity (and there have to be some because $\bar{y}_n \rightarrow \bar{y}$) has an incentive to expand production by ϵ because unit cost remains unaltered but the price increases, which contradicts the hypothesis that $\bar{y}_n$ is a CN equilibrium.

The example remains if the P correspondence is smoothed out provided it is upward sloping at the Walrasian equilibrium. We want to emphasize, however, that it is not the (nondegenerate) upward sloping demand that makes the example but the flatness (strict constant returns in this case) at equilibrium productions of the individual production set. Novshek and Sonnenschein (1978) have investigated limit situations with aggregate strict constant returns to scale but nonconvex individual production sets.

4   Proofs

For ease of presentation we will prove Theorem 2 before Proposition 1 and Theorem 1.

4.1   Proof of Theorem 2

The proof will proceed in four steps. Although it may appear long, its general structure is quite clear. The strategy pursued is to find, for the "right" dimension s (which turns out to be $2l-1$), C^1 maps G_n, G from some open set $V \subset R^s$ into R^s that have the properties: (i) the zeros of G (i.e., the solutions to $G(v) = 0$) yield the Walrasian solutions of $\mathcal{E}$, the particular regular equilibrium we are focusing upon being one of the solutions (typically the only one in V); (ii) the zeros of G_n yield the Cournot–Nash solutions for $\mathcal{E}_n$; (iii) G_n converges to G C^1 uniformly on V. We then obtain our approximating sequence in a straightforward manner via the implicit function theorem. The situation is pictured in Figure 7.15. The key aspect to note is that in spite of the number of agents of the economies $\mathcal{E}_n$ going to infinity, the maps G_n, G are all defined in a space of the same fixed dimension. Once this has been accomplished, the rest follows rather simply. We remark that the fixed dimension of the domain of G and the G_n's is $2l-1$, which is also independent of the number of types. In fact, our proof does not depend in any essential way on the finiteness of P. It can be extended without the slightest difficulty to the case where P is merely "compact."

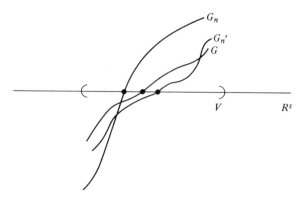

Figure 7.15

In Step 1 we construct the function G. Steps 2, 3, 4 build G_n. Actually, this is done in Step 4; Steps 2 and 3 are preparatory. Step 4 also carries out the application of the implicit function theorem.

Step 1. Let $\bar{p} \in R_{++}^{l-1}$ be the given regular Walrasian equilibrium price. Let $U \subset R_{++}^{l-1}$ be a small connected neighborhood of $\bar{p}$ on which Condition H is satisfied.
    Define $\xi : U \to R_{++}^{2l-1}$ by

$$\xi(p) = (p^1 d^1(p), \ldots, p^{l-1} d^{l-1}(p), d^l(p), s^1(p), \ldots, s^{l-1}(p))$$

To each p, ξ assigns the Walrasian vector of aggregate bids (denominated in numeraire units) and offers. We drop $s^l(p)$ because it can be derived from the other entries of the vector, that is, $s^l(p) = d^l(p) - \sum_{j=1}^{l-1} p^j f^j(p)$. Denote $\bar{z} = \xi(\bar{p})$. Those are the Walrasian equilibrium aggregate bids and offers. Note that ξ is a C^1 function.
    Define $\pi : R_{++}^{2l-1} \to R_{++}^{l-1}$ by $\pi(z) = ((z^1/z^{l+1}), \ldots, (z^{l-1}/z^{2l-1}))$. Given bids and offers z, $\pi(z)$ is to be thought as a vector of clearing prices. Note that in particular, $\pi(\bar{z}) = \bar{p}$ because $d^j(\bar{p}) = s^j(\bar{p})$ for all j.
    Let $V \subset R_{++}^{2l-1}$ be a neighborhood of $\bar{z}$ such that $\pi(V) \subset U$. Define then $G : V \to R^{2l-1}$ by $G(z) = \xi(\pi(z)) - z$. Observe that $G(z) = 0$ implies that $p = \pi(z)$ is a Walrasian equilibrium price because then for every j, $z^j = p^j d^j(p)$, $z^{l+j} = s^j(p)$ and $p^j = z^j/z^{l+j}$ which yields $d^j(p) = s^j(p)$. Conversely, if $f(p) = 0$ and $z = \pi(p) \in V$, then $G(z) = 0$ (in particular, $G(\bar{z}) = 0$). So, there is a natural one-to-one correspondence between the zeros of f and the zeros of G. The interpretation of the function G is simple enough. Given a vector of (aggregate) bids and offers z, $\xi(\pi(z))$ is the vector of optimal ("notional") Walrasian aggregate bids and

offers corresponding to the clearing prices $\pi(z)$. If they coincide with the z with which we started, we have an equilibrium.

It is clear enough that, being the equilibria in correspondence, we should expect that their regularity will also be.

Lemma 1. $Df(\bar{p})$ is nonsingular if and only if $DG(\bar{z})$ is nonsingular.

Proof. Of course, $\operatorname{rank} f(\bar{p}) = l-1$ if and only if

$$\operatorname{rank}(Dd'(\bar{p}) - Ds'(p)) = l-1,$$

where d', s' are the functions obtained from d, s by dropping the last coordinate. Consider the map $\pi(\xi(p)) - p$ with values in R_{++}^{l-1} and domain $U \subset R_{++}^{l-1}$. Of course, $\pi(\xi(\bar{p})) - \bar{p} = 0$. Denote by E the $(l-1) \times (l-1)$ diagonal matrix with generic entry $e_{jj} = \bar{p}^j/s^j(\bar{p}) \neq 0$. A simple computation yields $D(\pi(\xi(\bar{p})) - \bar{p}) = E(Dd'(\bar{p}) - Ds'(\bar{p}))$. Therefore, $Df(\bar{p})$ is nonsingular if and only if $D(\pi(\xi(\bar{p})) - \bar{p})$ is non-singular. Let A be the $(2l-1) \times (l-1)$ matrix $D\xi(\bar{p})$ and B the $(l-1) \times (2l-1)$ matrix $D\pi(\bar{z})$. Then $D(\pi(\xi(\bar{p})) - \bar{p}) = BA - I$. On the other hand, $DG(\bar{z}) = D(\xi(\pi(\bar{z})) - \bar{z}) = AB - I$. But $\operatorname{rank}(AB - I) = l-1$ if and only if $\operatorname{rank}(BA - I) = l-1$ (Proof: Let $(AB - I)v = 0$, $v \neq 0$. Then $w = Bv \neq 0$ and $(BA - I)w = 0$, which yields the desired conclusion.)

Step 2. In this step we consider a fixed type h. To save on notation we drop all subindexes h. Let $u: R_+^l \to R$ be a C^2 utility function for $\succeq$ with no critical point.

The sets $U \subset R_{++}^{l-1}$, $V \subset R_{++}^{2l-1}$ and the vectors $\bar{p}$, $\bar{z}$ are as in Step 1. Let $\bar{x} \in R^l$ be the vector: $\bar{x}^j = f_h^j(\bar{p})$ for $j \leq l-1$, $\bar{x}^l = -\bar{p} f_h(\bar{p})$. That is to say, $\bar{x}$ is the Walrasian equilibrium excess demand vector of type h. By assumption, $\bar{x} \gg -\omega$ and $\bar{x}^j \neq 0$ for all $j \leq l$. Let $J \subset R^l$ be a neighborhood of $\bar{x}$ with the properties: (i) $x + \omega \gg 0$ for all $x \in J$, (ii) $x^j \bar{x}^j > 0$ for all $j \leq l$ and $x \in J$, (iii) J is bounded, that is, there is $\epsilon > 0$ such that $\epsilon |x^j| < 1$ for all $x \in J$ and $j \leq l$.

Define a function $\eta: V \times (-\epsilon, \epsilon)^l \times J \to R^l$ by:

$$\eta^j(z, q, x) = \begin{cases} \dfrac{z^j}{z^{l+j}} (1 + q^j x^j) & \text{if } x^j < 0 \\[3mm] \dfrac{z^j}{z^{l+j}} \left(\dfrac{1}{1 - q^j x^j} \right) & \text{if } x^j > 0 \end{cases}$$

If we convene that $z^{2l} = z^l$, η^l is also well-defined. The function η is C^1. Observe that $\eta(z, 0, x)$ is the vector of clearing prices associated to z.

Hence, because $\bar{x}$ are the Walrasian demands associated with $\bar{z}$ and $\bar{x} + \omega \gg 0$ we have that for some $\bar{\lambda} \neq 0$: $\eta(\bar{z}, 0, \bar{x}) - \bar{\lambda}\partial u(\bar{x}) = 0$, and $\sum_{j=1}^{l-1}(\bar{z}^j/\bar{z}^{l+j})\bar{x}^j + \bar{x}^l = 0$. Therefore, $(\bar{z}, 0, \bar{x}, \bar{\lambda})$ satisfies the system of $l+1$ equations:

$$\eta(z, q, x) - \lambda\partial u(x) = 0$$

$$\sum_{j=1}^{l-1} \frac{z^j}{z^{l+j}} x^j + x^l = 0$$

At $(\bar{z}, 0, \bar{x}, \bar{\lambda})$ the Jacobian of this system with respect to the $(l+1)$ variables (x, λ) is

$$\left| \begin{matrix} -\partial^2 u(\bar{x}) & -\partial u(\bar{x}) \\ (\bar{p}^T, 1) & 0 \end{matrix} \right| = (-1)^{l+1}\bar{\lambda} \left| \begin{matrix} \partial^2 u(\bar{x}) & \partial u(\bar{x}) \\ (\partial u(\bar{x}))^T & 0 \end{matrix} \right| \neq 0$$

because of the nonzero curvature condition. Therefore, by the implicit function theorem (see, for example, Schwartz (1967)), there are $\bar{z} \in V' \subset V$, $0 < \epsilon' < \epsilon$, and C^1 functions $x(z, q)$, $\lambda(z, q)$ defined on $V' \times (-\epsilon', \epsilon)^l$ such that: $\eta(z, q, x(z, q)) - \lambda(z, q)\partial u(x(z, q)) = 0$ and

$$\sum_{j=1}^{l-1} \frac{z^j}{z^{l+j}} x^j(z, q) + x^l(z, q) = 0$$

for all $(z, q) \in V' \times (-\epsilon', \epsilon')^l$. Furthermore, for a neighborhood $J' \subset J$ of $\bar{x}$, we have that given z, q the only solution x to the system of equations with $x \in J'$ is $x(z, q)$. Because to begin with V, J, and ϵ can be chosen arbitrarily small we will, to save notation and without loss of generality, identify V', J', ϵ' with V, J, ϵ. The interpretation of $x(z, q)$ is clear. For $q=0$, $x(z, 0) = \hat{f}_h(\pi(z))$ is nothing but the Walrasian demand function (composed with π). In general, therefore, $x(z, q)$ is a kind of Walrasian demand with distortions (preventing full proportionality of prices and marginal utilities). The latter are represented by the vector q.

From now on V and ϵ will be as in the end of this step. For each type h we have a $x_h(z, q)$. There is no loss of generality if we take all the $x_h(z, q)$ to be defined on $V \times (-\epsilon, \epsilon)^l$. The range is contained in $J_h \subset R^l$. Remember that $x_h + \omega_h \gg 0$ for all $x_h \in J_h$.

Step 3. In this step we shall consider a fixed $\mathcal{E}_n : I_n \rightarrow P$. It will be convenient to represent bid, offer, and net trade functions as vectors: $m = (m_1, \ldots, m_n) \in R_+^{ln}$, $y = (y_1, \ldots, y_n) \in R_+^{ln}$, $x = (x_1, \ldots, x_n) \in R^{ln}$. The subscript i denotes an agent.

For each i, let $u_i : R_+^l \rightarrow R$ be the utility function chosen in the previous step for the type of preferences of the ith agent.

We let $V \subset R^{2l-1}$ be as at the end of Step 2. It shall be convenient to define the cone $V' \subset R^{2l}$ as $V' = \{z \in R^{2l} : \alpha(z^1, \ldots, z^{2l-1}) \in V$ for some $\alpha > 0$ and $z^{2l} = z^l\}$.

Suppose that $(z, x) \in V' \times R^{ln}$ satisfies:

$$z^j = \frac{z^j}{z^{l+j}} \sum_i \max\{0, x_i^j\}$$

(a) \qquad\qquad\qquad\qquad for all j

$$z^{l+j} = \sum_i \max\{0, -x_i^j\}$$

This is a kind of balance of demand and supply condition. Then if we define $(m, y) \in R^{2ln}$ by $m_i^j = (z^j/z^{l+j}) \max\{0, x_i^j\}$, $y_i^j = \max\{0, -x_i^j\}$ for all j, we immediately see that $x[m, y] = x$ where $x[m, y]$ is the net trade generated according to the rules of the trading game. Thus, if a pair of aggregate bid and offer vector z and net trade vector x satisfies the balancedness Condition (a), then compatible individual bids and offers vectors can be generated in the natural manner. We say that (m, y) *corresponds* to (z, y).

For each i, we now define an important auxiliary function $F_i : Q_i \rightarrow R^l$, $Q_i = \{(z, x_i) \in V' \times R^l : x_i^j > -z^{l+j}$ for all $j\}$ by:

$$F_i(z, x_i) = \begin{cases} \dfrac{x^j}{z^{l+j}}\left(1 + \dfrac{x^j}{z^{l+j}}\right) & \text{if } x_i^j < 0, \\[3mm] \dfrac{z^j}{z^{l+j}}\left(\dfrac{1}{1 - (x_i^j/z^{l+j})}\right) & \text{if } x_i^j > 0 \end{cases}$$

Given $(z, x) \in V' \times R^{ln}$ we state three more conditions on (z, x):
(b) for each i, $x_i \geqslant -\omega_i$;
(c) for each i, $\sum_{j=1}^{l}(z^j/z^{l+j})x_i^j = 0$;
(d) for each i, $x_i \in Q_i$ and $F_i(z, x_i) = \lambda_i \partial u_i(x_i)$ for some λ_i.

Lemma 2. Let $(\hat{z}, \hat{x}) \in V' \times R^{ln}$ satisfy (a), (b), (c), and (d). Then $\hat{x}$ is a CN net trade. The bids and offers vector $(\hat{m}, \hat{y}) \in R^{2ln}$ that correspond to $(\hat{z}, \hat{x})$ are the CN equilibria.

Proof. Condition (c) is the budget constraint. So, Condition (b) gives individual feasibility. We only need to verify the preference maximization condition.

Take an agent i. It will remain fixed for the rest of this proof. Denote $\bar{m} = \sum_{i' \neq i} \hat{m}_{i'}$, $\bar{y} = \sum_{i' \neq i} \hat{y}_{i'}$. By definition of $(\hat{m}, \hat{y})$ we have:

$$\text{if } \hat{x}_i^j < 0, \text{ then } \bar{m}^j = \hat{z}^j \text{ and } \bar{y}^j = \hat{z}^{l+j} + \hat{x}_i^j$$

(*)

$$\text{if } \hat{x}_i^j \geq 0, \quad \text{then} \quad \bar{m}^j = \hat{z}^j - \frac{\hat{z}^j}{\hat{z}^{l+j}} \hat{x}_i^j = \hat{z}^j \left(\frac{\hat{z}^{l+j} - \hat{x}_i^j}{\hat{z}^{l+j}} \right)$$

$$\text{and } \bar{y}^j = \hat{z}^{l+j}$$

Let $g(x_i) = \sum_{j=1}^l [\bar{m}^j/(\bar{y}^j - x_i^j)] x_i^j$. Note that $g(\hat{x}_i) = 0$ (use (*) and (b)). We saw in Section 2.2 that the constraint set of agent i in net trade space is $\{x_i \in R^l : g(x_i) \leq 0, -\omega_i \leq x_i \ll \bar{y}\}$. The shape of this set and its frontier (i.e., $g(x_i) = 0$) is pictured in Figure 7.2. At any $x_i < \bar{y}$, $\partial_j g(x) = \bar{m}^j \bar{y}^j/(\bar{y}^j - x_i^j)^2$ and $\partial_{jj} g(x) = [2\bar{m}^j \bar{y}^j/(\bar{y}^j - x_i^j)^3] > 0$. Hence, $\partial^2 g(x_i)$, which is diagonal, is positive definite, and we conclude that g is convex in the domain $x_i > \bar{y}$. Therefore, $\partial g(\hat{x}_i)(\hat{x}_i - x_i) \geq 0$ whenever $g(x_i) \leq 0$ and $x_i > \bar{y}$ (remember that $g(\hat{x}_i) = 0$). This implies that in order to guarantee preference maximization it will suffice to show that, for some $\lambda_i > 0$, we have $\partial g(\hat{x}_i) = \lambda_i \partial u_i(\hat{x}_i)$; see Figure 7.2. This follows from Condition (b) if we show $\partial g(\hat{x}_i) = F_i(\hat{z}, \hat{x}_i)$.

We have $\partial_j g(\hat{x}_i) = \bar{m}^j \bar{y}^j/(\bar{y}^j - \hat{x}_i^j)^2$. Using (*) this yields:

(i) if $\hat{x}_i^j < 0$, then $\partial_j g(\hat{x}_i) = [\hat{z}^j/(\hat{z}^{l+j})^2](\hat{z}^{l+j} + \hat{x}_i^j) = F_i^j(\hat{z}, \hat{x}_i)$

(ii) if $\hat{x}_i^j \geq 0$, then

$$d_j g(\hat{x}_i) = \bar{m}^j \hat{z}^{l+j}/(\hat{z}^{l+j} - \hat{x}_i^j)^2 = (\hat{z}^j/\hat{z}^{l+j})[\hat{z}^{l+j}/(\hat{z}^{l+j} - \hat{x}_i^j)] = F_i^j(\hat{z}, \hat{x}_i).$$

This ends the proof of the lemma.

A warning may be in order. The vector $F_i(z, x_i)$ does not generally represent the gradient of the frontier of the attainable region of agent i at the point x_i. This is the case only at equilibrium, that is, when the demand = supply Condition (a) is satisfied.

Step 4. In this step we put together the two previous ones, define the functions $G_n : V \to R^{2l-1}$ and apply the implicit function theorem.

For $\mathcal{E}_n$ denote by θ_n^h the fraction of agents of type h. Of course, $\theta_n^h \to \theta^h$.

Interpreting $z_n \in V$ as mean aggregate bids and offers we know from Step 3 that $z_n \in V$ and $(x_{1n}, \ldots, x_{mn}) \in R^{ln}$ yield a symmetric CN equilibrium if the following conditions are fulfilled (put $z_n^{2l} = z_n^l$):

(a)
$$z_n^j = \frac{z_n^j}{z_n^{j+l}} \sum_h \theta_n^h \max\{0, x_{hn}^j\}$$
$$\quad \text{for} \quad 1 \leq j \leq l$$
$$z_n^{j+l} = \sum_h \theta_n^h \max\{0, -x_{hn}^j\}$$

(b) $x_{hn} \geq -\omega_h$ for all h

(c) $\qquad \sum_{j=1}^{l} \dfrac{z_n^j}{z_n^{l+j}} x_{hn}^j = 0 \quad$ for all h

(d) $\qquad x_{hn} \in Q_h \quad$ and $\quad F_h(nz_n, x_{hn}) = \lambda_h u_h(x_{hn}), \quad \lambda_h > 0 \quad$ for all h

Let N be such that, for all $l+1 \leqslant j \leqslant 2l$ and $z \in V$, $Nz^j > 1/\epsilon$ where ϵ is as in Step 2 and we convene that $z^{2l} = z^l$. For any $z \in V$ define $q_n(z) \in (-\epsilon, \epsilon)^l$ by $q_n^j(z) = 1/z^{l+j}$.

Observe that, by definition, if $z \in V$, $x_{hn} \in J_h$ and $n > N$, then $x_{hn} \in Q_h$ and $F_h(nz_n, x_{hn}) = \eta_h(z_n, q_n(z_n), x_{hn})$. Therefore, Conditions (b), (c), and (d) will be satisfied by any $z_n \in V$ and the corresponding

$$x_{hn}(z_n, q_n(z_n)) \equiv x_{hn}(z_n), \quad 1 \leqslant h \leqslant m.$$

Note then that for any $z \in V$, $x_{hn}(z) \to \hat{f}_h(\pi(z))$. In fact, taking a smaller V if necessary, we can assume that $x_{hn} : V \to R^{l-1}$ converges to $\hat{f}_h \circ \pi$, C^1 uniformly.

Therefore, $\bar{z}_n \in V$ and $x_{hn}(\bar{z}_n)$, $1 \leqslant h \leqslant m$, $n > N$, will generate a symmetric CN equilibrium if Condition (a) is also satisfied, that is, if $\bar{z}_n$ is a zero of the function $G_n : V \to R^{2l-1}$ defined (with the usual convention $z^{2l} = z^l$) by:

$$G_n^j(z) = \begin{cases} \dfrac{z_n^j}{z_n^{j+l}} \sum_h \theta_n^h \max\{0, x_{hn}^j(z_n)\} - z_n^j, & 1 \leqslant j \leqslant l, \\[2ex] \sum_h \theta_n^h \max\{0, -x_{hn}^j(z_n)\} - z_n^j, & 1 \leqslant j \leqslant l-1 \end{cases}$$

It is clear that G_n converges to G, defined in Step 1, C^1 uniformly on V. Also, if $z_n \to z$, then for each h, $x_{hn}'(z_n) \to f_h'(\pi(z))$. Therefore, we can reduce the search for a suitable sequence of symmetric CN equilibria to the search for a sequence $z_n \to \bar{z}$ with $G(z_n) = 0$. The existence of a $N' \geqslant N$ and such a sequence for $n > N'$ is a consequence of the implicit function theorem. The following version of it will do (put first $G = G_\infty$, then let $M = \{\infty, 1, 2, \dots\}$, $d(n, m) = |(1/n) - (1/m)|$ and interpret $G(z, t) = G_t(z)$).

Implicit function theorem (see Schwartz (1967), ch. 3.8): Let $V \subset R^s$ be an open set and M a metric space. Let $G : V \times M \to R^s$ be continuous. Suppose that $D_z G(z, t)$ exists and depends continuously on (z, t) for all $(z, t) \in V \times M$. Suppose that $G(\bar{z}, \bar{t}) = 0$ and $D_z G(\bar{z}, \bar{t})$ is nonsingular. Then there are neighborhoods $\bar{z} \in V' \subset V$, $\bar{t}' \in M' \subset M$ and a continuous function $z : V' \to M'$ such that $G(z(t), t) = 0$ for all $t \in M'$. Further, $G(z, t) = 0$, $(z, t) \in V' \times M'$ implies $z = z(t)$.

One observation is in order. Strictly speaking, we have shown the existence and uniqueness of the approximating sequence only within the class of symmetric net trades. A careful reading of the proof (especially Step 4) will reveal, however, that uniqueness holds in general. Basically, one only has to systematically replace the subindex h by i. The functions G_n, G will still be perfectly well-defined on the space R^{2l-1}.

4.2   Proof of Proposition 1

The proof is unavoidably technical. Let $r > \omega_h^j$ for all j and h. We proceed by contradiction. Let x_n be a sequence of CN net trade equilibria for $\mathcal{E}_n : I_n \to P$. The corresponding aggregate bids and offers are z_n. It suffices to establish that

$$\max_{i \in I_n} |x_n^l(i)| \to \infty$$

does not hold. Suppose it does, then $z_n^{2l} \to \infty$ and we can assume $z_n^{2l} \geqslant 2r$. Call $p_n^j = z_n^j / z_n^{l+j}$ and normalize $\sum_j p_n^j = 1$. Because for all j, x_n^j is uniformly bounded below by $-r$, we should have $p_n^l \to 0$. We can also assume (extract a subsequence if necessary and relabel) that $p_n^1 > (1/l)$ for all n. The following properties are not difficult to verify (the uniform boundedness below of x_n is again the crucial fact): #$\{i : |x_n^j(i)| \leqslant r$, all $j\} \geqslant (n/2)$, there is $\epsilon > 0$ such that #$\{i : x_n^1(i) + \omega_n(i) \geqslant \epsilon\} \geqslant \epsilon n$ and #$\{i : 2x_n^1(i) \leqslant -z_n^{l+1}\} \geqslant n-2$. We can therefore assume that there is a sequence i_n and $v \in R^l$ such that $\mathcal{E}(i_n)$ is of the same type (say h) for all n, $v_n \equiv x_n(i_n) \to v$, $v_n^1 + \omega_h^1 > \epsilon$ and $2v_n^1 \geqslant -z_n^{l+1}$. Let now $q_n = \partial g(v_n)$, where g is the equation for the frontier of the attainable set of i_n in the economy $\mathcal{E}_n$ (see Figure 7.2). As in the proof of Lemma 2 (in Step 3 of the proof of Theorem 2) we have that if $v_n^j < 0$, then $q_n^j = p^j[1 + v_n^j / z_n^{l+j})]$ and if $v_n^j \geqslant 0$, then $q_n^j = p_n^j[1/(1 - (v_n^j / z_n^{l+j}))]$. Therefore, $q_n^1 \geqslant (1/2)p_n^1 \geqslant (1/2l)$, $q_n^l \leqslant 2p_n^l$, and we conclude $q_n^l / q_n^1 \to 0$. Define $w_n \in R^n$ by $w_n^1 = -q_n^l / q_n^1$, $w_n^j = 0$ for $1 < j < l$, $w_n^l = 1$. Then, for n sufficiently large, $\omega_h + v_n + w_n \geqslant 0$ and therefore $\omega_h + v_n \succsim_h \omega_h + v_n + w_n$ (because $q_n w_n = 0$ and $\succsim_h$ is a convex preference relation). By continuity of $\succsim_h$, $\omega_h + v \succsim_h \omega_h + v + w$, where $w_n \to w$. But this contradicts the strict monotonicity of $\succsim_h$ because $w \geqslant 0$ and $w \neq 0$. This contradiction establishes the proposition.

4.3   Proof of Theorem 1

Part (i) is a trivial consequence of Proposition 1 and the fact that a bounded set of measures on a compact metric space (in this case, K) is relatively compact. So, any sequence of such measures (in our case the μ_{nh}, $1 \leqslant h \leqslant m$) has a convergent subsequence. Because, in turn, any limit measure μ_h satisfies $\mu_h(K) = \lambda(I_h)$, it can be generated by a function $x_h : I_h \to R^l$.

The proof of Part (ii) is at this point very simple, the intuition for it being quite obvious: If aggregate bids and offers go to infinity, then no individual trader can seriously affect the prices at which he trades.

If $A = \phi$, then the claim follows vacuously. Let $A \neq \phi$ and denote by z_n the aggregate bids and offers underlying x_n. Clearly, $z_n^{l+j} \to \infty$. We normalize by taking $\sum_{j \in A}(z_n^j/z_n^{l+j}) = 1$. Call $p_n^j = z_n^j/z_n^{l+j}$, $j \in A$. Then we can assume that $p_n^j \to p^j$. By putting $p^j = 0$ if $j \notin A$, we have a vector $p \in R^l$. It is a simple exercise to verify that for (almost) all i, $px(i) = 0$. Suppose now by way of contradiction that for some i (strictly speaking for a set of i's of positive measure) $pv < 0$, $v^j = 0$ for $j \notin A$, $\omega_i + v \geq 0$ and $\omega_i + v \succ_i \omega_i + x(i)$. Let the type of i be h. Then we can find a sequence i_n such that the type of i_n is h and $\omega_h + v \succ_h \omega_h + x_n(i_n)$. Let g_n define the frontier of the attainable set of i_n in the economy $\mathcal{E}_n$. Then (see Section 2.2),

$$g_n(v) = \sum_j \frac{z_n^j - m_n^j(i_n)}{z_n^{l+j} - y_n^j(i_n) - v^j} v^j$$

But $z_n^{l+j} \to \infty$ and $y_n^j(i_n)$, $m_n^j(i_n)$ are uniformly bounded (by lr where r is an upper bound for the endowments of any commodity). So, for n large enough, $g_n(v) \leq 0$, but this contradicts the preference maximization requirement on $x_n(i_n)$.

4.4 Proof of Theorem 3

The proof is entirely similar, only even simpler, than the proof of Theorem 1. Let $q = P(\bar{y})$. Those are the obvious Walrasian equilibrium prices. Suppose that for some $i \in I$ (strictly speaking, for a set of i's of positive measure) we have $qv > qy(i)$ for some $v \in Y(i)$. Put $\epsilon = qv - qy(i)$. Then, for some N and $i_n \in I_n$, $n > N$, we have

$$qv > qy_n(i_n) + \epsilon/2, \quad v \in Y_n(i_n), \quad y_n(i_n) \to y(i)$$

Let $\bar{y}_n'$ be equal to y_n except that $y_n(i_n)$ is replaced by v. Then $\bar{y}_n' \to \bar{y}$ and $\bar{y}_n' \in \hat{Y} \subset J$. Therefore, by continuity of P, $P(\bar{y}_n') \to q$. So, for n large enough, $P(\bar{y}_n')v > P(\bar{y}_n')y_n(i_n)$, which contradicts the fact that y_n is a CN production.

4.5 Proof of Theorem 4

We shall only provide a concise argument. The reason is that we follow the same general proof strategy as for Theorem 2 and also that we have nothing to add to Roberts's (1980) proof. We refer to Mas–Colell (1981) for a careful proof of a generalization of Theorem 4 to the nonconvex case.

Let $\mathcal{E}_n$, $\mathcal{E}$, and (y, q) be as in the statement of the theorem. Let $A \subset J$, $B \subset R^l$, be as in the statement of Condition U. Take $B' \subset B$ bounded and such that $S(\bar{B}') \subset A$.

Consider type h with Walrasian production y_h. The hypothesis that S is a C^1 function on B implies, with the convexity and boundedness of each Y_h, that the supply correspondence of h, S_h, is a C^1 function on B. This is not obvious, but it can be proved. If we let L be a sufficiently small neighborhood of zero in the space of $l \times l$ real matrices and if B is taken sufficiently small, then the generalized demand correspondence $\xi_h : B \times L \to R^l$ defined by letting $\xi_h(v, L)$ be the solutions to the problem $\operatorname{Max}_{y_h \in Y_h}(vy_h + y_h L y_h)$, is also a C^1 function (see Roberts (1980) for a proof). Intuitively, the hypothesis that S_h is C^1 (hence, Lipschitzian) implies that the relevant region of the boundary of Y_h has nonzero curvature, which in turn yields that the generalized supply is a function (which is the essential fact). We may note that this curvature aspect is specific to the proof of this theorem and has no analog in the proof of Theorem 2 (for which the relevant convexity conditions are always satisfied).

In the arguments to follow we always take n to be large enough for them to be justified. Suppose that in the economy $\mathcal{E}_n$, $y_n : I_n \to R^l$ is an attainable allocation such that for all $i \in I_n$, if i is of type h, then $y_n(i) = \xi_h(p(\bar{y}_n), (1/2\#I_n)Dp(\bar{y}_n))$. We claim that y_n must be a CN production. To verify this it suffices to make two observations: (i) For each i, the direct computation yields that the gradients computed at $y(i)$ of the profit function used to define the generalized demand (with $v = p(\bar{y}_n)$, $L = (1/2\#I_n)Dp(\bar{y}_n)$) and of the Cournotian profit function are identical. In other words, the first-order conditions of the Cournot maximization problem are satisfied; (ii) Because of the same curvature arguments of the previous paragraph, if n is large, then the second-order sufficient conditions will be automatically satisfied. Indeed, the isoprofit manifolds of the Cournot problem are almost linear and the production sets are bounded, convex, and with boundaries having some curvature.

Let $A' \subset A$ be a neighborhood of $\bar{y}$ with $p(A') \subset B'$. For each sufficiently large n, define

$$H_n : A' \to R^l \quad \text{by} \quad H_n(z) = \sum_h \theta_n^h \xi_h\left(p(z), \frac{1}{2\#I_n} Dp(z)\right) - z$$

Then, if $H_n(z) = 0$, we can determine a CN production y_n by putting $y_n(i) = \xi_h(p(z), (1/2\#I_n)Dp(z))$ if agent i is of type h. We also define

$H : A' \to R^l$ by $H(z) = S(p(z)) - z$ and note that $H_n \to H$, C^1 uniformly. As in the proof of Theorem 2 one verifies that rank $DG(q) = l$ if and only if rank $DH(\bar{y}) = l$. Therefore, by the regularity condition and the implicit function theorem (see proof of Theorem 2) there is $z_n \to \bar{y}$, $H(z_n) = 0$. From this we derive CN productions $y_n \to y$ and conclude the proof. Observe that the dimensionality of the domain of H_n is independent of the number of types.

REFERENCES

Arrow, K. and Hahn, F. (1971). *General competitive analysis*. San Francisco: Holden-Day.

Aumann, R. (1964). Markets with a continuum of traders. *Econometrica* 32: 39–50.

Cournot, A. (1838). *Recherches sur les principes mathématiques de la théorie des richesses*. Paris: Rivière. Translated by Nathaniel T. Bacon (1897). *Researches into the mathematical principles of theory of wealth*. New York: Macmillan.

Debreu, G. (1959). *Theory of value*. New York: Wiley.

Debreu, G. (1970). Economies with a finite set of equilibria. *Econometrica* 38: 387–392.

Debreu, G. (1972). Smooth preferences. *Econometrica* 40:603–615.

Dierker, E. (1977). Regular economies: a survey. In *Frontiers of quantitative economics III*, M. Intriligator, ed. Amsterdam: North-Holland.

Dubey, P. (1981). Price-quantity strategic market games, *Econometrica* 50: 111–126.

Dubey, P., Mas-Colell, A. and Shubik, M. (1980). Efficiency properties of strategic market games: an axiomatic approach, *J. Econ. Theory,* Symposium issue, April 1980, pp. 339–363.

Dubey, P. and Shapley, L. (1977). Non-cooperative exchange with a continuum of traders, RAND Report P-5964, Santa Monica, California.

Dubey, P. and Shubik, M. (1977). A closed economic system with production and exchange modeled as a game of strategy, *J. Math. Economics* 4: 253–287.

Gabszewicz, J. and Vial, J. P. (1972). Oligopoly "à la Cournot" in a general equilibrium analysis. *J. Econ. Theory* 4: 381–400.

Hart, O. (1979a). Monopolistic competition in a large economy with differentiated commodities. *Rev. Econ. Stud.* 46: 1–30.

Hart, O. (1979b). On shareholders unanimity in large stock market economies. *Econometrica* 47: 1057–1085.

Hart, O. (1980). Perfect competition and optimal product differentiation. *J. Econ. Theory,* Symposium volume, April 1980, pp. 279–313.

Hildenbrand, W. (1974). *Core and equilibria of a large economy*. Princeton: Princeton University Press.

Jaynes, J., Okuno, M. and Schmeidler, D. (1978). Efficiency in an atomless economy with fiat money. *Internat. Econ. Rev.* 19: 149–157.

Journal of Economic Theory (1980), vol. 22, no. 2, April 1980, Symposium issue on *Noncooperative approaches to the theory of perfect competition.*

Makowski, L. (1980a). A characterization of perfectly competitive economies with production. *J. Econ. Theory,* Symposium issue, April 1980, pp. 208–222.

Makowski, L. (1980b). Perfect competition, the profit criterion, and the organization of economic activity. *J. Econ. Theory,* Symposium issue, April 1980, pp. 222–243.

Mas–Colell, A. (1981). Walrasian equilibria as limits of mixed strategy non-cooperative equilibria, CRM IP–293, University of California, Berkeley.

Mas–Colell, A. (1982). Perfect competition and the core. *Review of Econ. Studies* 44: 15–30.

Novshek, W. and Sonnenschein, H. (1978). Cournot and Walras equilibrium. *J. Econ. Theory* 19: 223–266.

Novshek, W. and Sonnenschein, H. (1979). Private communication.

Novshek, W. and Sonnenschein, H. (1980). Small efficient scale as a foundation for Walrasian equilibrium. *J. Econ. Theory,* Symposium issue, April 1980, pp. 243–256.

Ostroy, J. (1980). The no-surplus condition as a characterization of perfectly competitive equilibrium. *J. Econ. Theory,* Symposium issue, April 1980, pp. 183–208.

Pazner, E. and Schmeidler, D. (1976). Non-Walrasian equilibria and Arrow–Debreu economies. Mimeographed, University of Illinois, Urbana.

Pearce, I. (1952–53). Total demand curves and general equilibrium, *Rev. Econ. Stud.* 20: 216–227.

Postlewaite, A. and Schmeidler, D. (1978). Approximate efficiency of non-Walrasian Nash equilibria. *Econometrica* 46: 127–137.

Roberts, J. and Postlewaite, A. (1974). The incentives for price-taking behavior in large exchange economies. *Econometrica* 44: 115–127.

Roberts, J. and Sonnenschein, H. (1977). On the foundations of the theory of monopolistic competition, *Econometrica* 45: 101–113.

Roberts, K. (1980). The limit points of monopolistic competition. *J. Econ. Theory,* Symposium issue, pp. 256–279.

Schmeidler, D. (1980). Walrasian analysis via strategic outcome functions, *Econometrica* 48: 1585–1595.

Schwartz, L. (1967). *Cours d'Analyse I,* Paris: Hermann.

Shafer, W. and Sonnenschein, H. (1982). Market demand and excess demand functions. Chapter 14, in *Handbook of Mathematical Economics,* Vol II, K. Arrow and M. Intriligator, eds. Amsterdam: North-Holland.

Shapley, L. (1976). Non-cooperative general exchange. In *Theory and Measurement of Economic Externalities,* S. A. Y. Lin, ed. New York: Academic Press.

Shapley, L. and Shubik, M. (1977). Trade using one commodity as a means of payment. *J. Pol. Econ.* 85: 937–968.

Shubik, M. (1973). Commodity money, oligopoly, credit and bankruptcy in a general equilibrium model. *Western Econ. J.* 11: 24–28.

Simon, L. (1981). Bertrand and Walras equilibrium. *Econometric Research Memorandum,* No. 282, Princeton, N.J.

CHAPTER 8

Recent results on the existence of Cournot equilibrium when efficient scale is small relative to demand

Hugo Sonnenschein

1   Introduction

This chapter concerns a line of research that begins with William Nov-shek's remarkable Ph.D. dissertation, and then extends his result on the existence of Cournot partial equilibrium with entry to the case of general economic equilibrium. I plan to write about the purpose of this research and the recent discoveries that have been made. In addition, I will remark upon the important work that lies ahead. I will give only a broad outline, leaving out either proofs or details. I will try to provide some historical perspective, but will make no attempt to touch as many bases as might be expected in a survey.

First, let me explain why I feel that the problems under consideration are central to the theory of value. Put briefly, the lesson of the analysis of perfect competition that has been carried out over the past 25 to 30 years is this: It is possible to formulate a rigorous model of economic equilibrium for economies in which: (a) markets exist for all commodities, and (b) every agent in sight takes prices as given. Furthermore, under some rather general conditions, each economy has at least one equilibrium state, and there is a close relationship between the set of Pareto optima for economies and the set of equilibria. To me, this means that a logical next step to take in order to deepen our understanding of the workings of perfect competition is to address the following two questions. Under conditions of laissez faire, and assuming that agents are intelligent strategists: (a) What markets will exist, and (b)

When will agents behave as if prices are beyond their control? The research on which I will report represents an attempt to shed light on the second question. It is carried out in a setting that is suggested by the following standard informal argument; see Figure 8.1.

Let F denote an inverse demand function and AC an average cost curve associated with the employment of any one of an unlimited number of available units of an entrepreneurial factor. Perfect competition is taken to require three conditions: perfect knowledge, firms that are small relative to the market, and mobile resources. The price P^* is sometimes referred to as the perfectly competitive equilibrium price, and a tendency toward P^* is established as follows. Suppose $\bar{P}$ exceeds P^* by more than a little bit. By perfect knowledge, firms know $\bar{P}$ and the average cost function AC. Provided that a firm changes price very little by entering, a firm will make a profit by entering and producing at minimum average cost. Because efficient scale is small, a firm in fact changes price very little by entering. Since resources are mobile, firms can enter, and this shows that $\bar{P}$ is not viable. (Since firms are free to leave the market, no price below P^* is viable.)

I want to make three observations about this intuitive argument. First, although the argument might well be taken to require the price-taking hypothesis on the part of consumers, it does not do so on the part of producers. The argument suggests that firms are involved in a non-cooperative game and that they understand that their actions will have an influence on price. Second, the average cost curves associated with the use of the entrepreneurial factor are U-shaped. The technology of a firm is not convex. Efficient scale of firms, that is, the scale at which firms attain minimum average cost, is bounded away from zero (it is indicated in Figure 8.1 as one unit). It is a "big deal," at least in terms of its own scale of operations, for a firm to enter or leave the market. Third, the negative slope of the inverse demand function F plays a major role in the argument. In the case of partial equilibrium analysis, the assumption that demand slopes downward does not have the feeling of a serious requirement. Walras, in the *Elements,* appeared to have the idea of a downward sloping demand curve very much in mind when he wrote "...under free competition, if the selling price of a product exceeds the cost of the productive services for certain firms and a profit results, entrepreneurs will flow towards this branch of production or expand their output, so that the quantity of the product [on the market] will increase, its price will fall, and the difference between price and cost will be reduced..." (1874–77, p. 225). This is nothing less than a statement that F has a negative slope! Prices must give the correct "entry signals" for the above intuitive argument to work.

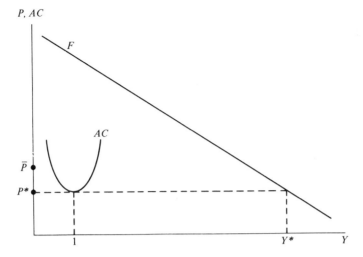

Figure 8.1

The purpose of the research that I will write about is to provide a formal foundation for the theory of perfect competition that captures the flavor of the intuitive argument presented above. In particular, I am interested in foundations that have firms behave as strategic actors, which, rather than being hypothesized to take prices as given, are forced in certain situations into actions that are well explained by price-taking behavior. In other words, this is an attempt to explain the price-taking assumption, and the attempt is along classical lines.

It should be clear that the Arrow–Debreu model, in its standard inter-pretation, does not capture the above intuition. First, firms are *assumed* to be price takers; strategic behavior on the part of firms is not allowed. Second, U-shaped average cost is not permitted by the theory. Third, the assumption of downward sloping demand plays no role in the analysis. Nevertheless, the foundations I will write about are intimately related to the Arrow–Debreu–McKenzie theory.

Finally, before I turn to definitions and theorems, two notes are in order. First, for the case in which average cost is constant and demand is linear, Cournot (1838) established a relationship between quantity-setting strategic equilibrium and price-taking equilibrium. Cournot's theorem applies to markets in which there are many firms, each of which acts noncooperatively. We know that he showed that prices are forced toward the value of average cost as the number of firms increases with-out bound. Observe that Cournot's result is false for the specification of Figure 8.1. The presence of an increasingly large number of active firms requires an increasingly high price so that firms can cover costs. As the number of firms grows, prices increase without bound, not to minimum average cost. This should convince us that Cournot's analysis does not apply to the situation at hand. Rather than forcing firms into the model, the intuitive description of perfect competition that I went through with the aid of Figure 8.1 allowed for the number of firms to be determined endogenously. This is quite important. The determination of the number of firms in a market is intimately connected to the U-shape of the average cost curves.

Second, I note that as the work described here has gone forth, a parallel theory has developed in which consumer agents, as opposed to entrepreneur agents, are assumed to make offers strategically, rather than to take prices as given. This theory is associated with the names of Shubik (1973) and Shapley (1976). Here, I will only say that there are natural reasons to separate the foundations of consumer price-taking theory from the foundations of producer price-taking theory. These parallel works should be regarded as complementary. They are not alternatives, but rather each is a part of a more fully integrated picture of competition. A recent issue of the *Journal of Economic Theory* brings together a collection of papers on the noncooperative theory of perfect competition (1980).

2   Novshek's theorem

Theorems on the existence of equilibrium in Cournot-type partial equilibrium models have been around for some time. Takashi Negishi (1961) extended these results to the case of general economic equilibrium. His pioneering work applies when technology is convex and when perceived demand is linear. This leads to concave profit functions and continuous reaction functions; the existence of equilibrium in such a setting is established via the Brouwer fixed point theorem. The work of Marshak and Selten (1974), Fitzroy (1974), and Arrow and Hahn (1971) all require concave profit functions and follow in this mold.

John Roberts and I (1977) presented an example that argued concave profit functions might be quite difficult to justify on theoretical grounds, even with convex production sets. In any case, the requirement of a convex technology for individual firms is extremely severe in the present context. In the spirit of the intuitive argument, we want to solve for the number of active firms in the market, and if production becomes more efficient with smaller scale (as with strict convexity), then this is not possible. But without strict convexity, one can only expect that the profit-maximizing action of agents will not vary continuously with the actions of other agents. The problem is much the same as with the discontinuity of supply in the Arrow–Debreu theory when production sets are not convex; however, the possibility of discontinuity is enlarged in the present context, because the isoprofit contours are no longer linear.

Following this early work, the first surprise was due to Novshek (1979). In a chapter of his dissertation, he made a major breakthrough when he proved the existence of quantity-setting Cournot equilibrium with entry for the economies of Figure 8.1 when efficient scale is small relative to demand. More specifically, he showed that in the tail of the sequence of economies obtained by replicating demand and adjusting units to per-capita terms, Cournot equilibrium always exists. Further, he noted that the Cournot equilibria of these economies converge to what I called the perfectly competitive equilibrium. I want to emphasize that Novshek's proof was very ingenious; he had to overcome some formidable obstacles, because continuous reaction functions are simply not available. (Ruffin [1971] worked with a similar model to explain P^*, but he did not go into the problem of existence.) Here is a brief recapitulation of Novshek's theorem (1980).

Assumptions: For the cost function $C(y)$,

$$(C) \qquad C(y) = 0 \quad \text{if} \quad y = 0,$$
$$= C_0 + v(y) \quad \text{if} \quad y > 0$$

where $C_0 > 0$ and for all $y \geqslant 0$, $v' > 0$, $v'' \geqslant 0$. Average cost is minimized uniquely at $y = 1$.

For the inverse demand function $F(Y)$, (F) $F \in C^2([0, \infty])$, with $F' < 0$ whenever $F > 0$, and there exists $Y^* > 0$ such that $F(Y^*) = C(1)$ (equals minimum average cost). Y^* is the competitive output.

Definitions: An α size firm corresponding to C is a firm with cost function $C_\alpha(y) = \alpha C(y/\alpha)$. For each α, C, and F, one considers a pool of available firms, each with cost function C_α, facing market inverse demand F.

Given C, F, and an $\alpha \in (0, \infty)$, an (α, C, F) market equilibrium with free entry is an integer n and a set $\{y_1, \ldots, y_n\}$ of positive outputs such that:

(a) $\{y_1, \ldots, y_n\}$ is an n firm Cournot equilibrium (without entry), that is, for all $i = 1, \ldots, n$,

$$F\left(\sum_{j \neq i} y_j + y_i\right) y_i - C_\alpha(y_i) \geqslant F\left(\sum_{j \neq i} y_j + y\right) y - C_\alpha(y)$$

for all $y \geqslant 0$, and

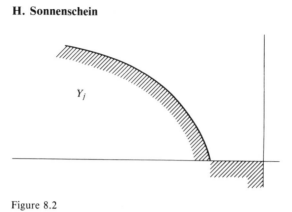

Figure 8.2

(b) entry is not profitable, that is,

$$F\left(\sum_{j=1}^{n} y_j + y\right)y - C_\alpha(y) \leq 0$$

for all $y \geq 0$. The set of all (α, C, F) market equilibria with free entry is denoted $E(\alpha, C, F)$.

It is easy to see that the Cournot equilibria exhibited converge to the competitive equilibrium Y^*; that is, given C satisfying (C), (F) satisfying (F) and $\alpha \in (0, \infty)$, if n, $\{y_1, y_2, \ldots, y_n\} \in E(\alpha, C, F)$, then $\sum_{j=1}^{n} y_j \in [Y^* - \alpha, Y^*]$. Novshek's theorem guarantees that Cournot equilibrium exists provided that efficient scale is sufficiently small relative to demand.

Theorem: Given C satisfying (C) and F satisfying (F), there exists $\alpha^* > 0$ such that for all $\alpha \in (0, \alpha^*]$, $E(\alpha, C, F) \neq \emptyset$.

3   Cournot general equilibrium

After Novshek's result, a natural next step was to take the analysis into a general equilibrium setting. One considers a basic economy $\mathcal{E} = (X_i, \omega_i, \succsim_i, Y_j, \Theta_{ij})$, specified just as in the Arrow–Debreu model, with one major exception: The sets Y_j are not convex. It is natural to think of the Y_j's as having a convex portion translated by a vector that indicates the presence of some fixed cost. See, for example, Figure 8.2.

Two related economies are associated with the basic economy $\mathcal{E}$. In the economy $\mathcal{E}(\alpha)$, for each j, there are a countable infinity of the production sets Y_j. When $(1/\alpha)$ is an integer, the economy $\mathcal{E}(\alpha)$ is to be thought of as a $(1/\alpha)$ fold replication of the consumer part of the basic economy $\mathcal{E}$, with an infinity of the basic production sets Y_j for each j.

As α gets small, the economies $\mathcal{E}(\alpha)$ converge to a limit economy $\hat{\mathcal{E}}$, which is formed by replacing each Y_j by the smallest convex cone that contains Y_j. In the spirit of the partial equilibrium treatment, one wants to show that the set of Cournot equilibria (with entry) of the economies $\mathcal{E}(\alpha)$ converges to the Walrasian equilibria of the limit economy $\hat{\mathcal{E}}$. There are substantial difficulties, however. For any given positive α an equilibrium may not exist, even in mixed strategies, for the economy $\mathcal{E}(\alpha)$. Novshek (1979) identified a strong condition on demand that was sufficient for the existence of equilibrium provided that α is sufficiently small. The condition is called interindustry complimentarity (IIC), and it is a restriction on the Walrasian equilibria of the limit economy $\hat{\mathcal{E}}$. Loosely speaking, it requires that at a Walrasian equilibrium of $\hat{\mathcal{E}}$, the profitability of a firm of the type defined by Y_j is increased by the entry of firms of the type defined by Y_k $(k \neq j)$ and diminished by the entry of firms of the type j.

Clearly, the condition IIC is too strong for acceptable general theorems. Novshek and I tried to weaken it to a condition we knew to be necessary for Cournot equilibrium; namely, that for each j, the profit of firms defined by Y_j varies inversely with the mass of active firms of the type j. This condition is called DSD since it generalizes the notion of downward sloping demand in partial equilibrium analysis. We were able to prove an existence theorem with IIC replaced by DSD, but only by allowing a limited amount of mixed strategy in the equilibrium. Without it, the theorem is false. Movement to consideration of mixed-strategy equilibria, even of a limited form, was for us a major decision. There is every reason to believe that the qualitative features of equilibrium will change with changes in the equilibrium concept. In any case, this is the setting of our first general existence theorem (1978, pp. 236–7).

Theorem: Given a basic economy $\mathcal{E}$ (more correctly, given an open dense set of basic economies) such that there is a DSD equilibrium in the limit economy $\hat{\mathcal{E}}$, every economy $\mathcal{E}(\alpha)$ in the tail of the sequence of economies generated by $\mathcal{E}$ has at least one Cournot equilibrium (with entry). Firms are allowed mixed strategies, but only a finite number of them (fixed in advance) play mixed strategies in the equilibria that are exhibited. These marginal firms make zero expected profit, while the remainder of active firms typically make positive profit. (Thus, the percentage of firms that adopt mixed strategies approaches zero.)

This existence theorem pretty well captures the intuitive argument that we started with. The coverage of the theorem is rather broad; it could not be much broader because DSD at an equilibrium Y^* of a limit economy $\hat{\mathcal{E}}$ is a necessary condition for there to exist a sequence of Cournot equilibria, one from each $\mathcal{E}(\alpha_n)$ $[\alpha_n \to 0]$ that converge to Y^*. Production sets need not be convex and firms are assumed to behave strategically. It is natural to inquire regarding the reasonableness of DSD, which plays a major role in the analysis. It is always satisfied for the case in which the consumer sector acts as a single agent; however, Novshek and I have constructed robust and not obviously pathological examples of economies in which DSD is not satisfied.

Recently, Andreu Mas–Colell (private communication) contributed a surprise to the investigation when he showed that, provided one assumes strict convexity of the production set in $\hat{\mathcal{E}}$ (associated with variations in the quality of the entrepreneurial factor), DSD can be dispensed with in the demonstration of the existence of Cournot equilibrium with entry. Roughly speaking, with strict convexity of the production sets of a limit economy $\hat{\mathcal{E}}$ and with mixed strategies allowed, all Walrasian equilibria of $\hat{\mathcal{E}}$ are limits of Cournot equilibria of the finite approximating economies. But I wish to emphasize that even with strict convexity, Walrasian equilibria of $\hat{\mathcal{E}}$ that do not satisfy DSD can never be the limits of pure strategy equilibria. In any case, Mas–Colell's result points out a striking qualitative discontinuity in the connection between Walrasian equilibira of $\hat{\mathcal{E}}$ and the mixed-strategy Cournot equilibria of approximating economies $\mathcal{E}(\alpha)$ when one passes to the case of aggregate constant returns to scale. The DSD condition is only relevant when we reach the case of aggregate constant returns to scale. This also serves to underscore the point that the relationship between Walrasian equilibrium and noncooperative equilibrium of approximating economies depends very much on the particular notion of noncooperative equilibrium that is adopted. I have the feeling that we have only begun to scratch the surface of understanding this relationship.

Before changing the subject, I want to recognize the important and much related work of Oliver Hart (1979), who, although not concerned with the existence of equilibrium, provided the first rather general equilibrium treatment of the asymptotic properties of equilibrium. Also, I note the early contributions of Gabszewicz and Vial (1972) and a very recent generalization of that work by Kevin Roberts (1980), and a paper presented at these meetings by Isabel Fradera (1980).

4   Entry dynamics

The condition DSD is related in an obvious way to the adequacy of the potential for profits, as a signal for entry, to guide an economy toward a Walrasian equilibrium. Just as tâtonnement dynamics will not always lead to equilibrium allocations, one cannot expect this of a naive entry dynamics. Nevertheless, it is natural to inquire regarding the range of situations in which entry dynamics, possibly based on fairly naive expectations, will lead to Walrasian allocations.

I have studied (1981) a simple dynamic equilibrium model with a continuum of firms, a continuum of commodities (differentiated products), and a continuum of consumers, each of whom demands one unit of one of the commodities. Given an initial density of firms, the initial equilibrium price function for commodities is defined by the condition that supply equals demand for all commodities. Each firm produces only one type of commodity at each point in time; however, firms adjust the commodity they produce by moving in the direction of higher profit at a velocity proportional to the rate of change in profit. Thus, the density of firms changes over time, and prices adjust so that at each instant supply equals demand. As prices change, the gradient of profit changes, which explains further changes in the distribution of firms, and so forth.

Despite the fact that the expectations of firms are extremely naive in this model, the system (formalized by means of a partial differential equation) converges over time to the unique zero profit Walrasian equilibrium. This happy result does not require that firms calculate an optimal plan for production over time. Indeed, agents are only required to know prices at each point in time (as opposed to for all time hence). I think it is interesting to inquire regarding the extent to which the result generalizes.

I will conclude by returning to the big picture. The purpose of this research is to study Walrasian equilibrium as a limiting case of a Cournot (with entry) regime. The results I have shown indicate it is possible to formulate a rigorous model of economic equilibrium in which the price-taking behavior of firms is explained rather than assumed. Furthermore, under some rather general conditions, it can be shown that every economy (with sufficiently small efficient scale) has at least one Cournot equilibrium state; in addition, when efficient scale is small relative to demand, Cournot equilibria are well-approximated by Walrasian equilibria. But this remains a wide-open area of inquiry. Quantity-setting Cournot equilibrium with entry (mixed strategies allowed) is only one of many interesting noncooperative solution concepts; in addition, there remain stability questions, welfare economics questions, and so on.

REFERENCES

Arrow, K. J. and Hahn, F. H. *General competitive analysis,* San Francisco: Holden-Day, 1971.

Cournot, A. A. *Recherches sur les principes mathématiques de la théorie des richesses.* Paris: Librairie des Sciences Politiques et Sociales, M. Riviere and Cie., 1838.

Fitzroy, R. Monopolistic equilibrium, non-convexity and inverse demand. *J. Econ. Theory* 7: 1–16, 1974.

Fradera, I. On the existence of Cournot equilibrium with technological non-convexities, presented at the World Congress of the Econometric Society, 1980, Aix-en-Provence.

Gabszewicz, J. J. and Vial, J-P. Oligopoly "à la Cournot" in general equilibrium analysis, *J. Econ. Theory* 4: 381–400, 1972.

Hart, O. Monopolistic competition in a large economy with differentiated commodities. *Rev. of Econ. Stud.* 46: 1–30, 1979.

Marschak, T. and Selten, R. *General equilibrium with price-setting firms.* Berlin, Heidelberg, and New York: Springer-Verlag, 1974.

Mas-Colell, A., ed. *Noncooperative approaches to the theory of perfect competition,* Symposium issue, *J. Econ. Theory,* 1980.

Negishi, T. Monopolistic competition and general equilibrium. *Rev. of Econ. Stud.* 28: 196–201, 1961.

Novshek, W. *Essays on equilibrium with free entry,* Ph.D. dissertation, Northwestern University, 1979.

Novshek, W. Cournot equilibrium with free entry. *Rev. of Econ. Stud.* 47: 473–486, 1980.

Novshek, W. and Sonnenschein, H. Cournot and Walras equilibrium. *J. Econ. Theory* 19: 223–266, 1978.

Roberts, J. and Sonnenschein, H. On the foundations of the theory of monopolistic competition. *Econometrica* 45: 101–113, 1977.

Roberts, K. The limit points of monopolistic competition. *J. Econ. Theory* 22: 256–278, 1980.

Ruffin, R. J. Cournot oligopoly and competitive behavior. *Rev. Econ. Stud.* 38: 493–502, 1971.

Shapley, L. Non-cooperative general exchange. In *Theory and measurement of externalities,* A. Y. Lin, ed. New York: Academic Press, 1976.

Shubik, M. Commodity money, oligopoly, credit and bankruptcy in a general equilibrium model. *Western Econ. J.* 11: 24–28, 1973.

Sonnenschein, H. Price dynamics and the disappearance of short run profits: an example. *J. Math. Econ.* 8: 201–204, 1981.

Walras, L. *Eléments d'économie politique pure.* Lausanne: Corbas, 1874–77. Translated by W. Jaffé as *Elements of pure economics.* Chicago: Irwin, 1954.

PART VI

APPLIED MACROECONOMICS

CHAPTER 9

Macroeconomic tradeoffs in
an international economy with
rational expectations

John B. Taylor

The purpose of this chapter is to study the macroeconomic policy trade-off between output and price stability confronting individual countries in an international economy linked by trade flows and a managed exchange-rate system. A tradeoff between output and price stability arises because of the tendency for wage and price decisions to be staggered over time. This prevents general price and wage levels in each country from adjusting quickly to changes in nominal variables – such as the money supply or the exchange rate – and creates an effect of these variables on real output and trade flows. Within each country, however, these real effects are tempered by expectations of future aggregate demand policy, both at home and abroad, and by exchange-rate policies generally. In this chapter we use the rational expectations approach to describe these expectations effects.

The policy implications of staggered wage setting and rational expectations have been studied in a closed-economy context by Taylor (1980a) and in a small open-economy context by Dornbusch (1980, Ch. 9). This chapter represents a multicountry extension of these earlier studies. Its main aim is the development of an applied econometric framework for

Prepared for the 1980 World Congress of the Econometric Society, Aix-en–Provence, France. I am grateful to Ates Dagli, Robert J. Gordon, Maurice Obstfeld, Edmund Phelps, and Stephen J. Turnovsky for useful comments and discussions. This research was supported by a grant from the National Science Foundation.

evaluating aggregate demand policies and exchange-rate rules under rational expectations.

Within a multicountry framework, it is possible in principle to determine an optimal set of policy rules for the world economy, given a social welfare function that depends on the macroeconomic goals of price and output stability in each country. The specific form of the optimal policy rules will of course be conditioned on parameters that need to be estimated empirically. Under certain conditions, the optimal rules will entail an exchange-rate regime in which each country makes its own decision regarding monetary accommodations although at the same time maintaining external stability. That is, each country chooses a point on its domestic tradeoff between output and price stability according to its own preferences and economic structure and independently of the preferences and economic structures abroad. But under other conditions, some coordination of aggregate demand policies is needed, for it is difficult to achieve isolation of each country from the preferences and economic structure of others. Not surprisingly, these conditions depend on how international price linkages, operating through import costs, affect the wage-price dynamics in each country. Such linkages have been studied by Bruno (1978) and Dornbusch and Krugman (1976) and emphasized in practical discussions of the vicious circle. An optimal aggregate demand and exchange-rate policy will reflect these price linkages. However, the analysis shows that the price linkages in turn depend on the policy rules through the effect of rational expectations. This is another example of the importance of the Lucas (1976) critique of econometric policy evaluations that generally ignore these expectations effects.

The chapter proceeds as follows. Section 1 outlines the major assumptions and the basic structure of the model. Because of the empirical aims of the analysis, we develop the model in terms of a general N-country framework. By introducing appropriate vector and matrix terminology, the N-country model can be described abstractly but simply as a vector generalization of the closed economy model. Many of the technical features of the analysis carry over directly from earlier studies by making matrix generalizations of scalar techniques. For example, matrix polynomial factorization is used in place of scalar polynomial factorization to obtain the rational expectations solution. In Section 2, we describe how the rational expectations solution is obtained and show how optimal aggregate demand and exchange-rate policy can be computed.

In Section 3, the policy problem of obtaining internal and external balance is considered and related to earlier work on the subject, in particular that of Corden (1969), who emphasized Phillips curve constraints. We show that, in the absence of direct price linkages between countries, it is possible for each country to choose a point on its own macroeconomic tradeoff and maintain external stability through variations in the exchange rate.

In Section 4, we show how maximum likelihood estimates of the model can be obtained subject to the rational expectations restrictions. It is important to note that in order to incorporate the rational expectations restrictions, it is necessary to estimate the policy and structural parameters simultaneously for all countries in the analysis. Although feasible and straightforward analytically, this is a computationally difficult task and has not yet been attempted. However, certain unrestricted reduced-form parameter estimates are shown to be useful for comparing policies across countries and for determining the extent of interaction between economies. Estimates of these parameters for 7 countries – the United States, West Germany, Italy, the United Kingdom, Canada, Japan, and France – during the 1970s are presented and compared. The results suggest that there are strong interactions between the policies in these countries. This indicates the potential for improving previous empirical international comparisons (see Taylor [1980b], for example) that have not incorporated this interaction. It also indicates the potential value of a full empirical multicountry analysis along the lines suggested here, despite the heavy econometric demands.

1   The model and assumptions

The structure of the demand side of the model can be summarized in the following equations representing each country $i = 1, \ldots, n$ at time t

$$(1) \qquad y_{it} = \sum_{j=1}^{n} \alpha_{ij}(m_{jt} - p_{jt}) + \sum_{\substack{j=1 \\ j \neq i}}^{n} \beta_{ij}(p_{jt} + e_{ijt} - p_{it}) + u_{it}$$

$$(2) \qquad z_{it} = \sum_{j=1}^{n} \gamma_{ij}(m_{jt} - p_{jt}) + \sum_{\substack{j=1 \\ j \neq i}}^{n} \delta_{ij}(p_{jt} + e_{ijt} - p_{it}) + v_{it}$$

where y_{it} = real output; z_{it} = trade deficit (+); m_{it} = money supply; p_{it} = aggregate price level; and e_{ijt} = exchange rate (currency i price of currency j). All variables except z_{it} are measured as detrended logarithms, thereby representing percentage deviations from a given trend. In order to be able to enforce the constraint that trade deficits sum to zero across countries while at the same time using units comparable to detrended logarithms, we measure z_{it} as the trade deficit of country i divided by the trend in world trade. Since $\sum_{i=1}^{n} z_{it}=0$ we can either drop one of the z_{it} equations or enforce the restriction that the coefficients of each explanatory variable sum to zero across the n countries.

Equation (1) is an aggregate demand relationship for the goods and services produced by each country. Aggregate demand is assumed to depend positively on the supply of money relative to the price level in each country and positively on the price of foreign goods ($p_{jt}+e_{ijt}$) relative to home goods p_{it}. That is $\alpha_{ij}>0$ and $\beta_{ij}>0$ for all i and j. Equation (1) reduces to a simple quantity theory equation for each country when $\alpha_{ii}=1$, $\alpha_{ij}=0$, and $\beta_{ij}=0$. Permitting $\alpha_{ii}\neq1$ is a generalization of such a quantity theory relationship. When $\alpha_{ij}>0$, a more stimulative aggregate demand policy[1] in country j spills over into country i by increasing demand for the exports of country i. When $\beta_{ij}>0$, then substitution effects reduce the demand for the exports of country i when either the price level or the exchange rate of country i rises, or the price level of country j falls. The random shock u_{it} is assumed to be serially uncorrelated with mean zero in the theoretical analysis but may be correlated across countries.

The trade deficit equation, Equation (2), depends on the same variables as Equation (1) and for similar reasons. For example, an increase in real balances, which increases demand in country i, will increase the imports demanded by country i and hence increase the trade deficit of country i ($\gamma_{ii}>0$) and reduce the trade deficit of all other countries ($\gamma_{ij}<0$). The trade deficit z_{it} does not feed back into any equations in the model. It is included here as an indicator of external balance to be incorporated in the criterion function for the analysis of optimal policy. The elasticities δ_{ij} should all be negative reflecting conventional substitution effects.

The main focus of the model is on the wage and price dynamics, which are summarized in the following three equations:

(3) $x_{it} = \phi_{i1}\pi_i(L^{-1})\hat{w}_{it} + \phi_{i2}\pi_i(L^{-1})\hat{p}_{it} + \phi_{i3}\pi_i(L^{-1})\hat{y}_{it} + \epsilon_{it}$

(4) $w_{it} = \pi_i(L)x_{it}$

(5) $p_{it} = \theta_{ii}w_{it} + \sum_{\substack{j=1 \\ j\neq i}}^{n} \theta_{ij}(p_{jt}+e_{ijt}) + \eta_{it} \quad \left(\theta_{ii}=1-\sum_{\substack{j=1 \\ j\neq i}}^{n}\theta_{ij}\right)$

where x_{it} is the contract wage and w_{it} is the aggregate wage. The hat over a variable represents its conditional expectation based on information through period $t-1$, and L is the lag operator ($L^s x_{it}=x_{it-s}$ and $L^{-s}\hat{x}_{it}=\hat{x}_{it+s}$). The term $\pi_i(L)$ represents a polynomial in the lag operator so that $\pi_i(L^{-1})\hat{w}_{it}$ represents a distributed lead in the expected aggregate wage.

As discussed earlier, the temporary rigidity in this model is due to the staggering of nominal wage contracts. We assume that there is a distribution of wage contracts by length, which is stable over time. The variable x_{it} is an index of contract wages signed at time t, and the weights in the polynomial $\pi_i(L)$ are determined by the distribution of wage contracts in this index. The average wage w_{it} is then a weighted average of past contract wages as indicated in Equation (3) where w_{it} is a distributed lag in the contract wage x_{it}.

Equation (3) describes how the nominal wage contracts are set. It is assumed that workers and firms setting wage contracts look ahead to the period during which the contract is set. As described in Taylor (1980a) the determinants of these contract wages within each country include the expected average wage w_{it}, which represents an estimate of the going wage during the contract period, and expected future demand conditions y_{it}, which represent labor market tightness. Labor market conditions in other countries do not directly affect wage decisions because of limited labor mobility across countries.[2] If prices tend on average to be set by a fixed markup over wages (as was assumed in the closed economy treatment of Taylor (1980a)), then incorporating future expected prices as well as future expected wages in the contract equation does not change the basic structure of the wage equation. (Essentially $\hat{p}_{it}$ can be replaced by $\hat{w}_{it}$.) However, if prices tend to be set on average by a fixed markup over wages *and* the costs of other factors of production, then clearly incorporating future expected prices in the contract equation does change the basic structure. Because in this analysis we wish to emphasize the direct international price linkage which comes from imported inputs to production, it is necessary to allow for the possibility that wage contracts will reflect future price movements, at least to a degree. Hence, $\hat{p}_{it}$ with weight ϕ_{i2} as well as $\hat{w}_{it}$ with weight ϕ_{i1} is incorporated in Equation (3). The markup pricing behavior is summarized in Equation (5), where the price level p_{it} is a markup over wages and import costs. The terms ϵ_{it} and η_{it} represent random shocks to wages and prices, which are assumed to be uncorrelated over time.

In order to close the model it is necessary to make assumptions about aggregate demand policy and exchange-rate policy. A general set of policy rules for these variables can be represented by[3]

(6) $$m_{it} = \sum_{j=1}^{n} g_{ij} p_{it}$$

and

(7) $$e_{ijt} = c_{it} - c_{jt}$$

where $c_{it} = \sum_{j=1}^{n} h_{ij} p_{jt}$. The monetary policy rule in Equation (6) allows for accommodation to domestic price movement g_{ii} as well as to foreign price movement. For a monetarist rule $g_{ij} = 0$, the money supply grows at its trend rate in each country. The exchange-rate rules in Equation (7) can be similarly accommodative to price movements. If $h_{ij} = 0$ for all i and j, then exchange rates are fixed except for any trend differences in the rates of inflation between countries (recall e_{ijt} is measured relative to trend). In general, however, exchange rates are accommodative to price movements in the sense that increases in the price level in a country lead to a depreciation of that country's exchange rate. Equation (7) with values for the h_{ij} describes a managed exchange-rate system. When obtaining the rational expectations solution of the model it will be necessary to assume that people know how this exchange-rate system works (that is, they know the h_{ij}).

Equations (1) through (7) describe the full model. The analysis of the model and the calculation of the rational expectations solution can be made considerably easier by introducing matrix notation. For this purpose, define the vector of country outputs $y_t = (y_{1t}, y_{2t}, \ldots, y_{nt})'$ and similarly define the vectors z_t, p_t, m_t, c_t, x_t, w_t, u_t, v_t, ϵ_t, and η_t.

Using the representation in Equation (7), substitute for the exchange rate in Equation (1) to obtain:

$$(8) \qquad y_{it} = \sum_{i=1}^{n} \alpha_{ij}(m_{jt} - p_{jt}) - \sum_{\substack{j=1 \\ j \neq i}}^{n} \beta_{ij}(c_{jt} - p_{jt}) + \sum_{\substack{j=1 \\ j \neq i}}^{n} \beta_{ij}(c_{it} - p_{it}) + u_{it}$$

$$(9) \qquad y_t = A(m_t - p_t) + B(c_t - p_t) + u_t$$

where

$$A = \begin{bmatrix} \alpha_{11} & \alpha_{12} & \cdots & \alpha_{1n} \\ \alpha_{21} & \alpha_{22} & \cdots & \alpha_{2n} \\ \vdots & & & \\ \alpha_{n1} & & & \alpha_{nn} \end{bmatrix}$$

and

$$B = \begin{bmatrix} \Sigma \beta_{ij} & -\beta_{12} & \cdots & -\beta_{1n} \\ -\beta_{21} & \Sigma \beta_{2j} & \cdots & -\beta_{2n} \\ \vdots & & & \\ -\beta_{n1} & & & \Sigma \beta_{nj} \end{bmatrix}$$

where the sum of the ith diagonal is from $j = 1, \ldots$, excluding i. Note that B is singular since the sum of each row is zero.

The trade deficit vector z_t can be represented in a similar way by substituting $e_{ijt} = c_{it} - c_{jt}$ into Equation (2) to obtain

(10) $z_t = \Gamma(m_t - p_t) + \Delta(c_t - p_t) + v_t$

where Γ and Δ are composed of the γ_{ii} and δ_{ij} in the same way that A and B are composed of α_{ij} and β_{ij}.

The policy rules in Equations (6) and (7) can be written as

(11) $m_t = Gp_t$

(12) $c_t' = Hp_t$

where G is the matrix with elements g_{ij} and H is the matrix with elements h_{ij}. Note that if $H = I$ then $e_{ijt} = p_{it} - p_{jt}$ which is a purchasing power parity rule.

The N equations in Equation (3) can be written:

(13) $x_t = \Phi_1 \pi(L^{-1})\hat{w}_t + \Phi_2 \pi(L^{-1})\hat{p}_t + \Phi_3 \pi(L^{-1})\hat{y}_t + \epsilon_t$

where Φ_1, Φ_2, and Φ_3 are diagonal matrices with the elements ϕ_{1i}, ϕ_{2i}, and ϕ_{3i} on the diagonal, and where $\pi(L^{-1})$ is a diagonal matrix polynomial with $\pi_i(L^{-1})$ at the ith diagonal element. Note that Equation (13) does not directly incorporate any intercountry effects. All off-diagonal elements in these matrices are zero. Given this definition of $\pi(.)$ Equation (4) can be written simply as

(14) $w_t = \pi(L)x_t$

To obtain a matrix expression for Equation (5) substitute for e_{ijt} to obtain

$$p_{it} = \theta_{ii}w_{it} + \sum_{\substack{j=1 \\ j \neq i}}^{n} \theta_{ij}(p_{jt} + c_{it} - c_{jt})$$

Define a matrix Θ in terms of the elements θ_{ij} in the same way that B and Δ were defined, and let D be the diagonal matrix consisting of the diagonal elements of Θ. Then

(15) $p_t = (I - D)w_t + \Theta c_t - (\Theta - D)p_t + \eta_t$

is a matrix representation for Equation (5).

2   Solution and properties of the model

Equations (9) through (15) represent the full model in vector form. To describe the properties of the model we begin by substituting the policy rules (11) and (12) into Equation (9) for the aggregate demand vector y_t to obtain

(16) $y_t = -Qp_t + u_t$

where $Q = A(I-G) + B(I-H)$.

The matrix Q is a world accommodation matrix. It is a representation of multicountry accommodation to price shocks and incorporates both aggregate demand policy G and exchange-rate policy H. Recall that $G=0$ represents a monetarist aggregate demand policy, while $H=0$ represents fixed exchange rates and $H=I$ (the identity matrix) represents "purchasing power parity" rules. When $Q=0$ the world economy is held at full employment regardless of price developments. This full employment rule can be obtained by setting $G=I$, which means full monetary accommodation in each country (real balances are held constant), and by setting $H=I$, which means full exchange-rate accommodation (a purchasing power parity rule). However, if price stability is desired it will not be optimal for Q to equal zero. As will be discussed below, when price linkages are negligible ($\theta_{ij}=0$ and $\phi_{i2}=0$), the optimal accommodation matrix Q is a diagonal matrix with positive diagonal elements: A price shock in one country should be followed by a slowing of real output growth in that country with no effects on output in other countries. Under a fixed exchange rate system ($H=0$) combined with monetarist money supply rules in each country ($G=0$), all elements of Q will be positive so that a price shock in one country will require the slowing of all other economies. Some unrestricted estimates of Q are reported in Section 4 for seven large countries during the 1970s.

Substituting the policy rules (11) and (12) into the trade deficit equation, (10), results in

(17) $z_t = -Rp_t + v_t$

where $R = \Gamma(I-G) + \Delta(I-H)$. The matrix R is analogous to Q. It is a world *external* accommodation matrix. External balances will be independent of price shocks under full monetary and exchange-rate accommodation. That is, $G=H=I$ implies that $R=0$. Note, however, that other values of G and H can also achieve this.

Equations (16) and (17) describe how internal and external balance is influenced by price movements for a given set of policy rules. We now proceed to derive the dynamics of prices and thereby close the system. According to Equation (13), the contract wage x_t depends on rationally expected wages, prices, and output during the contract period. From Equation (16) a forecast of output in future periods can be obtained in terms of a forecast of prices. Forecasts of prices in terms of wages can in turn be obtained by solving the markup Equation (15) for p_t. That is, by substituting the exchange rate rule into Equation (15) to obtain

$$(18) \qquad p_t = (I - D)w_t - (\theta(I - H) - D)p_t + \eta_t$$

Taking expectations in Equation (18) and solving for $\hat{p}_t$ results in

$$(19) \qquad \hat{p}_t = K\hat{w}_t$$

where $K = [I - D + \theta(I - H)]^{-1}(I - D)$ is the world markup matrix. According to Equation (19) expectations of future prices can be written in terms of expectations of future wages. Within each country markups determine prices in terms of wages and import costs. But, given an exchange-rate rule, import costs in turn are determined by prices in other countries and hence by wages in other countries. Therefore, the expected price in each country will depend in general on expected wages both at home and abroad. This line of reasoning depends heavily on the rational expectations assumption: An expected wage increase abroad will raise (if people understand the model and the exchange-rate system) expected prices abroad and thereby raise import costs and prices at home unless a purchasing power parity exchange-rate rule is in effect. The increase in prices at home will then raise prices abroad by a bit more by the same mechanism, and so on. Equation (19) represents the net effect of these interactions.[4]

Under certain conditions the world markup matrix K will be diagonal and direct wage-price linkages between countries will not appear. For example, if import costs do not get incorporated in the general price level (that is if $\theta_{ii} = 1$ and $\theta_{ij} = 0$ for each country i), then θ is diagonal and $K = I$. In that case $\hat{p}_{it} = \hat{w}_{it}$ in each country. However, exchange-rate policy can also interfere with the wage-price linkages. In particular, the purchasing power parity exchange rate rule ($H = I$) also results in $K = I$ and hence $\hat{p}_{it} = \hat{w}_{it}$ in each country i. In this case, any expected boom in wages in one country is offset by an expected depreciation of the currency, which leaves prices unchanged in other countries and the expected price level in the wage boom country marked up by the full extent of the expected wage boom.

Given the world markup equation, (19), the wage and price dynamics of the system can be determined as follows. Take expectations in Equation (16) and use (19) to obtain

$$(20) \qquad \hat{y}_t = -Q\hat{p}_t$$
$$= -QK\hat{w}_t$$

Substituting Equations (19) and (20) into the contract wage Equation (13) we have

(21) $x_t = [\pi(L^{-1})(\Phi_1 + (\Phi_2 - \Phi_3 Q)K)]\hat{w}_t + \epsilon_t$

which shows how contract wages set in each country will depend on expected average wages in all other countries during the contract period. Although π and Φ have been assumed to be diagonal to reflect the lack of labor mobility across countries, the world accommodation and mark-up matrices (Q and K) will not in general be diagonal as discussed above. If the off diagonal elements of Q are positive and large enough, then increases in expected wages in one country will have a depressing influence on contract wage negotiations in other countries, as workers and firms in those countries figure out that the restrictive policy response will cause a reduction in labor market tightness.

Taking expectations in Equation (21) and substituting for the average wage $\hat{w}_t$ in terms of the expected contract wages $\hat{x}_t$ using Equation (14) results in

(22) $[I - \pi(L^{-1})(\Phi_1 + (\Phi_2 - \Phi_3 Q)K)\pi(L)]\hat{x}_t = 0$

which is a two-sided vector difference equation in the contract wage vector. Solving this set of equations involves eliminating the expected future values of the expected contract wage, which can be accomplished by factoring the matrix polynomial on the left-hand side of Equation (22) into two polynomials, one which involves negative powers of L and one which involves positive powers of L. The solution for $\hat{x}_t$ in terms of past values of x_t can then be obtained by eliminating the polynomial in the negative powers of L. That is, Equation (22) can be written as

(23) $\psi(L^{-1})\Omega\psi(L)\hat{x}_t = 0 \quad (\psi_o = I)$,

where the polynomial $\psi(.)$ and the normalization matrix Ω depend on the polynomial π and the matrices Φ_1, Φ_2, Φ_3, Q, and K. Premultiplication of Equation (23) by $\Omega^{-1}\psi^{-1}(L^{-1})$ results in[5]

(24) $\psi(L)\hat{x}_t = 0$

and since $x_t - \hat{x}_t = \epsilon_t$ we obtain a reduced-form stochastic vector difference equation in the contract wages

(25) $\psi(L)x_t = \epsilon_t$

From the definition of the average wage we can now obtain a vector ARMA model for the average wage vector w_t; that is,

(26) $\psi(L)w_t = \pi(L)\epsilon_t$

The behavior of the price vector p_t is obtained from

(27) $p_t = Kw_t + [I - D + \theta(I - H)]^{-1}\eta_t$

and the behavior of the output vector and the trade balance vector follows directly from Equations (16) and (17).

Equations (26), (27), (16), and (17) describe the behavior of all variables in the multicountry model in terms of the structural parameters of each country and in terms of the policy parameter of the money supply and exchange-rate rules. These equations can be used for policy evaluation purposes simply by observing how the behavior of the system changes when the parameters of the policy rule changes. The equations can also be used for optimal policy calculation by maximizing a social welfare function with respect to the policy parameters. For example, suppose that high variability of output, aggregate prices, and the trade deficit reduce social welfare in each country. Then the optimal policy could be calculated by minimizing

(28) $E[y_t'\Lambda_1 y_t + p_t'\Lambda_2 p_t + z_t'\Lambda_3 z_t]$

with respect to G and H, where Λ_1 and Λ_2 are diagonal weighting matrices whose diagonal elements contain the relative weights on price and output fluctuations in each country's utility function. The dimensons of Λ_1, and Λ_2 are n. The elements of the diagonal matrix Λ_3 measure the importance of external stability. Clearly, the rank of Λ_3 should be $n-1$ because there are only $n-1$ degrees of freedom for z_t in the world economy. Without loss of generality, we assume that the first $n-1$ diagonal elements of n_3 are nonzero, whereas the nth element is zero.

In previous closed-economy analyses of models with contracts and rational expectations, the criterion of optimal policy for country i would simply be the minimization of $E[\lambda_i y_{it}^2 + (1-\lambda_i)p_{it}^2]$. By minimizing this quantity with respect to the policy parameters for various values of $0 \leq \lambda_i \leq 1$, a tradeoff between fluctuation in output (measured by Var y_{it}) is traced out. A tradeoff curve can then be represented in Var y_{it} and Var p_{it} space. An optimal policy is given by a point on this tradeoff curve. In the following section we examine how international considerations influence each country's attempts to maintain optimal policy as defined by a point on this tradeoff.

3   Internal and external stability[6]

One of the arguments in favor of flexible exchange rates – whether managed or not – is the freedom they give every country in an international economy to simultaneously achieve internal and external balance. In terms of the model in this chapter, external balance has the obvious interpretation as a situation where all elements of the trade balance vector z_t are constantly set to zero except for the unavoidable random shocks v_t. Internal balance is more difficult to define, however, because of the macroeconomic tradeoff that exists between output and price stability. One possible interpretation of internal balance is a full-employment policy where y_t is constantly held at zero except for unavoidable random shocks u_t. This corresponds to the notion of internal balance used in the early discussion by Corden (1960).

In order to achieve internal balance in this sense it is necessary to choose policies which generate $Q=0$ and $R=0$, thereby bringing y_t to full employment and z_t into balance except for the random shocks. It is of course possible to set Q and R to zero simultaneously, because the number of targets are equal to the number of instruments: The targets y_t and z_t have $2n-1$ independent elements, and the instruments m_t and c_t have $2n-1$ independent elements. The values of the policy parameters that achieve this are $G=I$ and $H=I$, fully accommodative monetary and exchange-rate policy. Note that both internal and external balance can be achieved in this case, whether or not there are direct price linkages across countries. When $H=I$, the world markup matrix K is equal to I so that price and wage developments in each country are independent of developments elsewhere. This is because $\Phi_1+(\Phi_2-\Phi_3 Q)K$ in the contract wage Equation (21) is diagonal when $Q=0$ and $K=I$.

There is a serious problem with this interpretation of internal balance, however. It focuses entirely on employment stability and ignores price stability. In fact, this fully accommodative monetary and exchange-rate strategy will lead to complete price instability. Equation (25) for the contract wage will be unstable.[7] Both output and price stability should be incorporated in the definition of internal balance when there is a tradeoff between the two as in this chapter. For this reason we interpret internal balance as a situation where each country is able to achieve whatever combination of output and price stabilty it prefers without regard to the preferences of those in other countries. This definition corresponds more closely with that used in more recent discussions of the question by Corden (1969) and Johnson (1969). Using this interpretation, internal balance is achieved by setting R equal to zero but setting Q equal to a diagonal matrix with the diagonal elements chosen to minimize

$$(29) \quad E[y_t'\Lambda_1 y_t + p_t'\Lambda_2 p_t]$$

Under such a policy, each country is isolated from economic developments and policy choices in other countries and is therefore able to determine its own point on the tradeoff between output and price stability. It is clearly possible to make Q diagonal and $R=0$ using the $2n-1$ instruments available.

The required mixture of exchange-rate and aggregate demand policies will have certain important features. To see these, suppose that there are only two countries, one with a fully accommodative policy $g_{11}=1$ and the other with a less accommodative policy $g_{22}<1$. Then for external balance, country 1 will have to expand its money supply when there is a price shock in country 2 in order to offset the contraction that the policy rule of country 2 requires. In addition the exchange rate (currency 1 price of currency 2) between the two countries should depreciate more when there is a price shock in country 1 than it appreciates when there is a price shock in country 2.

Note that, unlike the fully accommodative case, the isolation of the two countries disappears when there are price linkages between them. Policies that achieve an internal balance through a combination of price stability and output stability do not have the property that $H=I$. Hence, if there are price linkages $(\Theta \neq 0)$, then the world markup matrix will not be diagonal. This has two implications: (1) in a world where $\Theta \neq 0$ it is not possible for each country to choose a point on its internal tradeoff between output and price stability and be independent of policy choices elsewhere; and (2) the optimal policy which minimizes the criterion function in Equation (28) will not have the property of perfect external stability $(R=0)$. The optimal policy will entail a response of trade balances to purely nominal swings in prices caused, for example, by wage shocks or aggregate demand policy errors. In this sense the case where $\Theta \neq 0$ requires policy coordination between countries. Of course the policy rules which underlie this coordination will depend on the quantitative value of Θ as well as of the other parameters in the structural model. Moreover, the policy rules will not in general entail fixed exchange rates $(H=0)$.

4 Estimation

Econometric estimation of this model can be approached using constrained maximum likelihood techniques to enforce the rational expectations restrictions. Under the assumption that the vector $(u_t', v_t', \epsilon_t', \eta_t')'$ is normally distributed, the likelihood function of the observations on y_t, p_t, w_t, and z_t can be computed from the vector ARMA equations: (26), (27), (16), and (17). This likelihood function can then be maximized with respect to the structural parameters of the model using standard nonlinear techniques.[8] Note that in order to perform this constrained estimation it is necessary to estimate the structural equations and policy parameters for all countries simultaneously. Clearly, there are severe practical problems if such estimation is attempted without a number of approximations in addition to those already made. One possibility would be to consider a small number of large economies and aggregate the smaller economies into groups. Another possibility would be to use several two-step procedures as described in the previous note. Since degrees of freedom are likely to be in short supply the constraints provided by the rational expectations should be useful. Recall that it is necessary to have relatively stable monetary policies and exchange-rate rules during the estimation period if the approach is to be accurate.

In this section we report estimates of a simplified version of the model, which is illustrative of the basic approach and provides information useful for making international comparisons and determining the importance of interactions between the countries. We focus on seven large industrial economies: the United States, Germany, Italy, and United Kingdom, Canada, Japan, and France. The vector y_t consists of the linearly detrended log of output (real GNP or GDP) for these countries for quarterly time periods from 1970:1 through 1979:4. The vector p_t consists of the linearly detrended log of the output deflator.

Our main interest is in estimating the world accommodation matrix Q (under the approximation that these seven countries constitute the entire set of interactions in the world economy). Recall that the diagonal elements of Q indicate how accommodative each country is to its own price movements, and the off-diagonal elements indicate cross accommodation. Cross accommodation consists both of exchange-rate accommodation and of aggregate demand accommodation, but we do not attempt to disentangle these two forms of accommodation here.

To illustrate how Q might be estimated, assume that price linkages between countries are small so that $K=I$ and $\Phi_2=0$, and also that price movements parallel wage movements closely over the cycle. Then for the case where $\pi(L)$ is first order, we have from Section 2 that

$$(30) \qquad p_t = \psi p_{t-1} + 0.5(\epsilon_t + \epsilon_{t-1})$$

where ψ is related to the other parameter of the model by the constraint

$$(31) \qquad 4[2\psi + I + \psi^2]^{-1} = I - \Phi_3 Q$$

where Φ_3 is the diagonal matrix that describes how labor market pressures influence wage behavior in each country. If ϵ_t is uncorrelated with u_t in Equation (16), then the system consisting of Equations (30) and (16) is block recursive so that Q can be consistently estimated by ordinary least squares. Such estimates, however, will not in general be efficient, because they ignore the constraint, (31), across the equations,

Table 9.1. *Estimates of the accommodation matrix Q*

	US	Germany	Italy	UK	Canada	Japan	France
Estimates of Q constrained to be diagonal							
US	0.98						
Germany		0.38					
Italy			0.16				
UK				0.31			
Canada					0.31		
Japan						0.23	
France							0.65
Estimates of Q unconstrained							
US	0.80	0.78	0.01	0.12	−0.02	0.01	0.01
Germany	0.03	0.60	0.07	0.14	−0.44	0.14	0.55
Italy	0.29	0.44	−0.01	0.50	−1.18	0.18	0.51
UK	0.29	−0.19	−0.27	0.40	−0.52	0.15	0.79
Canada	0.53	−0.28	0.09	0.08	−0.42	−0.18	0.43
Japan	0.42	0.06	0.00	0.21	−0.75	0.33	0.86
France	0.38	0.05	0.23	0.05	−0.38	0.05	0.19

which is due to the rational expectations assumption. Note that in the special case where Q is diagonal, the model is just identified. If so, then the lack of correlation between ϵ_t and $u_{t'}$ along with the recursive nature of the model implies that (16) and (30) can be estimated separately. This is an important simplification, because joint estimation of Equations (16) and (30) requires dealing with a 14-dimensional constrained ARMA model. Even with the low orders considered here this is not an easy estimation problem.

Table 9.1 reports estimates of Q both unconstrained and constrained to be diagonal. In the diagonally constrained case all elements are positive but less than 1, thereby indicating partial accommodation. Note that these estimates indicate that Italy had the most accommodative policy during the 1970s whereas the United States had the least accommodative policy. Germany and France were more accommodative than the U.S. but less accommodative than the United Kingdom, Canada, and Japan.

However, the constraint that Q is diagonal can easily be rejected by the data. Hence, it is not appropriate to use this condition to estimate Φ_3 without jointly estimating Equations (30) and (16) together. Examining the unconstrained estimate of Q it is clear that these economies have not been achieving internal balance independently of economic developments elsewhere. Either suboptimal policy rules are keeping Q from becoming diagonal, as is required for independent internal balance, or price linkages are large enough that it is not optimal for Q to be diagonal.

The diagonal elements of the unconstrained Q indicate that, with respect to internal price movements, the United States and Germany have been the least accommodative, whereas Italy and Canada have been the most accommodative. Some of the cross-accommodation terms are quite large. The United States responds almost as strongly to German price shocks as it does to its own. On the other hand, Germany is almost completely isolated from U.S. price movements. All countries apply at least some restriction to their economies when U.S. inflation increases; not surprisingly Canada and Japan apply the most restrictive pressures whereas Germany applies the least. The most notable reverse responses in the Q matrix are those describing the reaction of countries to price increases in Canada.

5   Concluding remarks

This chapter has examined aggregate demand policy and exchange-rate policy rules in an international economy in which each country faces a tradeoff between the goals of output and price stability. An analytically convenient procedure for generalizing earlier closed-economy studies of staggered wage contracting with rational expectations was developed in order to provide a framework for this international study. Within this framework, policy evaluation, optimality calculations, and estimation – all subject to the rational expectations restrictions – can be performed. The problems of achieving internal and external stability and the potential needs for policy coordination across countries were examined within this framework.

Data from seven large industrial economies during the 1970s were used to estimate a world accommodation matrix that summarizes the aggregate demand policies and exchange-rate policies for these countries and how they respond to price shocks at home and abroad. Strong cross-accommodation effects were found in this accommodation matrix, which indicates that previous closed-economy or small open-economy frameworks would benefit from international generalizations of this kind. Such an international framework is apparently necessary for evaluating the effects of aggregate demand policy even if one is interested solely in the effects of policy on internal stability.

NOTES

1 A relationship between real balances and aggregate demand can formally be derived from a standard IS–LM framework; however, because expenditures depend on the real rate of interest, the reduced-form impact of real balances

on demand will depend on the expected rate of inflation. If market interest rates are thought to be the only channel through which real money influences demand, then our framework also requires an imperfect capital mobility assumption. An important extension of this model would be a full development of a capital market so that alternative assumptions about capital mobility could be analyzed. Fair (1979) has developed a quantitative model that includes international capital markets, but without rational expectations.

2 As will be clear in what follows, it is possible to modify the labor immobility assumption within this framework by allowing for cross effects in the contract wage equation.

3 The c_{it} notation is introduced for analytic convenience and does not restrict the class of exchange-rate policies. Note that $e_{ijt} = e_{ikt} + e_{kjt} = c_{it} - c_{kt} + (c_{kt} - c_{jt}) = c_{it} - c_{jt}$ as one should expect.

4 In effect, the price component of the "expected" vicious circle completes its rounds within the time period. The impact on wages occurs more slowly, however, because of the staggering of wage contracts.

5 Noting the analogy with the closed-economy case considered by Taylor (1980a) is useful at this point. In the closed-economy model the scalar contract wage x_t satisfied a two-sided scalar difference equation. A scalar polynomial in the lag operator was factored to obtain the constrained reduced-form differences equation in x_t. The same procedure is being used here except that we are working with matrix polynomials rather than vector polynomials.

6 Because there is only one instrument of aggregate demand policy in this model we have abstracted from the Mundell (1962) type of policy mix.

7 This follows from the closed-economy model, because with the fully accommodative policies the countries are isolated from each other.

8 Clearly, the policy rules could be estimated jointly with the structural parameters by adding stochastic terms to Equations (11) and (12) and joining these equations to (26), (27), (16), and (17). Alternatively, one can use a two-step procedure, estimating the policy rules first and taking these as given when estimating Equations (26), (27), (16), and (17).

REFERENCES

Bruno, M. (1968). Exchange rates, import costs, and wage-price dynamics. *Journal of Political Economy* 86: 379–403.

Corden, M. (1960). The geometric representation of policies to attain internal and external balance. *Review of Economic Studies* 28: 1–22.

Corden, M. (1969). International monetary reform and the developing countries: a mainly theoretical paper. In R. A. Mundell and A. K. Swaboda, ed. *Monetary reform in the international economy.* Chicago: University of Chicago Press.

Dornbusch, R. (1980). *Open Economy Macroeconomics.* New York: Basic Books.

Dornbusch, R., and Krugman, P. (1976). Flexible exchange rates in the short run. *Brookings Papers on Economic Activity* 3: 537–575.

Fair, R. A. (1979). A multicountry econometric model. Cowles Foundation Discussion Paper No. 541, Yale University.

Johnson, H. (1969). The case for flexible exchange rates, 1969, Federal Reserve Bank of St. Louis, *Review* 51 (June): 12–24.

Mundell, R. A. (1962). The appropriate use of monetary and fiscal policy for internal and external stability. *IMF Staff Papers* 9: 70–79.

Taylor, J. B. (1980a). Aggregate dynamics and staggered contracts. *Journal of Political Economy* 88: 1–23.

Taylor, J. B. (1980b). Output and price stability: an international comparison. *Journal of Economic Dynamics and Control* 2: 109–132.

CHAPTER 10

The new industrial organization and the economic analysis of modern markets

Richard Schmalensee

1 The new industrial organization

It is generally accepted that the modern field of industrial organization began with the work of Edward Mason and others at Harvard in the 1930s.[1] Lacking faith in the ability of available price theory to explain important aspects of industrial behavior, Mason called for detailed case studies of a wide variety of industries. It was hoped that relatively simple generalizations useful for antitrust policy, among other applications, would emerge from a sufficient number of careful studies. Perhaps because such generalizations were not actually uncovered very rapidly by case analysis, or perhaps because of easier access to data and computers, the case study approach was generally abandoned by the early 1960s. Most students of industrial organization followed Joe Bain (1951, 1956) and turned instead to cross-section studies, electing "to treat much of the rich detail as random noise, and to evaluate hypotheses by statistical tests of an interfirm or interindustry nature."[2] The need to describe each firm or industry in the sample by a small number of more or less readily available measures effectively limited consideration to relatively simple hypotheses not involving "the rich detail" so important to students of particular industries. Thus, the standard regression equation in this

It is a pleasure to acknowledge research support by the U.S. Federal Trade Commission and helpful comments from P. L. Joskow, J. P. Ponssard, F. M. Scherer, C. C. von Weizsäcker, and O. E. Williamson. Only I can be held responsible for this essay's flaws or the opinions it expresses.

253

literature specified some measure of profitability as a linear function of a concentration ratio and, usually, other similar variables. Bain's (1959, 1968) text, which dominated the U.S. market during the 1960s, similarly focused on simply-stated qualitative generalizations and contained almost no formal theory.

Leonard Weiss' (1971) impressive survey of "Quantitative Studies of Industrial Organization," prepared for the Econometric Society a decade ago, concentrated almost exclusively on cross-section econometric research. Commenting approvingly on that survey, William Comanor (1971, pp. 403–4) provided a crisp description of industrial organization circa 1970: "Despite the original prescription of Edward Mason, practitioners in this area have moved from an early reliance on case studies and toward the use of econometric methods of analysis. To a large extent, therefore, a review of econometric studies of industrial organization is a review of much of the content of the field." Recognizing that methods of scientific inquiry inevitably change, Weiss (1971, p. 398) opined at the end of his survey that "perhaps the right next step is back to the industry study, but this time with regression in hand."

Some econometric work on individual industries had of course been done when Weiss wrote; MacAvoy's (1962, 1965) studies of natural gas price formation and nineteenth century railroad cartels are particularly noteworthy. A great deal more of this sort of analysis was done during the 1970s, however. The investigations of insurance markets by Joskow (1973) and Smallwood (1975) and of airline regulation by Douglas and Miller (1975) are good examples. In contrast to the earlier cross-section work and even to some of the still earlier case studies, the industry-specific econometric analyses of the 1970s seem to have been more concerned with understanding the particular industry at hand than with developing or testing simple propositions that might apply to all markets. This may have reflected a shift in scientific interest toward the fine structure of markets. In the United States at least, it likely also reflected a rise in the importance of industry-specific regulation relative to antitrust policy. All the industries mentioned above were regulated in the United States. Regulation can at least in principle respond to an industry's idiosyncratic features in a way that is difficult for antitrust policy, which must ultimately be based on relatively simply stated rules that apply to all markets.

Not only were scholars pulled toward industry-specific analysis, they were pushed away from cross-section regressions. After Weiss (1971) wrote, critics such as Demsetz (1973), Mancke (1974), and Phillips (1976) began to demonstrate the extreme difficulty of drawing firm conclusions about causation from the sorts of cross-section regressions that began filling the journals in the 1960s.[3] Those regressions now seem much less central to the field of industrial organization than they were a decade ago.

Along with a shift in the focus of econometric analyses away from cross sections and toward particular industries has come an important change in the role and status of formal theory in industrial organization. The first, Masonian wave of case studies were explicitly part of an inductive enterprise distrustful of received theory. One also finds very little explicit theorizing in the cross-section literature; a priori arguments are typically limited to verbal justifications for the inclusion or exclusion of particular variables on the right-hand side of a single linear equation. In the 1960s, however, students in good graduate programs were learning that one had to have a formal structural model, not just a list of plausible candidate independent variables, in order to do serious econometrics. Thus, the empirical essays of Joskow (1973) and Smallwood (1975) mentioned above contain more explicit development and use of theory than most of the early, classic, book-length industry studies, and they are not atypical in this regard. In the early 1970s, Scherer's (1970, 1980) text, which made good use of microeconomic theory, replaced Bain's (1959, 1968) work as the standard graduate text in industrial organization.

The tools of theoretical analysis available to well-trained economists today are much more powerful than those Mason and his contemporaries had. In recent years, these tools have been employed with increasing frequency to construct formal models that either attempt to do justice to "the rich detail" of particular industries or promise to be helpful in the analysis of classes of real markets. Indeed, a sizeable literature has lately grown up in what can only be called "the pure theory of industrial organization"; theory that is designed to help one analyze individual real markets correctly, but that is not tied to or based upon any particular set of facts. To paraphrase Weiss, the rallying cry of many of those working in industrial organization in the 1970s seems to have been "back to the industry, but this time with the tools of modern economic theory in hand." Michael Spence has recently provided a revealing description of this approach:[4] "My instinct as an economist is to study industries on a case by case basis, applying and adapting models as appropriate. For those of us who do this kind of work, the differences among industries may seem more important or interesting than the similarities. And thus we are uncomfortable with general rules."

This new industrial organization of the 1970s differs from that of both classical industry studiers and cross-section regression-runners in a number of respects. First, more attention is paid to "the rich detail" of particular markets. Careful industry-specific econometric work and the "new institutional economics" of Williamson (1975, 1979) and others are making important contributions. Second, despite this focus on the particular, formal microeconomic theory is used intensively, and its power is appreciated. If nothing else, formal modeling serves as a check on the tendency of verbal argument to make any imaginable form of conduct sound plausible in small numbers situations, the same sort of check provided by close examination of actual conduct. Both checks are easily bypassed in the cross-section econometric approach. Third, in "applying and adapting models as appropriate," the investigator goes beyond mechanical use of textbook polar case analysis of competition and monopoly. Just as industrial organization economists began to become econometricians in the 1960s, many began to become theorists in the 1970s. Finally, the systematic search for simple generalizations of the sort that Mason hoped to find in case studies, the same sort that cross-section regressions seek, is essentially abandoned. This is not inconsistent with the emphasis on development of tractable, and thus simple, formal models, because these are taken to be tools useful for understanding "the rich detail" of reality. In any case, Spence's comments make it clear that faith in the adequacy of simple general rules for either market analysis or public policy is no longer universal.

These differences do not add up to a revolution. As Stigler (1968) and Scherer (1970, 1980) make clear, case studies and theoretical analyses were undertaken during the 1950s and 1960s. But these approaches became more important during the 1970s, and they seem likely to retain much of that importance in the 1980s.

Much of the interesting theoretical work in industrial organization deals with markets in which the offerings of rival sellers are essentially identical and buyers are well informed. Considerable attention is paid to oligopolistic interaction and to the strategic use by established sellers of first-mover advantages and economies of scale to protect monopoly profits from outside entry. Studies by Spence (1977, 1979), Dixit (1979, 1980) and others go beyond the familiar criticisms of the Bain–Sylos limit-pricing model, which was developed in the 1950s, to the construction of more satisfactory models of entry deterrence in which all actors behave rationally.[5]

In many real-world markets, however, buyers do not perceive all sellers' products as identical, and not all buyers are well-informed. Markets with product differentiation and nonprice competition were forcibly brought to economists' attention by Chamberlin (1933); they were not considered explicitly in the Marshallian price theory he inherited. Formal analysis of the consequences of imperfect buyer information about price seems to have begun with Stigler's (1961) seminal work. For many products, however, especially those sold in supermarkets and similar multibrand outlets, information about *quality* is at least equally important and much less perfect. In markets where products may differ and buyers may be unsure of the exact differences among them, a central element of seller conduct is product selection. Markets of this sort are more visible and important in modern economies – with cheap transportation, mass communication, and routine commercial application of the scientific method – than in the economies about which Adam Smith and Alfred Marshall wrote. They are thus referred to as "modern markets" here.

The remainder of this chapter considers problems that must be faced in the economic analysis of modern markets and the development of analytical tools to cope with those problems. I do not attempt to be comprehensive but rather focus on three sets of issues that seem to me both interesting and important. Section 2 is concerned with two of Bain's (1968) three key dimensions of market structure: concentration and product differentiation. The form of product differentiation is shown to have important implications for the appropriate measurement of concentration. Standard measures, which implicitly assume product homogeneity, can easily lead one to incorrect inferences about the nature of market interaction. A new measure of concentration that deals with these problems is presented.

Section 3 deals with Bain's (1968) third key dimension, conditions of entry. We focus on what he (1956, p. 216) found to be "the most important barrier to entry discovered by detailed study": product differentiation advantages of established sellers. Some suggestive evidence on the nature of those advantages is discussed. A simple model of rational buyer behavior under imperfect quality information is sketched in which differentiation advantages arise naturally. Implications for patterns of competition are discussed.

Finally, advertising is important in many modern markets, and buyer behavior therein involves problem solving in important respects. Section 4 concludes this chapter with a few general remarks about the treatment of advertising and consumer behavior in industrial organization.

2   Market concentration and product differentiation

Concentration is surely the most frequently quantified element of market structure. With no product differentiation, received doctrine holds that seller behavior will be more monopoly-like, at least in the short run before entry can occur, the fewer the sellers or the less equal their market shares.[6] In markets with homogeneous products, it is thus sensible to define and measure concentration by means of some function that is decreasing in the number of sellers and increasing in some measure of the inequality of their shares.[7] If concentration is to be used as a predictor of market conduct or performance, one would like to derive the exact form of this function from a generally accepted theory of oligopoly, but no such theory exists.[8]

Two derivations of concentration indices from models of market behavior nonetheless deserve mention. Following Rader (1972, pp. 269–273), let us consider Cournot equilibrium with constant costs.[9] Let c_i be the unit cost of firm i, with $i = 1, \ldots, N$, let q_i be firm i's output, let Q be the sum of the q_i, and let $P(Q)$ be the market inverse demand curve. Profits are then given by

(2.1) $\quad \pi_i = [P(Q) - c_i]q_i \quad i = 1, \ldots, N$

At Cournot equilibrium, firm i sets $\partial \pi_i / \partial q_i = 0$ assuming all other outputs fixed. If E is the absolute value of market demand elasticity, and $s_i = q_i / Q$ is firm i's market share, these equilibrium conditions can be written as

(2.2) $\quad (P - c_i)/P = s_i/E \quad i = 1, \ldots, N$

Letting Π be total industry profit, the sum of the π_i, one can multiply both sides of (2.2) by q_i/Q and sum over i to obtain

(2.3) $\quad \Pi/PQ = H/E$

where the H index of concentration is defined by

(2.4) $\quad H = \sum_{i=1}^{N} (s_i)^2$

Proceeding in a very different fashion, Stigler (1964) derives this same index as a measure of the likelihood of collusive behavior in a market with imperfect seller information. In markets with no product differentiation, the H index thus seems a sensible measure of concentration. I have elsewhere (Schmalensee (1977a)) attempted to show that it can be well approximated using published official data on concentration ratios.

In the Cournot model above, an increase in any one firm's output affects all other firms by reducing the market price. All are affected in proportion to their market shares. With product differentiation, however, this kind of symmetric or generalized interaction need not be present. If it is not, the theoretical rationale for market-wide concentration measures like (2.4) is weakened, as the development below establishes.

Markets with differentiated products began to receive serious attention from theorists in the 1920s. Two polar case models of market demand and seller interaction emerged at the very start of this work. The spatial model of Hotelling (1929) stressed buyer diversity; additional brands made it more likely that any individual buyer would find one well-suited to his particular tastes.[10] The symmetric model usually associated with Chamberlin (1933), on the other hand, involved a representative buyer who benefits from increased product variety. Both polar cases are still used extensively; compare the spatial analyses of Salop (1979a) and Schmalensee (1978b) with the symmetric models of Spence (1976) and Dixit and Stiglitz (1977).

In the original Hotelling model, brands (of cider in his example) are located along a line in the space of potential products. Buyers' ideal products are spread out along this same line. Each brand competes only with its two nearest neighbors, no matter how long the line is or how many brands it holds. (End brands have only one nearest neighbor.) Because rivalry is thus localized, each firm faces only a small number of actual rivals, no matter what standard marketwide concentration measures imply. Oligopolistic behavior would be predicted in markets of this sort even with many sellers.

In the 1930s, Kaldor (1934, 1935) argued strongly for the spatial view of differentiated markets, and he recognized that it implied a world of overlapping oligopolies. By the early 1950s, Chamberlin (1951, 1953) himself accepted the spatial model as the more useful of the two polar cases. He (1951, p. 68) also clearly recognized that it implied ubiquitous oligopoly, not the large-numbers case with which he is usually associated.

There is no reason to suppose that either extreme model is universally appropriate. One might model the automobile market in spatial terms, for instance, while analyzing the restaurant market in some locality with a symmetric model. In some markets, interactions among rival sellers might have more structure than the symmetric model implies but less than in a one-dimensional Hotelling framework. Lancaster's (1966, 1971) model of demand, where a linear technology converts purchases of goods into consumptions of characteristics about which buyers care, might be able to shed light on these intermediate cases, but so far very little has been done in this direction. As the analyses of Baumol (1967), Lancaster (1975), and Salop (1979a) have shown, the formal correspondence between Lancastrian models with two characteristics and one-dimensional spatial models is almost exact. In particular, the same localization of competition is preserved. Archibald and Rosenbluth (1975) have further shown that localization is preserved in models with three characteristics. In Lancastrian models with four or more characteristics, however, they demonstrate that in principle the average brand might have a large number of direct competitors. Conditions that would either guarantee or rule out this possibility are apparently not known, and no work within the Lancastrian framework has apparently sought useful summary statistics to describe intermediate degrees of localization.

The marketing literature contains both symmetric and spatial models, though the latter usually involve more than one dimension. A good deal of econometric work in marketing adopts the symmetric "us/us+them" specification.[11] On the other hand, the construction of "perceptual maps" of brands' locations in product space, based on various sorts of questionnaire data, has become commonplace.[12] These maps are some-what hard to interpret in economic terms, however, because the meaning of distance is rarely clear. Attempts have also been made to capture the structure of brand interactions by analysis of brand switching data and, recently, by the estimation of nested multinomial logic models based on forced-choice experimental data.[13] These approaches are designed to provide insight to those concerned with marketing actual existing brands or seeking profitable niches for new brands. They seem less helpful to an analyst concerned with the general nature of seller interaction in the market as a whole.

I now want to develop a measure of the overall extent to which rivalry is localized in a particular market.[14] This measure is in turn based on a measure of concentration that reflects the structure of brands' interac-tions. My approach is modeled on that leading to Equation (2.3), except that it is both easier and at least arguably more natural in the context of differentiated products to work with nonprice competition.

As I have argued elsewhere (Schmalensee (1976a, 1976b, 1977b)), the Nash/Cournot behavioral assumption is much more plausible in this context than in models of price/output competition. It might be even better to use a framework that, like Stigler's (1964), permits concentra-tion to affect the qualitative nature of seller interaction, but no frame-work of that sort usable here is apparent. In any case, I would argue that the measure developed here is no more dependent on the Nash/Cournot assumption than is the H index itself. Both arise in Nash/Cournot models; both are intended mainly for empirical use.

Assume that the difference between price and unit cost is a constant, m, for all firms, and assume that total market sales are fixed at $\bar{Q}$. Let a_i be firm i's effective advertising, with c_i the unit cost of that advertising. (Per dollar spent, high-quality brands may have more effective adver-tising.) If the s_i are market shares, as above, profits can be written as follows:

$$(2.6) \quad \pi_i = m\bar{Q}s_i - c_i a_i \quad i = 1, \ldots, N$$

In Nash/Cournot noncooperative equilibrium, with each firm maximizing its own profit taking the others' a's as fixed, it is easy to see that the ratio of actual profit to potential monopoly profit is given by

$$(2.7) \quad \Pi/m\bar{Q} = 1 - \sum_{i=1}^{N} a_i(\partial s_i/\partial a_i)$$

The most natural symmetric demand model in this framework is the following:[15]

$$(2.8) \quad s_i = a_i / \sum_{j=1}^{N} a_j \quad i = 1, \ldots, N$$

Straightforward differentiation yields

$$(2.9) \quad \partial s_i/\partial a_i = (1 - s_i)/\sum_{j=1}^{N} a_j \quad i = 1, \ldots, N$$

Substitution into (2.7) then gives us

$$(2.10) \quad \Pi/m\bar{Q} = 1 - \sum_{i=1}^{N} s_i(1 - s_i) = H$$

The H index thus emerges as a sensible concentration measure in differentiated markets in which competition is not localized at all. Note that (2.8) implies

$$(2.11) \quad \partial s_j/\partial a_i = -s_j/\sum_{k=1}^{N} a_k \quad i \neq j; \quad i,j = 1, \ldots, N$$

That is, rivals are affected by any brand's actions in proportion to their own market shares, just as in the homogenous product Cournot model above. Note also that if the c_i are nearly equal, so are the s_i, and H is then approximately $1/N$.

Now consider a spatial setup in which N brands are distributed evenly around a circle with unit circumference, and buyers are distributed uniformly around the same circle. Suppose that brands are numbered consecutively and that each brand competes only with its two nearest neighbors. A tractable demand structure with this property involves the following share equation:

$$(2.12) \quad s_i = 3a_i/N(a_{i-1} + a_i + a_{i+1}) \quad i = 2, \ldots, N-1$$

with the obvious modification for brands 1 and N.[16] If all the a_i are equal, this structure implies that all brands have shares of $1/N$, exactly as in the fully symmetric model, (2.8). Differentiation yields immediately

(2.13) $a_i(\partial s_i/\partial a_i) = s_i(a_{i-1} + a_{i+1})/(a_{i-1} + a_i + a_{i+1})$
$$= s_i[1 - (Ns_i/3)]   i = 2, \ldots, N-1$$

Because the first and last expressions are equal for $i=1$ and $i=N$ as well, direct substitution into (2.7) produces

(2.14) $\Pi/m\bar{Q} = 1 - \sum_{i=1}^{N} s_i[1 - (Ns_i/3)] = (N/3)H$

If costs are roughly equal, the ratio of actual to maximum profit is on the order of $1/3$, no matter how large N is. One can thus think of $(N/3)$ as measuring the extent of localization, or of $(3/N)$ as measuring the extent to which rivalry among the brands in this market is generalized.

In any real market, the investigator is likely to have incomplete information about the structure of firms' demands. Given high-quality estimates of the demand structure, of course, Equation (2.7) can be used directly to make predictions about conduct and performance. Unless one has a great deal of confidence in the second-order, curvature properties of these estimates, however, this is likely to be a risky undertaking. Suppose, for instance, that one admits the possibility of shares being determined by a simple generalization of (2.8):[17]

(2.8′) $s_i = (a_i)^e / \sum_{i=1}^{N} (a_j)^e   0 < e \leqslant 1,   i = 1, \ldots, N$

This is clearly a symmetric model, but (2.10) must now be replaced by

(2.10′) $\Pi/m\bar{Q} = 1 - \sum_{i=1}^{N} es_i(1 - s_i) = (1 - e) + eH$

The concentration measure developed below avoids dependence on difficult-to-obtain second-order information, like the value of e, by essentially building in curvature assumptions like those used to derive (2.10) and (2.14).

It is crucial, however, to have first-order information on the relative values of demand cross-derivatives. It is convenient to deal with that information in the following form:

(2.15) $\theta_{ij} = -(\partial s_j/\partial a_i)/(\partial s_i/\partial a_i)$
$$= k_{ij}s_j/(1-s_i)   i \neq j,   i,j = 1, \ldots, N$$

The first equality defines the θ_{ij}; the second defines the k_{ij}. It is reasonable to assume that all these quantities are nonnegative. Because market share must sum to one,

(2.16) $\sum_{j \neq i} \theta_{ij} = 1$ or $\sum_{j \neq i} k_{ij} s_j = (1 - s_i)$ $i = 1, \ldots, N$

The θ_{ij} indicate at whose expense firm i can increase its sales. One can have a good idea of who loses how much if i gains share, without having any information about how rapidly the marginal product of i's advertising is falling off.[18] In the basic symmetric model, (2.8), all the k_{ij} are equal to unity. When demand has more structure, as in (2.12), they differ in value. All else equal, one would like a concentration measure that increased in response to this sort of departure from symmetry.

I now proceed to construct such a measure. The summation in (2.10) is a share-weighted average of the shares of the total market held by each firm's rivals. Similarly, in (2.14) if the s_i are approximately $1/N$, the summation gives the share-weighted average of quantities approximately equal to $2/3$, the share of each firm's two rivals in the part of the market for which that firm is competing. The larger any firm is relative to its direct competitors in either case, the smaller is the corresponding term in the summation, and the larger is the ultimate concentration measure. This makes sense, both in terms of the diminishing returns built into (2.8) and (2.12) and in terms of more general notions of oligopoly interaction.

Suppose one thinks of (θ_{ij}/s_j) for $j \neq i$ as a sort of estimate of the reciprocal of the share of the total market held by i's rivals. These estimates are exact if (2.8) holds for all $j \neq i$, but in general they will differ. In order to obtain a single estimate, $\hat{s}_{-i}$, of the effective share of the market held by i's rivals for each i, let us weight these estimates by the θ_{ij}. These weights reflect the relative importance of the corresponding rival firms to firm i. This yields

(2.17) $\hat{s}_{-i} = 1 / \sum_{j \neq i} \theta_{ij}^2 / s_j$

On the reasoning above, the relevant quantity is not the share of the *total* market effectively held by i's rivals, but rather their effective share of that part of the market for which i competes. One can estimate this latter share simply as follows:

(2.18) $s^*_{-i} = \hat{s}_{-i} / [s_i + \hat{s}_{-i}]$

Proceeding by analogy with (2.10) and (2.14), our measure of concentration becomes

(2.19) $H^* = 1 - \sum_{i=1}^{N} s_i(s^*_{-i}) = \sum_{i=1}^{N} (s_i)^2 / G_i$

where substitution from (2.15)–(2.18) establishes

$$(2.20) \quad G_i = s_i + (1 - s_i)^2 / \sum_{j \neq i} (k_{ij})^2 s_j \quad i = 1, \ldots, N$$

It is straightforward to show that any single G_i is maximized subject to (2.16) and the nonnegativity of the k_{ij} if $k_{ij}=1$ for all i and j. In this fully symmetric case, $G_i=1$ and $H^*=H$, as one would hope. Because the summation in (2.20) is convex in the k_{ij}, H^* increases with deviations from this symmetric situation in much the same way that H increases with deviations from market share equality. It is clear that $G_i \geqslant s_i$ for all i, so that H^* has natural bounds:

$$H \leqslant H^* \leqslant 1$$

with the left inequality strict except in the symmetric case. These bounds induce limits on G^*, the natural measure of the extent to which rivalry is generalized among competing brands:

$$(2.21) \quad 0 \leqslant G^* = H/H^* \leqslant 1$$

Except in symmetric models like (2.8) or (2.8'), G^* is less than unity. In the spatial model (2.12) with equal costs, it is straightforward to show that $H^*=1/3$ and $G^*=3/N$, as above. One can think of $1/G^*$ as a measure of the extent of localization of rivalry.

I do not claim that H^* and G^* are the only measures of their general type or the best ones; they are merely the only such measures I have found. They are not intended primarily for theorem proving but for use in the analysis of actual modern markets. Two remarks about such applications thus seem in order. (I hope to have more to report in the reasonably near future.)

First, symmetric structures like Equations (2.8) or (2.8') are much easier to write down and estimate than nonsymmetric structures of any generality. It would thus seem sensible in most applications to test for deviations from symmetry before attempting to estimate a general matrix of k_{ij}. One can base such tests on arguments that under the null hypothesis of symmetry, the cross-equation disturbance covariance matrix from a properly specified system of estimated share equations should reflect the underlying symmetry in testable ways.

Second, closely related problems are posed by the existence of marketing instruments besides advertising and by firms selling multiple brands in the same market. In some cases, the pattern of cross-effects might be more or less invariant to the marketing instrument employed. That is, if an increase in firms 1's advertising would increase its sales mainly at the expense of firm 2, it might also be that firm 2 would be the main loser if firm 1 lowered price. In such cases, one could estimate the k_{ij} separately for each important instrument of rivalry and average them in almost any straightforward way. If rival firms belong to different strategic groups, in the sense of Caves and Porter (1977) and Porter (1979), these instrument-specific estimates might differ substantially, however. An increase in advertising might affect rivals who advertise a lot, whereas a cut in price might affect those who charge a low price and advertise little, for instance. In situations of this sort, it is not immediately obvious how substantially different sets of k_{ij} should be combined.

Similarly, if a firm sells multiple brands, it can take a variety of different actions when attempting to increase its overall share. The analysis above used "firm" and "brand" interchangeably, but in fact a single firm may sell several brands with different patterns of k_{ij}. It is again not immediately obvious how these should be combined if one wants a measure of concentration at the firm level, not the brand level. It should be possible to devise an appropriate generalization of H^* by beginning with models like Equation (2.8) in which firms sell multiple brands, but I have not yet attempted this.

3   Product differentiation advantages

Standard usage defines product differentiation by the consequences of its absence: Product differentiation is present whenever buyers do not treat the wares of competing sellers as perfect substitutes. It is also standard to follow Bain (1956, p. 3) and evaluate barriers to entry "by the advantages of established sellers in an industry over potential entrant sellers, those advantages being reflected in the extent to which established sellers can persistently raise their prices above a competitive level without attracting new firms to enter the industry." Adopting these definitions, there is no obvious reason why these two dimensions of market structure should be causally related or even correlated in cross-section. Indeed, one can think of examples of markets with considerable apparent differentiation in which entry barriers appear negligible (restaurants) and in which they are at least arguably substantial (breakfast cereals).[19]

In his seminal work on conditions of entry, Bain (1956, Ch. 4) observed that differentiation might in some instances translate into a preference for established brands over new brands and that this sort of product differentiation advantage could constitute a barrier to entry. Bain found this source of entry barriers to be very important in some of the markets he studied, and he sought (mainly through interviews) to understand the nature and origins of the corresponding buyer preferences in each case.

Summarizing his work on product differentiation advantages, Bain (1956, p. 143) concluded:

> All of these things might seem to suggest the existence of fundamental technical considerations, institutional developments, and more or less fundamental consumer traits which make possible or even very probable the development of strong and stable product-preference patterns. They may also suggest that advertising *per se* is not necessarily the main or most important key to the product-differentiation problem as it affects intra-industry competition and the condition of entry. Although instances are found in which it is, we may need in general to look past advertising to other things to get to the heart of the problem.

Despite this conclusion, most of the relevant cross-section econometric work on the determinants of profitability has followed Comanor and Wilson (1967) and used the ratio of advertising to sales as a proxy variable for both the importance of product differentiation and the significance of product differentiation advantages of established firms over potential entrants. Most of these studies have found a strong positive statistical relation between the advertising/sales ratio and various measures of profitability across industries. This has most commonly been interpreted as reflecting advertising's ability to enhance and protect monopoly profits of established firms. Because the theoretical case for such a causal relation between these variables is less than airtight, there are measurement problems associated with the standard practice of expensing advertising instead of capitalizing it, and the observed statistical relation must reflect firms' advertising budgeting rules as well as advertising's effect on market structure, the interpretation of the cross-section econometric results has been hotly debated.[20] Whatever the eventual outcome of that debate, these results cannot by their nature refute Bain's conclusion that advertising may not be "the main or most important key" to understanding the relation between product differentiation and conditions of entry, because advertising has generally been the only differentiation-related variable considered in cross-section econometric work.

Bain (1956, Ch. 4) does not explicitly assert the nature of this "key," but a number of his remarks suggest that he thinks that buyer uncertainty about product quality is at the heart of the mechanism involved. Thus he notes early in his discussion (p. 116), "There is a good *a priori* possibility, moreover, that most buyers will on balance prefer established and known products to new and unknown ones." Similarly, he states (p. 130) that within his sample, "the allegiance of consumers to established products in areas in which they are ignorant or uncertain concerning the actual properties of products is quite important." Finally, in summarizing (p. 142) the most common "strategic underlying considerations in strong product differentiation," he begins with "durability and complexity of the product (and corresponding infrequency of purchase by the individual consumer), generally associated with poor consumer knowledge or ability to appraise products, and thus with dependence on 'product reputation,' and also with dependence on customer-service organizations." All of this suggests that established firms' advantages in differentiated markets might often depend heavily on buyers' uncertainty about the attributes of new brands, so that being first in a market might often be much more important than merely spending a lot of money on advertising.[21]

Conventional wisdom in marketing and scattered recent empirical work both support the notion that there are important advantages of being the first entrant in some sorts of markets. Runyon (1977, p. 214) states the conventional wisdom clearly: "If the product is virtually identical with [established] competitive products, it has little chance of marketing success."[22] Bond and Lean (1977, 1979) find that important and long-lived advantages are enjoyed by pioneering brands of prescription drugs, advantages that can only be overcome by late entrants if they offer distinct therapeutic benefits. Whittin's (1979) study of cigarette market segments points in this same direction, as does the cross-section analysis of marketing costs by Buzzell and Farris (1976). Urban, Johnson, and Brudnick (1979) use pretest market analyses of buyer preferences to adjust for quality differences between first brands and later entrants. Based on data for 42 products in 16 consumer goods markets, they conclude that the second brand on average attains less than 60 percent of the first brand's share, the third brand obtains less than 40 percent, and so on. The problems faced by an actual entrant into the U.S. reconstituted lemon juice industry (Schmalensee (1979)) are at least consistent with this sort of disadvantage. Finally, experiments reported in the marketing literature by Tucker (1964), McConnell (1968), and others reveal that consumers are willing to pay a premium to continue purchasing brands with which they have acquired experience, even when all brands are identical in appearance and in fact.

A simple model involving rational buyer behavior serves to support the idea that product differentiation advantages can be built on differential information and to shed some light on the mechanism that might be involved.[23] Consider a narrowly defined product class, like bottled lemon juice, such that individual consumers can be sensibly modeled as using at most one brand in the class at a time. It is assumed that brands either "work" or "don't work"; they either perform as a brand in this class should, or they fail to perform acceptably. Whenever a new brand is introduced, all consumers are naturally uncertain about whether or not it will work. Assume that we have what Nelson (1970) christened "experience goods": The only way a consumer can resolve this uncertainty is to buy a brand and try it. One trial suffices to determine whether or not any brand works.

Let the function $F(v)$, $0 \leqslant v \leqslant V$ give the number of consumers willing to pay *at least* v for a unit of a brand in this class that works. Suppose that prior to the introduction of the first brand, all consumers have subjective probability π that it will not work, and all value a unit that doesn't work at $(-\phi v)$, with $\phi \geqslant 0$. (One might have $\phi > 0$ for a bleach that could ruin clothes, for instance.) Suppose that the time between purchases is constant, call it one period, and let the corresponding one-period discount rate, assumed common to all consumers, be r. Given market interest rates, more frequent purchase implies a smaller value of r. The assumption that all consumers have the same values of π, ϕ, and r is not as restrictive as it might seem, because the development below can be interpreted as applying only to a subset of consumers with the same values of these parameters, and the demand functions obtained can then be summed across all such subsets.

To simplify the analysis, let us assume that the prices of individual brands must be held constant over time. In Schmalensee (1980b) it is shown that the main conclusions developed below go through if price changes are allowed, but the details of the argument are too space-consuming for inclusion here. Let us also assume that consumers are risk-neutral, have infinite horizons, and behave perfectly rationally. Risk-neutrality and infinite longevity merely simplify, whereas perfect rationality could perhaps even be defended to a noneconomist in this context by noting that the consumer's decision problem is relatively straightforward.[24]

The solution to that problem is the heart of the model. Suppose that in order to try a new brand, a consumer ceases (for one period) to use a substitute that yields a nonnegative surplus (demand price minus purchase price) of s. Then it is rational to try a new brand selling at price p if and only if the following inequality is satisfied:

(3.1) $\pi[(-\phi v - p) + (s/r)] + (1-\pi)[(v-p)(1+r)/r] \geqslant s(1+r)/r$

The first bracketed term on the left gives discounted surplus if the new brand is tried, doesn't work, and the consumer switches back to the substitute. (It is assumed that one must use the entire unit of the new brand in order to evaluate it, so that its failure to work does not trigger early purchase of the substitute. This is not crucial to the argument.) Because the new brand need not be chosen once and for all, the consumer is willing to pay more than the expected gain vis à vis the substitute to try it. The second term on the left of Equation (3.1) capitalizes the stream of surplus associated with a brand that works, and the term on the right gives the benefit associated with continuing to purchase the substitute.

Inequality (3.1) can be rewritten as

$$(3.2) \quad p \leqslant (v - s) - \tau v$$

where the quantity τ is defined by

$$(3.3) \quad \tau = \pi r (1 + \phi)/(1 + r - \pi)$$

This quantity captures the premium that must be paid to induce trial. If $\tau = 0$, condition (3.2) indicates that the new brand will be purchased if and only if its net surplus, $v - p$, exceeds s. As one would expect, τ is increasing in ϕ and π. It is also increasing in r. Larger values of r reflect lower purchase frequency, this serves to increase the importance of any single purchase relative to the entire future stream of purchases, and this makes the risk associated with trying the new brand loom larger relative to the alternative of sticking with the substitute. As noted above, Bain (1956, p. 142) attaches some importance to low purchase frequency in this context.

For the first brand in some particular product class, it is reasonable to take $s = 0$. Without loss of generality, we can set the marginal utility of income for every consumer to unity. This means that before the appearance of the product category, every consumer receives zero surplus (on the definition used here) from the marginal unit of every commodity purchased. (We are assuming away indivisibilities.) If only a small fraction of total spending is devoted to the substitute product relevant here, so that income effects can be neglected, it follows that the forgone surplus from reducing spending on the substitute is zero. Alternatively, one can assume directly that overall utility is linear in spending on all goods and services outside the product class considered here.

If the first brand is priced at p_1 and announced to consumers who have $s = 0$, it follows immediately from Equation (3.2) that it will be tried by those with

$$(3.4) \quad v \geqslant p_1/(1 - \tau)$$

If we suppose for simplicity that the first brand in fact "works," then all who try it stick with it, and its demand function is given by

(3.5) $q_1 = F[p_1/(1 - \tau)]$

Note that the assumption that a brand always works is perfectly consistent with consumers' ex ante uncertainty about its quality. Pretrial advertising may be able to convey a great deal of product information, but as Nelson (1974) has noted, sophisticated consumers must be skeptical about quality assertions that they can directly verify only after purchase.[25] If one sets $V=1$ by choice of units and if $F(v)=1-v$ for $0 \leqslant v \leqslant 1$, so that consumers' valuations are uniformly distributed over the unit interval, equation (3.5) becomes

(3.6) $q_1 = 1 - p_1/(1 - \tau)$ $0 \leqslant p_1 \leqslant 1 - \tau$

Now suppose a second brand appears that is objectively identical to the first. Again, consumers know that it is worth v if it works and $(-\phi v)$ if it doesn't. Even though the second brand actually works, it is again reasonable for imperfectly informed consumers to attach some probability to its not working. If consumers do not talk to each other about this product class, as has been in effect assumed so far, those who did not try brand 1 have no reason to assign any value but π to the probability that brand 2 doesn't work. Those who have tried brand 1 and found it to work might assign a somewhat lower probability to brand 2's not working, because they know that it is at least possible to produce a brand in this class that works. For algebraic simplicity, I assume instead that they also have subjective probability π that brand 2 does not work. It is shown below that greater optimism on the part of this group improves brand 2's prospects in a continuous fashion. (That is, group members do not all rush to buy brand 2 if they are only a little bit more optimistic about its chances of working.)

The second brand's sales of course depend on the first brand's price. In order to highlight the problem of late entry, suppose that the first brand does not alter its price in response to new competition. This is a much more passive response than any considered in the recent literature on entry deterrence cited in Section 1, above. Empirically, it is easy to find cases in which price is reduced in response to attempted entry; see Schmalensee (1979) for an example. Further, unless one assumes that collusion is without cost or difficulty, successful entry that transforms a market from monopoly to duopoly must lower at least the expected value of price under any reasonable model of firm behavior. The assumption that p_1 will be held constant under all circumstances is thus surely the most optimistic assumption a potential entrant could plausibly hold.

Under this assumption, suppose that brand 2 enters and sets its price,

p_2, equal to p_1. Those consumers who did not find it optimal to try brand 1 then find it optimal not to try brand 2 either. If p_2 were slightly below p_1, a small number of this group would be induced to try brand 2 and, because brand 2 always works, they would stay with it indefinitely. Those consumers who did try brand 1 are now enjoying a surplus of $(v-p_1)$ on each purchase occasion. For any such person to try brand 2 would mean giving up this positive quantity, whereas trying brand 1 involved giving up a zero surplus. It is easy to see that nobody currently buying brand 1 will rationally try brand 2 unless it is discretely cheaper, because otherwise there is no point to bearing the risk of trial. Thus, if brand 2 enters with a price equal to brand 1's, it will sell *nothing at all*, and if it undercuts brand 1 a tiny bit, it will have correspondingly tiny sales. The demand conditions facing brand 2 are not the same as those that faced brand 1, because some consumers have made irreversible investments in learning about brand 1. In order to persuade them to make the same sort of investment in learning about brand 2, that brand must offer some advantage over brand 1. The only way to do that here is to charge a lower price.

In general, using Equations (3.2) and (3.4), brand 2 is tried and used by nonusers of brand 1 for whom

(3.7a) $\quad p_2 \leqslant (1-\tau)v \quad$ and $\quad v \leqslant p_1/(1-\tau)$

and it is tried and used thereafter by customers of brand 1 for whom

(3.7b) $\quad p_2 \leqslant p_1 - \tau v \quad$ and $\quad v \geqslant p_1/(1-\tau)$

Note that consumers with large values of v are least likely to try brand 2, even though they were most likely to try brand 1. This switch occurs because their high valuation of brand 1 gives them a high opportunity cost of trying brand 2 once they've learned that brand 1 works.

Conditions (3.7) are depicted in Figure 10.1. Before brand 2's entry, brand 1 has sales of $F[p_1/(1-\tau)]$, from (3.5). Upon entry, brand 2 is tried by those consumers with v's located between the intersections of the $p=p_2$ line and the solid kinked schedule. As the figure is drawn, brand 2 has sales of $\{F[p_2/(1-\tau)] - F[(p_1-p_2)/\tau]\}$, so that brand 1 has lost sales of $\{F[p_1/(1-\tau)] - F[(p_1-p_2)/\tau]\}$. Note that from (3.7b), brand 2 does not capture *any* of brand 1's customers unless $p_2 \leqslant p_1(1-2\tau)/(1-\tau)$.

If experience with brand 1 causes consumers to be more optimistic about brand 2, the first inequality in (3.7b) would involve some parameter τ' less than τ in place of τ. In terms of Figure 10.1, this would mean replacing the $(p=p_1-\tau v)$ locus with a flatter line having the same inter-

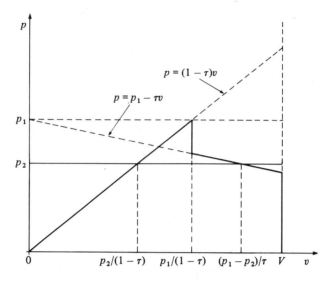

Figure 10.1. Demand for brand 2 from conditions (3.7)

cept and slope $(-\tau')$. Small changes in τ' would then clearly give rise to small changes in brand 2's prospects, as asserted above. As long as τ' is positive, brand 2 must charge a discrete amount less than brand 1 in order to capture *any* of the latter's customers.[26]

As they stand, conditions (3.7) imply the following demand function for brand 2:

$$(3.8a) \quad q_2 = F[p_2/(1 - \tau)] - F[p_1/(1 - \tau)],$$
$$(1 - 2\tau)p_1/(1 - \tau) \leqslant p_2 \leqslant p_1$$

$$(3.8b) \quad q_2 = F[p_2/(1 - \tau)] - F[(p_1 - p_2)/\tau],$$
$$p_1 - \tau V \leqslant p_2 \leqslant (1 - 2\tau)p_1/(1 - \tau)$$

$$(3.8c) \quad q_2 = F[p_2/(1 - \tau)] \quad p_2 \leqslant p_1 - \tau V$$

Only if p_2 is low enough to induce all of brand 1's customers, along with some nonusers, to invest in trial does brand 2 face the same demand curve as brand 1 did. Otherwise, brand 2's demand curve is below brand 1's, no matter what price brand 1 changes.

In order to show this difference, the demand function (3.8) is graphed in Figure 10.2 under the uniformity assumptions that gave rise to (3.6). The right-most dotted line is (3.6), the demand function that initially faced brand 1. Because brand 2 can make positive sales if it undercuts brand 1 by a tiny amount, its entry cannot be deterred under our

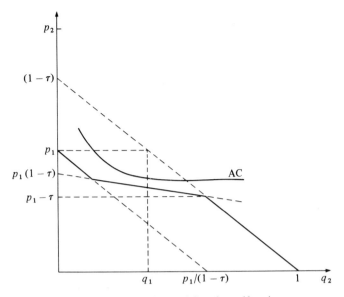

Figure 10.2. Demand for brands 1 and 2 under uniformity

assumptions if unit costs are constant and brand 1 is generating excess profit. If there are economies of scale, however, so that the long-run average cost curve looks like the curve labeled AC in Figure 10.2, brand 1 can enjoy excess profits and not worry about entry. In general, if pre-entry excess profits are possible for brand 1 and if there are any scale economies, the geometry of Figure 10.2 makes it clear that there is a barrier to entry in Bain's sense after brand 1 is established. This holds a fortiori if potential entrants are less optimistic than assumed here.

A number of comments about this barrier are in order. First, the second brand's handicap vanishes if $\tau = 0$ and, roughly, increases with τ. Because τ increases with ϕ and π, which measure the risk of trying a new brand, and with r, which varies inversely with purchase frequency, this model is broadly consistent with Bain's observations about risk and purchase frequency quoted above. Second, in this model consumers acquire information about new brands only by trying them or, perhaps, by exposure to advertising that is not fully credible. If information about new brands is valuable enough, however, one can expect consumers to use word-of-mouth and other channels to seek it. In this model, it is easy to show that if the expected value of perfect information about a new brand is positive, multiplying p, s, and v by any positive scalar k also multiplies that value by k. This means that information is worth more for products with a higher unit value, all else equal. This in turn suggests that the barrier modeled here may be most important, all else equal, for low-priced products, since consumer information seeking may be least important there.

Third, it is interesting to note that a barrier to entry arises in this framework only through the interaction of late entrants' demand disadvantage *and* brand-specific scale economies. Bain (1956, Ch. 4) was concerned about economies of scale in marketing in this context, but the present analysis implies that scale economies in production are also relevant. Fourth, it is worth noting explicitly that advertising plays no role in creating the entry barrier modeled here. This does not prove that advertising never creates product differentiation advantages that established sellers can use to protect monopoly profits from entry. It does suggest, at least, that Bain's (1956, p. 143) finding that "advertising *per se* is not necessarily the main or most important key to the product-differentiation problem" deserves to be taken more seriously than it generally has been. Finally, Porter (1974) has noted that for some products ("shopping goods"), retailers are important sources of information about quality. Where retailers can reliably evaluate quality and offer their reputations as hostages for the accuracy of those evaluations, one would expect the mechanism discussed here to be relatively unimportant.[27]

The model of this section is consistent with marketers' conventional wisdom that so-called me-too brands, brands that promise quality identical to established brands but sell at lower prices, are unlikely to be very successful in a set of consumer markets. This lends some theoretical respectability to the apparent fact that economists' most commonly assumed form of market rivalry, price-cutting with no quality change, is very rare in some such markets. In situations where the model developed here captures important aspects of market operation, the most natural and common form of rivalry must involve developing products that differ from existing ones, so that one's wares look like brand 1, not brand 2. Models of market interaction that focus on price may be utterly misleading in these cases, even when there are no technical obstacles to duplicating rivals' products.

In the model considered here, all parties are rational. Brand 1's advantage does not arise because its customers are lazy or stupid or because they are easily misled by advertising. This might lead one to suspect that an equilibrium in which brand 1 earns excess profits in perpetuity can have some sort of optimality properties. In fact, the brand 1s of this world have taken risks and been innovative. I see nothing in this framework that might link the size of the rewards from early entry to the social value of the corresponding innovation, however. The dependence of the barrier's height on the importance of scale economies makes it especially doubtful that this kind of permanent monopoly situation has any particularly attractive optimality properties. On the other hand, it is not obvious what sort of public policy would reliably enhance efficiency, because consumers are generally rational to worry about the quality of products with which they lack experience. More work is needed, as usual.

4 Advertising and consumer behavior

When they participate as buyers in modern markets, consumers often make purchase decisions under uncertainty about complex products. In many modern markets, sellers spend a substantial fraction of their revenue on advertising, attempting to affect those decisions. In such cases, it is reasonable to assume that, on average, advertising spending has some impact on firm or brand sales. A deeper set of issues involve the effect of these expenditures on market structure. Hypotheses about these latter effects must be based on explicit or implicit hypotheses about consumer behavior, since these effects must derive from shifts in the structure of consumer demand. I hope to show in this concluding section that widespread failure to recognize the implications of this straightforward observation and unwillingness to grapple with the rich detail of market operation has limited economists' understanding of advertising and thus impaired our ability to analyze modern markets.

In mainstream economic theory, households are almost always assumed to solve dynamic optimization problems under uncertainty correctly, no matter how hard the solutions are to characterize or compute. If the problem involved is relatively straightforward, as in the previous section or in Butters' (1977) interesting model of informative advertising, this may be empirically plausible. When consumers must solve complex dynamic programming problems correctly in order to behave rationally, however, most noneconomists and even some economists would doubt the value of imposing perfect rationality. This does not imply that rational behavior models cannot yield useful insights in complex situations, only that it may be misleading to take such models too seriously. One might, for instance, be willing to accept as a plausible hypothesis the prediction of Grossman, Kihlstrom, and Mirman (1977) that if larger purchases yield more useful information about product quality in a dynamic context, consumers will buy more than they would if information had no value, without having much faith in the ability of their complex optimization model to make correct quantitative or detailed predictions about behavior. Those who have taught introductory statistics or have been persuaded by the experimental evidence reported by Kahneman and Tversky (1979) and others might suspect that consumer behavior could deviate systematically from optimality even in simple situations involving uncertainty. In any case, one cannot appeal to natural selection and talk about *as if* optimization for households as is commonly done for competitive firms.[28] I am not trying to argue that it is *wrong* in any sense to make the assumption that consumers behave optimally at all times, just to suggest that this assumption lacks obvious empirical plausibility when real households are assumed to solve problems that economic theorists themselves find difficult to analyze.

Most discussions of advertising in industrial organization run no risk at all of taking the rationality assumption too seriously. Consumers are generally treated as responding more or less mechanically to advertising spending, not as intelligent agents consciously deciding how to react to the advertising they encounter. Sometimes, as in the work of Dixit and Norman (1979), it is explicitly assumed that advertising spending changes tastes in a predictable way, but it is more common to be less formal and less explicit about how consumers are being manipulated.[29] Again, I am not trying to argue that this view of consumer behavior is always wrong. But I would agree with its Chicago School critics that it misses important aspects of at least some situations.[30] Advertising sometimes does provide information that clearly improves consumers' decisions, if only by making them aware that new products exist. It seems odd to assert that consumers' tastes are changed by want ads or grocery store ads that stress price information, for instance. When the rational response to some particular advertisement or other market event is obvious to most economists, it seems a bit unreasonable to assume that most consumers will respond very differently.

Economists have generally left the detailed study of actual consumer decision making to psychologists and marketers. In the marketing literature, especially, one encounters descriptions of consumer behavior intermediate between the two extremes just discussed. Consumers are treated as boundedly rational, in Herbert Simon's phrase.[31] They are assumed to pursue reasonably stable objectives in a reasonably intelligent fashion, but not necessarily in the supremely rational fashion economists reflexively assume. As humans, consumers' effectiveness is sometimes limited by their finite abilities to receive, store, retrieve, and process information. Given their limits, they sometimes sensibly adopt rules of thumb to economize on decision-making time. Both introspection and considerable empirical work support this general view.[32]

Williamson (1975, 1979) has emphasized the importance of recognizing bounded rationality in the study of institutional and contractual structure. He argues that it becomes important to economize on human rationality when complex uncertainty is an important feature of the relevant environment. Contracts and institutions can be expected to reflect this. In simple situations, where uncertainty is either of minor importance or easy to describe, one loses little by ignoring the boundedness of rationality. By similar reasoning, one might expect the bounds on consumer rationality to be of negligible importance in some market situations, whereas in others they might be the prime determinants of observed behavior. Thus, if optimization is possible for reasonably intelligent people, optimal behavior is probably a good prediction. But if consumers face a problem for which the exact solution is either difficult or impossible to compute, it might be important to know what sort of heuristics and rules of thumb humans tend to employ in related contexts if one wishes to predict actual behavior. The noneconomic literature on consumer behavior thus suggests strongly that the most appropriate shorthand description of consumer behavior in general, and of consumer reaction to advertising in particular, might depend crucially on the details of the decision problem posed for consumers by the market considered.

This in turn suggests that the effects of advertising on market structure and competition can be expected to vary considerably, depending on both the initial market situation and the nature of the advertising involved. There is some empirical support for this hypothesis in the industrial organization literature. Benham (1972), for instance, finds that restrictions on eyeglass sellers' advertising tend to raise the price of eyeglasses, while Scherer (1980, pp. 380–3) documents the extraordinary price premia commanded by heavily nationally advertised brands in some markets. Boyer (1974) finds advertising intensity to be *negatively* associated with profitability in a sample of trade and service industries. Porter (1974) finds no association between advertising and profitability across markets in which retailers serve as an important source of consumer information. He finds a strong positive association in a sample of what he calls "convenience goods," which are usually purchased without consulting a retailer.[33] In later work, Porter (1976) finds suggestions that different media have different competitive effects. Finally, Lambin's (1976) detailed econometric analysis of 16 product classes in eight European countries supports the general impression of diversity.

Almost all the substantial literature recently surveyed by Comanor and Wilson (1979) is concerned with chosing between two simple generalizations: advertising is always procompetitive, or advertising is always anticompetitive. If the nature of advertising and of consumer response to it varies across markets in response to more fundamental market attributes as the discussion above implies, both of these are almost surely wrong. Adequate analysis of the role of advertising in any individual modern market likely requires the development or deployment of a model reflecting the key features of that market. In many models that prove useful for market analysis, consumers may be assumed supremely rational as a good approximation. In at least some situations, however, it may be necessary to deal explicitly with bounds on consumer rationality in order to explain observed behavior adequately. Sufficient analysis of actual modern markets, using the modern theoretical and econometric tools of the new industrial organization, can be expected to teach us something about the conditions under which various forms of advertising have desirable or undesirable effects on market structure and operation.

NOTES

1 Grether (1970) and Weiss (1971) discuss this early history. Mason (1939) is still worth reading on problems and methods. In this chapter I follow the U.S. convention and refer to *industrial organization* instead of the English (and, I think, preferable) *industrial economics.*

2 Weiss (1971, p. 362). This history doesn't describe the evolution of the Chicago School very well. Perhaps because of its early resistance to the Chamberlinian revolution in microeconomic theory, Chicago seems never to have lost faith in the ability of Marshallian price theory to explain the central features of observed market behavior. For whatever reason, formal theory is much more important and generalizations from cross-section evidence are much less important in Stigler (1968) than in Bain (1968).

3 For instance, most early cross-section studies find a positive correlation between concentration and profitability and interpret it as reflecting a positive causal relation between concentration and ease of collusion. In an important revisionist study, Peltzman (1977) argues that this correlation in fact mainly reflects a positive relation between cost-reducing innovative activity and increases in concentration. That is, Peltzman argues that profits are high mainly where costs of infra-marginal innovative firms with large market shares are relatively low. Careful readers of his study will come to appreciate the difficulty of using available data to discriminate among alternative models of these sorts.

4 Spence (1981, p. 58). Schmalensee (1979) takes a similar methodological position.

5 See also Salop (1979b), Eaton and Lipsey (1981), and Schmalensee (1981). Scherer (1980, Ch. 8) provides a good discussion of the limit-pricing model and its critics. Recent work by Kreps and Wilson (1980) and others they cite seems likely to deepen our understanding of predatory pricing and other strategic responses to entry.

6 In general terms, Bain (1968, Ch. 5) and Stigler (1968, pp. 29–36).

7 Hannah and Kay (1977, Ch. 4) provide a useful discussion of functions that have been employed to define and measure concentration; see also Scherer (1980, pp. 56–59) and the references he cites.

8 It is generally but not universally accepted that market concentration is of interest mainly for its predictive value. Dansby and Willig (1979) propose concentration measures that reflect the returns from government intervention under certain assumptions about the costs thereof, whereas Blackorby, Donaldson, and Weymark (1979) argue that concentration measures should be derived as part of a market performance index concerned directly with unequal firm shares.

9 Hannah and Kay (1977, pp. 11–12) have this same derivation. For other examples of the sort of approach taken here, see Dansby and Willig (1979) and Encaoua and Jacquemin (1980).

10 In retrospect, at least, some of Sraffa's (1926, pp. 182–197) language, which is cited approvingly by Hotelling (1929), is very suggestive of the spatial model.

11 Parsons and Schultz (1976, Ch. 7) provide a useful survey.

12 Discussions of alternative techniques and lists of references are provided by Hauser and Koppelman (1979) and Huber and Holbrook (1979). Clarke (1978) has explored the use of perceptual mapping data in econometric work.

13 Urban, Johnson, and Brudnick (1979) discuss the literature on the first of these approaches and present the second technique in detail.

14 Bernhardt and Mackensie (1968) propose a rather different approach to this problem of structural measurement.

15 Bell, Keeney, and Little (1975) and Barnett (1976) present axiomatic derivations of this basic functional form. Models of this sort are analyzed in detail in Schmalensee (1976a, 1976b).

16 This is *not* the most natural spatial model of nonprice competition. In the standard one-dimensional spatial model of price competition, each firm has only one rival for each half its market; see Salop (1979a) for a good discussion. Such a framework is a bit harder to work with here, however, and its use would not add much insight. Hannah and Kay (1977, pp. 12–15) have an interesting analysis of price setting in the standard model from which a multiple of the H index of concentration emerges, much as it does below.

17 Models of this sort and more general implications of related curvature properties are explored in Schmalensee (1976b, 1977b, 1978a).

18 If one is very lucky about the distribution of the a_i in some historical sample, for instance, one might be able to obtain useable estimates of the relative magnitudes of these cross-derivatives from ordinary linear regression, even though the underlying structure must be nonlinear. White (1980) provides a careful analysis of this approach.

19 An argument is given in Schmalensee (1978b).

20 That debate is surveyed by Comanor and Wilson (1979), Demsetz (1979), and Scherer (1980, Chs. 9 and 14). It is perhaps worth mentioning that the U.S. ready-to-eat breakfast cereal industry has generally had both very heavy advertising relative to sales and very high measured profitability. Whereas entry of new firms has been rare, entry of new brands sold by established firms has been quite common. Because most cereal advertising deals with the attributes of individual brands, if consumer goods advertising generally serves to inhibit new entry, it should have served to inhibit the introduction of new brands of cereal. As it apparently did not do so, the meaning of at least this one sample point in cross-section studies would seem to be in doubt. (Schmalensee [1978b])

21 Bain (1956, Ch. 4) mentions a number of other factors, including economies

of scale in advertising and pre-emption of scarce retail outlets, that are not directly addressed in the present analysis. On scale economies, see the references cited in note 20 and Schmalensee (1981).

22 Peckham (1966) makes essentially the same point.
23 This extends the model in the appendix to Schmalensee (1979) and is a special case of the model analyzed in Schmalensee (1982). Bond and Lean (1979) present a model that has the same sort of implications as the one in the text, but they focus on advertising and do not treat consumers as (necessarily) rational. A broadly similar setup is considered by von Weizsäcker (1980, Ch. 5), but his model is basically competitive and the one in the text is not. Shapiro (1980) has recently done closely related work.
24 The general status of the rationality assumption in this sort of context is discussed briefly in Section 4. It is worth noting explicitly that the consumers in this market are *not* knowledgeable and intelligent enough to infer brands' qualities from such signals as price, advertising, or availability. Because consumers need to know the costs of producing at different quality levels in order to interpret such signals, and because such costs are usually closely guarded secrets, this does not seem unrealistic for most markets.
25 On the limitations of Nelson's (1974) analysis, see Schmalensee (1978a) and Boyer, Kihlstrom, and Laffont (1978). Note that after the first period, all those buying the first brand are enjoying positive surplus. The first brand could raise its price to $p_1/(1-\tau)$ and lose no sales. The consequences of allowing pricing of this sort, which is commonly observed in new-brand introduction, are explored in Schmalensee (1982).
26 In Schmalensee (1982), brand 2 is allowed to charge a low price upon entry in order to induce trial and then to undercut brand 1 by any amount. Brand 2's disadvantage remains in this more complicated model.
27 I am indebted to Professor von Weizsäcker for this point. It seems consistent, at least, with Porter's (1974) cross-section regression results.
28 Several of the points made here are developed more fully in Schmalensee (1975).
29 See, for instance, the discussions in Comanor and Wilson (1967, 1979), Mann (1974), and Scherer (1980, Ch. 14). Kotowitz and Mathewson (1979b) develop a dynamic model of "persuasive" advertising, which is assumed mechanically to alter consumers' perceptions. See also their (1979a) model of "informative" advertising.
30 Telser (1964) provides an important early statement of this "advertising is information" viewpoint; see also Brozen (1974), Ferguson (1974), Nelson (1974), and Demsetz (1979).
31 Simon (1978) provides an excellent discussion of rationality in and out of economics that is directly relevant here.
32 This view of consumer behavior is presented most explicitly by Bettman (1979), who also surveys the relevant evidence. Other useful references in this literature include Howard (1977), Runyon (1977), and Engle, Blackwell, and Kollat (1978).
33 Howard (1977, p. 151) presents an interesting classification of products similar in spirit but apparently more general than that used by Porter (1974).

REFERENCES

Archibald, G. C. and Rosenbluth, G. The "new" theory of consumer demand

and monopolistic competition. *Quarterly Journal of Economics* 89 (February 1975): 569–590.

Bain, J. S. Relation of profit rate to industry concentration: American manufacturing, 1936–1940. *Quarterly Journal of Economics* 65 (August 1951): 293–324.

Bain, J. S. *Barriers to new competition.* Cambridge: Harvard University Press, 1956.

Bain, J. S. *Industrial organization,* 2nd ed. New York: John Wiley, 1968. (1st ed., 1959).

Barnett, A. I. More on a market share theorem. *Journal of Marketing Research* 13 (February 1976): 104–109.

Baumol, W. J. Calculation of optimal product and retailer characteristics: the abstract product approach. *Journal of Political Economy* 75 (October 1967): 674–685.

Bell, D. E., Keeney, R. E., and Little, J. D. C. A market share theorem. *Journal of Marketing Research* 12 (May 1975): 136–141.

Benham, L. The effects of advertising on the price of eyeglasses. *Journal of Law and Economics* 15 (October 1972): 337–352.

Bernhardt, I. and Mackensie, K. D. Measuring seller unconcentration, segmentation and product differentiation. *Western Economic Journal* 6 (December 1968): 395–405.

Bettman, J. R. *An information processing theory of consumer choice.* Reading, Mass.: Addison-Wesley, 1979.

Blackorby, C., Donaldson, D., and Weymark, J. A. A new theory of concentration indices and indicators of industrial performance. Economics Discussion Paper no. 79-34, University of British Columbia, October 1979.

Bond, R. S. and Lean, D. F. *Sales, promotion, and product differentiation in two prescription drug markets,* a staff report to the U.S. Federal Trade Commission. Washington, 1977.

Bond, R. S. and Lean, D. F. Consumer preference, advertising, and sales: on the advantage from early entry. Working Paper no. 14, Bureau of Economics, U.S. Federal Trade Commission, October 1979.

Boyer, K. D. Informative and goodwill advertising. *Review of Economics and Statistics* 56 (November 1974): 541–548.

Boyer, M., Kihlstrom, R. E., and Laffont, J. J. Misleading advertising, mimeographed, January 1978.

Brozen, Y. Entry barriers, advertising, and product differentiation. In *Industrial concentration: the new learning,* H. J. Goldschmid, et al., eds. Boston: Little, Brown, 1974.

Butters, G. Equilibrium distribution of prices and advertising. *Review of Economic Studies* 44 (October 1977): 465–492.

Buzzell, R. D. and Farris, P. W. Marketing costs in consumer goods industries. Report no. 76-111, Marketing Science Institute, Cambridge, August 1976.

Caves, R. E. and Porter, M. E. From entry barriers to mobility barriers. *Quarterly Journal of Economics* 91 (May 1977): 241–262.

Chamberlin, E. H. *The theory of monopolistic competition.* Cambridge: Harvard University Press, 1933. (8th ed., 1962).

Chamberlin, E. H. Monopolistic competition revisited. *Economica* 18 (August 1951): 343–62. Page citations to revision in Chamberlin (1957).

Chamberlin, E. H. The product as economic variable. *Quarterly Journal of Economics* 67 (February 1953): 1–29. Reprinted in Chamberlin (1957).

Chamberlin, E. H. *Towards a more general theory of value.* New York: Oxford University Press, 1957.

Clarke, D. G. Strategic advertising policy: merging multi-dimensional scaling and econometric analysis. *Management Science* 24 (December 1978): 1687–1699.

Comanor, W. S. Comments [on Weiss (1971)]. In *Frontiers of Quantitative Economics,* M. D. Intriligator, ed. Amsterdam: North-Holland, 1971.

Comanor, W. S. and Wilson, T. A. Advertising market structure and performance. *Review of Economics and Statistics* 49 (November 1967): 423–440.

Comanor, W. S. and Wilson, T. A. Advertising and competition: a survey. *Journal of Economic Literature* 17 (June 1979): 453–476.

Dansby, R. E. and Willig, R. D. Industry performance gradient indices. *American Economic Review* 69 (June 1979): 249–260.

Demsetz, H. Industry structure, market rivalry, and public policy. *Journal of Law and Economics* 16 (April 1973): 1–10.

Demsetz, H. Accounting for advertising as a barrier to entry. *Journal of Business* 52 (July 1979): 345–360.

Dixit, A. A Model of duopoly suggesting a theory of entry barriers. *Bell Journal of Economics* 9 (Spring 1979): 20–32.

Dixit, A. The role of investment in entry-deterrence. *Economic Journal* 90 (March 1980): 95–106.

Dixit, A. and Norman, V. Advertising and welfare. *Bell Journal of Economics* 9 (Spring 1978): 1–18.

Dixit, A. and Stiglitz, J. E. Monopolistic competition and optimum product diversity. *American Economic Review* 67 (June 1977): 297–308.

Douglas, G. W. and Miller, J. C. *Economic Regulation of Domestic Air Transport: Theory and Policy.* Washington: Brookings, 1975.

Eaton, B. C. and Lipsey, R. G. Capital, commitment, and entry equilibrium. *Bell Journal of Economics* 12 (Autumn 1981): 593–604.

Encaoua, D. and Jacquemin, A. Degree of monopoly, indices of concentration, and threat of entry. *International Economic Review* 21 (February 1980): 87–105.

Engle, J. F., Blackwell, R. D., and Kollat, D. T. *Consumer behavior,* 3rd ed. Hinsdale, Ill.: Dryden, 1978.

Ferguson, J. M. *Advertising and competition: theory, measurement, fact.* Cambridge, Mass.: Ballinger, 1974.

Grether, E. T. Industrial organization: past history and future problems. *American Economic Review* 60 (May 1970): 83–89.

Grossman, S. J., Kihlstrom, R. E., and Mirman, L. J. A Bayesian approach to the production of information and learning by doing. *Review of Economic Studies* 44 (October 1977): 537–547.

Hannah, E. and Kay, J. *Concentration in modern industry.* London: Humanities Press, 1977.

Hauser, J. R. and Koppelman, F. S. Alternative perceptual mapping techniques: relative accuracy and usefulness. *Journal of Marketing Research* 16 (November 1979): 495–506.

Hotelling, H. Stability in competition. *Economic Journal* 39 (March 1929): 41–57. Reprinted in Stigler and Boulding (1952).

Howard, J. A. *Consumer behavior: application of theory.* New York: McGraw-Hill, 1977.

Huber, J. and Holbrook, M. B. Using attribute ratings for product positioning: some distinctions among compositional approaches. *Journal of Marketing Research* 16 (November 1979): 507-516.

Joskow, P. L. Cartels, competition and regulation in the property-liability insurance industry. *Bell Journal of Economics* 4 (Autumn 1973): 375-427.

Kahneman, D. and Tversky, A. Prospect theory: an analysis of decision under risk. *Econometrica* 47 (March 1979): 263-292.

Kaldor, N. Mrs. Robinson's "economics of imperfect competition." *Economica* 1 (August 1934): 335-341.

Kaldor, N. Market imperfection and excess capacity. *Economica* 2 (February 1935): 35-50. Reprinted in Stigler and Boulding (1952).

Kotowitz, Y. and Mathewson, F. Informative advertising and welfare. *American Economic Review* 69 (June 1979): 284-294. (a)

Kotowitz, Y. and Mathewson, F. Advertising, consumer information, and product quality. *Bell Journal of Economics* 10 (Autumn 1979): 566-588. (b)

Kreps, D. M. and Wilson, R. On the chain-store paradox and predation: reputation for toughness, mimeographed, Stanford University, June 1980.

Lambin, J. J. *Advertising, competition, and market conduct in oligopoly over time.* Amsterdam: North-Holland, 1976.

Lancaster, K. J. A new approach to consumer theory. *Journal of Political Economy* 74 (April 1966): 132-157.

Lancaster, K. J. *Consumer demand: a new approach.* New York: Columbia University Press, 1971.

Lancaster, K. J. Socially optimal product differentiation. *American Economic Review* 65 (September 1975): 567-585.

MacAvoy, P. W. *Price formation in natural gas fields.* New Haven: Yale University Press, 1962.

MacAvoy, P. W. *The economic effects of regulation.* Cambridge, Mass.: M.I.T. Press, 1965.

Mancke, R. B. Causes of interfirm profitability differences. *Quarterly Journal of Economics* 88 (May 1974): 181-193.

Mann, H. M. Advertising, concentration, and profitability: the state of knowledge and directions for public policy. In *Industrial Concentration: The New Learning,* H. J. Goldschmid, et al., eds. Boston: Little, Brown, 1974.

Mason, E. S. Price and production policies of large-scale enterprise. *American Economic Review* 29 (March 1939): 61-74.

McConnell, J. D. The development of brand loyalty: an experimental study. *Journal of Marketing Research* 5 (February 1968): 13-19.

Nelson, P. Information and consumer behavior. *Journal of Political Economy* 78 (March/April 1970): 311-329.

Nelson, P. Advertising as information. *Journal of Political Economy* 82 (July/August 1974): 729-754.

Parsons, L. J. and Schultz, R. L. *Marketing models and econometric research.* Amsterdam: North-Holland, 1976.

Peckham, J. O. Can we relate advertising dollars to market share objectives? In *Proceedings of 12th Annual Conference.* New York: Advertising Research Foundation, 1966.

Peltzman, S. The gains and losses from industrial concentration. *Journal of Law and Economics* 20 (October 1977): 229-264.

Phillips, A. A Critique of empirical studies of relations between market structure and profitability. *Journal of Industrial Economics* 24 (June 1976): 241–249.

Porter, M. E. Consumer behavior, retailer power and market performance in consumer goods industries. *Review of Economics and Statistics* 56 (November 1974): 419–436.

Porter, M. E. Interbrand choice, media mix and market performance. *American Economic Review* 66 (May 1976): 398∴406.

Porter, M. E. The structure within industries and companies' performance. *Review of Economics and Statistics* 59 (May 1979): 214–227.

Rader, T. *Theory of microeconomics.* New York: Academic Press, 1972.

Runyon, K. E. *Consumer behavior and the practice of marketing.* Columbus, Ohio: Merrill, 1977.

Salop, S. C. Monopolistic competition with outside goods. *Bell Journal of Economics* 10 (Spring 1979): 141–156. (a)

Salop, S. C. Strategic entry deterrence. *American Economic Review* 69 (May 1979): 335–338. (b)

Scherer, F. M. *Industrial market structure and economic performance,* 2nd ed. Chicago: Rand McNally, 1980. (1st ed., 1970).

Schmalensee, R. Alternative models of bandit selection. *Journal of Economic Theory* 10 (June 1975): 333–342.

Schmalensee, R. Advertising and profitability: further implications of the null hypothesis. *Journal of Industrial Economics* 25 (September 1976): 45–54. (a)

Schmalensee, R. A model of promotional competition in oligopoly. *Review of Economic Studies* 43 (October 1976): 493–507. (b)

Schmalensee, R. Using the H index of concentration with published data. *Review of Economics and Statistics* 59 (May 1977): 186–193. (a)

Schmalensee, R. Comparative static properties of regulated airline oligopolies. *Bell Journal of Economics* 8 (Autumn 1977): 565–576. (b)

Schmalensee, R. A Model of advertising and product quality. *Journal of Political Economy* 87 (June 1978): 485–504. (a)

Schmalensee, R. Entry deterrence in the ready-to-eat breakfast cereal industry. *Bell Journal of Economics* 9 (Autumn 1978): 305–327. (b)

Schmalensee, R. On the use of economic models in antitrust: the ReaLemon case. *University of Pennsylvania Law Review* 127 (April 1979): 994–1050.

Schmalensee, R. Economies of scale and barriers to entry. *Journal of Political Economy* 89 (December 1981): 1228–1239.

Schmalensee, R. Product differentiation advantages of pioneering brands. *American Economic Review* 72 (1982): in press.

Shapiro, C. Consumer information, product quality and seller reputation, mimeographed, U.S. Federal Trade Commission, July 1980.

Smallwood, D. E. Competition, regulation, and product quality in the automobile insurance industry. In *Promoting competition in regulated markets,* A. Phillips, ed. Washington: Brookings, 1975.

Simon, H. A. Rationality as process and product of thought. *American Economic Review* 68 (May 1978): 1–16.

Spence, A. M. Product selection, fixed costs, and monopolistic competition. *Review of Economic Studies* 43 (June 1976): 217–235.

Spence, A. M. Entry, capacity, investment and oligopolistic pricing. *Bell Journal of Economics* 8 (Autumn 1977): 534–544.

Spence, A. M. Investment strategy and growth in a new market. *Bell Journal of Economics* 9 (Spring 1979): 1–19.

Spence, A. M. Competition, entry and antitrust policy. In *Strategy, predation and antitrust analysis,* S. C. Salop, ed. Washington: Federal Trade Commission, 1981.

Sraffa, P. The laws of return under competitive conditions. *Economic Journal* 36 (December 1926): 535–550. Page citations to reprint in Stigler and Boulding (1952).

Stigler, G. J. The economics of information. *Journal of Political Economy* 69 (June 1961): 213–225. Reprinted in Stigler (1968).

Stigler, G. J. A theory of oligopoly. *Journal of Political Economy* 72 (February 1964): 44–61. Reprinted in Stigler (1968).

Stigler, G. J. *The organization of industry.* Homewood, Ill.: R. D. Irwin, 1968.

Stigler, G. J. and Boulding, K. E., eds. *A.E.A. readings in price theory.* Chicago: R. D. Irwin, 1952.

Telser, L. G. Advertising and competition. *Journal of Political Economy* 72 (December 1964): 537–562.

Tucker, W. T. The development of brand loyalty. *Journal of Marketing Research* 3 (August 1964): 32–35.

Urban, G. L., Johnson, P. L., and Brudnick, R. H. Market entry strategy formulation: a hierarchical modeling and consumer measurement approach. Sloan School Working Paper no. 1103-80, M.I.T., December 1979.

Weiss, L. W. Quantitative studies of industrial organization. In *Frontiers of quantitative economics,* M. D. Intriligator, ed. Amsterdam: North-Holland, 1971.

Weizsäcker, C. C. v. *Barriers to entry: a theoretical treatment.* Berlin: Springer-verlag, 1980.

White, H. R. Using least squares to approximate unknown regression functions. *International Economic Review* 21 (February 1980): 149–170.

Whitten, I. T. *Brand performance in the cigarette industry and the advantages of early entry,* A staff report to the U.S. Federal Trade Commission. Washington, 1979.

Williamson, O. E. *Markets and hierarchies.* New York: Free Press, 1975.

Williamson, O. E. Transaction-cost economics: the governance of contractual relations. *Journal of Law and Economics* 22 (November 1979): 233–262.